Summary of Contents

Practical Intranet Development

John Colby

Gareth Downes-Powell

Jeffrey Haas

Darren James Harkness

Frank Pappas

Mike Parsons

Francis Storr

Inigo Surguy

Ruud Voigt

ISBN 978-1-59059-169-7   ISBN 978-1-4302-5354-9 (eBook)
DOI 10.1007/978-1-4302-5354-9

Practical Intranet Development

glasshaus

labor-saving devices for web professionals

© 2003 Apress
Originally published by glasshaus in 2003

Trademark Acknowledgments

Credits

Authors
John Colby
Gareth Downes-Powell
Jeffrey Haas
Darren James Harkness
Frank Pappas
Mike Parsons
Francis Storr
Inigo Surguy
Ruud Voigt

Technical Reviewers
Jon Stephens
David Schultz
Mark Horner
Martin Honnen
Rick Stones
Drew McLellan
Tim Luoma
Jody Kerr
Shefali Kulkarni
Mid Jamie

Proof Reader
Agnes Wiggers

Commissioning Editor
Amanda Kay

Technical Editors
Matt Machell
Alessandro Ansa

Publisher
Viv Emery

Communications Manager
Bruce Lawson

Project Managers
Sophie Edwards
Helen Cuthill

Graphic Editors
Rachel Taylor
Pippa Wonson

Cover
Dawn Chellingworth

Indexer
Adrian Axinte

About the Authors

John Colby

John Colby is a lecturer in computing at the University of Central England in Birmingham. Prior to this he was in the computer industry for twenty years in consultancy and engineering roles, and prior to that ten years in heavy engineering, anything from battleships to coal mines, taking in heavy haulage and machine tools on the way.

John has been building web sites since HTML 2.0 days and has had to come to grips with a variety of technologies on the way, becoming involved with an international company's intranet, the constructions, the politics, the ideals, and making the whole thing work on a variety of hardware and software platforms. Over a number of years this involved convincing users that web technology was correct for the tasks in hand, building and maintaining web servers, and integrating documentation functions into a web-based format. Along with this there were the almost inevitable expansions, share price crashes, takeovers, upsizing, downsizing, and reorganizations to cope with.

A fan of open source technologies and methods, he managed to save the company a lot of money in license fees in translating from proprietary programs to open source technologies. In particular the knowledge base changed and alternative systems were implemented so that knowledge was retained within the company rather than being forgotten when someone departed.

Currently John is preparing and teaching courses on Internet technologies and networking, and has a special interest in web standards-compliance in aiding the uptake of adaptive technologies, displaying web-based information using a variety of devices and bringing into use good practice so that web access is enabled for everyone.

Gareth Downes-Powell

Gareth Downes-Powell has been working in the computer industry for the last twelve years, primarily building and repairing PCs, and writing custom databases. He branched out onto the Internet five years ago, and started creating web sites and custom web applications. This is now his main area of expertise, and he uses a variety of languages including ASP and PHP, with SQL Server or MySQL back-end databases.

A partner in Buzz inet, *http://www.buzzinet.co.uk/*, an Internet company specializing in web design and hosting, he uses a wide range of Macromedia products, from Dreamweaver MX through to Flash and Director, for custom multimedia applications. Gareth maintains *http://ultradev.buzzinet.co.uk/* as a way of providing support for the whole Macromedia UltraDev and MX Community. There, he regularly adds new tutorials and custom-written extensions to this rapidly expanding site.

Gareth enjoys keeping up with the latest developments, and has been providing support to many users to help them use UltraDev and Dreamweaver MX with ASP or PHP on both Linux and Windows servers. Rarely offline, Gareth can always be found in the Macromedia forums (news: *forums.macromedia.com*), where he helps to answer many users' questions on a daily basis.

Jeffrey Haas

Jeffrey Haas is a content management specialist, Internet code warrior, and outspoken advocate of digital process. He has been working online since 1993 in content creation, technical production, management, and strategic advisor roles. As well as creating innovative digital storytelling techniques during three years at The Discovery Channel Canada, he has worked on web sites, intranets, and extranets for dozens of clients in the financial, telecommunications, and entertainment industries. His credits include managing the development and implementation of various network applications for Chart Magazine, Four Seasons Hotels and Resorts, HMV, ING Canada, Scotiabank, Sympatico, and several Warner Music recording artists.

Jeffrey is currently Manager of Technical Development for Spencer Francey Peters, a Toronto-based corporate branding and design agency. His responsibilities there include leading the implementation of sophisticated multi-lingual intranets and defining electronic workflow processes for global customers.

Outside of work hours, Jeffrey spends his time making music, studying martial arts, drinking coffee, writing, and developing personal digital projects.

I would like to thank my teachers for sharing their knowledge about computers, computer users, and corporate communication. Without you, I would have since succumbed: Andrew Adamson; Wayne Carrigan; Gergely Csaszar; Jeffrey Elliott; Aaron Goldstein; Veronica Holmes, for the value of process; Paul Kaliciak; Kevin Leflar; Liam Nickerson; Matthew Penzner; Kelly Peters; and Jeffrey Zeldman. I also want to thank my spiritual advisors for your friendship, support, and guidance: Darren Altbaum; Candine Blackbeard; Rachelle Burdman; Jessica Dean; Michael Dressler; Noah Egelnick; j. englishman; Gwyneth Evans; Geoff Girvitz; Susanna Haas; Shale Kazdan; Jay Lo; Howard Stellar; and, of course, Captain Q. Farf, Lord of the 4th Dimension. Finally, thank you to my parents, Paul and Sharon Haas, for the Commodore 64 in 1996 and so much more before and after that.

Darren James Harkness

Darren James Harkness is a creative engineer by day and a gypsy knife-eater by night. Darren is an old-school web developer, having developed several quality, content-driven web sites by hand since 1995. His qualifications include an instinctual understanding of W3C recommendations and graphic design, along with a solid understanding of back-end development. He feels most at home as a Jack-of-all-trades, dabbling in every aspect of the development process. You can find Darren online at *http://www.staticred.net*.

He'd like to thank his wonderful partner, Kirsten, for keeping him sane.

Frank Pappas

Frank Charles Pappas sang and danced his way through his early years, though innate good sense prompted him to escape the natural – and not so natural – disasters of southern California for a new and exciting life in Washington, DC.

Frank graduated with degrees in both Political Science and Spanish Language and Literature from the George Washington University in Washington, DC. When he's not busy lobbying GW's Elliot School of International Affiars to allow him to complete his Masters degree, Frank spends his free time at L'academie de Cuisine in Maryland, helping to teach fundamental cooking techniques while polishing his skills as patissier.

Now living inside the Beltway, Frank has spent the past ten years crafting an unparalleled track record in providing technology, branding, and marketing leadership to a wide array of clients, including Bush-Quayle '92, Swissair, Radisson and Regent Hotels, Brita, AOL-Time Warner, the Ford Motor Company, Viacom, and the Washington Post Company.

Mike Parsons

Mike is currently working for the advertising group McCann Erikson in the Netherlands. Although currently living in Amsterdam, he has worked for companies in New York and Sydney.

After working in radio and publishing he quickly fell in love with the Internet and has worked in this field since 1996. During that time worked for clients in the media, automotive, telecom, government, non-profit, and technology sectors.

The main theme in his career has been the balance of technology and business. As a result all of his work with technology is done with an entrepreneurial approach – achieving business goals with technology. To help achieve these goals he wrote the E-Business Integrity Methodology, a set of modules that create a framework for Internet projects and takes them from idea to execution.

Apart from being the Senior E-Business consultant at McCann Erikson he is also a feature writer for Europemedia.net and CM Focus. In his spare time he studies Managing the Digital Enterprise at North Carolina State University, USA.

Francis Storr

Francis Storr lives in South East England and is an intranet developer for a large international company. He works in XHTML, CSS, and JavaScript and currently has his nose buried in numerous books on XML. He is passionate about the promotion and implementation of Standards and Accessibility for the Web but tries not to annoy his colleagues by mentioning those subjects in every single conversation. He also firmly believes that one day he'll get around to building a site of his own.

When not working he spends time trying to evangelize the merits of The Wildhearts (the finest rock band in the world) to people who really should know better, tries to spot episodes of Matt Groening cartoons he hasn't seen before, and actively avoids doing the washing up.

Thanks to Amanda Kay, Alessandro Ansa, the reviewers, and the whole glasshaus team for getting me involved with this project. I've been told I have to say thanks to everyone at work, so "thanks to everyone at work" (especially Stevie for shouting loudly). Thanks also to Ali, Paula, and the Longplayer guys for getting me out of a hole, and also for so much fine music. Finally, thanks to my long-suffering family for everything.

Inigo Surguy

Inigo has spent five years working with intranets, content management systems, and XML for major international companies. These days, Inigo works as a consultant with a particular interest in knowledge management, usability, and web services.

I would like to thank Anu for introducing me to KM, Niki for her help with ECI, Rollo for being generally helpful, and Michelle for being great.

Table of Contents

Chapter 5: Development Techniques   71

Chapter 6: Designing Your Intranet to Be Useful
Usability and Information Architecture   105

Introduction

An intranet can be a powerful tool. A well-designed intranet becomes the key resource and communications platform for your organization, used by members of staff as their first destination for information. In contrast, a poorly designed intranet will sit unused, accumulating useless information, and eating up IT budgets. So, how do you avoid this situation, and make sure you design the most useful, and usable, intranet?

This book takes you through the steps you need to take to make an invaluable intranet, from identifying your users' needs and building an indispensable tool, to marketing the results. It guides you through the problems that may occur, passing on invaluable advice from people who have been through the process before.

We start by setting the scene, giving an overview of what intranets are and how to justify it to your organization. We then give you a rundown of the main areas you'll need to think about when developing an intranet, covering browsers, development techniques, usability, content management, security, and internal marketing. Finally, we'll take a look at what to do when the intranet moves beyond its original function, looking at remote access, extranets, and what to do when the intranet gets too big.

Who's This Book for?

This book is primarily aimed at the web professional who has been given the task of creating, or updating, their organization's intranet. It assumes a certain level of familiarity with the concepts of designing and developing for the Web, but no prior knowledge of intranets. Because the book offers a broad overview of the subject, it may also be suited to a technically minded project manager who has been given the task of leading intranet development.

What's Inside?

Chapter 1 is a brief introduction to intranets, and some of the issues we will be considering in the book.

In *Chapter 2* we take a look at justifying the intranet to your organization through calculating Return on Investment, and how this not only justifies the project, but points out the functionality that will be most valuable in your organization.

Chapter 3 is the first part of our intranet roadmap, and discusses where to start the process. We'll cover stakeholder interviews and how you can benefit from them.

In *Chapter 4* we'll look at the issue of browser base, and how an intranet gives you the bonus of knowing what browsers are viewing your content. We'll also discuss the issue of web standards, and their place in intranet development.

Chapter 5 delves further into development techniques, looking at how to manage the intranet project and the solutions that may suit your organization.

Chapter 6 is an overview of usability and information architecture in an intranet context, with tips on how to create the most usable interface for your intranet.

Chapter 7 is about controlling content, and how to avoid the common pitfalls of delivering information via an intranet.

In *Chapter 8* we look at Content Management Systems, and how they can be a benefit to any intranet. We'll also look at how to decide on a CMS, and the options available.

Chapter 9 is about taking the intranet further as a communications platform, how forums and other forms of online tools can enhance communication within your organization.

Security and Personalization is the subject for *Chapter 10*, where we'll give you an overview of the problems you'll face in securing your intranet. We'll also discuss how proper security can lead to a personalized experience for intranet users.

In *Chapter 11* we'll look at the issue of marketing an intranet once you have it, and how to make sure that employees know of the intranet's existence and keep coming back.

Chapter 12 is about the problems you may face when an intranet gets too big, and how restructuring may solve those problems.

Remote Users are the focus of *Chapter 13*, where we'll look at allowing employees to access an intranet from an external location.

Chapter 14 is about expanding your intranet to your clients and business partners, so that it becomes an extranet.

Support/Feedback

Although we aim for perfection, the sad fact of book publication is that a few errors will slip through. We would like to apologize for any errors that have reached this book despite our efforts. If you spot such an error, please let us know about it using the e-mail address *support@glasshaus.com*. If it's something that will help other readers then we'll put it up on the errata page at *http://www.glasshaus.com*.

This address can also be used to access our support network. If you have trouble running any of the code in this book, or have a related question that you feel that the book didn't answer, please mail your problem to the above address quoting the title of the book, the last 4 digits of its ISBN (**123X**), and the chapter and page number of your query.

Web Support

Feel free to visit our web site, at *http://www.glasshaus.com*. It features:

- Code Downloads: The example code for every glasshaus book can be downloaded from our site.

- Online Resource Center: We will be building up a definitive reference on the Web, containing all the up-to-date reference material that you'll need. We've decided to put this reference material on the Web rather than weighing down our books with hefty appendices. It will be added to over time, so if there is anything you feel isn't up there but should be, please let us know.

1

- What is an intranet?

- Key differences between intranet and Internet development

- The intranet development team

Author: Ruud Voigt

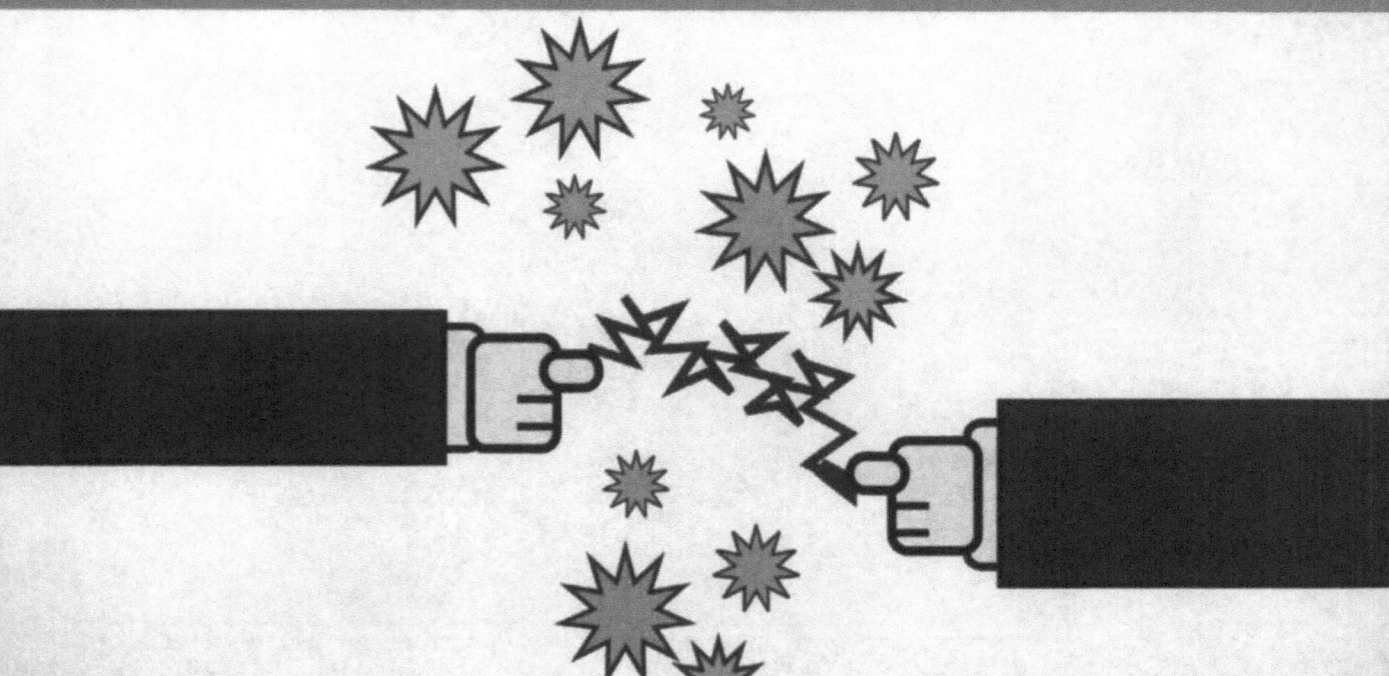

Introduction to Intranets

So, you've been given the responsibility for your company's intranet, where do you start? Before we start talking about the specifics of development it's worth looking at the basics; what exactly is an intranet anyway?

In this chapter we will introduce you to the concept of intranets, what they are and how they differ from the Internet in terms of content and development. We'll introduce the benefits an intranet can bring to your organization, and take a look at the different applications that an intranet might include. Since this chapter acts as a brief introduction to the concepts behind intranets, we will not cove the topics in detail; we will however point you in the direction of later chapters that expand on the points covered.

What Is an Intranet?

In the broadest sense of the word an intranet is a network of computers that communicate using Internet protocols, but are not part of World Wide Web. Usually an intranet is considered to be the internal computer network of an organization, but like many things, the intranet concept is a little more complicated than that.

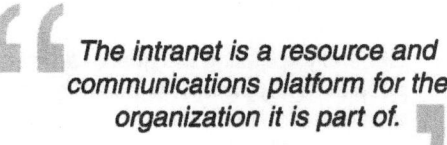

The intranet is a resource and communications platform for the organization it is part of.

It is also common to refer to the intranet as the specific web sites or applications that can be found on the network, not the network itself. Many organizations create a central portal on the network where a variety of company resources can be located through a web browser. These intranet resources can include all sorts of functionality: Common forms for the organization, reference material, customer relationship management systems, calendars, company news, contact databases, discussion forums, knowledge management utilities, and other applications. While this doesn't make the definition of the word intranet any clearer, it does make the intranet's usage more obvious: the intranet is a resource and communications platform for the organization it is part of.

Intranet, Extranet, and Internet

One of the key differences between the Internet and an intranet is that the intranet is not intended to be publicly available. On the contrary, many intranets are hidden behind multiple firewalls to protect sensitive company data from the prying eyes of the world. It would be easy to think that the intranet is simply internal to the organization's physical location, however this is not always the case, many companies open up their intranets to remote access via modem dial-in.

The matter of extranets complicates the matter further. An extranet holds a position somewhere between the Internet and an intranet. Extranets occur when limited intranet access is expanded to users external to the organization, usually a company's business clients. They are usually run on the company's internal network in order to make company resources available to users, but use the Internet for transport since the users are external to the organization's network. Again, the key is that the extranet is a closed resource for a specific group of users, and is not intended for public consumption. There is little point in debating whether any web site with a closed member area is an extranet or not, the definitions are not that exact. We'll discuss extranets further in *Chapter 14*.

Taking the above into account, another way of looking at the Internet, intranet, and extranets would be to say that the only difference between the three is the permissions you set on the resources.

Why Have an Intranet?

The first, and most obvious, reason for creating an intranet is to save money. Building and maintaining an intranet is a significant investment. It stands to reason that such an investment must give tangible benefits to the organization that builds it. If spending all this time and effort isn't going to have a beneficial effect on the bottom line, then you should question why you're undertaking the project.

Putting the right tools on the intranet can reduce costs dramatically. A typical example is saving printing costs for commonly updated resources by placing them online instead. How an intranet can save you money will depend on your organization, each has its own unique problems, you'll need to consider which routine tasks could be made more efficient by moving them to an intranet. Essentially, creating an intranet should provide a good **Return on Investment**, which we'll be taking a look at in detail in *Chapter 2*.

Generally speaking the goal of an intranet is to facilitate the sharing of data and information between people and applications, possibly spread over several locations, and to encourage the efficient use of information resources within an organization. How does an intranet make this possible? Let's look at some of the objectives that companies hope to achieve by implementing an intranet:

Increasing Efficiency

Many organizations possess a very large amount of data. Obviously there will have to be an employee and payment system, a financial system, and usually one or more systems that are directly concerned with day-to-day business activities. Besides this there is a large amount of data that is not part of any discreet system but is still valuable to the company.

Very often employees will need to take the time to research this data, without being aware of the fact that a colleague already possesses it. It would be much more efficient if that knowledge could be stored on a centralized resource so that there would be less duplication of effort. The key to a effective intranet in terms of efficiency is largely one of determining which of these resources might be useful to other members of the organization and of finding a way to let those people know the resource exists, preferably at the exact moment it is required.

Obviously this is not strictly possible, but it should be the goal to treat knowledge as a valuable company resource. Making these resources easily available will leave users more time to do the work they needed the information for.

Teleworking

By centralizing a company's data resources on the intranet employees will have more freedom to move around, within, or outside of the company's physical location. In a paper-based office, information from the personnel department, for example, could only be found in the personnel office, or possibly requested by internal mail, but on the intranet it can be interacted with from any location.

Users are no longer required to be in a specific place in order to access information. This makes it possible for users in flexible working locations, working 'on the road', and even working from home to access any company data needed to complete their tasks.

Community

As companies grow it becomes more and more difficult to give employees the feeling that they are part of an organization. Large companies spend a lot of money and resources to get employees motivated to work for the good of the company instead of just punching in and punching out on time.

An intranet can be designed to act as an interface between the company and its employees. Giving employees a central place where they can find information on the organization and their coworkers and communicate with other people in the organization can help to create a feeling of community among the workers.

Large companies in particular have an increasing need for this type of communication with their employees. An intranet can provide an ideal platform for distributing news, connecting employees, and discussing projects with workers on other sites.

Third Party Access

Centralizing company data on the intranet also creates possibilities for sharing data and knowledge with business partners and clients. This information can be made available for clients as an extranet. For example product information can be shared with resellers, stock with suppliers, and status information with customers. Besides increasing the exchange of information with the outside world, this will decrease the time needed to give out this information. Where we used to have to answer a phone or a letter to communicate with partners and customers, they can now get the information directly from the extranet freeing up time for the organization's customers. Some data could even be directly integrated into the intranets of business partners.

Differences between Intranet and Internet Development

There are some differences in working on intranet projects when compared to Internet projects. If you've never worked on an intranet before, chances are you'll finally get to use some of the more complex options of your server software. Where a lot of web sites tend to be run on shared ISP servers, intranets, by definition, are in the hands of the organization that uses it.

This doesn't mean you get to do whatever you want, intranet system administrators need to take care not to allow developers to create resource or security problems, but chances are that it will probably be a lot easier to convince your own company systems administrator to let you install some custom software than it will be to convince your ISP. Time to get out all your old books and look up the chapters you never got a chance to use before.

Known User Base

Unlike the Internet, on intranets you'll probably have a pretty good idea of what browsers and operating systems most of your users will be using. This allows for some freedom that is often missing in an Internet project. Coding for multiple browsers becomes less of a guessing game. For example, if you are using Internet Explorer then it is much easier to arrange the availability of customized ActiveX Components, whether you make them available over the network or go around and install them by hand. We'll cover the issue of browser base in more detail in *Chapter 4*.

> *Unlike the Internet, on intranets you'll probably have a pretty good idea of what browsers and operating systems most of your users will be using*

The user base has another side; for instance, mobile and handheld devices of all sorts are becoming increasingly common and are bound to become an important part of the business-IT world in the near future. Where it can be quite a painstaking process to build a WAP-site that will work in (or adapt to) every available WAP-enabled telephone, adapting a few key HTML interfaces to a specific mobile device is not that much of a project. The intranet gives you the possibility to work out these kinds of options to any extent you can come up with.

Another advantage of a knowing who your users are is that you can have a greater ability to solicit and make use of feedback. This is invaluable in the planning stage, as you will be able to accurately identify the needs of the users. It also allows you to quickly spot potential problems by testing the intranet with genuine users. Once the intranet is available knowing your users allows for a constant cycle of improvement, which is much less of a guessing game than in an Internet situation.

Type of Content

The type of content that makes up an intranet can be very different than on a web site. Whereas web sites generally contain general information available to the general public, intranets tend to concentrate on very specific data that is often part of the actual business process of an organization. You wouldn't, for example, want to publish the addresses and phone numbers of all the users of a web site, but creating a company-wide address/phonebook on the intranet is a popular and often one of the first applications created. Where a web site might contain a calendar with some public events, an intranet could make the schedules of all its employees available on the intranet (providing suitable security of course). The availability of this kind of operational data is what can make working on intranet projects such an exiting task.

Another advantage of intranets is that they often run between a hundred and a thousand times faster than most Internet users' web access, so it is much more feasible to use rich graphics and even multimedia and other advanced content on intranet pages. Not that you should just use such facilities because they are available, but certainly features like intranet-based training and induction information can benefit from rich media content.

Typically the amount of content also differs. Your organization may only have a cursory web presence of a few pages, but because of its position as a corporate resource and communications platform an intranet may contain thousands of documents split over departments and locations. This makes organizing the data efficiently much more difficult, and brings issues like usability and information architecture to the fore.

Privacy and Security

Privacy has been a hot issue on the Internet from the beginning and will continue to be in the future, and is just as vital on the intranet. Because organizations generally keep a lot of information on their employees there is a lot of data that needs to be secure. The more interesting the data, and the more applications that are created to use the data, the more privacy becomes an issue.

Many employees will applaud a better system to handle their administrative data efficiently, but this will evaporate quickly if that data is not kept from prying eyes. Giving the wrong people, even within an organization, access to the personal data of an organization's members can have serious legal and staff morale consequences.

Security is related to privacy and is a major concern in intranet development because of the kind of data available within a company on employees and about the company itself. Not only is there a legal requirement to secure data about people in the organization, but leaking out strategically important business information to other companies is a scenario many businesses fear.

An insecure network not only poses the risk of data becoming public or misused, it also creates the possibility of losing important company data to successful attempts by hackers to create havoc on your network. It's essential to track anyone who does get in. For this reason, many companies have opted to keep their internal network completely separate from the Internet or devise creative firewall constructions.

Unfortunately security is a favorite argument for people opposed to Internet-based IT projects in general and intranets specifically. Security is obviously a very important issue, but deciding against development for fear of the security issue is sort of like deciding never trying to do anything for fear that someday one thing will go wrong. While security is an issue for intranets, you should keep in mind that it is much easier to control than on the Internet. The closed nature of the intranet makes it much easier to track users and control their access. We'll talk more about security in *Chapter 10*.

The Intranet Team: People Involved

As with any project, having an effective team to back it is essential to building a successful intranet. An intranet is not like a building. You don't just build it and hand over the keys. As was discussed above, an intranet is a broad concept, a way to store and retrieve certain kinds of information within an organization. This means that the intranet must constantly adapt to changes within the organization in a number of different ways. This requires that you have a team who know your organization, and know the technologies used on the intranet.

Management

If management in general is not behind the intranet project it is already doomed to fail. Much of life in any organization, more so as they increase in size, is a matter of politics. Because an intranet, by definition, tends to work over the whole of an organization, setting it up is going to require the cooperation of a number of departments, and their managers. This means that for every bit of information needed to set up and maintain the intranet, you'll need the cooperation of that department and its management. If cooperation is lacking in some departments this will influence the quality of the content of the network and make it less likely for users to get into the habit of using the intranet. An important part of gaining trust from the managers of different departments is showing them the benefits the intranet will have for them.

Designers

Because an intranet will often use a web-like interface you'll need somebody to deal with the look and feel of the front end. This may include page layout, branding, usability and accessibility issues, and maybe a bit of information architecture. Don't be

> *Because an intranet, by definition, tends to work over the whole of an organization, setting it up is going to require the cooperation of a number of departments, and their managers*

tempted to think that these issues are purely cosmetic; a good design can make your intranet pleasant and easy to use, which will encourage people to make use of it and keep coming back.

Developers

As well as people to handle the front-end, you'll need somebody to code the back end. For a simple intranet this may be as basic as knowing how to put together some HTML, but if you are seeking to automate complex tasks via the intranet then you'll need somebody with knowledge of a suitable web scripting language, databases, or content management systems.

It is likely that you will be given the task of integrating existing systems with the intranet. If there are already a number of systems working within an organization, the chances are that you are not going to be familiar with all of them. Involving the developers who are responsible for these systems can only save you a lot of work.

Network Administrators

Since the intranet is run on the company's network you'll need the cooperation of the network administrator. Since the introduction of an intranet will have a major effect on a network, server use will increase, affecting server performance and the network itself will slow down as more information is transported over it. In addition, you will need somebody familiar with the security settings for the network to make sure information is kept secure. If you have the support of the systems administrator from the start, you can plan for the likely effects of the intranet, and make sure the correct infrastructure is in place to deal with them.

In order to use any of the company data that makes intranets so interesting to work on, you're going to need to get access to those systems. Very often access will turn out to be a matter of network access and user permissions. Getting a number of systems to work together seamlessly, ensuring privacy, security, and efficiency can be challenging enough. If on top of that you need to submit every little change in network setting to your administrator in triplicate hoping he or she is in an agreeable mood today is not going to make your life any easier.

A good administrator will also be familiar with the 'quirks' of his network. In real life networks are almost never exactly the same as the official network diagram indicates. In order to get an intranet off the ground, especially an interesting one, you'll need to know about these things. Getting the systems administrator in on an intranet project (and enthusiastic about it if you can) is essential and will save you a lot of frustration in the long run.

Content Contributors

The importance of content, and of content management, will come up many times in this book. No matter how revolutionary your intranet ideas are, how incredibly efficient your code is, or how many millions you invest in your internal network, if the intranet has nothing of practical use to offer its users, they will never use it. People are not going to

> *It is important that early on you identify who in your organization has information that should be present on the intranet, and who will be keeping it updated.*

search for data on the intranet if, from prior experience, it's not there. The more often this happens the less likely a user will even try to find information on the intranet. All of this comes down to content, and as a developer you probably won't be the one providing it. It is important to realize that if those people who are supposed to be responsible for maintaining the content of the intranet do not, the project will fail, completely. It is important that early on you identify who in your organization has information that should be present on the intranet, and who will be keeping it updated.

Users

Contrary to common belief, the success of a piece of software is not measured by how well it was designed or how efficiently it works, but in whether or not people will use it or not. What software will people use and what won't they? Well obviously it will have to be well designed, user-friendly, intuitive, and a very efficient way to work, but most importantly: it has to do what its users want it to do, what they expect it to do, and preferably do it in a way (or at least look like its doing it in a way) the user expects.

The goal of IT projects is to make existing processes work more efficiently. Who do you think knows more about those processes: management? A $250 an hour external analyst? A business expert? No, it's the people who carry them out 8 hours a day, 5 days a week. It's these people who will be using the system you are creating and it is these people who will determine the success of your project in the long run. These people are an immense resource of information about how an organization works. Not how it works on paper and not how it should work, but how it actually does. If you are designing an intranet without getting your users in on it from the very beginning you are not only wasting an invaluable resource, but your project will probably fail. Why? Because there is no way it's going to match your users' expectations.

We will talk much more about identifying your users needs in upcoming chapters, both in terms of identifying the best opportunities for return on investment, and making sure that the site is usable for the people whose day-to-day jobs will rely on the intranet.

Typical Intranet Applications and Content

An intranet can contain many applications and a variety of types of content. Though some will be specific to your organization, there are a number that are consistently useful to place on an intranet.

In its most basic form an intranet could be a simple workgroup with just a few PCs or an international corporate network spanning several countries. It might include the simple sharing of information over a shared network drive or folder, or the distribution of software applications through public folders. There are a great many small companies with this kind of network. Often these networks are used minimally, largely because even the knowledge needed to make better use of them is simply not available within the organization. However, these applications can form the building blocks for your intranet.

News, Messages, and Knowledge

Like the Internet, e-mail, messaging, bulletin boards, and e-mail discussion groups and lists are often the first and most used elements on an internal network. E-mail offers an immediacy, saves time moving around, and allows the person being mailed to choose a time suitable to them to read and respond, causing fewer interruptions and greater efficiency.

Although e-mail can be a great benefit to an organization, it can cause several problems. Because it is so often the default way of sharing information between individuals, it can result in the same information constantly being sent round, rather than being pooled in one place. Because you have to know the correct person to e-mail to get information, it can lead to the information being lost to other members of an organization, who don't know who to contact. An intranet offers many opportunities for archiving this useful information in a more accessible way, creating a knowledge base for frequently asked questions, or a discussion forum so that all users can easily contact topic experts.

We'll talk more about news and messages, and how they can make the intranet a communications platform for your organization in *Chapter 9*.

Contact Information

Address books and lists of available company resources are an essential part of most intranets. In large organizations with separated departments we are no longer 'walking around' the organization; because of this it becomes harder to get in touch with the right people within an organization. Having a central place on the intranet to find resources, whether they exist in the form of people, information, or applications can ensure greater and more efficient use of the intranet resources. As organizations become larger, and it becomes more and more difficult to keep track of the activities of all its users, this becomes more and more important.

Human Resources

According to the latest ideas in business the most important point of competition and possible advantage of one company over its competitors is found in its human resources. Companies are investing more and more money in their employees in the form of training and education.
All this can cost a lot in terms of company resources to maintain, resulting in increased interest in the development of internal HRM (Human Resource Management) systems for the organization and its employees. The intranet is an ideal place to disseminate this kind of information to employees.

Organization-Specific Applications

In any organization there is an area that can really benefit from automation in general and via the intranet specifically. Every organization has a number of processes that are specific to its day-to-day operations. Though there is good software available for a great variety of tasks, almost every organization has a number of processes that require software to be specifically written or customized. These specific applications give you a good chance of finding the 'killer app', the application that will be so useful that it makes the intranet a vital part of your organization's life. We'll talk much more about identifying which applications are needed on your company's intranet in future chapters.

Business-Critical Applications

As an intranet becomes a central resource and application platform for your organization, it is likely that you will be asked to integrate business-critical applications with the intranet. When business-critical applications are involved, some extra issues come into play. The first thing to think about is the reliability of the application. Business-critical applications need to be extensively tested, and safety procedures need to be in place for when the application does fail. One of the things that you'll probably notice is that the costs of hardware are often considerably higher for these types of application. Servers will need to have integrated backup systems, possibly RAID hard disks and special power supplies and even cooling to ensure minimal downtimes when problems occur.

Security is also a major issue. Not only do we now need to protect the data and its integrity as we would in any system, but for business-critical applications it is important that the system itself is secured against attacks, from both inside and outside the company. In large organizations with many employees this last issue should not be underestimated. Many security breaches are the result of problems within the organization.

Integrating Existing Systems

Whether or not an intranet already exists in an organization, chances are there are already one or more networked digital information systems of some sort being used. There are a number of different systems and technologies that are often used in these types of situations. Though the full details of integrating such systems go beyond the scope of this book, you should be aware that such options exist.

E-mail Servers

Microsoft's Exchange Server (*http://www.microsoft.com/exchange*) and IBM's Lotus Domino (http://www.lotus.com) are very popular applications for intranet use. Both not only manage e-mail communications, but also contacts, calendars, and scheduling tools. They can contain a great deal of very interesting information about the organization that uses it, the people that work with it, and their business contacts. Customizing these systems can provide a good starting point for the intranet, since they already provide a communications platform for a network.

SAP

SAP (*http://www.sap.com*), and a number of comparable systems such as Clarify, are basically SQL-compliant databases around which extensive software interfaces have been created for a variety of business purposes. On the intranet we will probably want to replace the proprietary interface with an HTML form or access certain data directly from within an application. In such cases these systems can best be viewed as complicated SQL-compliant databases. Since they are based on SQL, they can be accessed by a variety of means, dependent on platform, such as Microsoft's ActiveX Database Objects (ADO) or a similar interface.

Although they may run on a 'regular' SQL database, software systems such as these are very complex and very often you will need to consult a specialist to get the data you require. It is important to get this right, you can't just do test runs on an integrated administrative system without running the risk of compromising its data, with potential catastrophic consequences.

Databases and Spreadsheets

In business today a surprising number of administrative tasks are still done in Microsoft Access and even more in a spreadsheet like Microsoft Excel. Although these programs are not necessarily made for the task, the fact is that they are used a great deal. This is largely because many people have them installed already; Excel in particular, is often used because it is so easy to learn. The result is that most intranets will, sooner or later, need to connect and get some data from an Access database or an Excel sheet that can be found somewhere on the company network. And if that's not enough of a challenge, there are a host of other database systems that are commonly used in businesses, such as MS SQL Server, Oracle DBS, Progress, and more. If you are using a Microsoft platform then ODBC (Open Database Connectivity) and ADO (ActiveX Database Objects) are ideal for providing this sort of connectivity, but most web scripting languages offer methods for access of this kind.

XML

When considering integrating applications with the intranet it is well worth thinking about XML. Because it works so well as a structured data language XML is a great intermediate stage of transferring data between two systems, or in situations where security issues prevent direct access to a data source. When XML is used in this way it is much like a more structured version of the 'text-dump' we would have used for such a problem in the past.

> For more information on XML see Practical XML for the Web, glasshaus author team, glasshaus, ISBN 1-904151-08-6.

Summary

In this chapter we have covered the basic information you need to know before proceeding. We've touched on what an intranet is and what benefits it can bring to your organization. We've also covered how intranet development can differ from developing for the Internet, mainly in terms of type of content and the advantages of knowing your user base. We've also touched briefly on the people who will likely be involved in the development process and the types of applications that you might wish to develop for the intranet.

In the upcoming chapters we'll focus more on each of the problems you will encounter while developing your intranet, from the initial justification, through planning and development, to expanding the intranet to remote users and extranets.

2

- The value of Return on Investment (ROI)

- Arriving at an intranet ROI

- Avoiding problems with ROI

Author: Mike Parsons

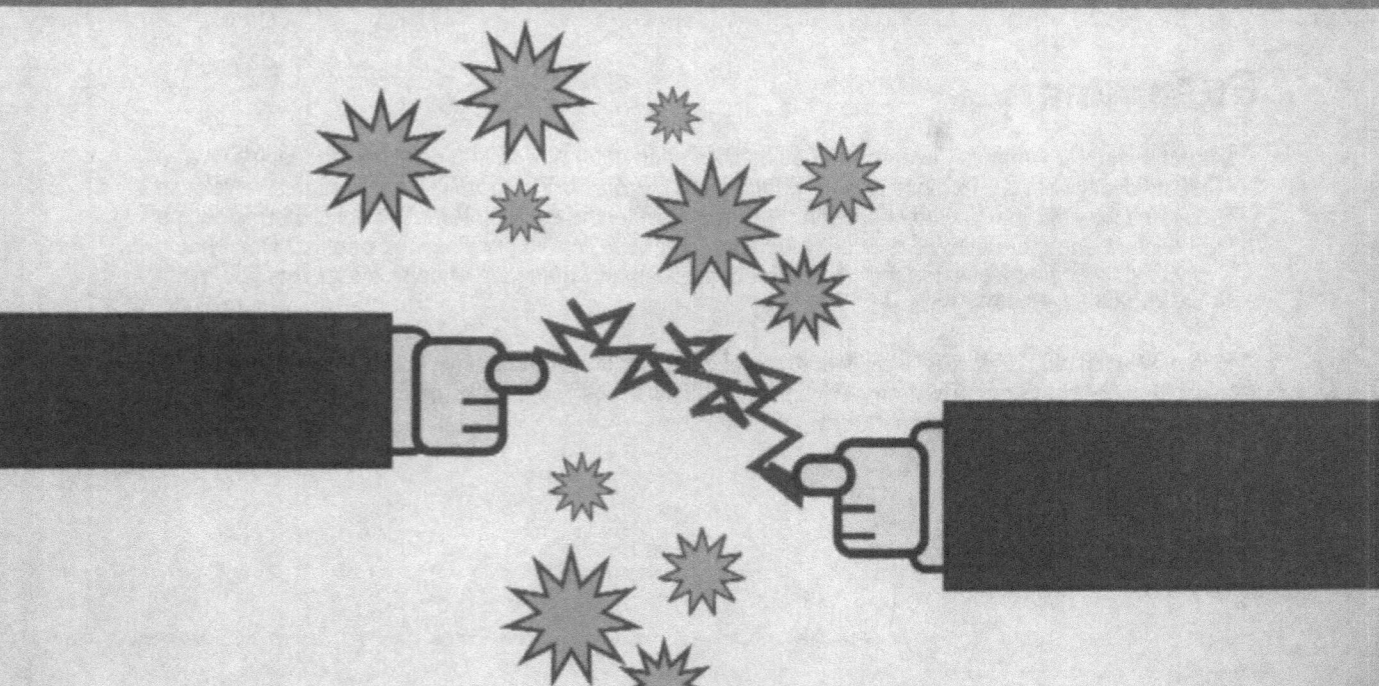

Intranet Justification

In this chapter we'll get down to determining the value of intranets and how we can communicate this to our peers and managers. In short, we'll endeavor to understand the relationship between intranets and business. That means we need to talk about money, costs, and spreadsheets. But don't let that get you down because that's not all we'll talk about. This chapter will not only help you to promote the value of intranets but also force you to look at how you can best serve your users.

To describe and measure intranet technology and its business impact we will use the term '**Return On Investment**'. **ROI** is a common term within the business and technology industries and is understood in the wider business community.

During this chapter we will cover the following topics:

- The definition of ROI

- What's the value of ROI?

- The ROI climate

- ROI types

- Possible ROI problems

- The ROI process

Definition of ROI

We all know the great impact the Internet has had on our work and personal lives. E-mail, Instant Messaging, and web surfing are now entrenched daily activities of millions of people. Increasingly, many workers are looking to their intranets to create order in a world of increasing information and interaction.

Web professionals are presented with a vast selection of functionalities for their intranet. This could range from simple document management, to sophisticated CRM (Customer Relationship Management) administration. Unfortunately we can't have everything and choices have to be made. The question becomes, how do we measure the value of the individual functionalities and make those choices? The answer is simple: **Return on Investment.**

Intranet **ROI** is an estimate of organization's total costs to build, maintain, and develop an intranet, and the organization's subsequent benefits. There are two main components to ROI: the costs and the benefits.

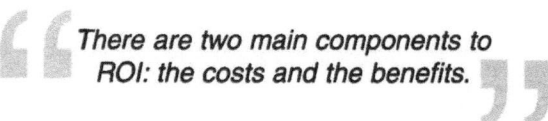

There are two main components to ROI: the costs and the benefits.

As a simple example, if you spend $120,000 to build an intranet and it generated $240,000 in cost-savings in one year – the ROI is $120,000.

$240,000	(Total savings)
- $120,000	(Total costs)
$120,000	Total ROI

The calculation is simple. But the real work is determining the figures that are entered into the formula.

What's the Value of Intranet ROI?

At this point you may be thinking: "I'm a web professional – not an accountant. I shouldn't have to do this ROI stuff!" Wrong. ROI has some very clear benefits for web professionals:

- Good ROI will sell your intranet project to managers.

- ROI aligns intranet with business strategy

- ROI improves decision-making

- ROI improves execution

Good ROI Will Sell Your Intranet Project to Managers.

I am sure you've all had those meetings where you're explaining your intranet and all its great new functionalities you've planned. At some point you start to notice the 'glazed' looks from your managers. It all becomes too technical and everyone, apart from you, was lost somewhere between Cascading Style Sheets and the SQL server.

The meeting would start much better if you said "We've found a way to save 8% of our annual printing costs – which is a total saving of $34,000". This should keep the attention of most managers. If you can show your project will save money, then you will have a much easier job selling the idea.

ROI Aligns Intranet with Business Strategy

A good intranet ROI will require that you understand the company's goals, and also allows for some measurement of success or failure based on a goal. During the ROI process members of management and different business units will participate and provide valuable insight into the goals of the business and how it plans to get there. At this point the opportunities for the intranet will start to become apparent. Therefore, it becomes logical to pursue functionalities that fit within the company's goals, rather than pursue the building of your own intranet kingdom.

Having the intranet aligned to broader objectives makes good sense. This alignment boosts the chance the intranet will be approved, and its development supported, as well as increasing the chances of its subsequent success.

ROI Improves Decision-making

Understanding the economics of your intranet gives you great clarity when it's crunch time. In fact, it can remove a great deal of tension that appears during decision-making times. How? When you have a fair measurement system the final numbers become indisputable. If you're forced to choose between two valuable functionalities in an intranet – just consult the ROI and choose the most effective functionality.

ROI Improves Execution

We all enjoy the visualization of our intranet after a tedious planning stage. However, it often seems our visual designs start to swim in a sea of buttons and icons. But when we understand the financial impact of functionality we can avoid critical areas of the intranet being neglected or plainly being left out.

Furthermore, intranet ROI requires an understanding of the typical worker's needs and daily tasks. As you guide your intranet project you ensure the user-interface will encourage and facilitate the execution of the tasks that bring the greatest ROI.

The Current Climate of ROI

ROI and technology is a hot topic in many companies right now. According to a study conducted by Forrester Research in 2002, ROI is the leading factor in prioritizing new IT projects. There are six areas that we need to consider in the current climate:

- Show me the money
- We need results today
- Who actually manages our intranet?
- I forgot about that cost
- We'll save millions
- Where's the ROI calculator?

Let's explore these trends and determine how we might respond to them in the context of an intranet project.

Show Me the Money

The measuring of the financial impact of an intranet is not such a bad thing for web professionals. Even if we don't enjoy spreadsheets and formulas, the result of a solid intranet ROI can provide insight for the development process. For example, during the planning process of the intranet you may be forced to make the choice between two different functionalities for the next release. Choosing between an employee directory and an expenses submission tool is not easy. Both are valuable for the employees and the organization – the intranet directory will have up-to-date contact information and the expense tool will make life easy for the accounts department. But looking at the ROI for both options can make the choice more obvious.

> *Even if we don't enjoy spreadsheets and formulas, the result of a solid intranet ROI can provide insight for the development process.*

If an intranet employee directory can reduce the printing of the 'hard copy' directory from six times a year down to one and access to up-to-date contact information represents a significant productivity improvement, the cost-saving on the printing could be measured at $75,000 and the time saved by employees can total an extra $50,000. But the expenses tool, despite being valuable, only represents a $12,000 saving on the current cost of handling employee expenses. The choice is easy.

In turn, the ROI will allow a project manager to brief technical and design teams far more effectively. It can be made clear to a developer that the update function is critical to the employee directory. We know this already because in the ROI analysis we saw access to recent and updated information represented a cost-saving of $50,000. Furthermore, when the designer creates a mock-up of the employee directory page it must clearly and easily allow the updating of contact information. This avoids the button or icon being hidden within the page and therefore not used by the employees.

We Need Results Today

Organizations are often looking more to the short term than they ever did during the nineties. Many companies are evaluating their activities based on what results it will produce in the next six to twelve months. And the only measurement is cash. If an intranet is not forecast to produce real cost-savings and productivity enhancements within 12 months, chances are it won't happen.

The 'quick-win' mentality of some companies can be a challenge to many intranet developers. Decision-makers are often reluctant to look beyond the next 12 months, and this can affect their attitudes towards intranets.

In response we must present intranets not only from an ROI perspective, but in a quick-win format as well. However, consider the long-term implications and risks of this approach. Without long-term planning your intranet runs the risk of being the sum of random quick-wins with no long-term cohesion. Issues such as scalability, flexibility, and integration are often the victims of short term planning.

Examples of intranet quick-wins:

- Employee Directory
- Expenses Declaration Forms
- Daily Lunch Menu
- Product and Service Information
- Company Document Templates (such as Fax, Proposals, Memo's, Project Management, etc)

If you're focusing on quick-wins also ask the following long-term ROI questions:

- What is the company's long-term strategy? How will this effect its technology needs?
- What is our vision for the intranet in 3-5 years? What will it look like and how will it function?
- What will our intranet needs be in terms of scalability, flexibility, and integration? What databases will talk to each other? Where do ERP (Enterprise Resource Planning) and CRM (Customer Relationship Management) meet?

Who Actually Manages Our Intranet?

Many intranets started as a side project for IT departments. As the intranet becomes more important, the responsibility of managing intranets has spread across several different areas of an organization such as Marketing, Human Resources, and Administration. Just who exactly is responsible for the ROI is often not clear.

Regardless of where the responsibility for your intranet sits, key representatives of the different parts of your company must play a role in determining the ROI of your next intranet project. As a web professional your insight into the company and its issues can be greatly increased by forecasting ROI for your colleagues. In their day-to-day activities your colleagues will see many different activities that can be improved with functionalities on the intranet.

At this point you need to make use of a **business steering group** and **user steering group.** Created for the intranet project, they bring together those with a stake in the intranet's design. The Business group should consist of a senior member of HR, Operations, Management, and Finance. This group is charged with establishing the main business goals and strategy – their participation creates a natural link between the intranet and business. The User group should consist of everyday users of the intranet. These people should represent the main categories of users within the organization (somebody from the accounts department, a sales person, and a receptionist). This group is charged with ensuring the intranet functionalities are relevant, easy to use, and effective.

Let's say your company has the goal of cutting costs by 10% over the next two years. The business steering group will be able to provide insight into the key areas of the business relevant to cost cutting. The areas may be purchasing, personnel, and time to market. Your chief financial officer may indicate to you that purchasing is a high-cost and inefficient process.

You can have a workshop with your user steering group the best improvements to make within purchasing tasks and process. You may determine that different business units buy their stationery separately. However, if they could combine their purchasing power they could negotiate a 12% discount with the supplier. In turn, your intranet could be a central interface of all purchasing with an application that facilitated group purchasing. When it's time to justify your intranet all you need to do is show the cost-saving on purchasing.

I Forgot About That Cost

Intranet costs are always a sum of more than the immediate cost of the server license and the billable hours of a developer. The success of an intranet is dependent on everyday workers using the intranet. These users need to be trained and supported. Also there are several operational activities that need to be covered and they all cost. In fact, personnel are usually the largest single cost of an intranet over time. Companies cannot afford to miss any of these costs; otherwise the intranet's chance of success becomes far lower. Web professionals often only attribute the direct infrastructure cost, yet it is sometimes the lowest of all costs. Many managers do not calculate the full costs of creating and managing content and the people required to do so. We'll discuss costs further in the ROI breakdown later in the chapter.

> The following research provides some insight into the real costs of an intranet: http://www.darwinmag.com/read/110101/intranet_cost_content.html.

We'll Save Millions

Did you forecast a 40% percent decrease in costs? Have you benchmarked this against other intranet case studies? Has your company ever made a cost-saving of similar proportions over the same period of time? It's better to always be on the safe side – don't set expectations too high. Clear and grounded assumptions on costs and returns need to be examined and approved before the champagne is opened. You can find a paper I wrote on specific cases of ROI at http://evolt.org/article/Optimising_Return_On_Investment_with_Intranets/25/35700. I also recommend http://www.cio.com/research/intranet/ and http://www.intranetjournal.com/.

In the previous paragraph we considered the real costs of an intranet. The logical next step in the process is to consider the real returns. However, when people discover the potential for some significant returns, they all too often jump the gun and tell the world without undergoing the proper checks and balances.

Let's set some general rules regarding over promising intranet ROI. Remember these are guidelines and you may find your company requires a special approach.

- Always take a hard line in your cost estimates. If your cost could be between $5,000 and $10,000 enter it as the higher.

- Always take a soft line with returns. For example if you think you could save $5 on the cost of handling a holiday request form, enter the saving at $4.50 or have a low and high ROI column.

- Any improvement over 50% is very high. Go back and triple-check all the numbers. Make sure you have significant evidence to support your forecast.

In very general terms (and these will differ from organization to organization):

- Any improvement over 25% is high.
- Any improvement between 10-25% sounds reasonable
- Any improvement between 0-10% is modest.

An important thing to remember is that the higher the forecast improvements, the more evidence you will need to prove them.

Where's the ROI Calculator?

Unfortunately there is no magic calculator where you can enter some data and out 'pops' a magic ROI number for your intranet. Every organization has its own unique problems, costs, and solutions. The challenge in creating an intranet ROI calculator is the very nature of intranets – internal. It's all done behind closed doors and companies are reluctant to share standards, performance benchmarks, and results. Furthermore, every company is different and finds its technology needs are unique in a particular way. But there are some things we can do to make our life easier:

- Setting benchmarks for intranet usage is very important. We want to know how regularly users visit the site, for how long, and what they do. Based on a detailed understanding of the user we can begin to see opportunities for improvement. Any further additions to the intranet can have a sound ROI based on past experiences. So make sure you use, and keep, your site stats.

- Work closely with your financial and operational people. These peers will give you insight into the business issues and by becoming familiar with those you'll start to gather insight into the relationship between business and intranet technology. Over time your thinking towards ROI will become more holistic and more insightful towards metrics and formulas.

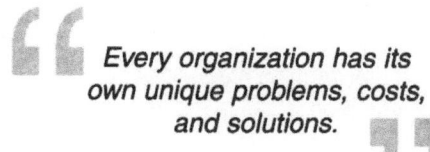

Every organization has its own unique problems, costs, and solutions.

The Different Types of ROI

Let's look at what we've covered up to this point before we jump into the types of ROI. We have a working definition of ROI and we've established its relevance to web professionals and their intranet projects. Remember, intranet ROI is an estimate of an organization's total costs to build, maintain, and develop an intranet, and the organization's subsequent benefits. There are two main components: the costs and the benefits.

So now you're dying to put ROI to work on your next intranet project. There are many different forms of ROI, however there are three popular types of ROI you may hear of within IT:

- **The Cost Benefit Approach** – This is a traditional method based on financial paradigms such as costs and returns. Types include Economic Value Added, Total Cost of Ownership, Total Economic Impact, and Rapid Economic Justification.

- **The Vendor Selection Approach** – Largely used as a risk-management tool helping managers choose between vendors and technology. Types include Balanced Scorecard, Information Economics, Portfolio Management, and IT Scorecard.

- **The Risk Management Approach** – A measure of probability that suits very large IT projects. Types include Real Options Valuation, Applied Information Economics.

The method you apply depends on what question you're looking to answer. For our intranet ROI we will be looking to measure the real benefits for the company. Risk and vendor selection will not be directly addressed in the following material. The model we will apply is the Cost Benefit Approach. I have selected this model as it keeps things simple and is easy for first-time users to implement and use. Before we look at implementing ROI let's be aware of some the problems organizations regularly have with the process.

I cannot stress enough how important simplicity is when approaching ROI. Complexity usually increases as you go through the process and touch on forecasting returns. The attributing of value to enhanced productivity can be complex as it's an estimate of future behavior not a measure of past behavior. Later in our intranet process I'll provide a framework for conducting ROI and we'll focus on keeping it simple and avoiding mistakes.

Rapid Economic Justification As an Advanced Model for Intranet ROI

REJ is very powerful because it incorporates an extensive approach to total costs and also seeks to align IT and business goals. The process begins with a quick scan of the organization and looks to uncover who the stakeholders are and their true expectations. Furthermore, it works on a roadmap basis to get the project to completion. This makes the model a great intermediary for business and IT executives.

Later in this chapter I will provide a basic framework for ROI that will get you started and avoid the common pitfalls. You may wish to develop your approach and I suggest you take some time to understand REJ to help you develop ROI forecasting.

The model was originally created by Microsoft as a way of understanding the value of technology projects. For more information about Rapid Economic Justification you can visit the Microsoft site or download this white paper:

http://www.microsoft.com/business/whitepapers/value/valuerejwp.asp
http://www.microsoft.com/business/downloads/value/rejwhitepaper.doc

A great discussion of the REJ model can be found at
http://knowledge.wharton.upenn.edu/microsoft/070302.html.

You may find REJ too much information. However, REJ provides a proven way to develop a company's approach towards business and technology and can go beyond the intranet.

Avoiding Problems with Intranet ROI

Although the basic principle is straightforward, the devil is in the details. So here are some rules to keep you out of trouble.

Business Impact, Not Cost Allocation

By calculating intranet ROI we're aiming to uncover an intranet's most powerful and profitable functionalities. We must uncover its true cost in order to determine ROI – but our job does not stop there. Equally, we must establish the improvement in company performance due to the intranet.

Remember the critical process in intranet ROI is the alignment of business and the intranet. You must be confident of determining the high-impact functionalities of an intranet. These functionalities must deliver benefits to the company in either a qualitative or financial way.

Poor Numbers In, Poor Numbers Out

If your basic numbers are incorrect or calculated on wildly optimistic formulas then your intranet project is doomed. In these circumstances history suggests everyone from management to sales will be expecting intranet utopia: an unrealistic utopia of cost reduction and productivity increases, none of which are actually forthcoming. It is important that you manage expectations, and don't give a false impression of how the intranet will benefit people. The fact is you must establish realistic numbers related to costs and forecasts in order to create a solid ROI.

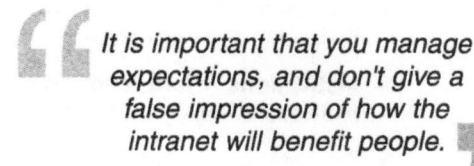

It is important that you manage expectations, and don't give a false impression of how the intranet will benefit people.

It's a Group Thing

One of the most powerful mechanisms in creating intranet ROI is group participation. No single individual can determine intranet ROI by them self. Often the result of a one-man ROI is a rather narrow and unrealistic document. A simple solution is to use the two groups we mentioned earlier, the **business steering group** and the **user steering group**. As a result of group involvement, the final intranet ROI has its foundation within the context of the overall business strategy and is connected to the daily lives of the employees.

Of course it may not be within the remit of the intranet developer to create groups like these. However, there may well be a business steering group or similar. If there is, then it is useful to get hold of the reports and documents that arise from their meetings, and make sure that these form a significant part of your decision-making process.

The Time Problem

Finally, as with all projects, time is bound to be an issue. You may not have the time you would like to put together an extensive ROI. One of the things you need to be successful in is research and background information, but it takes time to acquire and consolidate such information. Take care that pressure to get the re-design started and completed quickly doesn't lead to mistakes and oversights.

The ROI process and Data

The process you're about to read is a framework for delivering a cost-benefit ROI broken down into steps. In many cases a web professional or project manager may be working with someone from management or IT that is conducting an ROI plan. For that reason, the example focuses on true costs and how to determine realistic benefits.

Step 1: Quick-scan

The first stage is to create a very clear set of business goals and intranet functionalities that will help achieve them.

Create Background Document

- **Project History (Activities, People, Status)** – For example: Have we done an intranet before? Was it a success? Why? Who managed the project? What's their advice for this project? What does the current intranet look like? How is it performing?

- **Parties Involved (Internal, Vendors, Clients)** – Who is involved in this project and what are their roles and responsibilities?

- **Motivations (Hard and Soft)** – Hard motivations: more sales, less costs, etc. Soft motivations: happy staff, better knowledge-sharing, better culture.

- **Expectations** – What is going to be delivered? How will it be managed? How will it be communicated to the staff?

- **Current Intranet Overview** (include costs, benefits, and functionalities).

Project Plan

- **Aims** – A summary should be made of the Motivations and Expectations, with quantified statements.

- **Deliverables** – A shopping list of what will be created. Should include infrastructure, people, process, plans, and documents.

- **Communication** – List of all parties that will be communicated to. Then define objectives of communication: What will be communicated? What media will be communicated? How frequently will it be communicated? Who will communicate the information?

- **Roles and Responsibilities** (Who, What, When).

- **Critical Path** (A timeline of the project listed by deliverable).

- **Budget** (initial & ongoing).

Business Steering Group Meeting

Define business and intranet goals (including quick-wins). The meeting of this group must include senior managers from different parts of the company (technology, information, and finance directors, for example). The remaining members should be chosen according the goals of the intranet ROI. The main output of the meeting should be a mutually agreed chart like the one below. This outlines which functionalities have the greatest overall value.

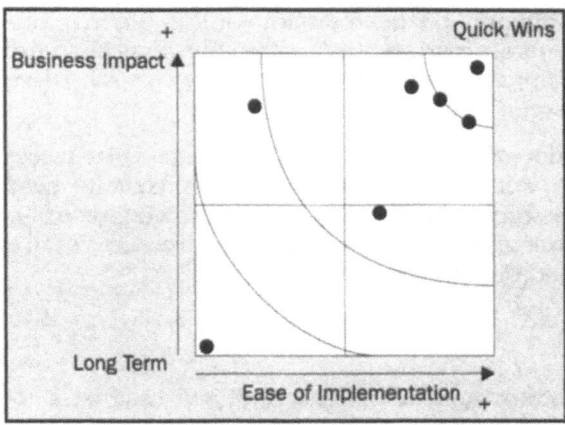

The diagram above demonstrates the business value of different functionalities within an intranet. For example an employee contact directory is usually easy to implement and has a large impact of ROI. However, an expense tool may have similar impact but is harder to implement. Therefore it moves towards the left of bottom axis.

User Steering Group

Define intranet functionalities. Working from the business goals and quick-wins determined by the Business Steering Group, the User Group would translate those into realistic functionalities. All functionalities should clearly connect to a business goal.

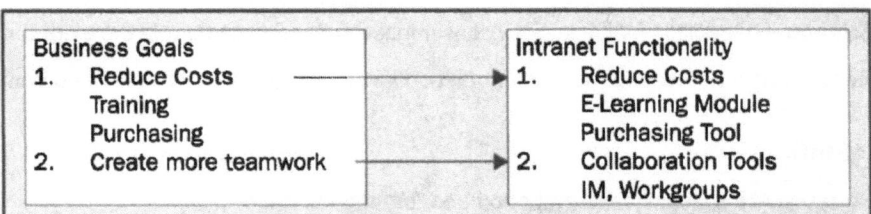

Step 2: Assumptions

The assumption step will establish how we arrive at the numbers that we enter into our formula. Make sure your CFO (Chief Financial Officer) is highly involved in this process. Your CFO will have a lot of input in this stage so I will cover some fundamentals of intranet ROI and you should add specific items related to the way your company works. Here's a list of assumptions that should be covered:

- **Define cost allocation between departments and corporation.** – In larger-sized organizations this can be a huge issue. Make sure you're clear if a business unit or head office pays a cost. For example, a server could be covered by head office but a special software package for an individual business unit is likely to be charged to the business unit.

- **Define interest charges and depreciation.** – Publicly traded companies especially will have policies on how these charges are handled. For example the cost of a server and its depreciated value may be spread over three years by the finance department. Your ROI should do likewise.

- **Define calculation of employee time usage.** – Later in the process you will estimate time-savings and their worth. Here we need to be clear on how we measured current time usage. I suggest using a logbook with a small sample group over a one or two week period. That way you can safely outline the average tasks and time allocations of an employee (as with all user questioning, avoid influencing the results).

Step 3: Costs

The next step is to work out the costs. Make sure you consider all of the items below when calculating the true costs of your project:

Infrastructure:

- **Servers** – You should include operating system, web server software, and security.

- **Routers** – Make sure you have enough routing capacity for the 'forecast' traffic.

- **Load balancing** – Ensure you network administrator has the required load balance capacity across servers at peak times (usually the morning on an intranet).

- **Databases** – You have both proprietary and open source solutions in this space. Make sure you cover licenses and support.

- **Storage** – Especially for backup purposes, make sure you can handle the extra data created.

- **Bandwidth** – Forecast bandwidth when you link externally and provide video content.

Central Staff:

- **Consultants** – Usually external people for strategy and tactics.

- **Project managers** – These can be internal and external.

- **Management team** – Ensure you allocate staff time costs as determined by HR policy.

- **Designers** – These can be internal and external.

- **Developers** – These can be internal and external.

- **System administrators** – These can be internal and external.

Content / Service Production and Maintenance:

- **Editor and Content Management System operator** – Who will enter content, publish material, and plan content needs.

- **HTML tools** – Do you need Dreamweaver or Frontpage? Or do you have a custom-made CMS?

- **Multimedia Tools** – Tools such as Real Producer and Final Cut Pro.

- **Application tools** – Tools that build your application environment such as JRUN, Delphi, etc.

Users' Wasted Time:

Name conventions – How much will it cost if the name of buttons and sections do not relate to the users?

User interface – How much will it cost if the layout of the intranet does not improve activities?

Search Engine – The more data on an intranet, the more people will use Search. How much will it cost if users cannot find information quickly and easily?

Other Items

Training – This includes manuals and live sessions.

Promotion – What means will be used to promote the intranet, such as Posters, Newsletters, Parties, etc.

Support – How will users be serviced when they have a problem with the intranet?

Log analyzer software – Software used to understand user behavior on a site.

Step 4: Benefits

There are two main categories of benefits – tangible and non-tangible. Tangible benefits consist of cost-savings and productivity increases. The non-tangibles include staff morale, openness, flexibility, etc. For some organizations the non-tangibles will be more important than others.

Example of Costs Reduced – Employee Directory Annual Intranet ROI

Using an no-hard-copy delivery, printable version available for download:

$213,000	(Total cost-saving – Printed 6 times per year + shipping)
- $ 34,000	(Cost of development and maintenance)
$179,000	Total ROI per year.
520%	ROI within one year

Please note: Employee Directory via the intranet is always a great return. Don't expect this ROI on every function within an intranet.

Example of Productivity Increases – Intranet Sales Kit

Many sales executives complain about not having enough information to do their job. An intranet can be very effective in delivering information directly to the sales executive. Furthermore, access to templates and materials for sales can improve the time spent on a proposal and its effectiveness. For example:

- 57% of sales persons' activities are directly related to sales

- 43% of their time on is spent on no sales activities (see log books for more information)

- By providing rapid delivery of sales information, access to order status and sales templates via our intranet we can save 10% of their time.

- Assuming this extra time is spent on sales

$17,520.00	Weekly revenue per sales person from 57% of their time
$ 3,073.69 +	10% increase in time allocated to sales-related activities
$20,593.69	Total revenue per sales person
$ 3,073.69	Revenue increase per sales person
200 x	Number of sales persons
$614,738.00	Total increase in sales
$614,738.00	(Total increased revenue)
$140,300.00	(Cost of development and maintenance)
$474,438.00	Total ROI within one year
	338% ROI within one year

These examples provide you with the format for estimating tangible benefits. However, never forget to list the intangibles as well. Here's a list of benefits that may be relevant to your intranet projects:

- **Becoming a knowledge and innovation company** – Sharing knowledge between employees has two major benefits. The first, employees learn from each other and avoid duplicating mistakes, thus making activities cost less. The second benefit of knowledge-sharing is innovation. Knowledge-sharing can stimulate employees and help them see opportunities both inside and out.

- **Better quality information for decision-making** – Some companies are starting to create digital dashboards on their intranets. GE and Cisco already have the ability to get daily data regarding many aspects of the company performance via their digital dashboards. The benefit is that the business information is centralized in the intranet. Executives can then access and update information on a daily basis. As a result they can immediately identify changes in their customer behavior and respond accordingly.

- **More content and empowered staff** – Many employee activities can be supported. Activities such as transfers, stock options management, pension, leave and holiday, payroll, overtime, discussions, and feedback can all be supported online. At Cisco, they reduced staff turnover by 50% after the launch of the employee self-services intranet. This not only supports the notion that staff were happier but also has bottom-line benefits given the cost of hiring and training people.

- **Breaking down barriers to information** – Many companies struggle to share information among departments. This is a culture and structure issue foremost. But intranets can be the underlying infrastructure that facilitates the sharing process. Employees can begin to discover what exists beyond their office.

Finally, before you run through the cafeteria shouting, "The intranet will solve all our problems!" you and your peers should ask yourselves these questions:

- "Am I confident that I am aware of all the possible costs?"

- "Are the benefits and improvements really achievable?"

- "Would I sign this document and present it to the CEO?"

Summary

In this chapter we set out to define the benefits and value of intranets – the relationship between business and technology. We used the term **Return on Investment** to describe this value. And we defined **ROI** as an estimate of organization's total costs to build, maintain, and develop an intranet, and the organization's subsequent benefits. There are two main components: the costs and the benefits.

A well-thought out ROI is especially useful in communicating the business-value of having an intranet to your peers and managers, creating support for your project. Another key value factor of ROI is that it can be instrumental in making your intranet more effective.

Our next step was to get into the nuts and bolts of ROI within the organization. Crucially we identified that managers are looking for results in the short term. These results must really hit the bottom line in terms of cash flow and profit. Also we identified the issue of really understanding the true costs of an intranet project.

Keep focused on your goal of establishing the value of intranets and you will unlock the huge potential of intranets within your organization.

The model we chose for forecasting ROI was a traditional cost benefit model. The problems we tried to avoid included 'poor numbers in, poor numbers out' and 'I forgot about that cost'.

We finished with the basic process for defining ROI. In performing this process the single most important aspect is to keep the process simple. Keep focused on your goal of establishing the value of intranets and you will unlock the huge potential of intranets within your organization.

3

- Identifying stakeholders
- Choosing the tools
- Planning the development

Author: Darren James Harkness

Where Do I Start?

In previous chapters, we discussed what an intranet is, why it can be useful for your organization to have one, and how to justify one. You're probably already itching get started, but, like any good adventurer, you'll want to prepare for your journey first.

Many web developers dive headlong into an intranet project without first sitting down and properly planning it through. In this chapter, we'll discuss how to do this by:

- Identifying the stakeholders in your organization's intranet and categorizing them into groups
- Creating a specific set of questions to ask your stakeholders to help guide the intranet's development
- Finding the "killer app"
- Identifying common problems met by each of your intranet development team
- Creating a development schedule for your organization's intranet
- Planning a release schedule for features on the intranet
- Building hardware specifications

We'll try to prepare you as much as we can in this chapter, but be forewarned: there may be other issues that emerge, which are specific to each individual organization, such as personalities or relative importance of individual departments.

Whether you have an existing intranet and you plan to improve it, or you're starting from scratch, make sure you have management buy-in before you do *anything*. Nothing is worse than spending hours on a project, only to have it killed because management didn't know you were working on it. Getting management buy-in can be a simple process, if you follow the steps in the previous chapter. Once you have it, you can start the most time-consuming, but most important, stage of intranet development: the planning and research stage.

I Love It When a Plan Comes Together

Before you even begin thinking of how to develop your intranet from a technical standpoint, you need to sit down and plan the development of your intranet from a human standpoint. If an intranet doesn't meet the needs of the people using it, the hours of technical work put into it will be worthless. The best way to do this is to bring together the people who will be using the intranet and the people who will develop the intranet, to discuss what is needed.

Identifying the Stakeholders

Before you start building the intranet, you need to know what will be there. In the introductory chapter, we discussed the various people involved in the intranet team: Management, Content Contributors, Developers, Designers, the Network Administrator, and the enduser.

Each of these is a member of the intranet process, and is extremely important to its successful launch.

- The **Management** budgets for the intranet, and depends on its successful operation.

- The **Content Contributors** create and coordinate information on the intranet.

- The **Developer** creates the back end of the intranet, ensuring information can be shared seamlessly and securely.

- The **Designer** creates the front end of the intranet, crafting an interface that's intuitive and easy to use.

- The **Network Administrator** is responsible for the (hopefully) stable and secure operation of the network the intranet is hosted on.

- The **Enduser** is the primary audience for the intranet, and therefore the most important person in the organization to its success. This group contains both internal users of your intranet and external users such as strategic business partners, vendors and customers who might benefit from a higher level of communication with your organization.

> *The management and endusers make up the* **stakeholders** *in your organization's intranet — the people who either make or break its success.*

Miss one of these groups, and the whole project can self-destruct. However, of all the members in your intranet development process, two are of more importance than the rest: management, and the enduser. Both have more of a vested interest in the success of your organization's intranet and have a symbiotic relationship: management has to show that the ROI justifies the intranet's development costs, which is best shown by the amount of use it receives from the endusers. As we discussed in *Chapter 2*, proving the ROI to the Management can be a relatively painless process given the right preparation.

The stakeholders will let you know:

- What the scope of the intranet should be. Intranets can be as small as sharing contact and appointment data, or complete information and productivity portals.

- What information the intranet should contain. This goes hand-in-hand with the previous point; once you decide what level of detail (basic forms or specific project information) the intranet will contain, your stakeholders will help you to decide what that information is.

- The budget for the project.

- A time estimate for the intranet's initial development.

Questionnaires

The best way to start planning the development of the intranet is to draft up a short questionnaire, which you can use to direct conversations with your stakeholders. The questionnaire will help you to extract a significant amount of information from the stakeholders, if it is written clearly and succinctly. Avoid using technical jargon in the questions; ensure they can be understood by anyone within the company, regardless of technical prowess.

Here's a sample stakeholder questionnaire. Let's assume for this example that we're installing an intranet at a software development company. Our stakeholder questionnaire might look something like this:

The questionnaire will help you to extract a significant amount of information from the stakeholders, if it is written clearly and succinctly.

1 What is your department and position?

2 How would you rate your need for a centralized resource for information on the network?

- ☐ Critical

- ☐ Important

- ☐ Somewhat important

- ☐ Average

- ☐ Not Important

3 How often do you find yourself e-mailing common information back and forth to other members of your organization?

- ☐ Many times daily

- ☐ Daily

- ☐ Weekly

- ☐ Monthly

- ☐ Never

4 How would you rate the need for a method of group communication on the network?

- ☐ Critical
- ☐ Important
- ☐ Somewhat Important
- ☐ Average
- ☐ Not Important

5 On a 1-10 scale, where 1 is not important, and 10 is critical, how would you rate the following features if they were added to the network?

- ☐ Discussion forums
- ☐ File Database
- ☐ Secure filesharing between different groups
- ☐ Common office forms
- ☐ Customer relations management
- ☐ Support Database
- ☐ Other

6 What do you feel is currently missing as a method of communication among members of your organization?

7 What daily tasks do you currently find cumbersome and inefficient?

8 On a 1-10 scale, where 1 is minor, and 10 is major, rate how the above tasks would improve by making these resources available on the network

- ☐ Substantial improvement in productivity
- ☐ Increased productivity
- ☐ Moderate amount of productivity
- ☐ No increase in productivity
- ☐ Decrease in productivity

Creating a short, but effective stakeholder questionnaire is extremely important in the beginning stages of planning your intranet. Try to keep the questionnaire to about one or two pages; you are going to have a hard enough time convincing people to spare a moment to complete it; if it is short and to the point, then you are more likely to get a good level of response.

The answers obtained from these questionnaires will be invaluable tools in your decision-making process. The more insight you get, the more the intranet will match the needs of the users.

Because of its short nature, you need to pack as much punch into the questions as possible. Go for the following key pieces of information:

Keep in mind that organizations will have different levels of technical knowledge, beware of using too much technical jargon in the questionnaire. Avoid asking leading questions (questions that imply the answer you want). Both of these problems could skew your results.

- If an intranet exists, identify what is currently missing

- Identify what resources the stakeholders feel the intranet should have, and why

- Identify what roadblocks are in the way of users accessing your organization's resources

The results of your stakeholder questionnaire will help you to determine your **Functional Needs Analysis**, which we will discuss further in *Chapter 5*. The questions should be designed in such a way as to give you a broad overview of what it is your users want and how useful it will be to them.

Stakeholder Meeting

A great way to kick off development is to book a few hours to sit down with the developers, designers, content creators, and one or two endusers to roughly map out how the intranet should look and function. Even a small organization should be able to appoint a content contributor, a developer, a designer, and two end users. If you are outsourcing your developer or designer, ask them to be present at this meeting.

Each group will have valuable contributions towards the ultimate framework of the intranet: the developers and designers will help to guide the information architecture of the intranet, the content creators will help guide the content of the intranet, and the users will help guide the process overall, by giving you first-hand comments on the suggestions the various team members are making.

Some important questions should be addressed in this discussion, including:

- Do the content creators need an administrative portal to enter the content?

- Are the content creators' requests possible from the developer's point of view? Can the developer think of a more efficient or viable solution?

- How complex is the intranet? Is it a file-sharing service, a collaborative tool, or a central part of their job function?

- If your organization consists of several different groups, how do those groups interact with the information on the intranet, and each other?

- Should the developer create a custom intranet, or should they use an out-of-the-box solution?

When you hold this discussion, bring lots of pencils and paper. Have each member detail a wish list for the intranet, and show relations between information and groups using the intranet. Have the designer show roughly how navigation would work throughout it. The end users will be valuable gauges for the suggestions your developer and designer make.

Don't be too worried about details such as color or wording just yet, instead try to pin down a basic plan.

Choosing Your Tools

Once you have decided *what* you are going to develop on your intranet, you need to decide *how* you are going to do it. This means sitting down and working out what hardware your intranet will use, and what software it will run on. This is probably the most difficult task for most web developers working on an intranet. Most have a basic idea of what hardware *should* be used, but don't have much of an idea of exactly what they should be looking for. In this section, we'll discuss some of the basics. From there you can go to your IT department and manager, feeling more confident about discussing your needs.

Choosing Hardware.

Your hardware is just as important a choice as the software you choose to run your intranet on. Many web developers do not care a whit about the hardware they are using, so long as it works. Which is unfortunate, since this is an extremely important decision to make. Poor hardware choices will cause performance drops, which will be painfully noticeable to your intranet's users.

Horsepower

There are three things that will make or break a server's performance: CPU, RAM, and hard drive space. Don't go crazy – a 5-person organization doesn't have the same resource requirements as a 500-person organization does.

Regardless, you are better off going with a server-level solution from a respected retailer such as Dell or HP. If you are planning on performing resource-heavy applications, such as a complex database system, or a complicated intranet application, you will want to look into a fairly high-powered CPU – possibly even a dual-CPU system. If you are only planning on hosting static pages, with an online form here or there, a lower-powered CPU will work just fine.

Whichever choice you make for CPU power, you will want to put lots of RAM into your intranet server – the more the better. This is especially true for larger organizations, who may potentially be serving hundreds of users at once.

You'll also want to place a large amount of hard drive storage in the server. Since a large amount of information will be transmitted through, stored on, or be created by the intranet, the last thing you want is to run out of storage space.

RAID and Backup Solutions

If you are hosting mission-critical data on the intranet server, you may want to investigate installing a RAID (Redundant Array of Inexpensive Disks). The theory behind the RAID is that data on your server is redundantly stored across several hard drives; if one hard drive fails, you avoid data loss. This does tend to add to the hardware purchase cost, as a RAID takes at least two hard drives and works much quicker on SCSI hard drives than on IDE.

In addition, you should also create a plan for backing up information on your intranet. It will be a valuable resource, and you don't want to lose all the information it contains. Ideally, you would back up the data nightly onto magnetic tape (or CD or DVD depending on preference); once a week, you would take this backup to a secure off-site location as protection against theft or property damage.

Network Hardware

Depending on the current size of your network, you may want to consider upgrading your current network equipment to handle the extra stress of the intranet traffic, which will be considerable if daily tasks are moved to the intranet. This could be as simple as upgrading from 10MB Ethernet to 100MB Ethernet, or as complicated as installing routers on the network.

Hardware Life Span

Something to keep in mind is that most hardware has a replacement cycle of two to five years. When creating your budget for intranet hardware, you should count on replacing the entire system on an average of every three years. If you already have existing intranet hardware, you should find out how far along it is in the hardware replacement cycle. If it is past the two-year mark, you will want to budget in new hardware as a replacement.

Ask your IT department to compare the cost of leasing versus buying your server hardware. Many system integrators offer excellent lease prices. The benefit to leasing is that when your lease term is over, you can trade up to new hardware without wasting resources.

Special Considerations

If you have remote users, or want users to be able to connect to the intranet from home, you may have to make special network considerations, such as providing remote dial-in facilities or creating a demilitarized zone (DMZ). A DMZ is a segregated network within your organization that allows remote users to access your intranet without compromising the rest of your internal network.

If you plan to do something like this, you will need to add networking hardware such as hubs and routers to your IT budget. Make sure you present preliminary budgets to management once you have decided what hardware to use for your intranet, to avoid having to scramble at the last minute to meet your budget.

Choosing Software

The first place to start when you're developing your intranet is to decide whether to use an out-of-the-box intranet software package, a hosted solution, or to custom-build your own intranet software. Each choice has definite advantages and disadvantages, depending on your organization's size and budget. Though we will get into more detail in *Chapter 5*, you will want to decide now which of the above you are going to use.

Out-of-the-Box Solutions

The Internet abounds with out-of-the-box intranet solutions. The biggest players are Microsoft Exchange and Lotus Notes, though there are literally hundreds of other contenders.

Out-of-the-box solutions come in two forms: in-house and hosted. In-house intranet packages are installed on your own network, giving you complete control over access and a small level of customization. Hosted solutions are housed on a remote server, freeing up your IT staff for other projects.

Software packages, such as Lotus Notes, or Microsoft Exchange are very popular for organizations with limited IT budgets, or no development staff. These applications offer a lower over-all TCO (Total Cost of Ownership) than custom solutions, as well as support, but offer far less customization.

The big benefit, however, is that you can have a fully functional intranet in a day or two, without a significant investment in development time. This is valuable for smaller organizations with a limited IT staff; it allows them to get back to other projects within a relatively short amount of time.

Though out-of-the-box solutions seem a relatively cheap and easy way of putting up an intranet, they are not always the best solution. These solutions cover a very general range of functions for an intranet, giving features such as expense reporting, online discussions, and calendars. However, industry or company-specific functions such as software bug tracking, customer incident reports, or customer relationship management (CRM) tools will not be included, and may be expensive add-ons.

Customizing out-of-the-box solutions can often be a painful process. With out-of-the-box solutions, you are forced to adapt to the software, rather than the software adapting to you. This will add to development time for customization, as well as to training time. It may be that you spend so much time altering existing software, that you may as well have written your own in the first place.

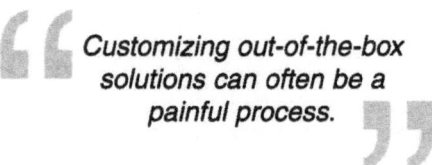
Customizing out-of-the-box solutions can often be a painful process.

Finally, many intranet software packages feature per-seat licensing costs, limiting you to the amount of users that can connect to your intranet. Though this is not necessarily a concern for smaller organizations, this can drastically increase the cost for larger organizations.

We will discuss out-of-the-box solutions in more details in coming chapters.

Hosted Solutions

A growing choice in Intranet software is the hosted solution. With this solution, your Intranet is maintained and hosted by a third party, outside your network. Hosted solutions have the advantage of incredibly fast implementation time. All you need to do with a hosted solution is to specify what content and features you want the solution provider to give you. There are also no direct hardware purchase or maintenance costs, which can be a distinct advantage if you have few in house support staff.

There are some distinct disadvantages to these solutions, the most obvious being cost. For a small organization, this might be negligible when compared to custom development, but for larger organizations, licensing fees can quickly add up.

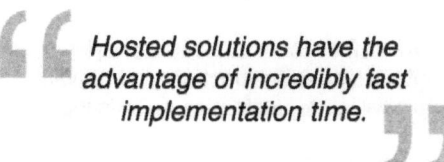

Hosted solutions have the advantage of incredibly fast implementation time.

There will also be very little potential for customization. Since the hosting solution hosts more than just your intranet, they will generally have a template, which is used for all of their clients. Though you may be able to customize within this template, there will still be limits to what you can do. If you have very specific non-standard requirements, this approach may not be the best for you.

Security is also an issue. Although the solution provider will do all they can to ensure the privacy of your data, it is still is also an issue for these solutions, since information will be traveling over the Internet, unless security is properly handled the system could be prone to eavesdropping.

Home-brew

If you have a developer you can dedicate to the creation and upkeep of your intranet, then home-brew is definitely the way to go. Although it can make for a higher total cost of ownership overall, developing your own intranet software offers you a much larger potential for customization, and will match your organization's needs more accurately.

The advantages of building your own intranet software are more significant for larger organizations, but include:

- The intranet is custom-built to your organization's needs.

- Your developers do not need to work around someone else's sourcecode. As a result, development of custom applications should go faster, overall.

- In-house support of your intranet. You don't have to wait for the vendor's support department to get back to you if any issues emerge, nor do you have to pay additional support fees.

- No licensing fees. For larger organizations, a custom built intranet can often be less expensive than out-of-the-box solutions, due to per-seat licensing fees.

3

There are still some disadvantages to building your own Intranet software, however:

- Development time. Building your own intranet software will add considerably to your development time, since it effectively has to be built from scratch.

- Bugs. As with all software development projects, unintended 'features' will appear in the intranet software from time to time. If you put a strong Quality Assurance (QA) system in place on the intranet development, however, this should be kept to a minimum.

Given that there are several open source applications available throughout the Internet for many intranet-specific functions, going with a home-brew solution may work better in the long run if you are willing to customize an existing piece of software, rather than build everything from scratch.

Another benefit of using a home-brew is the lack of licensing costs for most applications. You can also add and remove modules, expand on feature sets, or remove redundant ones as time progresses. In the coming chapters, we'll talk about the process of developing your own software in more detail.

Choosing an Operating System

Before you start installing or developing software for your intranet, you need to decide what Operating System (OS) your hardware will run. Several factors come into play when choosing an OS for your intranet:

- Which OS is currently in place?

- Do you already have a dedicated internal intranet server?

- Does your organization have licensing agreements with a major OS provider, which locks you into a specific OS?

- Are there licensing fees to consider?

- What are your performance requirements?

- Which OS do most of your users already use?

At the moment the two most common options when it comes to a server-level operating system: Windows and Linux/BSD. Each has its advantages and disadvantages:

Advantages and Disadvantages of Windows

Windows has quite a few advantages, which makes sense when you consider that it's one of the most prevalent operating systems in the business world. Some of these advantages are:

- Many application suites are available.

- Easy integration of Windows authentication systems and scripting.

- Much written documentation on Windows.

- 24-hour commercial support and maintenance plans available.

- Easy-to-use GUI administration interface. Administrating a Windows system is a relatively straightforward process.

Being an extremely popular choice has its downfalls, however. These include:

- Licensing costs – If you have a medium- to enterprise-sized organization, licensing costs on Windows (and intranet suites commonly built for Windows) can be a crippling addition to the initial cost of your intranet. It also presents scalability problems, as you may grow larger than your licensing scheme.

- Stability – Windows products have a bad reputation for being unstable.

- Resources – Undertaking identical tasks, Windows servers often require more resources than Linux-based servers.

- Security – Windows has its share of problems with vulnerabilities, security problems, and viruses, largely because it is so common and has proven to be so easy to exploit due to poor configuration.

- Less frequent updates – Major operating system updates only come every few months in the form of service packs.

- 'Black box' development model – The Windows source is a shrouded mystery. Though this gives the illusion of security through obscurity, it also gives you far less control over the finer details of the operating system.

Some of the disadvantages of Windows such as stability and security can be remedied by making sure the system is configured correctly in the first place, but this requires that you have the correct technical knowledge available in your organization already.

Advantages and Disadvantages of Linux/BSD

Linux and BSD offer a number of advantages to the intranet developer:

- Many open source applications are available, with sourcecode available to make for easy customization

- Linux/BSD is developed in a 'crystal box' environment. In other words, the source for Linux/BSD is open for review, which means weaknesses are constantly and consistently being found and fixed in the operating system's core. It also means you can change the operating system if you feel brave enough.

- Uses less machine resources than Windows. Linux still runs admirably on a 486.

- Frequent update cycle. Linux kernels (the core of the operating system) are released as often as possible. This quick release cycle helps to minimize vulnerabilities and bugs within the core operating system.

- Vulnerabilities are addressed and patched swiftly. It is not uncommon for a fix to be released within 24 hours of the vulnerability being announced.

- Cost. Linux has a much more attractive purchase price than Windows; most distributions are free for download and installation, and feature no per-seat licensing fees.

- Proven server architecture – most of the Internet is served by Linux/UNIX servers

- Large online support base. You can usually get answers in newsgroups, and from web sites such as *http://linux.com/*. You can find hundreds of software applications at *http://www.freshmeat.net*. The online support is so broad, that Google has a completely separate portal for Linux at *http://www.google.com/linux*.

Linux does have some disadvantages:

- Higher learning curve – Much of the administration is done through a command-line interface instead of a GUI, which is harder to grasp.

- That crystal-box development – As I said above, the Linux sourcecode is available for review at any given time; though I'd like to believe everyone looking at it for vulnerabilities had the best interests of the Linux community at heart, I know better.

- Less commercial support – Only a few of the Linux distributions offer commercial support packages; the rest offer support through web forums, and documentation only. Unless you have Linux-savvy staff, this can make supporting the hardware more problematic.

- Though most server and workstation hardware is now supported in Linux, there may still be a lack of support for your specific hardware under Linux.

- Because of lack of familiarity, it can often be difficult to convince management to go with Linux.

Other Software Considerations

There are a number of important software considerations besides operating system and how you are going to go about choosing the solution. Even an out-of-the-box solution may require a particular scripting language or database be installed before it can function.

Programming Languages

If you decide to develop your own intranet software in-house, you will need to decide which programming language to use (PHP, PERL, ASP 3, .NET, JSP, or others). Each language has its strengths and weaknesses, and some are more suited for specific tasks. Choosing depends upon a few criteria:

- What experience do you already have in-house? It makes sense to use the resources already available to you, rather than contracting out the programming, or hiring new developers.

- Is your intranet server running on Windows or Linux? ASP 3 and .NET are more suited to a Windows environment, where PERL and PHP will be more at home on a Linux environment.

- What are your performance requirements? If you are building an intranet for a small organization that has a limited amount of dynamic information, then you can use any of the above languages without taking a performance hit. However, if you are building an intranet for a larger organization, then JSP or .NET may be more effective.

Databases

Databases allow you to store information in a central location, which can be pulled out and placed into documents on your intranet. This allows you to replicate information in several places throughout your web site, making maintenance much easier. However, databases do more than simply making your life easier as a developer; they can be used to help transport information between the users of your intranet, through online forms, discussion forums, and contact management software.

Though a database is a godsend when it comes to managing information, your intranet server will take a slight performance hit every time it has to access the database. This may not be noticeable in a small organization, where only a few people are using the intranet at any given time, it will definitely be noticeable in an enterprise setting, where hundreds of people are using the intranet at once.

The general rule for deciding what to place in a database would be to look at how often the information is being updated. If a document is updated once or twice a year, then it can happily be made into a static HTML file on the server. If it needs to be updated once or twice an hour (such as an internal discussion forum), then placing it in a database is probably a very good idea for your sanity.

If you decide to make use of a database to store your intranet's content, you should budget time to build a front end for the database; your content contributors, designers, and developers will need a relatively easy way to access and update the intranet's content.

There are many database formats to choose from: Oracle, Interbase, MS SQL Server, Access, and MySQL are just some of them. Much like choosing a programming language, there are licensing fees, performance, and interoperability to consider. You may already be making use of a particular database in your organization, which will often make sticking with that a cheaper option.

A simple database such as Access will work well for small sites that don't require many concurrent users. A large organization may want to look into a more powerful database, such as Interbase or Oracle. Popular choices for intranets include Microsoft's SQL Server and the open source MySQL, because these integrate well with web scripting languages like ASP and PHP.

Licensing

Any conversation about software usually sparks a discussion of licensing schemes. As mundane an issue as this may seem, it's extremely important from a development *and* budgetary point of view to pin down the licensing schemes of the operating systems **and** software you wish to use.

Commercial operating systems such as Windows XP, Windows 2000, and MacOS and enterprise-level intranet software usually have per-seat licensing fees. Essentially, an organization is charged a fee on a per-user basis. In the case of operating systems, this means that your organization would be charged for each workstation or server the OS is installed on.

In the case of enterprise-level intranet software, this means your organization is charged per user connecting to the Intranet. For small organizations this isn't much of an issue; it may in fact be less expensive to license Intranet software than it is to custom-build. For larger organizations, licensing fees can quickly add up; a custom solution will often have a considerably lower TCO when compared against yearly licensing fees.

Plan the Work, Then Work the Plan.

Like any endeavor, the key to a successful journey is to plan ahead of time. In the following pages, we will discuss the roles of each member of your intranet development team, problems they may encounter, and strategies to keep development going.

What Information Should Go on the Intranet?

The content contributors provide the keystone of a successful intranet: the content. As simple as the content contributor's task sounds, it is the most time-consuming and important task of all the intranet development team. They must coordinate with both the managers and the end-users to determine what needs to be placed on the intranet and when.

Will your organization's intranet be used solely as a clearing house for brochure content? Brochure content consists of non-interactive content, such as commonly used forms, manuals, and policy guides. Though this information *is* valuable to the enduser, and a good way to populate the intranet with content, it does not really give them a reason to visit the intranet on a regular basis. Users, in this instance, will only visit the intranet when they need to fill out a form, or consult one of the policy guides.

Basic Services

As we mentioned before, there are some basic services an intranet is almost expected to have by its users. This includes (but by no means is limited to):

- Basic forms, such as expense reports, medical claim forms, and timesheets.

- An internal contact database, listing employees' names, extensions, and e-mail addresses.

- Quick company facts. The intranet at one organization has a "Who do I speak to about...?" section, which serves as an invaluable resource for new employees trying to find information.

- Company News. This could be as simple as a weekly listing of happenings throughout the company, given to you by the HR department. You can extend this by allowing employees within your organization to submit news items.

These basic services do not necessarily require much development time to put in place, since they mostly rely on static content (with the exception of the contact database). A rudimentary content management system (CMS) can help to make maintenance of this information relatively painless.

If you are putting a security model into place on your intranet, you can combine the user database for authentication with the user database for the contact list. When you create the user database, simply add fields for information you want to view in the contact database: full name, e-mail address, phone extension, and even their place on the seating plan if one exists.

Interactive Content

A good way to extend the basic content of the brochure-ware site is to replace some of the non-interactive content with interactive alternatives. Do your salespeople need to use an expense form on a regular basis? Replace the expense form on the intranet with an interactive one. You increase your sales team's productivity by reducing the time it takes to complete the form, and you also tie them into using the intranet on a regular basis. Once you hook the employees, they will start to explore the intranet to see what other benefits it offers.

The above example brings forth a very good question: should you tie the employee's job to the intranet? It is a two-edged sword. On the one hand, it ensures you get your ROI by forcing people to use the intranet to function within the company. On the other, it can backfire if you do not tie it seamlessly into their regular work routine. Endusers will either love you for it, or rue your very existence.

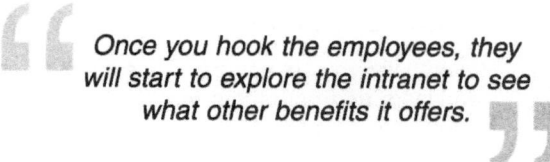

Once you hook the employees, they will start to explore the intranet to see what other benefits it offers.

If you can develop a "killer application", which makes the end-user actually enjoy their intranet experience, you will have a much happier user-base. We will discuss the "killer app" – and the forms it can take – later in this chapter.

Department-Specific Information.

Does a department share a large amount of information among its members? Do members of a department need to collaborate and discuss details of their projects? Placing department-specific information such as project budgets, functional specifications, or even a message board on the intranet can provide a valuable service. No longer do members of the same department have to hold large, sprawling conversations through e-mail; they can now collaborate using a single, central, public resource.

Department-specific information can also be contained, by only making it available to users within the department. This takes sophisticated user management, however, which we will discuss in Chapters 5 and 10.

What Information is Critical to the Intranet's Success?

Most endusers have some fixed expectations when it comes to information on the intranet. The first of these is contact information. In a large organization especially, tracking people down can be a difficult exercise at best. By providing your intranet users with a (preferably searchable) contact list, you provide them with a service they expect, and make their lives a little easier in the process. You can also plan to expand the basic functionality of an internal contact list by allowing users to create their own contact lists, and share them between other members of your organization. In this way, members of your sales group can share contact information, and even add notes to each contact.

In addition to a contact list, common forms are another resource endusers expect to find on an intranet: expense reports, medical forms, product and policy documentation, and the like. The last thing people in your organization want to do is hunt down forms they need on a daily basis. By placing these on the intranet, you provide them with a central resource. As mentioned above, you can even convert these to interactive forms; this gives you control over their distribution as well, allowing you to make changes without having to worry whether they're working off the intranet version, or a local copy on their hard drive.

Other Considerations

Eventually, you are going to come across a situation where you want to share information with some endusers and not others. An example of this would be a functional design specification (usually referred to as a funcspec) for your development team. You will want to start gathering your content and endusers and matching them up in groups.

Another consideration to keep in mind for the development process is approval time. Content may need approval by senior management before placing it on the intranet. Add a little extra time on to your development schedule to account for approval delays, or try to get content pre-approved. Also add development time if you need to rely on other individuals within the organization for content. These individuals may not share the same enthusiasm about developing the intranet as you do.

The final consideration for a content contributor is whether other employees within your organization can submit content for inclusion in the intranet. People are already talking within your organization, whether it is through ad-hoc mailing lists, e-mail, or their own internal web servers, creating a primitive, uncontrolled intranet. By giving them a central, authorized place to hold these discussions, you give them a true voice within your organization. A good source of information on this is the Cluetrain Manifesto, which can be found online at *http://www.cluetrain.com*.

Setting Priority

Once you have determined what information should be included with the intranet, you need to determine a level of priority for each desired component. This will be revealed, at least partially, by the stakeholder interviews you carried out earlier. Common trends will begin to emerge when you analyze the responses. Users may feel that filling out forms online would increase their productivity. Likewise, they may feel that simply having the information available in a central location is enough.

The nice thing about setting priorities is you can stagger the development of content, delaying the development of less important content until after the initial release. Once you have decided what is being included on the intranet and when, the developer and designer can start their work.

Developing the Intranet's Content

The developer and the designer work hand-in-hand while developing the intranet; the developer works on the back end and content delivery systems, and other information-managing systems, while the designer works with both the developer and the content creators to determine what is the most effective and usable way to present the content to the enduser. The developer will need to know some basic information before working on the content delivery systems:

Intranet Content

If the intranet is merely a brochure content site, your developer's task is really quite simple. They merely need to coordinate with the designer to ensure the information is laid out in a logical fashion. Brochure content should be organized in the same way as the company. For example, all HR documents should be placed in an 'HR' section; all product documentation should be in a 'support' section, and so on. For a brochure content site, this makes a fair amount of logical sense.

If the site contains interactive content, this may or may not be possible however. In this event, you will want to organize the content in a more natural manner; perhaps having an 'online forms' section, which is then broken down by department along with a 'documentation' section, again broken down by department. Usability techniques will be discussed in more detail in *Chapter 6*.

Content Contribution

Do the content contributors need an administrative portal to manage the content? The chances are good that the answer to this question is a 'yes'. Content management systems (CMS) greatly increase the productivity of the Content Contributors. Instead of spending their time messing about with HTML, scripting, file placement, and other mundane technical tasks, the Content Contributors can simply select the area of the site they want to edit and paste text into a text field.

This does pose a problem for the developer, however, as it adds much more development time onto the schedule to either install and configure or develop a CMS. In addition, the developer will need to know how complex a workflow the CMS will need to have. Do the Content Contributors want several users to be able to post information to the intranet? If so, they may want the ability to approve or reject submissions before they are made public. We will see more on CMS in *Chapter 8*.

Security

Another consideration at this stage is security. Will information placed on the intranet be sensitive to specific groups within the organization? If so, the developer will have to plan for a security model, using either a form of network authentication, or an authentication method specific to the intranet. It is important that you are aware of these considerations now, as it is easier to build them in from the start, than retrofit them later.

If possible, it's best to use a network-based authentication method, such as LDAP or Active Directory to automatically authenticate users on the intranet. For more on security, see *Chapter 10*

Plan for the Future.

Though you may have the world's best plan for rolling out your intranet, it will be a dismal failure if you haven't planned what happens *after* its launch. The best time to make plans for the future is during this initial planning process. Things you should plan for include:

- Updating content. Who will be updating the content after the intranet's initial release? Will they also be responsible for maintaining it? It is useful to set up a single content editor, who takes information from each department within the organization and coordinates it for placement on the intranet. In turn, these departmental sources would gather and coordinate information inside of each department. It may seem hierarchical, but it will be an excellent filtering method to ensure that only important, useful information is posted to the Intranet.

- Future Development. Unless your developer is a programming deity, the chances of launching your intranet with all the features your users would like to see are slim. Plan out a release schedule for features on your Intranet.

- Hardware and software upgrades. What is the life cycle of your intranet's hardware? How often will software patches and service packs need to be applied to the server? Coordinate with the IT department to get the answers to these questions, and work out a maintenance schedule.

Build it, and They Will Come.

In an ideal world, you would generally have 6 to 12 months to design, develop, and test a usable intranet that answers everybody's needs. You and I both know that the real world is much different; there is a much better chance you'll have to develop it within 2 to 3 months, concurrent with other major projects. This means some sacrifices have to be made.

> *It is better to roll out the core functionality quickly, and then leave extras for later iterations.*

First, forget adding every feature requested by your stakeholders into the intranet; there just isn't enough time. Look through the interviews and the collaborative discussions to pin down commonly requested features, or common weaknesses in the current methods of communication. It is better to roll out the core functionality quickly, and then leave extras for later iterations.

- Do most of the departments complain about a lack of communication? Make it easy for users of the intranet to talk to each other. This could mean forum software, the ability to make comments on content within the intranet, or even an intranet messaging service.

- Do people complain files are hard to find? Spend time developing the site structure, and develop an advanced search application on the intranet.

"Killer Apps"

I think it's best to take a moment here and tell you what most intranet developers have to learn the hard way: At some point during the development of the intranet, somebody will ask, "So how are we going to get people to use this thing?"

The answer seems simple at first: "Have a killer application."

> *The killer app not only brings the users to the Intranet; it brings them back.*

If you want people to use the intranet you are about to spend so much time developing, you need to give them a very good reason to use it. Unless the intranet provides something that makes the users' lives seem so wonderful and complete when they're using it regularly, it just won't be successful. This is where the "killer app" comes in. The killer application not only brings the users to the Intranet; it brings them back.

The answer seems much less simple when you actually have to figure out what that "killer app" is. It could be as simple as a way for salespeople to make feature requests to the developers, or as advanced as a complete system to track customer relations and support issues. Your stakeholder interviews will be valuable here; they can be used to identify trends in commonly requested features.

The easy way out is to ensure the intranet plays a part in their day-to-day life as an employee. This can be relatively easy for development and QA staff, by including something like a bug-tracking database. For sales staff, building a Customer Relations Manager would be an excellent option.

So, you know you need a killer application to bring users back to the Intranet. But what is it? What your particular killer application will end up being depends on what your stakeholder interviews and functional needs assessment hold within them.

Some of the best killer applications are the most basic. Take, for example, a software company I used to work with. The killer application in their case was an off-the-shelf open source bug-tracking suite. Since the company was entering a long research and development process, a system that allowed developers and QA testers to collaborate on software development was a perfect addition to the organization.

It allowed the QA team to effectively communicate potential problems to the development team, without clogging up the e-mail server with messages that might be forgotten or ignored by the developers. It also gave management a way to track the developer's progress without hovering over and watching their every move.

For a sales-driven organization, a solid Customer Relations Management (CRM) system might be the killer application you need to hook them into the intranet. A good CRM can be integrated with a support database, to provide both salespeople and product managers with valuable information about product trends.

Your killer app will be specific to your organization, it could even be as basic as a searchable contact database, with pictures and a dynamic seating plan. The key to finding your killer application is asking the questions: "What will bring users to the Intranet?" and "what will keep them there?".

> *The key to finding your killer application is asking the questions: "What will bring users to the Intranet?" and "what will keep them there?"*

Scheduling

Now you have a basic plan in place for the intranet, an idea for a "killer app", and a basic idea of who is doing what. Do not plan to start everybody off at once; your developer and designer will only be spinning their wheels until they know what they are dealing with for content. If all your development team members start working, the disastrous will happen: your developer will start building a database that isn't scalable to the variety of information the content contributors need to classify; the designer will come up with a visually beautiful, yet functionally vacant design for the intranet; finally, the Management will look at the entire mess, and decide that it is just not worth the trouble to follow through.

Instead, plot each intranet team member's schedules on a graph; MS Project and Outlook are very useful Windows tools for this task. Linux users can install the above tools using Crossover Office (http://www.codeweavers.com/products/office/), or can turn to an open source solution, such as Evolution (http://www.ximian.com/products/evolution/). Any of the above tools will help you to better visualize how the different team members interact; you can see a sample in the diagram to follow.

Something to keep in mind is that not all members of your intranet team are going to start working on the intranet immediately. Some processes cannot be started until others are well under way, or even complete. For example, the developer cannot create the database until they know what information it has to contain. Likewise, your designer cannot display information if there is no content to pull out of the database.

Ask your developer and designer to give you an estimate on their part of the intranet. Things to consider are:

- How dependent on the content are they?

- Can they work off a basic outline and refine from there?

- How long will it take the designers to come up with a usable look and feel for the intranet?

- How much can they work on without content? How much artwork needs to be created by them?

- If the developer is installing an out of the box solution, how long will it take to configure and customize?

That's not to say that each member of the intranet team has to wait until the other is done before proceeding, however. Tasks can – and should – overlap each other, as seen in the following diagram. In this way, information can pass both up and down the development team. This will also help you to avoid costly delays, by having all members in full communication with each other.

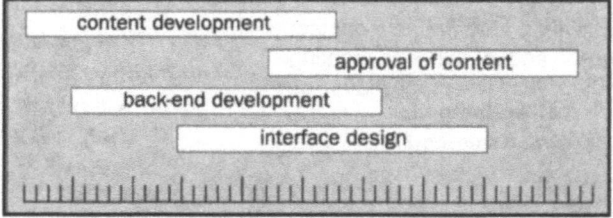

Ensure there is a high level of conversation between the various people on your development team. Things will change once development starts; a high level of communication between members of your development team (and between the development team and the stakeholders) will help to reduce any delays that occur.

Nothing is better for stable development than lots of conversation between the people developing it. Create a temporary forum on an internal web server, or ask your IT department to set up an internal mailing list for the members of the intranet development team.

Your intranet is all about getting people to communicate with each other; it seems fitting that you should place communication among your development team as a high priority as well.

4

- Advantages of knowing the browser base
- Why web standards are still important
- Dealing with microsites

Author: Francis Storr

Summary

Once you have a tentative plan and schedule, you can now move on to the development stage, which we will discuss in the coming chapters.

Remember that as the business benefits of using an intranet grow, so will the additional management issues of maintaining them. If this has not been factored in during the preparation stage, all that hard-earned management buy-in will be for naught. By sticking close to the plan you have made with your stakeholders, your content contributors, your developers and your designers, you can avoid costly delays in your intranet development.

In the upcoming chapters, we will discuss different browser platforms, development techniques, usability, managing content, internal communication through the intranet, internally marketing your intranet, and strategies to deal with large intranets and remote users. We will also discuss extending the intranet to an extranet.

Hold on to your britches, it's going to be a wild ride.

3

Where Do I Start?

Knowing the Browser Base

This chapter will look at the pros and cons of designing for just one target browser. While it can give you a nice warm feeling inside knowing that your audience all have exactly the same browser, should we really be taking the same care and consideration over our code that we would take if we were coding for the Web?

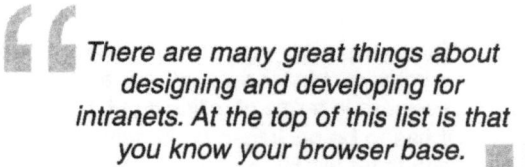
There are many great things about designing and developing for intranets. At the top of this list is that you know your browser base.

In the outside world where there is a proliferation of operating systems and browsers, developers have to work hard to achieve consistent presentation across all of these. Browsers have vastly varying levels of support for even the most basic of standards, and this lack of a common standard is what makes Internet development so "interesting" at times. In an intranet environment however, where there will be just the one type of browser, we are in a much stronger position and can happily produce code with just the one browser in mind and forget about the rest. This may make our lives easier, but is it a good idea? We're going to be looking at the following areas over the course of this chapter:

- The browser upgrade process can be significantly slower on an intranet than it is in a home environment

- The need to ensure that existing sites are coded to standards so that they will work both now and in the future

- The possible legal implications of not coding to standards and making your site inaccessible to your colleagues

- The benefits of using standards and appropriate W3C technologies

- Trying to keep standards within the business

- What can you do with your existing browser base?

There are many great things about designing and developing for intranets. At the top of this list is that you know your browser base. You don't have to sit there with Internet Explorer, Netscape, Mozilla, Opera, Lynx et al. open, *Alt*-tabbing and refreshing to see whether everything looks okay. You can happily design for the one browser that you have in-house and forget about the rest. It's proprietary standards a go-go and here's to an easy life. Really? Is that wise? Let's think about this…

Browser Selection in Businesses

We all know what it's like at home: you find out that one of the browser manufacturers have released an upgrade. After a bit of "shall I overwrite my old browser with this new one" thinking, you bite the bullet. The thing installs, you check your own sites, and have a good surf around the Web to see how your new toy works. After that, it's a case of seeing what level of support the new browser has for CSS, XML, and so on, before either roundly applauding the work of the company concerned or deploring the fact that you've been waiting years for a particular feature to be supported only to find out that it still isn't!

Well, on an intranet it's often a bit different, usually slower. Businesses will always have their eye on the bottom line, and there will be plenty of other things further up the budget pecking order than a browser upgrade. Browsers may not actually cost money to purchase, but there will be a cost to the business in terms of rolling it out. It may be that it has to be packaged up in network distribution software, it will need testing before it is rolled out, and there will be the post-install support needed for all of the businesses non-tech people who are suddenly faced with a new bit of software that they don't recognize. In the grand scheme of things, you could well be fighting it out against Human Resource's desire for a nice glossy staff magazine, a business re-branding, or perhaps even an office refurbishment program.

> *Browsers may not actually cost money to purchase, but there will be a cost to the business in terms of rolling it out.*

In a large corporate environment, probably the only people really pushing for the installation of a new browser will be the people like us – the ones that design and develop intranets. You may well find that the attitude is that of "well, the existing browser works, the pages work, our people can see what they need to, so what's the big deal?". And if you take a step back from being a web professional for a bit, your colleagues are right. As frustrating as this is, deep down you know that you really can do without that CSS `position:fixed` or that you could probably find a workaround for something you've been wanting to use XML for.

Large organizations tend to have a central browser rollout – that is every computer attached to the network will get an updated browser at the same time. The larger the organization becomes the more complex, and prone to problems, this process is, and the time between upgrades lengthens. This means that you can be waiting several years to upgrade from, for example, Internet Explorer 5 to Internet Explorer 6 (missing out 5.5 altogether). In fact, what you might find is that you'll get a browser upgrade along with a new operating system, which will probably be Windows-based. So, if you're currently on Windows 2000 with IE5.5 keep those fingers crossed for IE6, or resign yourself to waiting for the successor of Windows XP and IE7+.

Unless you're the person in the company that decides what goes with the intranet, there will pretty much always be someone above you that has the final say on things. You'll hopefully be asked for your opinion, but the end decision may well not be what you wanted. This is why coding to standards is important. The Gecko-based browsers are much pickier when it comes to rendering code, which is a good thing. Internet Explorer on the other hand will happily ignore some errors and display the page, which can lull you into a false sense of security. If somebody else makes a decision to switch, your pages must be able to cope with it.

Modern businesses will tend to gravitate towards the known, which is why Windows is used predominately. This will usually mean that Internet Explorer is the browser of choice in this environment. It obviously makes sense to use a browser that integrates well with the operating system and is easily updatable.

However, not all organizations will be using Windows exclusively. If your company includes a design department, they may be working with Mac OS X, some organizations may have some brand of Solaris workstation. This disparity can mean that the IT department has opted for a browser that will be consistent on the majority of systems, or it may mean that you have an obscure mix of browsers. In this situation you may be forced to take account of more than one browser on more than one platform.

A Brief Overview of Web Standards

Most probably you will have heard of the term "Standards" in relation to web sites. We'll start by having a look at what exactly standards are, and what they mean to the Web.

HTML (Hyper Text Markup Language) has been around since the World Wide Web was created. The language was initially designed to mark up a document for a web browser, that is, HTML defines a chunk of text as a paragraph, another as a heading, and another as a link to another document, or it can be used for formatting text, adding underlines, bold areas, and other sections.

As the Internet became increasingly popular, and it became a business in itself, new HTML elements were created to handle graphics and other more presentational elements. This is when the language started to be corrupted by people using it incorrectly. For example, HTML comes with a set of `<H1>` elements that are used to denote headings in a document. Developers have a tendency to bypass these and, for some strange reason, create a larger text size by using something like `<font size="7">`. By doing this, the browser has no idea about the structure of the document – all it sees is larger text, not a heading. This is just one example of the corruption that is commonplace in HTML.

When talking about valid code, the emphasis is on creating a page that complies with the W3C standards for that language, whether it is (X)HTML, SVG (Scalable Vector Graphics), XML or one of the many other languages controlled by them. The W3C is the World Wide Web Consortium, *http://www.w3.org*, a body that was founded in 1994 by Tim Berners-Lee, the inventor of the Web. The long-term goals of the W3C include making the Web accessible to all, to promote the semantic web and to create a "web of trust". The benefit of writing valid code is that the user agent should interpret the page as the standards dictate. There will always be bugs in browsers but the use of valid, well-written code with (wherever possible) no deprecated elements will mean that a web site will stand a much greater chance of working in as many browsers as possible. It will also remain fairly maintenance-free in years to come as browsers progress and slowly drop support for old code.

There is a lot of emphasis on valid code these days because of the "browser wars" circa versions 3 and 4 of Netscape and IE. We are in a situation today where Internet Explorer is the most used browser, but this wasn't always the case. In the early days of the Internet, Netscape had the edge and were pioneering things such as JavaScript. To try and add value to their browsers, the various manufacturers started adding their own proprietary code such as Internet Explorer's `<marquee>` and Netscape's `<blink>` elements. After a few years of this the Web was a mess of lax standards and proprietary insanity, with people more concerned about the look of their page rather than the fact that the code behind it was approaching tag soup. Web developers had to create multiple version of each site and use complex sniffing scripts to redirect users to a version of a site that would work in their browser

Luckily, following the work of such bodies as the Web Standards Project (WaSP, *http://webstandards.org*), we are in a much better position to starting developing one site that will work in all modern browsers. Developers are starting to take the attitude of "my site will work in all modern browsers, if it breaks, looks like a wreck in your version 4 software, or you only get a degraded presentation, it's your problem, not mine". This is a great step forward which started off with individual blog sites and worked its way up to large organizations such as Lycos and Wired who have both converted to table-less CSS layouts. By this I mean that these sites no longer use tables to construct their pages. The `<table>` element is a perfectly valid piece of HTML, except that it should be used for the presentation of tabular data rather than to actually structure the layout of a document. With CSS you can position objects themselves rather than having to start building complex nested tables filled with transparent spacer images. Again, this type of design is a corruption of HTML, which is something that, finally, we are getting away from.

 By writing code that complies with the rules and specifications laid down by the W3C, our web sites will be viewable to as many people as possible

By writing code that complies with the rules and specifications laid down by the W3C, our web sites will be viewable to as many people as possible. As more new methods of accessing online content become available (PDAs, mobile phones, and so on), it becomes increasingly important to ensure that each one of these devices is able to view our content. Coding to standards will help to ensure that everyone should be able to access our information with ease. We'll cover coding for other devices in *Chapter 13*.

Why Coding to Standards Is Important

As we've already mentioned, one of the joys of working on an intranet is that you don't have to worry about whether everything works OK in more than one browser. If it works in yours, it will stand a much better chance of working on everyone else's. Oh quiet and happy life!

If we think about this a little bit more, we'll see that this attitude may be a little misguided. What happens if your intranet has been coded to work explicitly with IE – you've got all those lovely ActiveX controls and filters in place that work wonderfully. Then your boss comes up to you and says that they'd really like to open up part of the intranet to some external clients. Bang – we're back into the realms of cross-browser testing! A company can't turn round to a client and say "well, it's designed to work only on Internet Explorer 6 or above, you'll need to change your browsers to view our site and do business with us".

With the push towards standards-compliance from all corners these days the wealth of code that we can write that will display correctly in all browsers is increasing. If we take a look at the WaSP site (*http://www.webstandards.org*) which was coded in XHTML and CSS, we can see that it displays correctly not only in modern browsers but also in devices that weren't even considered during the design process such as the Palm Pilot. See the following post at their site for more information: *http://www.webstandards.org/buzz/archive/2002_06.html#a000053*

Writing to standards, and using CSS to separate content from presentation, also has the advantage of making your code easier to maintain. In an intranet environment where you know your browser base, you will be fully aware of whether your browser is CSS-enabled and what level of support it has. If you ever have the fear of revisiting a

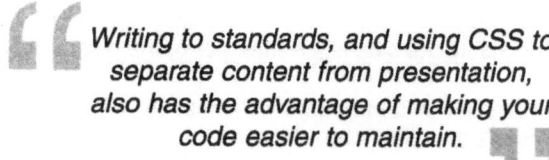

Writing to standards, and using CSS to separate content from presentation, also has the advantage of making your code easier to maintain.

document you haven't touched in a while because it is so full of extraneous code, or you've inherited badly written pages from a previous developer, you should use standards to make your life easier. Using external, linked stylesheets will mean that you can make global changes to the formatting of, for example, your text just by editing the stylesheet. You won't have to visit every single page that requires changing. It also means that when you move to a new job you can leave knowing that whoever follows you won't be cursing you from here to eternity for your bad practices!

This, surely, is the way that we should be moving forward with web development. With the possibility that parts of our intranet could be opened up to clients, it is essential to consider the technologies used when putting your site together.

Future-Proofing Your Code

Hopefully "future-proofing" (also sometimes referred to as forward-compatibility) is a term that you've heard before. Future-proofing is basically ensuring that your code is of a high enough standard to not need constant editing and attention. Browser manufacturers are moving more and more into compliance with the W3C specifications so we can be sure that, as long we are coding to those rather than to any proprietary standards, we won't have too many nasty surprises in the future. An example of this move towards standards can be seen with Internet Explorer's CSS colored scrollbars which Microsoft introduced as a proprietary CSS standard with IE5.5. However, such is the emphasis these days towards standards, that if you try to use these in IE6 in standards mode, IE won't render the color.

By writing to standards and separating as much content from presentation as possible, we can avoid situations in which our intranet fails when future browsers are rolled out across the company. Sleepless nights about whether that integral DHTML menu system will fail or not, are not something that anyone wants. By and large the main browsers are good at supporting the current XHTML standards, although Internet Explorer 6 still doesn't support the entire 4.01 / XHTML 1.0 recommendation.

If you need to check the validity of your HTML or XHTML, then the W3C provides a free validation service at: http://validator.w3.org. If you are using Opera, right-click on any page, then select Frame > Validate Source (or press control+alt+V) and it will automatically upload the rendered version of the page to the validator

Accessibility Considerations

By now you've probably heard of the American Section 508 law that covers accessibility in government-funded web sites. You may well have also heard about the cases of the Australian Olympic Committee web site that was the subject of a lawsuit. But what of intranets? Are they covered by the scope of such Acts as Section 508 (*http://www.section508.gov*) and the UK Disability Discrimination Act 2004 (*http://www.hmso.gov.uk/acts/acts1995/1995050.htm*)? Well, an intranet is technically a web site so the answer should be "yes". However, we need to think about exactly who is using the site. Is it a member of the public or someone else?

In terms of a pure intranet, the users will be our staff. The provision of the "usual" disabled facilities such as toilets and wheelchair ramps are the obvious things that companies do for disabled staff. But what about their intranet? In the UK at least, an intranet could be classed as a workplace arrangement, which means that if an employee who is disabled cannot do their job because the site is inaccessible, this could create a case where an employer would be obliged to make a "reasonable adjustment".

Interestingly, in the UK at least, although the 1995 Disability Discrimination Act covers any company that employs more than 15 people, in its "What Employers need To Know" document (which can be downloaded from *http://www.drc-gb.org/drc/InformationAndLegislation/Page313.asp*) it states that companies don't have to start making adjustments until after they have employed someone with disabilities. However, as with many such issues, it is better to have them in place from the start, than have to spend a long time retrofitting a site.

Putting in alt *text for every image doesn't take that much time if you do it as you go along. Having to revisit your entire site, page by page, to put in the* alt *text that you didn't do the first time around could take a colossal amount of time and money.*

There are many countries that either have legislation regarding accessibility or are soon to be introducing it. Anyone that develops for an intranet should seriously consider making their pages accessible. Cases involving accessibility legislation are still in their infancy and therefore attract global publicity, which is something that your company will want to avoid. Even if you currently don't employ anyone who has a disability that would prevent them from using your intranet, you probably will do at some point in the future. Starting with the attitude that your intranet should be accessible to all will stand you in good stead for the future.

The Web Accessibility Initiative

In 1999 the W3C introduced the **Web Accessibility Initiative** (WAI) and its related Web Content Accessibility Guidelines (WCAG) (*http://www.w3c.org/wai*). This is a set of rules and guidelines that show web developers how to create pages that are accessible to people with disabilities. It is these guidelines that are becoming the de facto rules against which all sites are deemed accessible. Levels of conformance are divided into three separate levels: A, AA, and AAA (with A being the lowest). The WAI also publishes a series of checkpoints against which to audit your site. There are numerous organizations that you can hire to audit your site but the majority of them will be working against the WAI, so you can save your company some money and do it yourself!

Auditing your own site is a fairly simple if slightly time-consuming task (although one that should be considered essential). The first step is to print off a copy of the WCAG checkpoints that can be found here: *http://www.w3.org/TR/WCAG10/full-checklist.html*. There are online tools such as the Bobby (*http://bobby.watchfire.com/bobby*) and Site Valet (*http://valet.webthing.com*) that are very useful for checking the accessibility of your pages, and will be useful at the auditing stage.

What you then have to do is to systematically examine each checkpoint and mark your intranet against each one. Each checkpoint is listed with its own reference number which can be clicked on and which will take you to the relevant part of the full WAI standard. From there you can follow links to look at techniques for achieving the standard. When auditing yourself you have to be ruthless; there is no point in saying "oh well, we're sort of there, I'll mark that as a Yes" if in reality you've failed or only partially passed the checkpoint. Should the worst come to the worst and you end up in a court of law, you'll only have yourself to blame.

Depending on the size of your site and how well you know it, self-auditing could take between an afternoon and about two days. A best practice after that would be to fully write up your findings and then go about planning to change things. Again, if the worst did come to the worst but you have proof that you are aware of your site's failings but you were actively working towards accessibility, this could potentially help your case.

Plugins and Specifics of the WAI

The W3C, through its Conformance and Quality Assurance program (*http://www.w3.org/QA/2002/07/WebAgency-Requirements*) is telling developers to use PNGs for all raster images and SVG for every other type of image.

The use of PNGs on an intranet is an example of the WAI's "use W3C technologies when they are available and appropriate for a task and use the latest versions when supported". This would mean using PNGs for all bitmap images instead of GIFs or JPGs and the use of SVG, MathML, and other XML-related technologies in their rightful places. Herein lies a problem. If we look at the PNG as a graphic format, there is no doubt that it offers much more than both GIFs and JPGs – it can have varying degrees of transparency, can happily deal with large areas of flat color and also more complex images and photographs. But, if we want to natively view a MNG (an animated PNG) without the use of a plugin, unless we're running Netscape 6+ or Mozilla 1+, we can forget about it!

The problem lies with browser support. Netscape 7 and Mozilla 1.1 both have excellent support for the PNG format, but unfortunately IE6 does not. Bearing in mind that many intranets will be based around IE, in the world of complete standards support we have a problem. Realistically, however, we're going to be using GIFs and JPGs for some time.

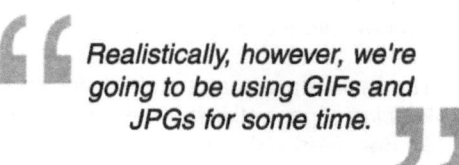

Realistically, however, we're going to be using GIFs and JPGs for some time.

We have the same mixture of benefits and problems with the XML-based language SVG. Images created in SVG can be made accessible, they can be zoomed into and panned around using a mouse and keyboard, which gives them a massive edge. Because an SVG file is just text (you can right-click and view source just as you can on any normal web page) you can improve accessibility by adding textual descriptions of the image using the `<desc>` element. Text in SVG images is real text that can be copied and pasted into other applications such as Word which could never happen with a bitmap image. For more information on the accessibility features of SVG, see: *http://www.w3.org/TR/SVG-access/#What*. However, at present, SVG requires a viewer to be able to work in a browser. This can be downloaded from *http://www.adobe.com/svg/viewer/install/main.html*. This is all well and good for the individual user who can download and install it, but what about distribution across a network or intranets?

As we have mentioned earlier, many things determine the pace of change within a corporate environment and an intranet most likely won't be at the top of the list. So what can we do? Well, if we want to present technical data as images (for example a pie chart of last month's sales figures) we can use a bitmap image and use the HTML `<longdesc>` element to provide a link to a page that has a plain-text description of that image.

If you are using Dreamweaver MX as your development tool, it comes with several accessibility options that can be turned on via *Edit > Preferences > Accessibility*. Turning on Form Objects, Frames, Media, Images, and Tables will make Dreamweaver prompt you for the required accessibility options when inserting an object. For example when you place an image on a page it will prompt you for an `alt` attribute and also the URL of any `<longdesc>` page you might have set up.

This is a very brief overview of a massive topic. For more information on Accessibility and web sites, read *Constructing Accessible Web Sites* (Jim Thatcher et al., glasshaus ISBN 1-904151-00-0).

Micro Sites

Micro sites are parts of an intranet that are "owned" and populated by people within an organization that may not be part of the main intranet team. For example an insurance company may have a main intranet team that develops the architecture and templates. They are experts in this field, but will know nothing about the numerous underwriting conditions that the company covers. It is in these situations that micro sites come into existence, with small pockets of people starting to spring up within the business that have the required expertise in their particular field and are also prepared to publish onto the intranet directly.

The main issue that standards-focused developers will come across with micro sites is that of keeping pages valid. As I mentioned above, you need to have micro site owners (sometimes known as **devolved publishers**) who are willing to work on the intranet. There will be some situations where someone, because of their position, has intranet publishing as a consequence of their job. For example, in our insurance company, you may have one team responsible for all policy referrals, and within that team there is one person responsible for communicating that to the rest of the business. Computers and web sites are not something that inherently interest them, but they are involved in this field as a consequence of their job. Although they will be concerned that the intranet page looks as it should and all of the information is up to date and accurate, they probably won't care at all about the underlying code. If you care about standards, this can be a nightmare!

Take this line of code which can easily be generated by a WYSIWYG editor:

```
<p><font face="Arial"><font color="#000000"><font size="2"></font><b><i>
</i></b><font size="2"><a href="#TOP">TOP</a></font><i></i></font></font></p>
```

This makes me have panic attacks just looking at it! The only part of the code above that we actually need is hidden right in the middle. The rest is presentational code that simply bloats the size of the page. What we really need is this:

```
<p><a href="#top">Top</a></p>
```

If you think that the above line of mangled code is something you'd never find, think again! Having devolved publishers who don't really have an interest in the Web but have to publish to the intranet as a consequence of their job is something that you will have to live with.

What Can We Do to Try and Resolve This Situation?

There are plenty of ways to create the micro-site HTML files. We'll look at a couple of the different ways and see what is best from a standards perspective.

"Save As HTML"

Microsoft Office programs such as Word, PowerPoint, and Excel all come with "*Save as HTML*" functions. In theory these are great and allow the easy creation of HTML files that can be viewed in a browser. This is all well and good, but have you ever looked at the code that is produced? If you are in any way fussy about your code it will immediately turn you off this approach. Office 97 will fill the code with endless font element bloat and add alignment to every single table cell even when it was completely unnecessary. Office XP now adds several hundred lines of style information before even getting to the main page body. It also clutters up pages with totally unnecessary bloat, which can increase download times. Take this example for an empty paragraph that was generated in Word XP:

```
<p class=MsoNormal><span lang=EN-GB><o:p> </o:p></span></p>
```

When all that was needed was:

```
<p> </p>
```

Save as HTML maybe handy, but it is not really the way to go. There are ways to correct it, such as Macromedia Dreamweaver's *Clean Up Word HTML* command, or the Office 2000 HTML filter (*http://office.microsoft.com/downloads/2000/Msohtmf2.aspx*), but neither of these options are a substitute for using correct code in the first place, and add an extra step to the creation process.

WYSIWYG Editors

The best way that a devolved publisher can create documents to put onto the intranet will be by using a WYSIWYG editor such as Dreamweaver, GoLive, or FrontPage. This setup will allow them to produce intranet content themselves which will free up the main intranet development team.

Some of these editors are better than others. If we are looking at both coding to standards and accessibility, Dreamweaver MX should be high on your shopping list. It codes both HTML and XHTML (and can convert one to the other pretty well), has much improved CSS support, and also now comes with a large amount of accessibility options and a built-in validator. The Web Standards Project (*http://webstandards.org*) has been involved with the development of this piece of software, so we can be confident that it is pretty good. A less expensive option, also from Macromedia, is Contribute. This new piece of software allows a non-technical person to update an HTML page, and allows an administrator to lock certain areas of a template, so the updates don't break the page, its standards-compliance, or accessibility. Adobe's Golive also has a built-in accessibility checker, and a free plugin called InSightLE for checking section 508-compliance.

However, just because a program supports standards, it doesn't follow that the micro-site creators will know how to use them. It is therefore important to make sure they receive the relevant basic training if you want to avoid problems, and the compliance of the site breaking.

Cascading Style Sheets

One way that we can help to reduce the type of tag soup that we have seen above is to use CSS. Setting up a stylesheet for parts of the intranet that a devolved publisher will use will dramatically increase the quality of the code and also make everyone's life easier. For example you could quite easily set up styles to enhance the presentation of standard HTML elements. For example, you might want space between your bullets in a list. Instead of this:

```
<ul>
<li>Grant Lee Buffalo<br /><br /></li>
<li>Tom Waits<br /><br /></li>
<li>Chantal Kreviazuk<br /><br /></li>
</ul>
```

we could just have written a style declaration along the lines of:

```
li {margin-bottom:2em;}
```

which would give you approximately the same effect and would mean that you would only ever have to code:

```
<ul>
<li>Grant Lee Buffalo</li>
<li>Tom Waits</li>
<li>Chantal Kreviazuk</li>
</ul>
```

Using this in a linked, external stylesheet means we can use this over and over again. Our code is cleaner and if we ever want to change the spacing, we'll only have to alter the stylesheet and not hunt out every unordered list we've written.

Another example of this would be to use CSS to set the background color and text style of your table headers. This would mean that every time a new table is created, it will look the same which is ideal for a corporate intranet. Dreamweaver's CSS pallet is useful for this. One of the intranet developers can set up a stylesheet with all the required styles in it, which can easily be applied by anyone with a small amount of training.

Branding Issues

As mentioned above, separating content from presentation is an excellent way to future-proof your intranet. Consider this situation:

You are working for a company that has a large and successful intranet consisting of several thousand standards-compliant pages and which is extensively branded with the company colors from the main logo to the color of the `<H1>` elements. Then let's say that your business is bought out by a company who want to change all your internal branding in the intranet; this branding is not just the color scheme but they also want the font changing from Arial to Verdana and the underlines for hyperlinks must be in purple, not the default blue.

This may seem like an extreme scenario, but it's not an unrealistic one. I know that I'd much rather spend a few hours adjusting my stylesheets and then testing to make sure all is OK rather than manually altering every instance of a font or changing an image on every page that I could have placed on a page using CSS.

Coding with proprietary elements and hacks will take just as long as coding to standards will, except that you'll end up in a situation where you'll have a site that might not work in the future. This leads to the question as to why anyone would want to use proprietary code. You're never going to be 100% certain that your company will stay with one make of browser. Internet Explorer is currently the global browser of choice, but that hasn't always been the case. If we look at the way that the Gecko rendering engine is being pushed forward maybe Netscape will become dominant again, or perhaps even Opera will suddenly take off in spectacular fashion. Who knows!

An Example of Working with One Specific Browser

Working with one specific browser has both benefits and flaws. In this section we'll take a look at an example case. Due to the prevalence of Windows as an operating system and Internet Explorer as the current browser of choice, we will be focusing on this set p. As we've mentioned previously, standards are the way to go to help ensure that our sites are both usable on multiple browsers but also to set you up for the future. Let's look at what can be achieved on IE5 upwards that will also work both in IE6, Netscape 7, and Mozilla 1.1. This will give us a broad base for what we can achieve now and also what will work well in the future.

Choosing a DOCTYPE

One of the most important things to consider when coding pages is which DOCTYPE to use. A DOCTYPE should be the first line of code in a page and tells the browser exactly what type of document it is looking at, that is, is it an HTML 4.01 Transitional document, an XHTML 1.0 frameset, or maybe an XHTML 1.1 page? A DOCTYPE isn't mandatory on a web page, but should always be included if you want your code to validate. In HTML4.01 and XHTML1.0, there are three different DOCTYTPES available: Transitional, Strict , and Frameset (*http://www.w3.org/TR/REC-html40/struct/global.html#h-7.2* and *http://www.w3.org/TR/xhtml1/#dtds* respectively). These tell the browser what type of document it is looking at, and how it should interpret the code.

Pages with Transitional DOCTYPEs will include depreciated (X)HTML elements, pages with Strict DOCTYPES should include none, (and browsers such as Internet Explorer 6 will switch and display CSS more correctly). The Frameset DOCTYPE should be used, not unsurprisingly, for framesets. As the push towards standards increases, more and more WYSIWYG editors are adding DOCTYPES automatically. Dreamweaver MX now contains a partial HTML4.01 Transitional DOCTYPE with all new pages.

If you are currently working with a browser earlier than version 6, I would recommend using an HTML 4.01 Transitional DOCTYPE that doesn't contain the final URI:

```
<!DOCTYPE HTML PUBLIC "-//W3C//DTD HTML 4.01 Transitional//EN">
```

While not being an ideal solution standards-wise, using this has several advantages for intranets:

- A page with this DOCTYPE will still validate without the URI – a document with no DOCTYPE will not validate at all even if the rest of your code is perfect. In some intranet environments, because of the many security features your company will have installed, you may not be able to use an online valuator. Dreamweaver MX now comes with a built-in Results panel that will validate to, amongst other things, HTML4.0, all three "flavors" of XHTML1.0 and WML. The excellent TopStyle (*http://www.bradsoft.com*) also includes validators for both XHTML and CSS.

- Since this DOCTYPE triggers "quirks" mode in newer browsers it will look the same in older browsers and newer ones. If you suddenly change to Netscape 6+ you won't find that your images have large blocks of whitespace beneath them (see *http://devedge.netscape.com/viewsource/2002/img-table/* for information on this). It also won't trigger "standards mode" if you suddenly switch to Internet Explorer 6 which may be a good thing if you use a lot of CSS for layout. since there are major differences in the box model (see sidebar).

Versions of Internet Explorer earlier than version 6 didn't implement the CSS box model well. The box model allows everything on a page to be thought of as being in a box to which padding, a border, and a margin can be applied *http://www.w3.org/TR/REC-CSS2/box.html*. The incorrect model in IE5 or less causes no end of problems which has led to several hacks having to be used, the most famous of which is Tantek's Box Model Hack, a description of which can be found here: *http://www.tantek.com/CSS/Examples/boxmodelhack.html*. Internet Explorer 6's DOCTYPE switching means that by altering the DOCTYPE of a page you can change the way that the browser interprets standards.

Cascading Style Sheets

Cascading Style Sheets allow you to customize the presentation of pages and, with a little knowledge and care, keep them looking the same in all browsers. Stylesheets are also the major tool for controlling the presentation of XHTML and XML documents. For example, you might be using the `bordercolor` attribute of the table element to apply a color to the border of your table. That's all well and good, but it's an IE-only attribute, and as such won't validate or work in non-IE browsers. You can however happily use CSS to apply this to all tables. For example:

In your external stylesheet file (`mystylesheet.css`) you would have:

```
.datatable, td, th {border: 1px solid #eee;}
.datatable th {background-color:#fc0; color:#009;}
```

and then in your actual HTML page you would apply a class to the table, allowing it to be formatted accordingly.

```
<!DOCTYPE HTML PUBLIC "-//W3C//DTD HTML 4.01 Transitional//EN">
<html>
<head>
<title>Music</title>
<link rel="stylesheet" href="mystylesheet.css" type="text/css">
</head>
<body>
<table width="580" cellpadding="0" cellspacing="0" class="datatable" summary="table
of rock bands">
<caption>Music from across the globe</caption>
<tr>
<th>Name</th><th>Genre</th><th>Comments</th>
</tr>
<tr>
<td>The Wildhearts</td><td>Rock</td><td>Excellent UK based rock group</td>
</tr>
<tr>
<td>Godspeed You! Black Emperor</td><td>Post Rock</td><td>Canadian 9 piece, mainly
instrumental</td>
</tr>
</table>
</body>
</html>
```

Now you can get consistent colors on any table that has the class of `datatable`. Every time you use a `<th>` element for table heading information you will get the same formatting and color scheme. This is incredibly useful, and by using a linked external stylesheet on all pages you can have consistent presentation across the entire intranet.

Internet Explorer 5 tends to get a bad rap when it comes to implementation of the CSS standards. To be fair, it is an older browser, but one that is probably still used a great deal in companies who had computers with IE5 pre-installed. It is capable of handling a good part of the recommendations but does fall down on some things that are quite frustrating such as not understanding how to center using `margin-left:auto; margin-right:auto;` (to fix this, use `text-align:center;` in the body element and then `text-align-left;` on everything else). For a full list of exactly which browser supports what, the following link has an up-to-date list of the main browsers: *http://www.westciv.com.au/style_master/academy/browser_support/index.html*

You can still produce some quite complex table-less page layouts in IE5. If you're looking for a good starting point for this, the Layout Reservoir at *http://www.bluerobot.com/web/layouts* is a good place to start. It contains examples of many common page layouts, which you can take and customize for your own use.

JavaScript DOM support

Internet Explorer 5 was the version of Microsoft's browser to start supporting the W3C DOM. However, it was below average to say the least and still contains much proprietary functionality, meaning that at the time it was still essential to write endless browser sniffing checks to see exactly which browser the user had. As intranet developers we do have the luxury of knowing what the browsers are capable of and the standards that they support. So a suitable choice here might be to use the minimum of DOM-based JavaScript that will work, and avoid other code since it may break when upgrades occur.

XML support

Internet Explorer 5 has only a partial implementation of the XML standard. When that browser was released Microsoft based its implementation on the XML Working Draft specification, which differed from the final release. You can implement XML using IE5 but you have to include numerous workarounds, making it a far from ideal solution. IE5.5 + browsers support the full XML 1.0 specification. Total support for the XML 1.0 standard is still not complete in any modern browser, which is fairly shocking as it has been complete since 1998.

Summary

In this chapter we've covered information to help you make an informed decision about your intranet browser base decisions. We've looked at how Internet Explorer has the obvious benefit that it is part of the Windows operating system, and can integrate with other Windows products. We've also mentioned how you should never take for granted the fact that we only have one browser to code for, as generally this decision is out of our hands, and the situation may change in the future. We've talked about web standards and touched on how to code them with confidence for more streamlined code, make it more maintainable, and enhance accessibility.

As browsers progress, their support for W3C technologies such as the JavaScript DOM, XML, and CSS is improving. This is fantastic news for the intranet developer as we can move our intranets forward and, as long as we keep to the standards, our work in the future will be much easier.

5

- Functional needs analysis
- Software and tools
- The production process

Development Techniques

This chapter is a step-by-step process outline detailing how an organization's political will to create an intranet can be transformed into a functioning intranet. It will define the process for people who need a roadmap, and encourage them to conduct proper planning themselves.

Converting the intention to build a corporate intranet into a deployed site can be a challenge for even the most experienced project managers. This is because stakeholders' expectations are usually not set properly or adequately managed.

As a project evolves through planning, development, deployment, and approval stages, the number of requests for clarification of detail is always surprising. Issues that you may have thought were clear as spring water are actually murky in some people's minds or completely disparate from what you had intended and likely explained. Often, people will walk away from the same meeting with a perception of concepts and an expectation of results that you never intended them to have. And then you'll be expected to deliver on those.

Everything must be documented clearly and explicitly.

The most common complaint of intranet project managers is that they need to meet impossible deadlines and fulfill unrealistic expectations with inadequate resources. If you don't want to be mouthing these words one day, it's important for you to make sure everyone is clear on what the project's deliverables are going to be; and the only way to do that is to make sure everyone sees the same picture.

The planning stage of an intranet project is its most important part. Do yourself a favor and don't forget this or rush through it. Planning correctly and thoroughly will allow you to explicitly define deliverables, schedule, and cost. More importantly, it will also allow you to set and correct expectations among all stakeholders. You want to avoid being vague anywhere as fuzzy deliverables are dangerous – they can result in you trying to extract perceptions from the subconscious of middle and upper management.

After you've defined all the necessary parameters in the planning stage, you'll be able to control the project properly during the development and deployment cycles. Then, when something (inevitably) changes inside the project's scope, you will be able to manage expectations by showing people the significance of how the changes will impact the deliverables, schedule, and cost.

Also, note that having a quick reference to the implication of project scope change will often prevent casual outside suggestions from becoming your additional deliverables. Telling someone in a serious tone that their idea will cost an extra $30,000 and two weeks extra development time (for example) will necessitate them making sure their ideas are thought-out and approved through proper channels. Also, "change request forms" can be considered if you're a particularly process-oriented individual.

During your planning stage, you will be creating a number of documents. Make sure that they are all accessible to non-technical stakeholders. This doesn't mean that these should be written at a grade-school level, but that they are comprehensible for people who are willing to learn a bit about the vocabulary. Including a glossary in an appendix can be valuable, as it is next to impossible to write a technical document that is completely devoid of jargon.

As well, network diagrams, wire frame concepts, site maps, and timelines should be included as images for people who don't like to read or who will just be scanning your documents. It might sound silly, but including pictures in documentation can make a huge difference for those who need visuals in order to understand concepts.

Functional Needs Analysis – Checklist

You need to define an intranet's functional requirements in the planning stage – well before beginning production. Content in many forms is assumed as a constant (text, video, audio, PDF documents, etc.). It's the other features that need to be determined early. This section includes a list of functional components commonly used in intranets. They are sometimes referred to as "killer apps" which make an intranet invaluable to an organization. Look for something that will eliminate or streamline a cumbersome and inefficient process. Finding the right component (and implementing it well) can be a spectacular career move.

Every organization is different and your killer application may be unique to your company.

Review the following list and classify the functional components that your organization finds compelling into "need to have at launch", "nice to have at launch", "need to have soon", "nice to have soon", or just a "want to have". Once you've organized them by priority, gather information on the technical requirements, cost, and development time required for each item's implementation. Quite often, this data will be the final factor that determines whether an identified "need" makes it into the final Project Scope Document.

We will now take a look at some of the functional components typically implemented as part of corporate intranets.

Brochure Content (Text and Images)

A very basic intranet without a large budget or significant requirements can be quite simple, yet still elegant and useful. If a company just wants to make a limited amount of textual and graphical information available to employees, then this approach can be sufficient. Including links to a public site and other resources is a good way to make this content compelling.

Some companies go forward with this type of idea to begin with. These cases will include information about lines of business, products, services, business hierarchy, and internal policies. As it grows, however, it will typically become difficult to maintain. This is where Content Management Systems and dynamic templating systems become valuable.

A large intranet site with informational utility and no interactivity can be created from brochure content, but the perception may be that it doesn't "DO" anything or that it is just marketing fluff. In addition, long-term maintenance of this content will be difficult.

Basic Content Management System (CMS)

Creating or purchasing a basic content management system can be extremely empowering for an organization. It allows non-technical staff to add, edit, and delete content on the intranet in a quick, efficient manner after minimal training. They do this from a graphical web interface to a database where they can read and write information. This information in the database is then dynamically presented to site users.

A basic CMS would typically allow an organization to manage text and images for multiple content areas, including news, press releases, organizational information, and other business data. It would also allow for the definition and implementation of a workflow for developing, validating, and publishing content.

Some excellent CMS systems of commercial quality are available as open source freeware.

There are many ways to approach the creation of a CMS and they are discussed later on in *Chapter 8*.

Sophisticated CMS with Dynamic Menu Systems

Sophisticated content management systems can act as complete site management tools that allow new content areas to be created by a range of users with different roles and responsibilities. Every aspect of an intranet site, from navigation hierarchy to content, formatting, and functionality can be controlled through a web-based system. Roles and responsibilities can be defined where some administrators can only add content to the database but not publish it to the intranet, while others can add content, edit it, and publish it to the intranet.

Developing or purchasing a system like this can give non-technical administrators (with some training) the ability to maintain a large, complex web site. This is done through the use of pre-defined templates that will usually have been customized by your development team in consultation with your design team.

More information on CMS systems is available in Chapter 8.

File Management Utility

Among the most valuable benefits an intranet offers an organization is its information centralization. This can give all employees access to corporate data in a single location, and reduce the cost and time required for maintaining multiple file servers.

While most organizations have unique IT infrastructures, there are some that configure their intranets to run on machines that are also accessible through a local network. In instances where this is the case, Microsoft Office and some other collaborative systems such as Lotus Notes allow "Workgroup Templates" to be defined (any local or network directory path is valid). If this is possible in your organization, you may want to consider allowing this due to the seamless integration it offers with various products by Microsoft and other vendors. While it may seem redundant to make the documents available through both channels, there will typically be numerous instances where a user can access the intranet but not the local network (public web access to the intranet might be allowed by your systems administrators but not Virtual Private Network access to local drives).

From an informational perspective, an intranet should be used for more than just the dissemination of raw and processed data. It should be used as a primary method for distributing and maintaining a document repository for all employees. Instead of making sure that all employees have the most current Microsoft Word templates, PowerPoint files, and corporate logos installed on their machines, all these documents should be located on the corporate intranet. This will become the default destination for users seeking these files.

A file management utility will allow select administrators to add, edit, and delete documents through a web-based (HTTP) interface instead of requiring File Transfer Protocol (FTP) access to the intranet server's document repository – a significant security benefit. It can also tie into a User Management system to check user profiles for required permission levels to access certain documents and document areas. Delegating the maintenance for areas of what can become a significant file store will ensure that someone has responsibility for every file group.

Basic User Management

Most intranets include significant amounts of sensitive corporate data. This is why it is important to have at least a basic degree of password-protection in place to restrict access to approved users. If the intranet is available via HTTP to users outside the corporate firewall, then this should be considered mandatory.

Many intranets just have a generic corporate password for all users. This happens when access needs to be restricted to employees only and a systems administrator simply password-protects the intranet's root directory on the web server. This results in a password prompt appearing the first time any user attempts to access any page or document within that root folder. If the user enters the correct password, they are authenticated as having permission to access everything in the folder.

What often makes these generic passwords inappropriate is that they get stale-dated. When personnel changes occur, ex-employees tend to retain their access privileges because system administrators don't want to change the password for all employees. This can obviously represent a significant security risk.

A Basic User Management system will allow individual users to each have their own access ID and password. An administrator will be able to add, edit, and delete user privileges as requests come in from Human Resources or other appropriate departments. These systems are quite simple to develop, or to purchase and implement.

See Chapter 10 for more information on intranet security.

Sophisticated User Management

A Sophisticated User Management system will allow an administrator to place intranet users into categorized groups, and then define access privileges for each group. These privileges will regulate which users and groups have access to certain areas of the intranet, including content and functional areas. This is so that marketing staff can enter their timesheets (in a hypothetical situation where timesheet entry is part of an intranet), but will only be able to see their own time, whereas a Vice President will be able to enter their own time as well as view and create reports on all employees' timesheets. Most other functional components that can be personalized and customized, such as calendaring, appointment, and CMS systems, would logically be integrated with a sophisticated user management application.

A system like this is recommended for more complex intranets with many users across multiple departments and lines of business. New users can just be added into defined groups according to their role in the company, and old users can be deleted from all groups in a single place.

Something to consider when discussing the need for a User Management system for the intranet is whether or not it should tie into a CMS (if one is being deployed) or other security systems. Minimizing the number of passwords employees need to remember is a good thing, but there are some security drawbacks to this as well. Read *Chapter 10* for more information on the Single Sign-On issue and general intranet security.

Contact Management Utility

Most companies have thousands of business contacts, including clients, prospective clients, partners, suppliers, professional service providers, and miscellaneous friends. The personal information for these contacts is normally distributed across various people in an organization, with some staff having the proper address and phone number for a client while other staff have an old address, but correct birth date, mobile phone number, and e-mail address. Centralizing this information in a database to which all users have access is a way of ensuring that everybody has access to the correct contact information (assuming the right contact information exists in the system), and that data redundancy is reduced.

To add significant utility to a system like this, include a component that allows for contact reports – where staff can add detailed notes about conversations and meetings with the contact, ideally accompanied by a date for follow-up (if applicable). The Contact Management Utility could then display the Contact's contact information, with dates and details of contacts available, too. An added feature would be to have this tool automatically generate a reminder e-mail to the person who entered a contact report when the date for following-up with the contact arrives. Also worth considering is a feature whereby each contact can have a "single-point of contact" within the business listed against their name.

Time/Project Management Utility

Tracking projects and resource time spent on projects across an organization is a considerable task for any organization that wants to quantify the work. Calculating the profitability of staff and projects is obviously very important in an environment where the bottom line is relevant.

A Time/Project Management Utility allows company administrators to create **project profiles** with estimated budget breakdowns, project details, contact and scheduling information. Once a Project Profile exists, staff can track the time they allocate to each project and reports can be generated periodically during a project's development cycle and again at its end. This is an excellent way to control expectations for multiple projects in any size of company.

The level of sophistication in a system like this can vary greatly. Fortunately for someone considering implementing a Time/Project Management Utility, there are numerous commercially available products which can be evaluated for research purposes or for purchase.

Discussion Forums

Discussion forums, when used seriously, can be incredible resources for companies. Staff can use them for any type of collaborative feedback and discussion processes where extended physical meetings are impossible. They allow for paced review, thought, and response in a way that is very similar to group e-mails, but quite distinct.

Once a discussion has started, people can read previously posted comments and post their own thoughts in response to them, or as a new comment. The distinction here is that discussion forums have the potential for multi-threaded discussions where a graphical representation of a discussion's flow of posts and responses is available to users. This is something that is very difficult to do through e-mail and is unique to this type of tool.

As well, a discussion that continues for several months over the course of a project can sometimes lack all the relevant information in context. Use of a forum like this, however, will allow for quick, efficient references to previous points and issues.

Private discussion forums can be created for specific projects, initiatives, and departments, and public discussions forums can be utilized for general corporate questions and answers. A key feature that should be included in any discussion forum is *search*, so users can search for words and phrases in specific discussions and across all discussions (as per requirements and permissions, to restrict access where necessary).

Calendar Utility

A Calendar utility on an intranet can be helpful for communicating holidays, significant corporate events, and other general reminders (tax filing dates, etc.) to staff. This would appear universally for all intranet users on a Calendar page, or as a secondary item on a main page.

Calendars can be a real killer application in settings where people are often in and out of the office, as it increases the possibility of face-to-face communication among staff. The drawback of this, like many other tools, is that it will only be as valuable as the integrity of its data. If people don't keep their schedules up-to-date or its adoption rate isn't very high, then the data will be unreliable and the components' chance at success will suffer.

Employee Directory

A searchable Employee Directory can be invaluable on an intranet, particularly in large organizations. This type of component can be as simple as a searchable phone book or as sophisticated as an all-encompassing Human Resources information system where all employees' data is stored, but the level of access to personal information is restricted according to users' access privileges. In the latter case, individuals would have access to most of their own data, but only names, titles, and phone numbers of other employees, while HR group members would have access to all users' data.

An implementation of an employee directory should include an extended search capability that allows users to search for employees by keyword and sort results by name, location, department, and title. User profiles should include all relevant contact information, including mail address, e-mail address, phone number(s), title, and department. If available, a photograph should also be included – this is a great way for new employees to learn the names of their peers, and for security personnel to verify employees' identities.

An extra "Wow" factor can be built into this system by cross-referencing the complete Organization Chart with staff profiles for multiple methods of navigation. As well as keyword searching, the employee directory could be developed to function like a drill-down database application. This would include listing names and titles for each employee's, who they report to directly, and their supervisor in individual profiles. These names would be clickable and take users to the appropriate profile where they could continue up or down the organizational hierarchy.

Typically, an employee directory will be part of a centralized **directory service** that multiple components will access to determine who a user is and what their access privileges are. Human Resources or another appropriately delegated administrator would be responsible for administrating it. This would cause authorized updates to staff profiles (when employment status changes) to be reflected in this system and any other systems or components that rely on its data.

Personalization

Personalization cannot be introduced into a project's scope without some level of security (user authentication) either already in place or scheduled for development.

Once a security system is functioning and a user has been identified by it, matching categorized content with their corporate roles and responsibilities (or groupings) can be done by either:

- a general application server
- a specialized one-to-one application server
- a specific personalization engine.

The resulting personalized pages will also usually include some elements defined by the user as per their unique preferences. These elements will typically be limited to basic presentation-layer modifications such as color preferences and how content and functionality elements are organized

See Chapter 10 for more information on Personalization.

Web Access

Many intranets are only available to internal corporate users who are inside a firewall. This is understandable due to security concerns and some internal corporate policies that want to regulate from where the intranet is accessed. When advanced functional components, such as those discussed in this section, are included in an intranet, there will be circumstances where opening access to outside users should be considered. If mission-critical items like a time/project management utility or contact manager are going to be included in an intranet, their immense utility to staff will necessitate allowing them access while they are away from the office (at home, at a client's office, or at a conference, for example).

There are a number of ways to attend to this, but your network administrators should address this issue as its primary concerns regard corporate IT security policy.

Remote Web Access should be considered during the Need Analysis to ensure network administrators properly scope it out (and estimate related costs and implementation time) for inclusion in the Project Scope Document (more on this later).

Boardroom/Resource Booking Engine

Even the most sophisticated organizations are often challenged by how to manage their meeting rooms and hardware resources. This is because many existing booking systems are too vague, too cumbersome, or just badly implemented. Quite often, established reservation procedures are ignored, meeting rooms and technical resources (laptops, projectors, etc.) get double-booked (or booked and not used).

Implementing a usable, web-based Boardroom/Resource booking engine can make an intranet project manager into a corporate hero by replacing an inefficient, often-hated offline process.

Searchable Content

A commonly-held misperception is that an intranet site can easily be indexed and made searchable by keyword. This is not true in most cases.

An intranet site's searchability depends on the following factors:

- What will the searchable contents of the intranet site consist of?

- Will only the HTML files need to be searchable? Or will there be numerous other documents in multiple formats (.pdf, .doc, .ppt, .xls, etc.) that will also need to be searchable?

- If meta information (title, keywords, and short description) about the other documents exists within the HTML files (or CMS database), then it might not be necessary to make them searchable as they will still be accessible through a simple search.

- How will the content and documents be stored: inside a CMS, or as individual files?

Once these technology and content formatting factors have been clearly resolved, the Search function can be defined. There are many ways to approach this. Note that there is a *"Search Solutions"* section later in this chapter.

Expense Reports

Creating an online utility that allows authenticated users to file their expense reports will be greatly appreciated by users. This process normally involves lots of paper, processing, and waiting for reimbursements. If you can reunite people with their money in an expedited fashion, you will have found your "killer app".

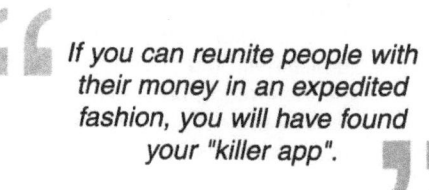

If you can reunite people with their money in an expedited fashion, you will have found your "killer app".

Job Listings

One content group which is normally an afterthought but that should definitely exist in your planning is for internal job listings. Companies should post all employment positions internally so that staff considering career moves stay internal and their corporate knowledge is not lost. Furthermore, this is the type of information that people really appreciate having access to.

A Final Word About Functional Components

Many of the functional components discussed above can easily exist independently of each other, but in many cases should not. While you can either purchase or lease some components and develop others internally, thought should be given to how the items selected on your Needs Analysis checklist will work with each other. As a general rule you want to minimize the potential for redundant data (having the same information exist in multiple instances) because it will be difficult to track which data is the most correct over time. So if you're going to create an Employee Directory, Calendar Utility, and Resource Management tool (or any other set of components that will rely on common data – in this case user profiles), ensure your technology team approaches their solution holistically.

If the components are going to exist across multiple systems and/or networks, consider implementing a centralized user directory based on Lightweight Directory Access Protocol (LDAP) or Microsoft's Active Directory. With that in place, other applications could access it through Simple Object Access Protocol (SOAP), which is basically a XML packet (information object) that components can request from the user directory to determine if users are authorized to access systems, what their group privileges are, and what details are included in their individual profiles.

Available Technical Resources

When the Needs Analysis has been completed and you have a checklist of the functional components identified for inclusion in the intranet, you will need to find people who can make it happen.

The first person you need on your side is your technical lead, the senior developer who will either do most (or all) of the coding or manage a team that does it. This person should have a very lucid comprehension of your existing corporate IT structure and understand the theory of how a web site will function in relation to it. Actual experience developing web sites isn't as important as their appreciation of the process and their ability to manage technically minded people.

Take some time to discuss some of the more complicated components identified in the Needs Analysis with your senior developer. Ideally they will have been part of that phase and already be familiar with the underlying rationale for the decisions made during it. You don't need to understand the technology, but you should get a clear understanding of the issues so that you can relay them to various project stakeholders. If your senior developer doesn't communicate well with you and you aren't comfortable, try to find someone else to fill the role. When things inevitably get complicated, it's very important that you have someone on your side with whom you can talk plainly.

When you're comfortable with your senior developer, you will need to work with them to make some decisions in regard to development approach, hosting platform, and scripting language(s). The resolution of all these issues will determine what skill sets will be required for the development and implementation of your intranet.

If resources with the required skill sets exist internally, you will need to make sure these resources will be available for the development cycle. If they do not exist or are not going to have the availability for your project, you will need to obtain a budget to hire some resources.

There are three distinct options for hiring outside resources. In each case, before making your final decision, have your senior developer meet the resources to determine a level of confidence in their work. A few compelling questions can separate the wheat from the chaff fairly quickly.

The options are:

- Hire experienced professionals on a full-time or contract basis. Make sure the resources have the required skill sets, sample URLs (to view their previous work) and references. If they don't have sample URLs or CD portfolios of work, then they aren't serious about their profession. Even students and newbies who take pride in their work will create a sample site to demonstrate their skills. For something as mission-critical as a significant intranet project, you don't want to pay people to learn on the job. And you definitely don't want to rely on undependable or unprofessional staff.

- Hire a small web design agency with experience creating intranets similar in scope and scale to the one you will be building. This agency will typically consist of one to five designers and developers who own and operate their own small firm. Each project tends to be extremely unique to them, and this normally results in innovation and creativity, but sometimes at the expense of efficiency, process, and clear meeting of expectations. Occasionally they will contract out complicated work to specialized professionals when they are busy or project scopes are out of their depth. They will almost never turn work away or say they can't deliver a project on time, on schedule, or on budget. These firms tend to be "hungry," on the cutting edge of development techniques and quite interesting. That being said, make sure to obtain references from people who aren't their friends or family, and be satisfied with their portfolio. Once an agency grows beyond eight or nine staff, they stop being a small web design company and their "process" becomes more defined. Simultaneously, the volume of their documentation and for-hire rates increases.

- Hire a professional firm. This is typically a company that started as a small web design agency and evolved to either a high-end boutique shop or a full-solution Internet development organization that takes care of "all your web needs" from copywriting to design and implementation. This breadth of work is normally possible due to the staff's depth of experience with smaller companies and projects. The result of this experience is usually greater attention to documentation, preparation, planning, and meeting expectations.

While these firms' rates can be quite expensive at times, a level of confidence and comfort in the firm's experience and professionalism usually offsets the cost. Do be very clear in your contract about delivery dates and budgets because cost overruns due to delays on your part can be quite upsetting with some of these agencies (you pay for their developers' time even if they aren't working because they are waiting for you to deliver assets, designs, approvals, or something else required to continue or commence their work).

Remember: All your resources should make you comfortable with their skills.

Additionally, remember to think about who will be doing maintenance on your system(s) after launch. If you're hiring external developers, will they deliver adequate training to your staff so all updates won't result in additional charges? Or would you prefer to contract maintenance to an external staff at a fixed rate or on a retainer? These things should all be considered and budgeted for (if necessary). Don't be left high and dry.

Development Approaches

Once the development team has been assembled and briefed, decisions need to be made about how the intranet will be developed. Generally, the decision comes down to whether the production is done by an in-house team, external contractors, or outsourced to an ASP (Application Service Provider). Specifically, the decision relates to a "build or buy" issue that may resolve with a decision to create a hybrid site.

There are six potential approaches to intranet development. They are:

- Developing an intranet internally with proprietary code
- Purchasing an existing intranet application and customize it
- Developing a hybrid intranet with basic components (usually templates) developed in-house and other more sophisticated functional components developed by third parties.
- ASP Model (complete outsourcing)
- Open source portal adoption
- Leveraging existing enterprise technology to create an intranet or intranet components

We will look at each of these in detail now.

Developing an Intranet Internally

This is a time-honored and trusted approach that makes sense when there are strong internet designers and developers in an organization. The development team typically knows the company and its processes better than any outside contractor and can create a new system that specifically solves existing problems instead of just customizing an existing system for another client.

On the other side of this approach is the "not being able to see the forest for the trees" syndrome where a development team can be too focused on the details to see the bigger picture. Also worth considering is whether the internal resources are actually internet developers or just IT staff who are sure they can create an intranet if they're given a chance. Be wary of these situations.

While there is no license cost for using your own technology, there are some drawbacks to developing a proprietary code base for your intranet. Unlike commercial products or software developed by the open source community, nobody else will be working on potential updates for you. If you want to add a new feature, your only option will likely be to have internal or external developers create it for you. That is not to say you cannot use open source components or purchase third-party tools that will allow you to extend your intranet, but integrating these components with your existing system can be very difficult if extensibility was not considered during initial development.

Purchasing an Existing Intranet

There are a number of commercial intranet development companies who concentrate on a single code base and use it for all their clients. In most cases, the product is highly customizable and is available to their own development clients and external clients in a component-based fee structure. This could allow you to potentially take the list of functional components determined in your Needs Analysis and cross-reference them with different vendors' products to find a package that meets your needs.

The advantage of choosing a package like this is that you can purchase it outright (although some vendors have annual licensing fees), have your team customize it with your design and content, and then host it on the web server of your choice. It gives you autonomous control over the growth and management of the site over time. And it allows you to take advantage of a well-developed system, ideally, that's been tried and tested over time.

The disadvantages of this type of package relate to the expense, time, and energy required to make minor or major changes, and to fix problems when they occur. While upgrades to newer versions can solve some problems and "known bugs," the process of upgrading can be difficult since any modifications made to older installations will probably have to be redone (though this isn't always the case now that many developers are separating content and layout from functionality within their applications, and even separating subelements of their own functional components).

Many vendors offer support service subscriptions, but their staff won't be as dedicated to your problems as your internal IT staff would be if they knew how the system worked. When an issue needs serious attention (for example, when it crashes the night before a major event and can't be restarted), their support staff may not be available to help. This can obviously lead towards frustration (and that leads to Anger, and eventually the Dark Side). The alternative option of hiring an independent consultant (or someone from the vendor) to provide a fix can be quite expensive, depending on the amount of work required. So you may want to consider investing in training for some of your IT staff to become knowledgeable about the innerworkings of the product.

Some of the leading vendors in this ready-made product area (applications that will work right out of the box with some minor customizations) are:

- Deep Blue Creative (*http://www.deepbluecreative.com*)

- Elleance (*http://www.elliance.com*)

- GroupSpace (*https://www.groupspace.info*)

- Intranet Connections (*http://www.intranetconnections.com*)

- Klick Interactive (*http://www.klickit.com*)

- Process Software (*http://www.process.com*)

- Kaorg (*http://www.kaorg.com*)

Developing a Hybrid Intranet

One of the wonderful things about the Internet is that a global community of developers has gathered to create and innovate, and to share. Many developers work on their own or in collaborative groups to create code, tools, applications, and tutorial web sites where other developers can learn, beg, borrow, buy, and steal from them. As a legitimate corporate intranet builder, you are an elite client for many of these developers and will probably get very positive responses when you begin shopping for functional components.

The best place to start looking for the additional functionality pieces of your intranet is by searching the Web for specific components or going directly to a developer community site like *http://www.evolt.org*, *http://www.sitepoint.com* or *http://www.siteexperts.com*. Most of these sites have discussion groups where you can post e-mail queries and requests for proposal (RFP).

Another option is to visit community code portals like *http://www.aspin.com*, *http://www.planet-source-code.com*, and *http://www.programmersresource.com* and literally browse and compare products like you were shopping in a retail establishment.

While the cost of this type of solution is attractive, the drawbacks are similar to those articulated in the section on developing an intranet internally.

Application Service Provider (ASP) Model

One of the most profound changes in intranet development has been the emergence of Application Service Providers (ASPs) over the past several years. These companies provide full end-to-end solutions for companies that want to build corporate intranets, and offer them for substantially less money than it would normally cost to develop a proprietary application.

The ASP providers have built their businesses on the fact that companies who pay for their own development, maintenance, and staffing costs related to their intranets are never guaranteed a good product. They offer an alternative to this uncertainty.

Development Techniques

5

ASP products will typically be fully customizable. You can integrate your own corporate designs for all the relevant templates (using a friendly web-based interface in most cases) or select a set of their standard designs and just add your logo to them. You can also choose from many different functional components that they make available, and pay only for what you want. This allows you to build your intranet site to the specifications outlined in your Needs Analysis and not worry about all the technical details (which will be a highly subjective positive or negative factor).

There are many ASP intranet companies in the marketplace today, and more emerging every few months. Some of the top-tier companies to consider are:

- *http://www.intranets.com*
- *http://www.intranetfactory.com*
- *http://www.infostreet.com*
- *http://www.intrasmart.com*
- *http://www.sitescape.com*

The benefits of going with an ASP company are that only a minimal amount of technical resources will be required to set up the intranet site, and that non-technical staff will be able to maintain it through a CMS. In addition, the ASPs will typically have 24-7 technical support available.

The drawback to this type of solution is that the investment will be ongoing, with cost formulas based on raw usage, number of users, amount of storage space used, components selected, and miscellaneous other factors (each model is unique to the company). Furthermore, they all have monthly or annual fees that your company will have to continue paying to keep your intranet site located there. And, unfortunately, if you change your mind and want to deploy your intranet internally later, most of the integration work done with the ASP will be lost. Additionally, consider the financial health of the ASP because if its business fails, your intranet may as well.

Open Source Portal Adoption

There are a number of excellent open source internet portals and web logs (blogs) that have been developed in recent years. These applications are quite popular and can easily be deployed inside an organization specifically for intranet purposes. This type of solution will allow you to tap into a global movement of developers who are constantly improving and developing these applications for a variety of motivational factors. This means that support for technical problems is never very far and that proactive administrators who follow mailing list discussions will often be made aware of bug problems before they are ever noticed internally.

The development of these open source portals and donation-ware blog software has been instrumental in the recent surge of community web sites. Many of these tools are quite sophisticated and include advanced CMS functionality and interactivity as part of their base installation package.

Some of the systems worth evaluating if you choose to proceed on this route are:

- *http://www.phpnuke.org*
- *http://www.moveabletype.org*
- *http://www.drupal.org*
- *http://scoop.kuro5hin.org*
- *http://www.pmachine.com*
- *http://www.aenovo.com*

The drawbacks of using this type of system relate to the fact that the software's full code is in the public domain. Unless an administrator in your organization is going to actively follow the development of the chosen application (through mailing lists or discussion boards), it is possible that a security issue can become publicly known and remain unfixed in your installation. This could result in a compromise of system integrity or a successful hacking attempt. Your IT team can address this by putting the intranet inside the corporate firewall, but this issue needs to be thoroughly explored before a solution like this is chosen.

Leveraging Existing Enterprise Technology

Some corporate environments already have existing enterprise solutions in place for e-mail communication and management of business process. The most-deployed products in this category are Lotus Notes and Microsoft Exchange. Both of these platforms can be extended to some degree to create a proper intranet that runs parallel to existing systems and leverages existing technology (such as user authentication).

Neither of these systems are thought of very favorably in the development community because the intranet extensions were generally an afterthought to the products' development. That being said, both IBM and Microsoft are working on improving this (through WebSphere and .NET, respectively) and it might be worthwhile to explore this option if the system is already in place. It would allow you to centralize your processes (probably running on the same machines) and have current IT staff extend their responsibilities to cover these areas, too.

Hosting Environment

Depending on the development approach chosen, there are a number of options available with respect to intranet site hosting environments. A full ASP model where your complete enterprise intranet is located on a third party's server(s) will not require you to make any intranet host decisions, but every other solution will. This is because you will need to find a physical location to locate the machine running your intranet and ensure your users have access to it through their network(s).

A web server is different from a typical network file server and an e-mail server. While all these servers can be made to run from the same physical machine, each requires a certain configuration to optimize its performance. To place them all on one machine would necessitate generalizing the configuration and reducing the efficiency of all the processes. That is why IT teams generally separate the roles of different machines for distinct purposes. A web server, and a database server (if a database is included in your project's scope), will typically be placed on a specific machine, or on two separate machines to optimize the performance of each.

The decisions that have to be made are:

- Should the web server(s) be located inside your organization or outside it, probably at an outsourced hosting provider?

- If the intranet is hosted internally, should it be inside or outside the firewall? If it's outside the firewall, people will be able to access the intranet externally from other offices and while traveling. If it's inside the firewall, they can still get access, but only if your IT team gives their permission – and this does pose a security risk. See Chapter 10 for more information on this issue.

- If the intranet is hosted externally, should it be on the hosting provider's machine(s) or on your machines, which you configure and physically transfer to their hosting facility (called co-location hosting).

- Should the computer(s) be Unix or NT (Windows 2000)?

- Should the platform be Internet Information Server (IIS) or Apache?

- Should the database and web server be placed on separate machines?

- What database platform should be used (SQL, MySQL, Oracle, DB2, Access)?

In all likelihood, this will be a discussion between your senior developer and IT team.

Scripting Languages

When the hosting environment has been determined, it is necessary to determine what server-side scripting language will be used during the development of your intranet. It will be used for reading and writing information to your database(s) and for dynamic generation of the intranet pages.

The choice here will depend mostly on what hosting environment has been chosen (Unix or NT) and what scripting languages are supported on the web server(s). Another relevant point is what skill sets are available to you through existing resources. If the only languages that are known to your existing resources were last used in the last millennium, then it's advised to find another resource.

Also consider what the corporate standard is. If your IT team developed a sophisticated internet site that they maintain, then it is very likely that they would be very up-to-date on the development environment used to create it. If that's the corporate "standard," then you should take advantage of it to maximize the effectiveness of that knowledge and experience to your organization.

The socially acceptable scripting languages in the year 2003 are: Cold Fusion, ASP, PHP, JSP, and ASP.NET.

It is irresponsible to create a static site that does not leverage a technology that allows for some degree of separation between content and formatting. Still, however, many companies move forwards with HTML-based intranets due to the attractiveness of short-term cost saving. This book stresses that the medium-term maintenance costs will far outweigh the short-term savings.

When making a decision about these languages, keep in mind the future growth of your company's intranet. If your current system (Windows 2000 and IIS) proves to be unmanageable and you decide to change it, what technologies can you bring with you versus what will you have to start over with? For example, if you lock yourself into MS/ASP and IIS and decide that you're tired of patching IIS 10 hours a week and want to move to Apache, you may have to leave ASP behind (though Chilisoft publishes software that allows ASP to run on Unix machines). Since solutions such as PHP and MySQL are available cross-platform, that combination should be a strong contender during your consideration process.

XML and Databases

An intranet doesn't *have* to use XML or databases of any kind. Every page can be static HTML with hard-coded content, format, and function – although the amount of functionality that will be available to static HTML pages will be quite limited.

The reason why XML or databases *should* be used in the implementation of your intranet is because they allow for the simple separation of content from format and functionality. This makes long-term maintenance of the intranet more efficient (thus less expensive). It also allows you to retain the value of your content because it will be easily reusable in other formats (wireless phones, PDAs, WebTV, etc.) and delivery channels can be created quite quickly.

A database should be used to store your data. This will likely be what the back-end of your CMS reads from and writes to. Also, any information from the functional components hosted on your own server will likely be tracked here.

XML comes into the picture when data needs to be transferred from one server to another (this is because transferring entire databases can be prohibitive due to their size). Depending on what system your IT department puts in place for your intranet, you may need to use XML to transfer information between servers.

Personalization

As stated previously, personalization is impossible without some level of security. This is because access to private information that you are likely to find in a personalized intranet needs to be restricted to only that user. There are many corporate policies and laws in some jurisdictions to this effect.

Very simple personalization such as a "*Good morning Gwyneth*" prompt, user defined color scheme, or itemized layout selections *can* be selected in forms and saved in cookies on users' machines, but this approach isn't recommended. The preference settings will not be transferable to other computers the user might move to. And extending the personalization to include personal information at a later date will necessitate taking one step backwards before taking a step forwards.

Practical, intelligent personalization involves authenticating users and then tracking their user sessions with either session variables (a relationship between the web server and a user's web browser) or token variables (a unique identifier which is passed as a string in the URL of all the intranet pages). Note that the latter method is less secure than the former.

Once you've authenticated a user and started to track them, you can display any personalized content to them that you (or they) might want. All you need to do is define *what* content and function pages should be personalized, and then make sure that information is detailed in the Project Scope Document.

See *Chapter 10* for more information on Personalization.

The Production Process

There are many resources in print and online that provide information on project management techniques for planning, building, and deploying technology solutions. Also, there are globally recognized methodologies you can study and receive accreditations for. The two most common of these are the Microsoft Solutions Framework (MSF – *http://www.microsoft.com/business/services/framework.asp*) and the Project Management Institute (PMI – *http://www.pmi.org*) certifications. These courses and resources can provide you with an extensive degree of information and techniques not covered in this chapter.

> *What this chapter will do for you is provide you with a solid roadmap to follow when you become responsible for planning, building, and deploying a corporate intranet. There are 20 steps listed in the following sections, and each one of them is important. Try to provide an output at each step for documentation and meetings.*

Step 1: Conduct Needs Analysis

Do you know why you're building an intranet? Is it meant to solve problems, improve efficiency, or just to bring your organization into the 21st century? Or are you just setting out to improve the existing intranet that your company's Vice-President's best friend's nephew designed in 1997? All of these are legitimate reasons, but you need a breadth and depth of understanding with respect to all issues before you can go any further.

Make sure to solicit feedback from the people who will use the intranet to increase the likelihood that it will provide them with utility

Assess the current site (if it exists) and understand where it is hosted, who was originally responsible for creating it, what the history of the site is and who is currently responsible for maintaining it. Create a site map at this time so you're clear about how everything works (and you can refer to it when you're creating the new one).

Consider preparing a survey for all stakeholders that solicits their opinions on content, functionality, and design (including usability issues). Get feedback on current intranet (if it exists) as well as identifying "Needs" for the new intranet. Remember that the intranet should be for employees, and for making their work lives easier; it's not exclusively for managers of various departments and lines of business. Make sure to solicit feedback from the people who will use the intranet to increase the likelihood that it will be useful to them.

Aggregate all the information gathered during the Needs Analysis and prepare a document that states the particulars of the current site situation and what needs have been identified for the new site.

Step 2: Prepare Project Scope Document

Using the document you created during your needs analysis, create a detailed plan for what types of content and functionality will be included in the new intranet and how it will be organized. Each type of content and specific functionality should be described in as much detail as possible. If some fine points aren't available or decided upon, they should be noted so they can be reviewed, discussed, and settled during the scope document approval process.

As well as your written descriptions, it is recommended that you include an illustrated site map in your scope document. It should depict the hierarchy of information in the new intranet and allow people studying it to visualize what the user experience will be from a pure information-flow perspective. If you're not an artist and have access to a digital production artist, give them a roughly drawn sketch with specific details and have them create something slick and compelling (note that including basic symbols and a legend always goes over well with visually-oriented people). If you're going to produce it yourself and you're not an artist, then keep it simple and straightforward.

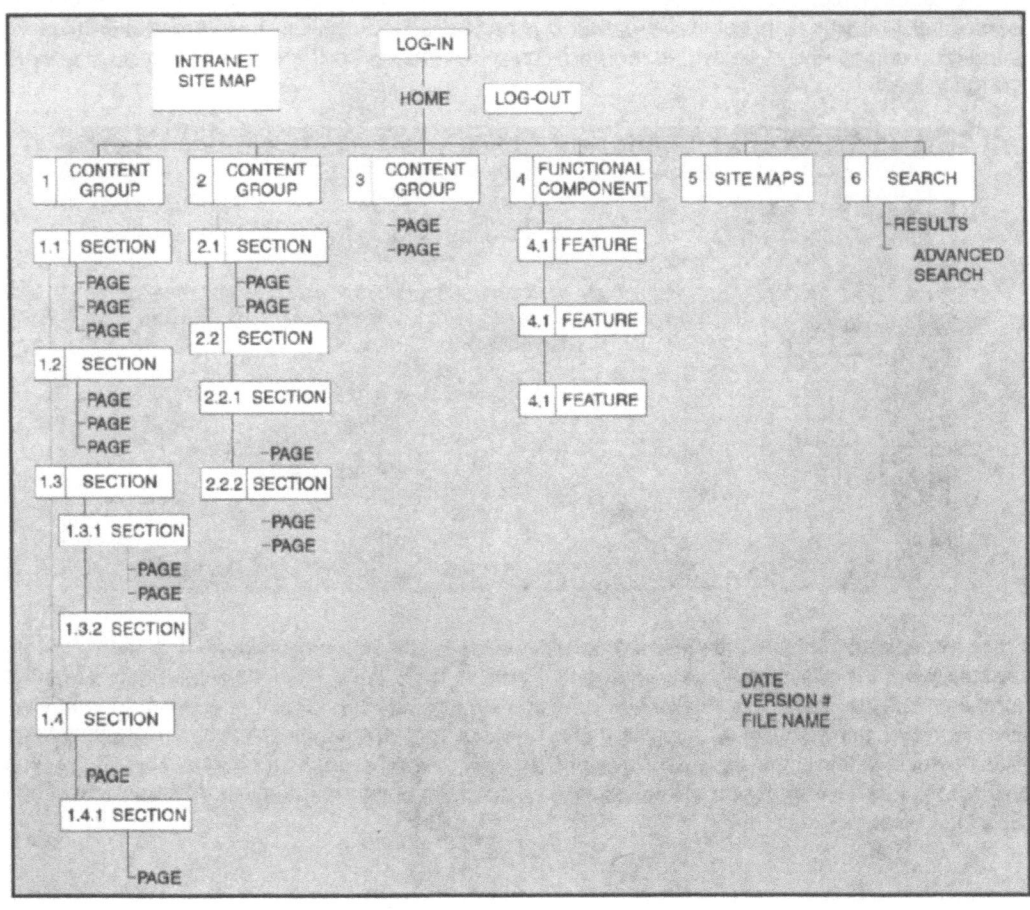

Once you know what you intend to do and how it will be done, it is important to determine: what resources are likely to be available for this project (technical personnel, non-technical personnel, and funds); what the development approach will be; where the site will be hosted; and what degree of personalization and security will be required. This information is necessary for determining scheduling and costs.

Ask each resource how much time will be required to complete their various aspects of the development process, and then double their estimate before including it in your schedule. This might seem excessive to someone who hasn't worked on projects like this before, but it is an unfortunate reality that almost all initial estimates by qualified, experienced professionals working on web-based projects fall short by approximately 50%. In cases where a "buffer zone" of 100% is not added to original time estimates and a deadline is inflexible, considerable overtime will be worked in order to meet the deadline. So, to keep the resources and their project manager less-stressed and more-loved, use the Factor of 2 Rule as a matter of course.

When all the time estimates have been gathered, prepare a Gantt Chart (using Microsoft Project, Visio, or some other project management software) that shows all the tasks required for your intranet's development and deployment. Each task should have a brief descriptive name (1-4 words), and should indicate what resources are required to complete it. It is also important to create relationships between the tasks and to state what preceding tasks must be completed before another one can begin. By creating a project schedule with an interdependent task list, managing changes and delays (and their bottom-line impact on the entire project's schedule) will be much easier.

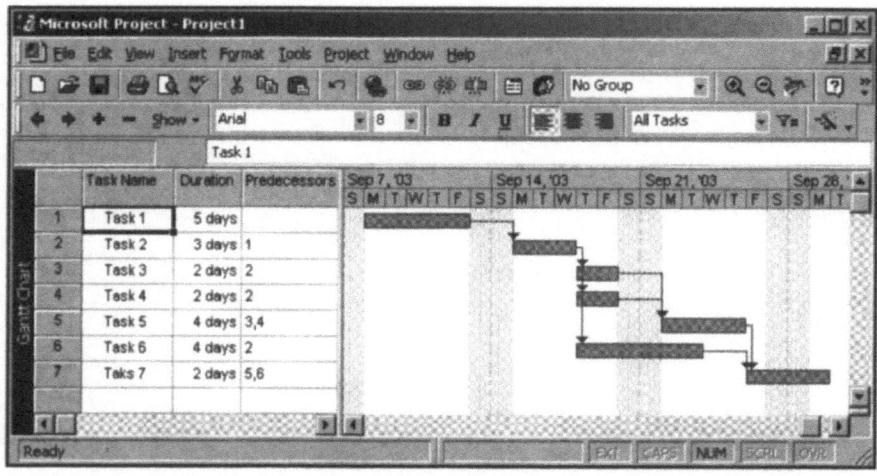

Once the scope and schedule have been determined, a cost must be calculated. If all resources are on salary in your organization, then attributing a cost to the project will depend on your company's algorithms. It's best to discuss this with your accounting department, if it is relevant to your project. There are certainly many cases where the only costs that are important to an organization are outside costs. If this is the case, obtain quotes from your various suppliers (if necessary) and reserve the right to ask for new quotes if the scope of work changes during the revision and approval of your Scope Document.

Once your deliverables, schedule, and cost have been established, finesse them all into your Project Scope Document. Take extra care to be realistic and explicit. Don't promise more than you can deliver. Being realistic means setting expectations that you can meet; and being explicit means including as many details as possible instead of generalizations. This applies to everything in your Scope Document. Remember that you don't want to be making the complaint that you need to meet impossible deadlines and fulfill unrealistic expectations with inadequate resources. This is one of your key opportunities to make sure this doesn't happen.

Step 3: Review, Revise, & Approve Project Scope Document

Once the Project Scope Document has been completed, it should be distributed for review to all relevant stakeholders and decision-makers. You should request that they read it thoroughly and provide comments and questions. This will help you ensure everything is clear to those who are going to be involved. If necessary, have a meeting to review the document.

Regardless of the how spectacular, intricate, and fascinating your Project Scope Document is, the question you will typically hear most often at this stage will be similar to this: "what will it look like?". Sometimes people will be able to articulate this clearly and ask: "Can I see the new design before I review this document, so I can see the context in which the content and functionality will fit?". Regardless of how they ask to see the designs first, it is important to explain that designing the look of the GUI is not part of the planning phase; it is part of the production phase. While visually oriented people may not appreciate that, explaining it in terms they might (designing a product without approved definition will cost time & money) will help.

Discuss the Project Scope Document to whatever degree is required and make revisions until consensus is reached among stakeholders. This document will be the master plan for your efforts. If some aspect of your project is not explicitly captured inside, it will not be delivered. That being said, there will still be people who give their approval, then contact you shortly thereafter with requests for modifications and additions.

Step 4: Managing Changes

It is important to define a process for managing changes from this point forward. A formal "Change Request Form" and approval process for making amendments to your Project Scope Document will eliminate the lion's share of requests (many of which will be frivolous). The rest of them should be detailed by the person making the request and submitted to you. You should

Remember to manage expectations. If you do this, you will live longer.

then determine the cost and time required to implement the change(s) and calculate how this will affect the greater project definitions. Also, you should make a recommendation about the degree to which the request is reasonable. Your information, with the original request, should then be reviewed and approved through appropriate channels. When approval is received, revise your Project Scope Document and make sure all stakeholders receive a current version.

Step 5: Create Detailed Site Map

Using the site map in your approved Project Scope Document as a base, work with your designer and information architect (if you have one) to determine a detailed site map. Define a hierarchy of all the information on the site and organize it from an intelligent perspective. If you want to know if it's intelligent, show it to some potential users for some feedback.

The detailed site map will identify the number and type of different template pages that require design. Normally, designs will be required for:

- The splash page (if desired – this is a matter of personal preference). This can also be the user login page.

- The home page.

- The primary content group page (if required for sites with hierarchical groups of content).

- The individual content page for a news story or content item.

- Functionality pages (for search results, discussion forums, address books, and other interactive functions listed in the Needs Analysis section of this chapter).

- CMS interface (if required).

Step 6: Create First Draft of GUI

The first draft of the Graphic User Interface (GUI) should be derived directly from the information hierarchy defined in the Detailed Site Map. Attention should be paid to the varying degrees of importance that some content types and functionality will have over others.

It is recommended that the creation of the First Draft include the production of three distinctly different design concepts. These concepts should each consist of designs for all defined template pages. The differences between the concepts should primarily be in regard to navigation approaches (how the site will be used) as color schemes for intranets usually come from standardized corporate palettes.

The rationale for three designs is that it allows a designer to conduct an exploration of possibilities that is ideally a lucid, thorough thinking process. If they understand good web design and usable interface theory, there are many GUI variations that can arise. As they think of different approaches, they may return to earlier ones and refine them.

The more significant benefit of multiple GUI concepts is that the stakeholder group will have a selection to review, analyze, and discuss. People with minimal interface design experience will point to aspects of concepts they like and don't like, and use a visual language that can more clearly state their intention than a halting non-technical vocabulary.

 Try to accommodate the non-technical people as much as possible, and listen to what they're saying even if they're not using the standard web designer lexicon

Before the GUI designs leave the realm of the designer, it is important that your project's senior technical developer and usability expert review them.

The developer needs to review the designs to make sure they are technically possible. They should advise you (and the designer) if they cannot be implemented at all (which may happen) in accordance with the schedule defined in the Project Scope Document. Remember the Factor of 2 Rule.

The usability expert should review the designs to make sure the design is intelligent. Sometimes a great flat design will become a nightmare when it becomes a fully functional web site. It's the usability expert's role to predict this and make appropriate recommendations.

When the team that is going to implement one of the designs has given their nod of approval to each of them, call a meeting of stakeholders. The meeting will be for the presentation and discussion of the three design concepts. If possible, have the senior developer and designer attend to answer specific questions and get first-hand exposure to the feedback. Bring printouts for people to refer to. And prepare for chaos.

If someone during the meeting is trying to convey an idea that they can't articulate, request that they provide a sample URL where the group can review their suggestion. Try to accommodate the non-technical people as much as possible, and listen to what they're saying even if they're not using the standard web designer lexicon.

The goal of the meeting is to walk away with either a stated preference for one of the presented concepts or at least a very clear understanding of what type of design is wanted by the stakeholder group. The meeting attendees should be told that a refinement of the chosen concept will be created by the designer and two variations of the final design will be forwarded to them as per the original schedule.

During the meeting, take extensive notes. If you can't do this while presenting, have someone meticulous take care of this for you. Note suggestions, who made them, what was agreed on, what was dismissed (sometimes good ideas can be disregarded and brought back to life later), and what the action items moving forwards are going to be. Then create two reports, one for your personal use (with all the specific details) and one for distribution to the stakeholders (a detailed summary).

Your personal document should include information about which stakeholder didn't say much and might need a one-on-one visit to get them on board or answer questions and address concerns. The intranet can be a highly political animal because it touches all departments, lines of business, and individuals within an organization. So be politically savvy when necessary, but remember to protect yourself with extensive documentation.

Make sure that all legal requirements are fulfilled – if your company employs people who are visually challenged or physically challenged the intranet should be accessible to them – or be prepared to spend time answering questions in court. See Chapter 6 on usability for more information on the implications of this.

The group document should be a comprehensive summary of the discussion outlining what was agreed to and an itemized schedule for next steps. Make this document one to two pages, if possible, but don't sacrifice detail for space when needed. Noting "the idea to have a webcam stream pictures from the Grand Canyon was dismissed as impractical and expensive" can keep you from having to explain later why it wasn't included when someone thought it would be.

Step 7: Second Draft of GUI

Use the feedback from the presentation of the First Draft concepts to create the Second Draft. This design iteration should be a refined concept with polish. It is recommended that a variation on the Second Draft be created as part of this design round so two refined concepts can be submitted to the stakeholder group for review or approval. This allows them to compare designs and state a preference (perhaps a request for further changes submitted with comments) instead of just returning a single concept with a request for further revisions.

Make revisions as necessary until the design for all templates has been approved.

Step 8: Obtain Approval for GUI and Start Developing

The GUI approval can take weeks or months to arrive. This is because it is the only really concrete stage of your intranet development that can be approved by non-technical stakeholders. As such, many corporate communications and design department members will want to have their say. After this stage, these stakeholders will have to wait until the project is about 90% done before they will see anything else. So be prepared to receive a plethora of opinions from corporate communications team members who want to have their say about the design. Stick to your guns here and remember that you're building the site for its users.

While you can certainly have the technical teams and content aggregators working concurrently with the designer, they may reach a point where they can do no further work without the final design. This can result in team members sitting idle, causing cost overruns and other miscellaneous problems.

Step 9: Create GUI Design Specifications Document

After the final GUI has been approved (and concurrently with the following steps, if you wish), ask its designer to create a GUI Design Specifications Document. It should be considered an addendum to the Project Scope Document and distributed to all members of the development team. This document will serve as a design bible during development and likely include (but not be limited to):

- A palette with HTML hexadecimal color values for all the colors used in the design.

- An explanation of what HTML colors should be used on the template pages for various text, table cell backgrounds, body backgrounds, and links (including active links, selected links, and visited links).

- Instructions on how link behavior should be implemented, in regard to mouse-hovering, underlines, and title texts.

- A font guide that includes information on all the fonts to be used in the site. This should include all the particulars your developer will implement in the site-wide Cascading Style Sheets.

- An explanation of usability and accessibility features and a detailed explanation (perhaps with illustrations) of how they should be implemented.

Step 10: Start Gathering Content

The Detailed Site Map outlines all the content areas that will exist in your new intranet. Each content area will have content items in it. You or someone on your team will need to make sure all this content is aggregated and organized so it can be included in the new site. These documents will usually exist in multiple formats across numerous locations and require various personal connections to obtain.

Meticulously tracking the particulars of all this information during this phase is important. Depending on the scale of this work, a master Excel spreadsheet might be useful. This can serve as a guide for the person responsible for the work, for the person managing the project, and for the developer or data-entry person who moves the content into the new system.

Creating a backup version of the content in its original format before conversion is always a good idea. This allows for comparison of original content with new, reformatted content, to verify data integrity. It also provides some insurance in case of problems.

Step 11: Design Conversion

To convert the designer's work into HTML, the developer will require individual images for various components of the design. The designer and developer need to discuss the specifics of this to make sure the developer gets exactly what they need.

Typically, designers creating templates for web sites will use a program like Adobe Photoshop to create multi-layered .psd images that can be displayed as a single flattened image ("flattened" refers to the multiple layers all being reduced to one flat layer when the image is printed or saved in another format). .psd files, however, cannot be used in an intranet site because web browsers don't display them. The only formats that can currently be used for images are .jpg, .gif, .png, and .swf (flash). Usually, however, .jpg and .gif files are those most often utilized.

A designer can't simply save their .psd file as a .gif or .jpg. This is because an intranet site consists of images and text, and it's considered bad practice to simply overlay text on top of a large image. Instead, the designer should convert their .jpg into a series of smaller web-ready images that can be used in HTML pages to accurately convey the visual effect of the design. The developer who will be creating the HTML templates can normally bestadvise the designer on exactly how to do this to make the HTML pages efficient.

When the designer converts their single image to a series of smaller images, they should keep some things in mind:

- The files should be optimized to have small file sizes for increasing the efficiency of page download times. This can be done with Adobe ImageReady, Macromedia Fireworks or Debabilizer. There may be some resistance to this by a designer who thinks an intranet is always accessed on a high-speed local network, but remind them that this process is considered best practice for web design and that some users may access the intranet from a dial-up account.

- File formats (.gif, .jpg, .png) for images should be carefully chosen based on requirements. Your designers will typically know quite well the issues surrounding the differences between formats.

- The filenames should be short, but descriptive (that is, `title.jpg`, `logo.gif`, `icon-print.jpg`, etc.). Numbered image names are discouraged. Also, images automatically given cryptic names when processed by Adobe software should be renamed.

- Numerous templates will probably all be converted to web-ready images at the same time. These templates' images should be placed into their own respective directories (for example, `/images/splash/` and `/images/home/`), with common files such as logos placed in (`/images/`). This organization will make a difference in the short-term development cycle and become invaluable to site maintenance staff in the long-term.

- Whole, uncut images should be included in web format in a reference directory (`/images/reference/`). This allows a developer who is implementing the site to compare the presentation of their HTML pages with the original design.

- The original .psd files should be included in their own directory (`/images/PSD/`) as a proactive long-term measure. This will make updating the intranet's visual components in the future significantly easier on designers who may succeed the site's original designer.

- If the designer has time, they should create a basic wireframe for each template design that indicates the height and width of every image and content area. This can help a developer, but it is a "nice to have" and not a "need to have."

Step 12: Develop HTML Templates

When the design conversion has been completed by the designer, the developer can create HTML versions of the templates. Prepared with the reference images, the GUI Design Specifications Document, the web-ready images, and possibly a wireframe outline for each template, he will be able to accurately recreate the approved design in HTML.

HTML is used to describe the coding language because it is probably going to be the major part of the technology used during this phase. It is possible and perfectly acceptable for the HTML templates to be developed in XHTML or a scripting language and appear as CFM, ASP, JSP, PHP files, or a number of languages. In any case, the technology will be transparent in this phase.

When developing the HTML templates, it is important that an intelligent architecture be created. Planning and implementing this now will allow the rest of the intranet site to expand over this framework and be exponentially more manageable over the long term

Intelligent architecture, in this instance, refers to a clear separation of content, presentation, and functionality. An example of this would be an HTML content page with information about a corporate division's historical milestones. The actual HTML page (`milestones.html`) will just consist of the HTML layout and the content. The information about how the content is formatted (the colors and font information defined in the GUI Design Specifications Document) will be in a separate Cascading Style Sheet file (`/includes/css/format.css`). And the information about how the page behaves (image rollovers, document object triggers, etc.) will all be in a JavaScript file (`/includes/js/rollover.js`).

The formatting and functionality documents will be referenced by the content page's HTML sourcecode. This code will instruct users' web browsers to download the appropriate include files and process them when it is being displayed in their browser. When these include files have been downloaded for the user's intranet session, they will just need to be downloaded once, and then all other content files can refer to them. This can have a dramatic effect on page load times when compared to having all formatting and functionality embedded in every page.

The additional advantage of this method is its extra-special selling point. By clearly separating the content from the presentation and the functionality, any of these three things can be changed without affecting the others. If the design evolves and/or users want larger font sizes, one CSS file can be changed to update every content page's layout. The functionality, similarly, can also be modified in the same way and to the same effect.

Referring to single CSS and JS files is probably an oversimplification of your intranet needs. You are more likely to have multiple CSS files for different templates (for example, all templates will use the same `/includes/css/global.css` global font definitions, but the splash page and discussion forum page won't need the `/includes/css/navigation.css` navigation font definitions).

While HTML files can theoretically refer to an unlimited number of CSS and JS files, the goal here is to create an intelligent architecture that will be extensible, maintainable, and sensible over time. Be careful not to micromanage functionality and layout to an extensive degree.

The last item to mention here is in regards to scripting languages. There are many advantages to using these technologies, but plan your implementation well, as per the above. Use the `/includes/templates/template-top.inc` and `/includes/templates/template-bottom.inc` include files to separate the advanced functionality of some sections from the formatting elements (note that the file structure of the site that is referred to here will be discussed later on). The advantages are also great in regards to organization and long-term maintenance, but the savings are more recognizable on the server-side (corporate benefits) than the client-side (user benefits).

Step 13: Test Templates

Your organization's IT department has most probably defined a standard software installation for all desktop computers. This is almost always an evolving standard, with some users just getting upgraded to the current configuration and others slowly moving past it. Two components of this standard that you have to become very familiar with are:

- What machines are currently deployed in the organization (platform, operating system, bandwidth capability)?
- What web browser software is installed on these machines?

You need to know what computers and software your users are running so you can test your templates on appropriately configured machines. Many problems about how users will see the intranet can be identified, trouble-shot and resolved at this stage by previewing the static HTML pages on typical machines.

A major advantage of standardized software deployment is that you can know a lot about your users in advance of your launch. Public internet development is often complicated by an ever-increasing number of web browsers that display HTML pages in their own special ways. Be thankful for corporate IT standards, if they exist.

Test all the template pages in the web browser and computer configurations included in your IT standard. If there are errors, make revisions as necessary.

Development Techniques

Step 14: Develop CMS

Develop the CMS (if required) as per the specifications in the Project Scope Document. Integrate it with the user authentication system (if necessary) and then test all the required functionality from different user profiles with distinct access privileges. Also port some sample content into the system for testing purposes. This can be "lorem ipsum" mock Latin text to make the selection of sample text easier.

You should now have a functioning navigation that defines a "sense of place" for the user within the intranet site. As well, the CMS should be ready for content to be added.

When the CMS has been completed, an instruction manual on its use and administration should be created. This manual should be distributed to the relevant administrators, and also be posted inside the CMS for other users who will be making updates in the future.

The developers can begin this process by including inline comments in their code to serve as basic documentation for future developers. These comments are like notes in the margin that are not read by the intranet server but are visible to people who are reviewing and editing the code now and in the future.

Step 15: Develop Functional Components

All the functional components identified in the Project Scope Document need to be developed and transparently integrated with the CMS. Regardless of development approach, hosting environment and scripting language, the look and feel of the site should be consistent across all functional areas. This is because the users for whom you are building the intranet site should not ever notice the technology that powers it.

If the site is based on a hybrid development approach, attempt to have all components use the same dynamic templating system. If that's not possible due to incompatibilities in scripting format, at least use the same HTML template and make absolute references to common images, CSS and JavaScript files.

When development is done, ask the developers to properly comment their code. This means that they should review and insert lines of text into their code that explain their rationale for approaching various sections of logic the way they did. This will make updating the code much more efficient in the future because less time will be required for other developers to learn how the code works.

One thing to remember as the process continues is that you must document everything. Sending summary e-mails to relevant stakeholders after conversations and meetings will allow you to prevent he said/she said arguments. These e-mails should include details about participants, decisions and action items. Not only will they include and inform the right people on the project's development, but it will also give you a paper trail to reference if things start heading in an awkward direction.

Step 16: Monitor Progress

There is no substitute for a periodic formal review of development with all the people involved in the design, development and implementation of the site. The team should review progress towards the expectations (technical goals, schedule, and cost) and discuss any concerns. To make these meetings constructive, do not attempt to assign blame if problems arise; instead, seek out a solution as a group. And remember to manage the expectations of your stakeholders.

Step 17: Integration of Content

When the CMS is complete, the aggregated content should be added to the site in accordance with the Detailed Site Map. A content administrator should do this. He should obtain a copy of the CMS manual and follow directions to create the correct content structure.

If any problems occur during this process, they should be reported to the project manager and the senior technical developer. As well, changes to the manual should be suggested at this time if some areas are inaccurate or incomplete.

Step 18: Small Group Testing

The Small Group Testing stage should include all the developers, designers, content aggregators and people involved in the production process. This is because these people will know the intranet best and be able to thoroughly test it ensure expectations are being met.

Upload the site to a live server, but don't activate it to the public yet. A good way of doing this is to have the root folder's default file (that is, `index.html`) have a "coming soon" message and to have the test intranet's main page available at another location (for example, `index2.html`). Communicate that URL to the Small Testing Group and ask them to return comments, feedback, and suggestions within a defined time frame.

When the comments, feedback, and suggestions come back, review them with an open mind, but be careful about making changes to anything outlined in the Project Scope Document. Defer those for the next testing stage. For everything else, modify the various functions, content, and design as necessary.

In larger organizations, remind your IT department to load-test your intranet server(s) to make sure they can deal with numerous simultaneous users. Having the site crash on the day it launches will not look good.

Note that Quality Assurance and Testing companies (known simply as QA firms) are available to do this testing for you, if you wish. They will evaluate a site's design, usability, content structure, and overall impact for a reasonable fee.

Step 19: Large Group Testing

Large Group Testing should occur when you are reasonably sure the Project Scope Document's promises have been met. This means that expectations regarding its appearance, usability, and technical functionality should all have been delivered. If this is the case, schedule a presentation of the intranet site to all stakeholder groups and review the developed intranet. Any changes that were deferred should be discussed at this point, and appropriate action should be taken.

Unless approval to launch the intranet is given at this meeting (possible, but unlikely), provide the stakeholder group with the test URL on the live server and ask them to send you comments, feedback, and suggestions within a defined time frame. Make changes as necessary and ask for approval to launch the site.

Make sure to allow time after testing and before approvals for the development team to fix any bugs and address other issues which may have arisen during testing.

5

Development Techniques

Step 20: Approvals

When approval to go live arrives (probably 3 to 6 months after starting the project), do a little happy dance and twirl around. Then send word to your senior developer that the test URL should be changed so that everyone in the organization has access to it.

Step 21: Launch

Typically, the best way to launch an intranet site is to send out a company-wide broadcast e-mail announcing the launch and inviting people to visit it. Do be careful, specifically in larger organizations, to be sure that load-testing has occurred before this, so the site's servers don't fail minutes after the corporate launch.

File and Directory Naming Conventions

Part of creating an intelligent architecture in the beginning of a development cycle is adopting good file and directory naming conventions. This was briefly discussed above in regard to the following structure:

```
/index.html
/images/
/includes/css/global.css
/includes/css/format.css
/includes/js/rollover.css
/includes/templates/template-top.inc
/includes/templates/template-bottom.inc
```

This directory and file structure implies some things that need to be clearly stated. These are:

- File and directory names should contain all lowercase letters

- File and directory names cannot contain any spaces or special characters (?, %, #, @, etc.)

- File and directory names should be brief and not overly descriptive

- Files and directories should be organized into subdirectories that reflect the structure of your site as well as your business. Some dynamic CMS systems will render this point redundant, but others will require defining directory paths. Be smart about that.

Software and Tools

There are many companies that create software and tools for intranet sites. Most of their products relate to the functionality options detailed in the *Needs Analysis* section above. These products are generally provided as hosted solutions for companies that don't have the technical resources or budgets to build proprietary solutions or make outright software purchases.

Many of these items are covered in some detail earlier in this chapter. One that does need special attention, however, is Search. This is a functionality that is almost always a priority in a Project Scope Document, is very difficult to implement well, and can cause some sincere complications for a development team.

Search Solutions

The 'search' function on a web site can be a very valuable resource to users. It adds a high degree of usability because it allows users to look for the information they're actually looking for, instead of the information your information architects thought they would be looking for when they designed your site's navigation schema. Even the most capable team of human factor engineers (usability experts) will never be able to take into account all your users' information needs in respect to specific words or phrases. That's why having a search function is a really good idea.

Unfortunately, there are numerous circumstances in which a company will be unable to simply include a search function on their intranet site when the need for one arises. The technical complexity inherent in searching for keywords or phrases embedded in HTML is often beyond the level of technology used in the creation, implementation, and maintenance of a site.

Many web sites are static, meaning that each of its pages is an individual file where the content (text and images) is integrated with the formatting (page layout, font information, text size, image alignment, etc.). There are various degrees of dynamic templating and scripting that can be implemented to make maintenance of individual pages' content and an entire site's graphical "look and feel" more efficient, but any site that does not store its content in a database is still a static site at its core. That means it's a series of individual digital pages that have only superficial relationships to each other and searching them from within the site will be impossible.

In order to make a site searchable in this scenario, there are two possible solutions:

- Invest what may amount to substantial resources migrating your site onto a database-driven platform that will allow your developers to create a search function. This will typically involve developing or purchasing a content management system that includes a Boolean search capability (allows use of 'and', 'or', 'not', and other advanced operators to fine-tune search requests).

- Outsource your search functionality to a Remote Site Search Service that will place your search engine on a web server which is distinct from the one where your web site is hosted. This will allow you to let someone else handle most of the technical issues, and allow you to likely realize substantial savings over solution #1.

   If you're interested in learning more about the first option, you should read Chapter 8 on Content Management Systems.

The Remote Site Search Service option mentioned briefly in solution #2 above encompasses a wide choice of services and service providers. The different packages vary in cost from free to very expensive and have numerous value-added options that were implemented in efforts to distinguish themselves from their competition.

All Remote Site Search Services rely on the same basic precept: they function like any of the major search engines, but limit their results to those found on the pages specified for indexing by their clients. Essentially, the remote searcher's "web spider" crawls your site and stores your pages' information in an indexed database on their server. When one of your users enters a query from a search form on your site, the query goes by HTTP to the search provider. The search provider looks up the query in their index, formats the results in a format specified by you (which is likely to be derived from your existing web templates), and then displays them on their web site. The results' links, when selected, take the user back to the appropriate page on your site.

Note that, if the results page is formatted properly, this process can be hidden from your users and they will never be made aware of the fact they're leaving and returning to your site during their searches.

Where the service providers diverge in their offerings is in their core technology, their features, and their pricing. Some service providers offer straightforward search capability (simple text and phrases only) while others provide a more complex search capability that includes date-ranging, relevance ranking, and proximity operators (NEAR). As well, a key feature that is very valuable to most site administrators is the availability of statistical reporting on search usage that includes aggregate data and allows for a better ongoing understanding of what users are looking for on a site.

In regard to pricing, the range is significant, from free to tens of thousands of dollars (US) per month. An overview of some of the services is below. Following that, there will be a recommendation and a brief section on limitations.

Remote Site Search Service Options

Name of Service	Comments	Price (US$)
AltaVista's Enterprise Search	Top-quality global search product with exceptionally fast servers and technicians Mild customization (your logo on their pages) More details available at http://services.altavista.com/	Pricing is by CPM (cost per thousand searches). Actual cost n/a.
Atomz.com (free)	Full customization of layout Atomz.com logo added to results page Powerful Web interface Statistical reporting included (w/ aggregate data and detailed breakdown) Will index up to 500 pages on a weekly basis Excellent product http://www.atomz.com/search/trial_account.htm	free
Atomz.com (paid)	Same as above, but allows re-indexing of up to 1000 pages on a daily basis (at the base end of their pricing) Includes PDF and Flash support Allows private domain labeling Includes advanced linguistic support in 19 languages and other advanced features located at http://www.atomz.com/search/features/	Starts at $5000/year for 1000 pages in index
FreeFind.com (free)	Limited customization of layout Includes advertising banners and logo Indexing allowed daily, weekly, monthly or at any time on request Includes automated "site-map" and "what's new" pages No limit on number of pages Statistical reporting is very basic	Free
FreeFind.com (paid)	All of the above, but no advertising Support for PDF documents Higher-priority service and support Plans cost between $5/month and $79/month. For more information on packages, see: http://www.freefind.com/plans.html	$5/month and $79/month. See URL for more info.
Google (free)	Allows co-branding of Google's search results pages, with your logo and theirs (limiting their results to pages on your site). Some further customization also allowed. Includes advertising Update schedule is arbitrary. And there is no guarantee that all your pages will be crawled No reporting available More info available at: http://www.google.com/services/free.html	

Google (SilverSearch)	Fully customizable Supports all languages supported by Google Includes full reporting *http://www.google.com/services/silver_gold.html*	USD$599 monthly fee, USD$10 CPM beyond 1 million queries per year
Google (GoldSearch)	Same as above, but designed for large sites	USD$1,999 monthly fee, USD$8 CPM beyond 4 million queries
MondoSoft's MondoSearch	Includes vast list of features detailed at *http://www.mondosoft.com/ms-features.asp* Includes indexing and searching of HTML, PDF, and Microsoft Office documents Statistics reports cost additional $400/month Technology includes "stemming" search inputs (corrects grammatical mistakes)	$1440 setup $315/month
SiteMiner	Unlimited re-indexing to accommodate new content Real-time reports on all searches performed on your site No promotional advertising on search box or search results pages Fully customizable formatting options	$19.95 per month or $199.00 per year. (up to 1500 pages)

Limitations

While there are numerous benefits to using a Remote Site Search Service (such as no load on your servers and the features mentioned above), there are some drawbacks to consider as well:

● Your Internet site will be dependent on an outside service. If that service is under peak-period strain of overuse, the response time may be slow.

● Some RSSS providers will have their own features which may not be customizable to the rather special requirements of your intranet system.

● If your data changes frequently (hourly or daily in some cases), the results will not automatically be updated, unless your plan includes frequent updates.

● There is sometimes a limit on capacity where a remote search service has a page limit from 150-5000 pages in their index. If your intranet is larger than that, it might not be entirely searchable. You'll need to evaluate the packages offered by your chosen provider and compare that with the estimated launch size of your intranet site (the number of pages and documents that will exist) and the projected size over the medium and long term. Note that this may substantially affect the cost of this service.

● You must pay a regular fee that is not an investment in your own core technologies.

Summary

This chapter detailed the process involved in developing an intranet for your organization. It covered many of the different planning stages that need to be completed thoroughly before any designers or developers start their work. Extensive planning is definitely the single most important aspect of the process.

The second most important part of your process is documentation. Capturing all information at every step as concretely, explicitly, and clearly as possible will allow you to get your project done on time, on schedule, and on budget. These three factors may change, but as long as expectations are managed properly during a project's evolution, they can become your revised deliverables.

6

- The useful intranet

- User testing

- Practical usability techniques

Author: Inigo Surguy

Designing Your Intranet to Be Useful – Usability and Information Architecture

In *Chapters 3, 4* and *5*, we've discussed some of the technology involved in creating an intranet. In this chapter, we'll take a step back from the technology and focus on the problems that users will face when using the intranet and how to solve them.

The problems that we'll be looking at in this chapter are:

- If you have an existing intranet, how to identify and fix its usability problems

- If you're starting from scratch, how to use iterative design to identify usability problems

- How to increase the usability of intranet navigation

- How to improve intranet search usability

- How to make the intranet fast to use

To tackle these problems, we'll take a user-centered approach. This means focusing on the aspects of the intranet that are important for the user, rather than the intranet developers or authors. The purpose of an intranet is to support users in the performance of their jobs, so it is vital to actively involve the users in the development and testing of the intranet.

We'll look at ways of considering the needs of your users in the design process, and of testing your intranet to see whether it meets those needs. We'll discuss justifying the costs of usability, and then go on to look at some specific intranet techniques and when they should be used.

Usability is about making a product – in this case your intranet – easy to use. It's not just about making it easy to learn for someone who hasn't seen it before; it is also about making it efficient to use for someone who uses it frequently.

A more formal definition is provided by the ISO standard for usability, ISO 13407: "The extent to which a product can be used by specified users to achieve specified goals with effectiveness, efficiency, and satisfaction in a specified context of use". Unfortunately, ISO standards are not freely available online, but you can purchase them from http://www.iso.org/.

Information Architecture sounds very academic, but it's essentially about organizing your intranet so people can find the information they are looking for.

There is a lot of overlap between usability and information architecture; in this chapter we'll take a practical approach and handle them together as one field instead of distinguishing between the two.

Planning the Useful Intranet

Know Your Audience...

The key point of usability is having an understanding of your users so that you can create to match their requirements and create an intranet with your audience in mind. The users of the intranet are more important than the developers or the designers; and your role as a creator of the intranet is to support them in their day-to-day tasks.

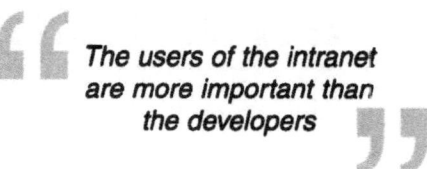

The users of the intranet are more important than the developers

You cannot assume that you know what is appropriate for your users. You probably have significantly more experience with computers than they do, and you will use the intranet for different day-to-day tasks than they will. Nor can a book like this one tell you what is right for your set of users; the only ways of telling what is appropriate for your individual audience is to employ user-centered techniques, such as the ones described in this chapter.

If you already have an intranet, then you need to identify how well your audiences are currently supported by intranet content. If there is an information void in a valuable area, then you need to identify it and target content to fill it. You cannot do this by using server statistics to identify the most and least used areas of the intranet, because the required information may not be on the intranet! Instead, you must use techniques such as user interviews and analyzing the words used in intranet searches to find out where information is missing.

... But You Have Lots of Audiences!

The problem when designing an intranet is that you have a number of different audiences, all of whom need to be supported. For example, possible audiences for your intranet might include:

- A new employee looking for site maps, HR information, and an address book with photos to help him put names to faces.

- An experienced employee who fills in timesheets and searches the company address book several times a day.

- A member of a Customer Service team, who needs fast access to customer information and support databases while on the phone to customers.

- A press officer, who needs to ensure that internal staff are aware of company-related news.

- A salesman out on the road, who needs fast access to his client information over a modem or from a PDA.

- A department manager who wants to keep the company informed about what her department is doing, to help her team work together well, and to assess the company's performance.

- A member of the web development team, who needs to maintain and update the intranet effectively, and view logs to see how the intranet is being used.

Each poses different usability challenges.

For example, new employees won't understand the company jargon. For them, the layout of the intranet must be easy to understand, and the intranet applications should be simple to learn. They will also need specific content, for example a glossary of company-specific terms.

The experienced employees value efficiency more than ease of learning. The intranet is a tool for them, and they want to use it as quickly as possible to get the results they want. Although a step-by-step "Timesheet wizard" might be useful for the newcomer, it will just frustrate an experienced employee because they know what they want to do and just want to do it quickly.

We'll talk more about the problems the salesman faces, and their solutions, in *Chapter 13*.

You shouldn't assume that these categories are fixed. For example, the experienced employee who knows the timesheet system inside out, and all its shortcuts, may still be flummoxed when she tries to enter an expense report over the intranet, or needs to visit an area of the intranet that she hasn't seen before.

However, despite the problem of multiple audiences, in some ways it is easier to improve the usability of an intranet rather than an Internet site. Although an intranet may have more distinct audiences than an Internet site, the intranet users are also easier to reach for tasks such as usability testing than Internet users are (they are probably all listed in your company address book). They also have a vested interest in increasing the usability of the intranet, as doing so will allow them to do their jobs more efficiently. In addition, you know what the business goals of your organization are, so you can build the intranet to effectively support these goals, whereas if you're working on an Internet site, you're unlikely to know the goals of your users.

So, what can we conclude? Designing a usable intranet is difficult? Yes, it is, as demonstrated by the many company intranets that are not usable, but by listening to (all) your users and having their needs in mind you can make your intranet usable. The rest of this chapter will be about methods to do just that.

6

Usability and Information Architecture

Peoplewatching

In *Chapter 3*, we described the process of "stakeholder interviews" to find out what your users believe should be available on the intranet. This process should be repeated to find out how your users believe the intranet should be organized and how it should work in terms of usability.

You can carry out formal user interviews, but this is often unnecessary. Just chatting to people at their desks for quarter of an hour about the intranet can be very informative. Ask about their problems with the current intranet, what they like, the parts of their daily routine that could be made more productive by it, and whatever else they want to talk about. Make sure you have a notebook to jot down their ideas. However, in a large organization it may not be possible for you to visit representatives of each of your audiences – be careful that you don't skew the intranet design to reflect the needs of those people that you are close to at the expense of other staff such as those in branch offices.

Another useful approach is not to ask people what they need, but to watch them doing their everyday work instead. Sometimes, you will find more information this way than by an interview, perhaps because they are reluctant to tell you their problems for fear of appearing stupid, or perhaps because they are so used to a problem that they work around it without even noticing. This approach can be time consuming; an alternative that can have some of the same benefits is to ask a user to log their intranet usage for a day on a sheet of paper. As they perform a task on the intranet (or perform a task that could have been done via the intranet), they should jot it down, and note what worked well and what didn't. This will often stir their memories as they look critically at the tasks they perform.

It's important to make people feel that the intranet is being created around their needs, rather than purely for the imparting of corporate news. User interviews are an important step towards that, as long as results are seen to be acted upon.

You can also find out a lot about how an existing intranet is being used by checking its server logs – you should be able to see which parts of it are frequently used, and which intranet applications are being totally ignored. You may also be able to use a tool to analyze user data by individual or by group to see what pages and applications are being used by which intranet audiences. Never take this as the final word; after all, there's no way of telling from the logs whether an intranet application is not used because it's hard to use, or because it's not useful, or because users don't know it's there, or because there's a better alternative used in practice. Instead, use it as a basis to steer your conversations with users.

Lots of companies nowadays have intranets so users, particularly new employees at your company, may have experience of several other company intranets. Pick their brains about the best and worst aspects of the previous intranets they've used – there may be ideas you can use, or pitfalls to avoid.

For more information on effective ways of using of server logs to improve usability see Practical Web Traffic Analysis (Fletcher, et al., glasshaus ISBN 1-904151-18-3).

When speaking to users, there are some techniques you should bear in mind:

- Avoid leading questions – you want to find out what the user thinks. By asking leading questions, you give them clues as to what you think the "right" answer is, and they may simply agree with you. This can provide reassurance to you, but it's not useful in improving usability.

- Ask open-ended questions that elicit further responses. Avoid simple yes/no questions; very few questions regarding usability are so clear-cut that these are useful.

- Be enthusiastic and interested – this will encourage the user to talk to you, and help convince them that you are going to act on the results of your talk.

- At the end, you may find it helpful to ask for feedback on your own user-interviewing technique, to help you improve your user interviews in future.

- Make sure the user knows how to contact you if they have further thoughts.

A good source of interviewing techniques is *How to Get Beneath the Surface in Focus Groups* (George Silverman, available on the web at *http://www.mnav.com/bensurf.htm.*) Although it's aimed specifically at organizing focus group discussions, it's got a lot of useful advice for user interviews in general.

The goal of interviews and field observations is to determine how people are actually using the intranet, rather than how you think they should be using the intranet.

One company decided that they could cut costs and increase efficiency by putting their company address book on the intranet. They did so, but several months afterwards found that very few people were using it. They investigated, and found that everyone was still using the old-fashioned paper address books, because it allowed them to scrawl useful notes in the margin – not possible with the online version.

In this case, there was an obvious solution to increasing the usefulness of the online address book, simply allow users to add personal annotations online as they did in the printed version. If the company had asked the users what they found most useful about the paper address book, then the intranet address book could have been useful from the start.

In fact, this example could be taken one stage further. With the intranet address book, it would be possible for each user to share their annotations with their colleagues, and to search them – converting the initial usability problem into an advantage!

Heuristic Evaluation

For a usability technique, "heuristic evaluation" doesn't have a very usable name. A heuristic is a rule of thumb; a common-sense rule that is usually right.

So, a heuristic evaluation is an inspection of an interface, in this case an intranet, to find areas where it doesn't conform to usability principles; these are the heuristics. You could call it a "usability checklist" instead if "heuristic evaluation" puts people off.

It generally involves one or more people looking through a list of intranet pages. As each finds problems, they mark them down, saying what the problem is and whether it is major or minor. Afterwards, all the results are brought together, and the combined list of problems can be used as a basis for a redesign.

Some Example Heuristics and Questions

This isn't intended as a definite list of questions – instead, it should be thought of as a set of rules of thumb which are appropriate for intranet design, and some example questions that illustrate those rules. Not all of the specific questions will be appropriate for your intranet; it will depend on the size of your company, the aims of the intranet, and the expectations of your users. However, the broad areas should be appropriate for all company intranets.

There are any number of heuristics that could be used; although they're not specifically intended for intranets, there are some more example usability heuristics listed at *http://www.asktog.com/basics/ firstPrinciples.html*, and at *http://www.useit.com/ papers/heuristic/heuristic_list.html*.

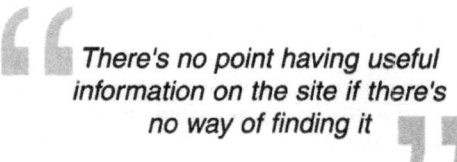

There's no point having useful information on the site if there's no way of finding it

Easy to Find Your Way Around

There's no point having useful information on the site if there's no way of finding it – so useful navigation is very important to usability. Navigation elements should be consistent and logical.

- Is the layout of the navigation logical? Having read the top-level headings, would you be able to work out what type of content is under each one?

- Are the most frequently used tasks emphasized? This can be difficult on an intranet, because different users will use different areas of the site. Implicit or explicit personalization can help by allowing different users to have different tasks emphasized to them. Implicit personalization is automatic personalization based on the user's profile and browsing habits, such as Amazon's "People who bought this book also bought…". Explicit personalization is allowing users to customize the information they see, for example by selecting the items that appear on their intranet homepage.

- Is there a site map that helps you visualize the entire structure of the site?

- Is there easy access to a site search? Ideally, there should be a search box on every page, rather than a link to a separate search page.

- Is the site layout consistent?

- Are names of links meaningful and unambiguous? For example: 'Company phone book' rather than 'extensions'.

- Is it possible to find similar pages to the one that you're currently looking at? One approach to doing this is using an automatic "People who bookmarked this page also bookmarked…" similar to the Amazon implicit personalization described above. However, there are problems doing this on an intranet; unless you are careful, you are likely to simply find the most popular intranet applications referenced from every page. An alternative approach is to have authors provide links to related pages when they create a page.

Obvious Where You Are in the Site

It's an important usability principle to make the system status visible to the user at all times. For an intranet, part of this corresponds to making it obvious where the user is in the site.

- Is there a "breadcrumb trail" visible on every page? (A "breadcrumb trail" is a hierarchical list of the section that the page is in – for example "*Company Offices -> Europe -> UK -> London*").

- Is the navigation entry for the current page highlighted?

- Is it easy to find your way back to the homepage?

Easy to Find Information Again

It's not enough to be able to find content easily once. It should be easy to find the same information quickly when you look for it a week later, without having to go through a lengthy search process again.

- Are there different link colors for visited and unvisited links, so you can see where you've been in a site, and easily retrace your steps?

- Are there distinctive colors and images for different areas of the intranet? For many people, these act as memory cues – it's easier to remember that a document was in the "blue" section with a picture of a dandelion near it, than it is to remember the exact route to it.

- Are there accurate page titles that make it easy to organize your browser bookmarks?

- Are the URLs easy to quote over the phone? For example, "*http://intranet/ humanresources/firstaid.html*" is memorable and can be read over the phone, "*http://jar-jar-binks:9811/Web-APPL/Generator.cgi/01326923746,4392946,3329282209.html*" is not.

- Are frames avoided? Pages within frames are harder to bookmark, and often have misleading titles.

Easy to Tell If Information Is Relevant and Valid

Ideally all pages are kept up-to-date and irrelevant or unimportant information is removed from the intranet, but often the best you can do is make it clear what the source of the information is, and how old it is.

- Is the "Last updated" date obvious on each page? Obviously, some pages date faster than others – a company stock ticker changes hourly, but the head office address may never change.

- Is the page author obvious on each page, with a link to their contact details? This lets you get more up-to-date or specific information directly from the author, and can let you know the validity of the information.

- Is there an obvious mechanism for a user to report inaccurate content? For example, some intranets allow users to annotate content, or even to edit it directly without going via the page author.

Does Your Intranet Speak the Users' Language?

The intranet shouldn't be seen as a "separate world" from the normal day-to-day business of the company – it should use the same language as the business, and be linked in to business processes. A major purpose of many intranets is to put different people into contact with each other, and this should be simple for the user.

- Are appropriate specialist terms used in the intranet navigation and content, rather than computer jargon or general terms that are less precise?

- Is it easy to get information about the author of a page, so you can understand where they are coming from? For example, if you read an item in a technical company knowledgebase, it's useful to know how much experience the author has with the technology being discussed.

- Is it easy to find the experts on a subject within the company?

Is Site Behavior Consistent?

This doesn't necessarily mean that the whole site should look exactly the same – but it does mean that it should behave the same in every area.

- Is navigation in the same place on every page? This also includes keeping the search box or link in the same place.

- If there are keyboard shortcuts defined for pages or forms, do they behave the same everywhere in the site?

- Are there separate systems (that work together), that can speed up the work for an expert user, and at the same time guide the way for a new one?

Responsiveness

This doesn't just mean that pages are fast to download (although that's good), but also that there's feedback to the user on tasks in progress.

- Do lengthy processes (over 10 seconds, or thereabouts) have some sort of progress meter (as a minimum to show that they are still working, and preferably to estimate time remaining)?

- Is there feedback as to how far through a process you are? For example, in an intranet application that requires you to fill in a multi-page form, are there indicators that you are currently on "Page 3 of 7"?

- If image buttons are used, is there an "onClick" graphic that gives an immediate indication that the button has been clicked?

Accessibility

This is particularly an issue for publicly funded organizations, but it needs to be considered by most large companies. Accessibility doesn't just mean making your intranet accessible to users who are blind – it's also about making it accessible to your visually impaired 65-year-old managing director, the 10% of people who are colorblind, and those employees with poor motor skills.

Intranet accessibility may be covered by laws such as Section 508 in the US and the Disability Discrimination Act in the UK. These essentially state that companies must take "reasonable steps" to avoid discrimination against disabled employees – quite what this means for intranets is as yet ambiguous, since very few cases have been brought under them. In any case, increasing the effectiveness of disabled employees by enabling them to use the intranet efficiently is going to benefit your company, regardless of the law.

There is more information on accessibility available from *Accessible Web Sites* (Thatcher, et al., glasshaus ISBN: 1-904151-00-0). On the web, the W3C's Web Accessibility Initiative is an excellent source of information, and their list of Web Content Accessibility Guidelines is at *http://www.w3.org/TR/WAI-WEBCONTENT/*. Another good source of information is Dive Into Accessibility at *http://diveintoaccessibility.org/*.

Read the W3C's recommendations for a full list of checkpoints. A few that are particularly relevant to intranets are:

- Is text resizable?

- Are site colors high-contrast? Can they be altered? In the HTML 4 standard, it is possible to provide alternative stylesheets for web pages, but switching to an alternative server-supplied stylesheet is not supported in Internet Explorer. There is an article at *http://www.alistapart.com/stories/alternate/* that describes how to provide alternative stylesheets in Internet Explorer as well as Mozilla/Netscape 6+.

- Is the intranet usable without JavaScript? For example, forms that provide client-side JavaScript input validation also require server-side validation if JavaScript is disabled, and JavaScript intranet navigation needs to degrade gracefully such that it is still usable without JavaScript.

- Are there keyboard shortcuts defined for the intranet? This not only speeds up access for frequent users, but it also helps employees with poor motor control. There is more information on this later in the chapter.

- Is there alternative text available for all images? One common mistake is to use spacer images for layout, and use the alternative text "Spacer image" for each one – it is permissible (and in this case recommended) to have the image `alt` attribute defined but set to a blank string.

Is It Possible to Undo Bad Decisions?

In order to learn any interface, including an intranet, users must be able to make mistakes without their experimentation causing serious problems (for example, losing half an hour's worth of form-filling by one careless click). This builds user's confidence in their actions.

- Can you return to the homepage of the current section of the site easily if you get lost?

- Do multi-page forms allow you to return to the previous page? Can you step back several pages, change an item and step forward again without having to re-enter data? Is a summary of the data presented back to you before any final *Submit* buttons?

- Can you easily repeat tasks with slightly different information? For example, is there a *search again* box on the search results page that is initialized with the text of the last search?

- Does the site store previous versions of documents?

- Are links that create new windows used carefully? In a newly created pop-up window, the browser's "Back" button will not work.

Usability and Information Architecture

When Should You Use a Heuristic Evaluation?

This technique is cheap and fast. It's best carried out with a small number of people (four or five), but you can still get useful results by using it on your own if you have to. You don't even need a finished design to use this technique – you can use it very early in the design process to assess the merits of mock-up designs on paper.

In the next section, we'll talk about another technique for assessing usability – user testing. It's best to use a heuristic evaluation to identify and remove the most obvious usability problems before beginning user testing. This stops you from wasting your users' time by having them identify problems that you already know about. Then, the user testing can efficiently find the problems that the heuristic evaluation has missed.

User Testing

User testing is perceived as expensive and difficult – and this impression is reinforced when you read about usability labs with video equipment, one-way mirrors, teams of usability specialists, and even user heart-rate monitors! But, fortunately, all you really need to do very effective user tests is a user and a notebook.

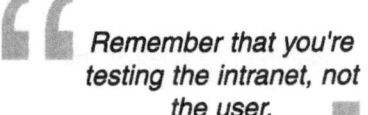

All you really need to do very effective user tests is a user and a notebook

User testing is something that should be done early on in the design process, and then repeated before the intranet site is put live. If you already have an intranet that you're working to improve, then of course you can test with the existing site. If not, then you need a skeleton of an intranet and some working intranet applications, or at the very least a paper mock-up of the site.

If you've already carried out usability testing for an Internet web site, then you'll be familiar with the process. The differences are that it's easier to get hold of users (you have a captive audience) and there should be more of a focus on using intranet applications (such as an address book) than on site navigation.

First, Catch Your User...

Four or five people is a good number for user tests (although you should test with each person individually) – it's enough people to get several perspectives on the site, but still keeps the tests short. If you've carried out a survey, as we suggested earlier, then you should have a list of people willing to take part – otherwise, your HR department might be able to help. You should try to get a mix of users from the different audiences that will be using the intranet – it may be worthwhile to try and randomize the users you test. If you can't get enough people, don't worry – even one user can provide very valuable information.

Remember that you're testing the intranet, not the user.

You can carry out the tests at the user's desk, and doing so will give you useful information such as how often they are normally interrupted and what their work involves. On the other hand, you may be wasting time by just listening to the user deal with unrelated problems and find it more productive to use your own office or an empty office.

Don't have more than two people watching the test – it can be intimidating for the user. If you have to convey your results to a larger team, then you can use a video camera, but it's often more effective to rotate the position of "second observer" around the team (especially because in most companies persuading your managers that you need to buy a video camera for web site testing is likely to be an uphill struggle).

It's important to remember that you're testing the intranet, not the user. If they can't find things, or can't use applications, then it's the fault of the design, not them. Also, ask them a few questions to see how much experience they have with the Web in general (although you should avoid testing users who have no web experience at all since you don't want to waste time explaining basic concepts), and with the company intranet in particular (if there is one). Also find out how long they've been at the company – it will determine whether they understand your company's standard terminology or not.

During the Test

You should provide the user with a list of tasks that you'd like them to try and achieve. Run through this list yourself beforehand to find out how long it takes you – and if you can't perform the tasks, then sort these problems out before you involve any users! Good tasks for your intranet might be:

- Finding the phone number of someone who can fix the user's computer
- Finding a map and directions to the London office
- Filling in a timesheet or expense report
- Scheduling a meeting and booking a room for it
- Updating their personal information in the company address book
- Finding and using the intranet A-Z

In general, think about what kind of tasks the user will be performing on the intranet, and how frequently they will need to perform each task.

Ask the user to think aloud – and note down what they say. What's going through the user's mind is as important as what they actually do. Also notice if they spend a long time pondering where to find something or reading a page. You should also make it clear that the user can stop performing any task, or stop the whole test itself, anytime that they want to.

Watch out for problems in the site. Typical problems discovered by user testing include:

- **Confusing titles** – in the navigation (perhaps company jargon that doesn't mean anything to a newcomer?)
- **Logical organization** – is it always clear where to look for site pages?
- **Unclear forms** – is it obvious exactly what goes in each box? Are form elements being ignored when they should be mandatory? Or mandatory when they're not really that important?
- **Unclear pages** – is it easy to find the important information on pages? Maybe greater use of bullet points and highlighting could help?

6

Usability and Information Architecture

- **Headings and sidebars ignored** – much like the phenomenon of "banner-blindness" on the Internet, "heading-blindness" is a problem on intranets. Users will often focus on what they consider to be the content of the page, and not bother reading areas they perceive as peripheral.

- **Ineffective site search** – is your site search easy to find and is it easy to scan the list of results to find the relevant ones? If users have to open ten different web pages from the search to find the one page that they're interested in, then maybe you should rethink the way you display search results.

I've always found the hardest challenge in usability testing to be keeping quiet while the user misses the "obvious" links and does entirely the wrong thing! Make sure that any other observers that are with you understand the importance of this.

The chances are that user testing will show up problems that you never expected – which is why it's so useful.

After the Test

Take the opportunity to ask the user for their general impressions of the intranet, and what they'd like to see on it. Also listen to their suggestions for improvements – after all, the users know what their everyday tasks involve better than you do.

Usability testing should be an enjoyable experience – after the first batch of tests, you might find other users queuing up to demand their turn! This is especially true if users can feel that they are having an impact on the intranet as the problems they identify are fixed.

Keep a record of how long each task took, and record it where you can reference it later. This can be very useful if you make changes after the user testing, and then test again. By comparing the times taken, you can see how much employee time you've saved by the redesign – which is very helpful when justifying your user-testing costs!

Dealing with the Results

The hardest part of user testing can be trying to convince the web site designers that there actually is a problem with the current design; it's far easier to blame "stupid users" than it is to consider that your own design may be flawed. This is one of the reasons that it's good to make sure that the members of your development team sit in on at least one user test session each (or that you video the tests if your team is too large for each person to observe a session). After seeing one user make a mistake, it's easy to dismiss it as user error – when you've seen five in a row make the same mistake, then it's more convincing.

You need to analyze the data that you have obtained from the tests. The big problems should be obvious – for example, if every user has encountered a problem with one specific form, then that form needs to be redesigned. Other data, such as the time required to complete each task, and the percentage of task completions, need to be evaluated statistically. I've found it simplest to do this with a spreadsheet program such as MS Excel. You can generate means and standard deviations automatically, and it may be helpful to generate graphs to spot trends in the data.

User testing isn't a complete solution of course, any more than any of the approaches in this chapter are. Just because you've identified a problem, doesn't mean that you know how to solve it. You need to make judgment calls about what should change and how, based on the results of the tests. Still, it can give very valuable information, and is one of the best techniques for increasing site usability.

After completing one round of user testing, it's usually worthwhile to spend time fixing the problems that were shown up, and then conduct another user test. The more testing you do, the greater chance you have of your intranet meeting your users' requirements – which means happier, more productive intranet users.

Stay in touch with your users! An intranet will change over time, and so will the way that people use it. Don't treat user testing as just something to be done in the initial design process – instead, every 6 months or so spend a day or two performing another test and re-evaluating your intranet usability.

Finding More Information About User Testing

An excellent source of user testing information on the Web is the "Usability Methods Toolbox" at *http://jthom.best.vwh.net/usability/*. This site has lots of in-depth information on usability testing techniques

A good book about user testing is the *Handbook of Usability Testing* (Jeffrey Rubin Wiley; ISBN 0-471594-03-2). This is not intranet (or even web)-specific, but it has a lot of practical advice and is a good all-round reference. To find out how some major web sites such as eBay, the BBC, evolt, and others carry out their user testing see *Usability: The Site Speaks for Itself* (Adrian Roselli, Don Synstelien, et al., glasshaus ISBN 1-904151-03-5). Another good book that is web-specific, but only touches lightly on user testing is *Don't Make Me Think* (Steve Krug, Que, ISBN 0-789723-10-7).

Other Ways to Keep In-Touch with Users

One big advantage that you have when trying to create a usable intranet, rather than an Internet site, is that you are one of your own target audiences. If you're not using the intranet on a regular basis, then why not? What would make you do so? How could you improve it to benefit yourself?

This "scratch your own itch" motivation can be very useful. If you find it inconvenient to use the intranet's timesheets application, then you can be sure that many other people in the organization are inconvenienced by it too. If you can increase its usability, then you can make your life easier as well as everyone else's.

However, do always remember that you're not the only audience. It's likely that you're more technically adept than the majority of users, and what seems easy to use for you may be baffling for other users. It's always worth, at the very least, calling in someone from the next office to have a look over every user interface change that you'd like to make to see whether it makes any sense to them.

I've found it helpful to keep a notebook handy at all times (or better still, a lightweight CMS system). If I have trouble using or finding something on the intranet, then I jot the problem down. Later, I can chat to other people and see if they've encountered the same problem. If they have, then it's probably affecting other people too – if not, then maybe I just had a temporary mental block.

Usability and Information Architecture

Seminars

As well as being useful for promoting the intranet, seminars can be useful for increasing its usefulness. A seminar is a good opportunity for finding out what people want from the intranet, and allows informal user training. It's also a good way for users to share information with each other – you may not know what is in an obscure section of a large intranet, but the chances are that someone will. Information can then be disseminated from the seminar attendees.

Have an Intranet "Suggestion Box"

Earlier we mentioned an important principle of intranet design, that on every page it should be easy to see who the authors of that page are and how to get in contact with them. This principle applies to the intranet homepage just as much as it does to all the others. It's a good idea to have a way of contacting the intranet team on the homepage itself, so suggestions for improvement can be gathered.

Another way of keeping in touch is to use Instant Messaging. If you have an internal IM server, such as Jabber, then intranet users can talk to you immediately, to ask questions, raise a problem, or make comments. The best source of information is always a knowledgeable human, rather than an intranet. However, this is only really practical in a very small intranet, or in a larger intranet with dedicated full-time intranet-user support staff. There's more information on Instant Messaging in *Chapter 9*.

The most important challenge here is to make sure that all suggestions are responded to, and that at least some of them are acted upon – otherwise users can feel that they are being ignored.

Iterative Development

So, user-centered design is no problem? Just find out what the users want and then do it?

Sadly, users usually don't know exactly what they want, or they want conflicting features, or they want technically infeasible features. And it's a lot easier to see what's wrong with an existing design, than it is to work out what would be a successful design.

The solution is to use iterative development. Create a simple prototype, test it, fix the problems, test again, and repeat as necessary. You won't find all the problems the first time, but as long as you involve users in the design process and they can see they impact on the design, you'll be removing problems each time.

Iterative development is cheaper than other forms of development. In general, if you can catch a usability problem early on, then it's easier and cheaper to fix than if it's identified after the intranet has been rolled out to everyone.

Justifying Usability

Although investing in usability can return significant benefits, there is usually a need to quantify those benefits to demonstrate that the time and money spent on usability is worthwhile. We have already looked, in *Chapter 2*, at the ROI of the intranet as a whole. Here we'll look specifically at the ROI of usability.

It's easy to work out the **costs of usability** – it's the cost of employing the intranet developers (and the users they work with) for the time taken to carry out the users tests, the evaluations, and the subsequent reworkings of the intranet site. It's much harder to quantify exactly what **benefits** it gives.

Estimating Usability Benefits

A simple, if naïve, formula for estimating savings from intranet usability is:

- Find the time taken to perform tasks on the original intranet site. This is information that you should be recording as part of the user testing process. If you are designing an intranet from scratch, then this can be the results of the first user testing of the early intranet designs.

- Compare it to the time taken to perform tasks on the final version of the intranet site, after you have identified and fixed the problems. Hopefully, the second figure is lower!

- Multiply the time difference between the two figures by the number of users that will perform the task.

- Multiply again by the number of times that users will perform the task per day.

- Multiply again by the average wage of the users.

- Multiply again by the number of days worked per year, to obtain the total savings per year.

For example, imagine an intranet application that is used on average twice a day, by a thousand people within your company. If your usability improvements speed up their use of it by one minute each, then that's 2000 minutes (about 30 hours) saved per day. If the average hourly wage is £10 per hour, then that's £300 saved per day. If users work for about 250 days per year, that comes to a saving of £75,000 – certainly enough to justify a few days of usability testing.

There are several criticisms that could be made of this approach:

- It assumes that users will use the time saved for useful productive work.

- A user's salary is not their actual cost to the company – the actual cost includes such things as equipment, support staff, electricity bills, rent on facilities, and so on, and is generally estimated at about twice the salary.

- It assumes that all usability savings are made in terms of timesavings. Other advantages can be increased use of the intranet reducing the cost of other business functions, increased accuracy of information available to the business, and reduced errors in data entry.

- It takes no account of reduced training costs and reduced support costs.

Still, it provides a workable estimate that will tend to err on the low side. If you need to make a case for usability to your managers, it's best to be conservative with the estimates of savings; an over-optimistic estimate is too easy to discredit.

Even though this formula will give a conservative estimate, it is still likely to show that investing in usability pays for itself many times over, simply because every improvement in intranet usability is multiplied hugely by the number of people that it benefits and the number of times it benefits them. In one usability study, by Clare-Marie Karat of IBM, savings of $6.8 million were estimated from an investment of $60,000 in usability – a hundred-fold return on investment.

Further Information

There are helpful real-world examples of money saved by usability at the Usability Professionals' Association web site (*http://www.upassoc.org/outreach/real.world.ex.html*). It includes reports of major savings attributable directly to usability research made by companies including Ford, Microsoft, and the USAA. Their site has a number of references to studies that have shown significant savings from usability (*http://www.upassoc.org/outreach/benefits.html*). There is also useful information in the article "A Business Case for Usability" from the WebWord usability newsletter at *http://webword.com/moving/businesscase.html*.

Practical Techniques for Increasing Usability

We've looked at the user-centered approach that you need to build a useful intranet; now we'll look at some specific techniques to use in your intranet, and some pitfalls to avoid. Although it's very important to know your audience well, as we describe above, there are some aspects of usability that apply to everyone.

We'll focus here on the aspects of web usability that are specific to the intranet, or particularly important for intranets.

Creating Effective Site Navigation

An intranet can be full of useful information, but if a user cannot find any of it, then it might as well not be there. For this reason, it's just as important to put effort into a usable site navigation as it is into the content creation process.

There's more information on creating site navigation for intranet and Internet sites, including useful code examples, in the book *Usable Web Menus* (Andy Beaumont, et al., glasshaus ISBN 1-904151-02-7).

The Card-Sorting Approach to Designing Site Navigation

A common approach to finding an effective web site navigation is to use "card sorting".

Assemble a small group of users (maybe three or four), and give them a stack of cards with the name of a category on each. Ask them, as a group, to sort the cards into piles that make logical sense to them. Then ask them to label each pile – these labels will become the names of the top-level menu items.

Of course, you need to provide a set of cards for the users to work from. Fifty to a hundred is a reasonable number. This will take between half an hour and several hours, depending on the number of cards and the number of users involved. If you have an existing intranet, then you can take the card topics from that; if not, then write the cards based on what you've identified as important intranet items from speaking to users and content owners.

It's best to decide approximately how many piles (that is, top-level menu items) you want before the session. Although exactly how many piles are created is up to the users, it's useful to them if you can provide some guidance. With an intranet, it's better to err in the direction of a broad, shallow navigation hierarchy (a larger number of top-level categories with fewer items in each) than a narrower, deeper hierarchy. This makes it easier for the intranet to grow over time while keeping the top-level categories the same.

If you're designing the intranet for a large company, then it's worth repeating this process with users drawn from different internal audiences over several days.

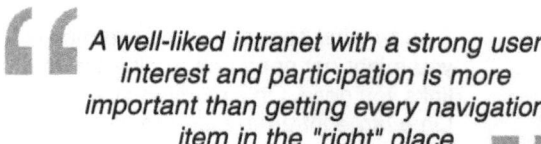

This technique can tell you:

- How the users think the intranet content should be organized

- To what extent different user groups agree on the site navigation structure

- Whether the names you've chosen for pages in the navigation are clear

It's also a good opportunity to get general feedback on what will be on the intranet – because the users can see an overview of what will be on the site, anything left out will be apparent.

It won't give you a final navigation design – particularly if different groups of users disagree on the organization. However, it gives a good base to work from.

One of the most valuable results of the card-sorting exercise can be an increased sense of user involvement in the intranet. Users who feel that they designed the intranet will like it more than if they weren't consulted. A well-liked intranet with a strong user interest and participation is more important than getting every navigation item in the "right" place!

Many intranets organize their content purely by company department. Although this is a simple approach, it's best to avoid it. It's not good for finding pages, since most employees won't know everything that all the departments do.

It can also lead to unfortunate politics – in some companies every department will fight to have as big a share of the intranet as all the other departments, even though they might not have enough useful content to fill their section!

Site Maps

An intranet site map is a web page that displays a list of links to the major intranet areas. Typically, these are grouped to represent the structure of the web site. A good, usable site map has three advantages:

- It helps users find pages on the site quickly – particularly if they know more or less what they're looking for

- It helps users see what is available on the site

- It gives an overview that helps users understand the structure of the site – so subsequent navigation around the site should be easier

It's important that a site map is a simple HTML page, with as much visible at once as possible. Some sites use Flash, JavaScript, and Java applets to produce hierarchical, unfolding site maps – although these may be fine for the purpose of finding things, it makes it harder for the user to understand the site structure, and they can also present accessibility issues.

6

Usability and Information Architecture

Exactly what appears on the site map is a question of the size of your intranet. On a small intranet, you might not need one at all – the front page of the intranet might be sufficient to display all the links you need. On a medium-size intranet, the site map will probably link to site pages or sections. On a large intranet, then the natural unit to appear on the site map is a subsite. As your intranet grows, you'll need to re-evaluate the site map every 6 months or so to see if you should change its scale.

As we suggested above for site navigation, it's not always a good idea to organize your site map by internal department. It's better to consider the tasks that a user might want to perform, and what types of information they are looking for when they come to the site map.

This is what the site map from CNET News looks like (*http://news.cnet.com/*):

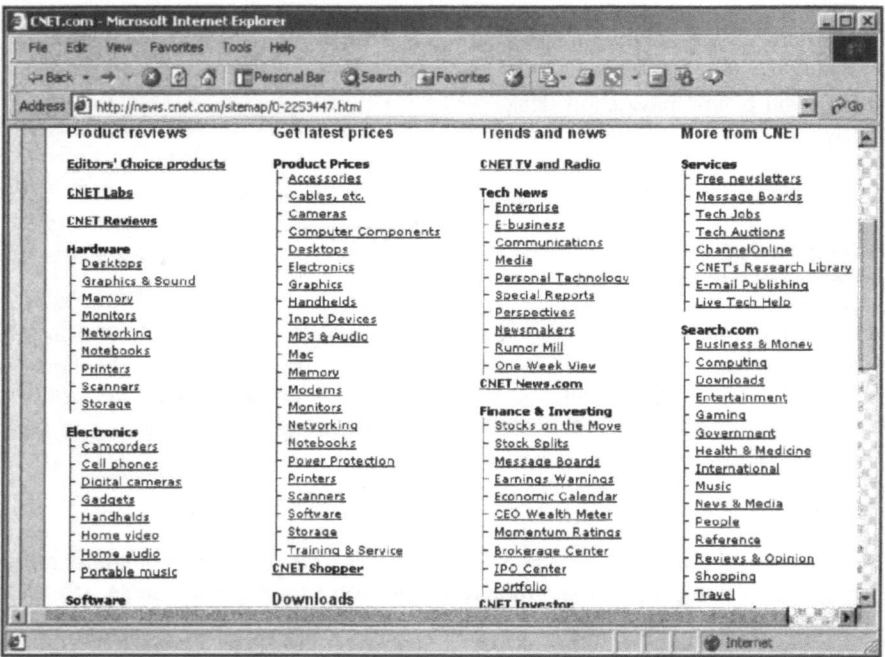

This is a good example of a site map. It's organized by task - for example "*Get latest prices*" or "*View Product reviews*". The structure is clear – there's very little space wasted. The whole site map fits on one page.

One way to improve it might be to add additional metadata – for example, the most commonly visited sections of the site could be highlighted with a "*Most popular*" icon. This increases usability by directing the user towards the site areas which others find useful.

We discussed the disadvantages of organizing your site navigation by department earlier. However, there are some times when it makes sense to an employee to locate a task by the department that is responsible for it. It often makes sense to have a separate departmental site map that presents an alternative view of the intranet's organization.

A simple improvement to the usability of a site map can be made by adding the HTML title attribute to the links in the site map. For example:

```
<a href="desktops.html" title="Independent reviews of PC desktop
computers">Desktops</a>
```

In most common web browsers, the title *information will appear when the mouse pointer hovers over the link. This adds useful information to the link, without wasting any of the screen space which is at a premium in a site map.*

If there is description *metadata on the referenced pages, this can be kept up-to-date with minimal effort – in most CMS systems or web programming languages, it's a simple job to load each of the referenced pages, pull out the metadata, and add it to the link.*

Site A-Z

A Site A-Z (sometimes called a Site Index) provides an A-Z listing of the major areas of an intranet.

This is the A-Z index for the BBC web site (*http://www.bbc.co.uk/*). It is a good example of a highly usable site A-Z:

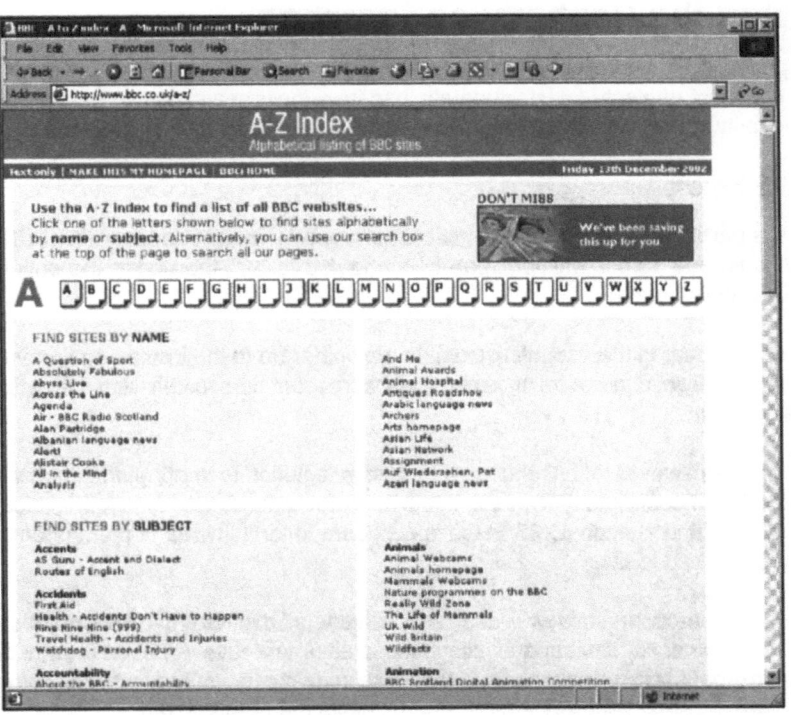

The display is split into two parts. In the *Find Site by Name* section there is an alphabetical list of BBC television programme names. In the *Find Sites by Subject* section, there is an alphabetical list of categories,

In the *Find Site by Name* section, each programme appears only once, but in the *Find Sites by Subject* a programme may appear in multiple categories. For example, the programme *Home Front*, a popular home and garden design programme, is listed in the *Design*, the *Interior Design,* and the *Gardening* categories.

Find Site by Name works well for the BBC because it has a large number of clearly identified TV programmes that can be unambiguously referenced by name. If your company is in a similar position (perhaps it produces a wide range of products, and each has a section on the intranet?), then this approach could be useful for your intranet.

More commonly, an approach similar to the *Find Sites by Subject* is useful for intranets. Important sections of the intranet need to be manually categorized (either by adding category metadata as the pages are created, or after the fact) and listed under an alphabetical list of categories. This does **not** mean that you have to catalog every page on the intranet – only the important sections. For a larger intranet, the A-Z page is likely to provide a list of microsites rather than a list of pages.

To decide on the list of categories, the card-sorting approach described earlier comes in useful. For an existing intranet, looking at the search terms recorded by the search engine can also give clues as to what users expect to be categories.

Improving the Usability of Searches

Search is perhaps the most important way of finding information on an intranet – but it also tends to be one of the most neglected. Unfortunately, because most search engines come with "out-of-the-box" functionality, it's rare for companies to tweak it extensively to their own needs.

Where to Search

Searches are particularly useful for the typical "overgrown" intranet described in *Chapter 12*. When information is spread across multiple, barely connected "silos", then often the only way of finding it effectively is with a search.

The problem with finding the useful information is transferred to the intranet maintainer – how do you efficiently index a large number of intranet silos spread across different servers, each using a different technology?

There is no simple answer to this. The best long-term solution is to bring all the information together in a single content management system, but this takes time, and has other disadvantages (for example, it's hard to find a single CMS that's appropriate for all types of content on a large intranet) that might make it a bad idea.

Most commercial search engines will search a variety of different data sources, such as SQL databases, Lotus Notes, flat files, and existing web sites. Alternatively, if each area of the intranet is currently indexed separately, then it's not too hard to write your own meta-search engine that submits a query to each separate search and displays the results together.

If you're starting an intranet from scratch, or your current intranet is small, then you have far fewer problems. You can use a CMS from the start and take advantage of its searching capabilities, but this can be expensive.

It's also important to have good content to index. A CMS can help here as well, by enforcing that metadata is added to pages as they are entered. It's also useful to ensure that outdated or inaccurate content is removed from the intranet – or it may appear in search results. We'll go into this more in *Chapter 8* and *Chapter 12*.

For the moment, we'll assume that a search engine is set up and working well (some options are described later), and focus on how to make the search page and the results usable.

Making a Usable Search Page

For most searches, a search page shouldn't be used at all! The majority of search queries, both on the Internet and the intranet, are only one or two words. This kind of search is best served by having a "*search*" textbox in the corner of every intranet page.

Intranet developers writing a meta-search application to search numerous data silos often wonder how best to combine the results from the different searches. Is an item from a Lotus Domino search with a relevance score of 78% just as relevant as one from an AltaVista search with a score of 78%? What if the relevance isn't a percentage? Or if there's only a date and no relevance score?

Often the most usable solution is to ignore the problem entirely! Display the search results from each source separately, with a title above each section giving the source of the results, and then it's easier for the user to tell whether they're relevant or not.

This is an example of a good search box that appears on every Forrester Research (*http://www.forrester.com/*) web page:

It's clearly labeled as a search, has an additional link to an "advanced search" page, and there are no other textboxes nearby with which it could be confused. Although the *Go* button is an image, it also has the `alt` tag containing the text "*Go*" for the benefit of users who are visually impaired or those not using images. The search box appears at the top right of every page, where it is easy to find by a user scanning for it. Something like this is all that a typical intranet user will use most of the time.

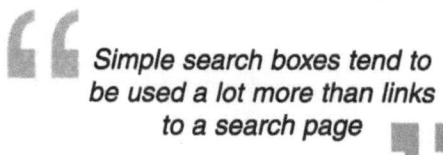

Simple search boxes tend to be used a lot more than links to a search page

Simple search boxes like this tend to be used a lot more than links to a search page. In fact, a study by usability expert Jakob Nielsen reports "When I changed the useit.com homepage to include a search box instead of a link, search engine use increased by 91%" (*http://www.useit.com/alertbox/20010513.html*).

It's usually worthwhile to have an advanced search page, even though it won't be frequently used. Most search engines provide Boolean search logic, date ranges, and any number of other things for free – so it would be a shame not to make them available (but if you're writing your own search routines, then don't bother to write advanced searches unless you're sure you need to). You can increase the use of advanced searches by providing search training – at the very least, an online Help page that details the syntax used by your search engine, and examples of searches. There is searching advice targeted at users of Internet searches that might give benefits to your users at *http://www.searchenginewatch.com/facts/index.html*.

6

Usability and Information Architecture

Just because the search page is simple doesn't mean that it can't be doing clever things behind the scenes. It's good to use a search engine that will correct misspelled search queries. It's also useful to use one that will search synonyms – if you are creating a site vocabulary (as described in the next section), then part of the compilation process should be to list the synonyms of each word so they can be fed into the search engine's configuration.

For searching intranet address books, it's useful to support the "Soundex" algorithm developed for the US census. This encodes names by the way they sound, rather than just by the way they are spelled, and can make it easier to find the details of someone whose name you've only heard. Many search engines and databases can be made to implement Soundex, and there are implementations for most computer languages available freely on the Web. It is intended only for standard English pronunciation – so might not be useful if your company is global.

There is documentation for using Soundex in PHP at http://php.benscom.com/manual/en/function.soundex.php, and an article about Soundex support in databases at http://databases.about.com/library/weekly/aa042901a.htm.

Searching by Area

When the intranet content is divided naturally into different zones (for example, when it's on different intranet servers), some sites will provide a "*Search only zone XXX*" option. For example, the Microsoft site has a search page that looks like this:

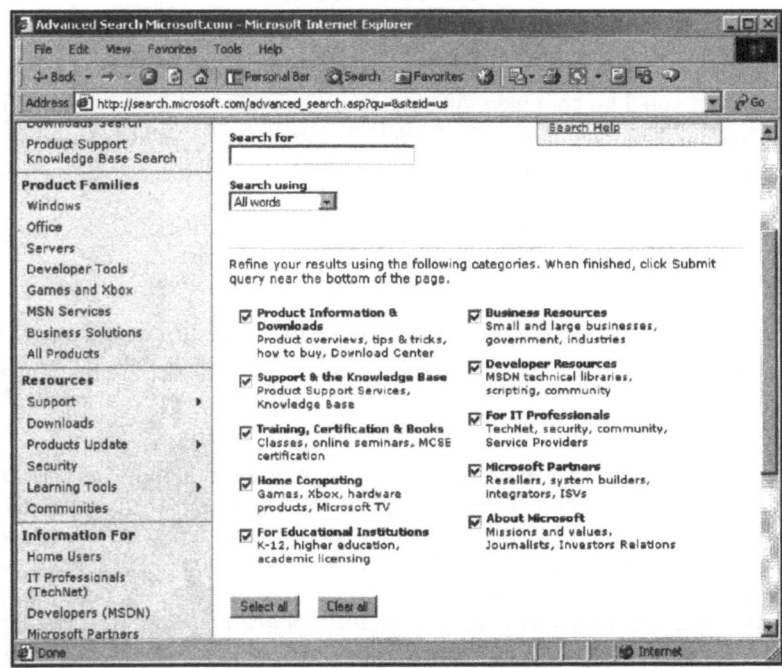

Only those areas of the site that are ticked will be searched.

Although this is appropriate and useful if you have very clearly distinguished and obvious zones, it can cause usability problems and needs careful consideration before being included. Users may be unsure which zone they should be looking in (I have a problem with programming JavaScript in Internet Explorer. Is that Support? Or Developer Resources? I'm an IT Professional, should I look there? Maybe it's in Product Information – that has tips and tricks?). They will require several searches to find an appropriate result, or just give up assuming the content isn't there. An alternative approach that is worth considering is to search all site areas, but to return the results grouped by the area that they came from.

It can also be appropriate to divide searches by zone if there are significant speed differences in the time that it takes for searching different zones. In this case, it would make sense to carry out the fast searches, and then provide a link at the top and bottom of the results page:

"*This search only searches the most commonly used content. If you didn't find what you were looking for, you can repeat your search over the entire intranet which will take approximately thirty seconds*"

Of course, speeding up the slowest search to the speed of the others is by far the best option if it's possible.

Increasing the Usability of Search Results

A search results page with good usability allows the user to make an accurate judgment of which pages are relevant to them just by scanning through it. A results page with bad usability requires that every result be loaded and read through before the user can tell whether each is useful or not. For example, compare the following two search results from a search for "web server":

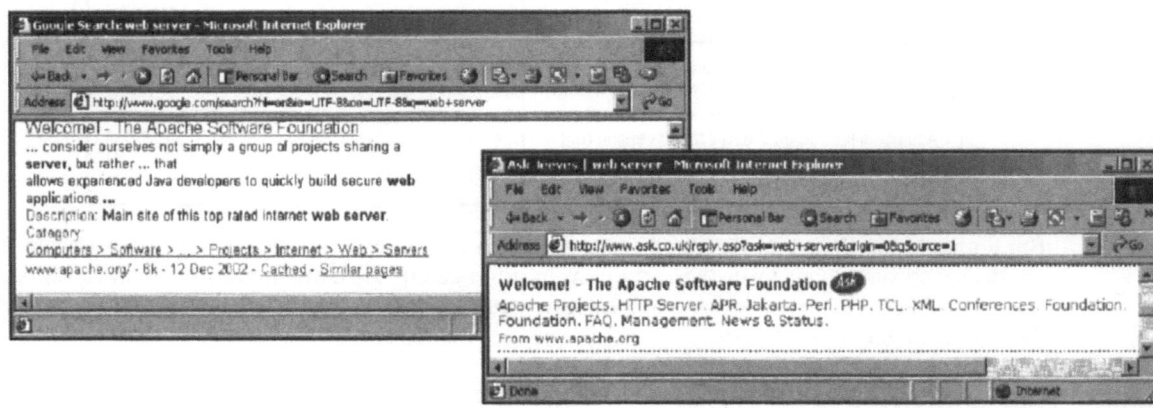

The first, on the left, is from Google (*http://www.google.com/*), the second from Ask Jeeves (*http://www.ask.co.uk/*). Both are search results for the same site, the home of the Apache web server (*http://www.apache.org/*). But the result from Google is much clearer and more usable than that from Ask Jeeves. The differences are summarized in the table overleaf:

Google Search Result for "web server"	Ask Jeeves Search Result for "web server"
Link uses standard browser link colors (blue for unvisited link, purple for visited link). It comes from the HTML `title` element of the page.	Link to the site is in black, not underlined. It's not immediately obvious that it's a link (although an underline appears when the mouse hovers over it).
Link is direct to the site (and uses purple for a visited link). This is very useful in a long list of results – it's typical searcher behavior to visit several of the links on the list, and revisit the results page to access others. It's much easier if it's clear which links have already been visited.	Although the link turns purple when it has been visited, it is not direct to the site and the link destination changes every time (it uses a query string to redirect traffic via a logging script). Thus, on reloading the results page, there is no indication whether the link has previously been visited.
The main text is the context in which the search text appears in the page. This gives valuable clues as to whether the result is relevant or not.	The main text is the left hand navigation of the Apache web page – which is mostly a list of programming languages supported by Apache. If you didn't know that an "HTTP server" was a web server, then there would be no clue that this result was relevant.
Where the text "web server" appears, it is highlighted in bold. This makes it faster to scan through the results list.	There is no mention of the text "web server" at all (from other search results, if there had been then it wouldn't have been highlighted).
The description text "Top rated internet web server" has been manually added to the search database (it doesn't appear in the page at all) On an intranet, it would be easier to edit the page to add metadata, but that's not an option on the Internet.	There is no additional description.
The category of the page "*Computer* > .... *Web* > *Servers*" is listed. On an intranet, this would correspond to displaying the breadcrumb trail for the intranet page.	No page category appears.
The page size is listed, so modem users can judge whether it's worth trying to download it.	No metadata about the page appears.
Additional links appear to a cached version (not very useful on an intranet) and to a "Similar pages" search (potentially very useful)	No additional links appear.

So, it should be clear that exactly the same search results can be made much more usable by carefully choosing what to display and how. In any search, there will inevitably be inappropriate results returned – but by ensuring that the search results are displayed in a usable way, you can help the user pick out the best ones.

Manually Improve the Search Results

Although it may seem to go against the point of having a search engine in the first place, most search engines will allow you to manually tune the results they provide. It's often worth checking the intranet logs to find out what the most common ten (or twenty, or thirty…) searches are, finding the most appropriate pages on the intranet for them yourself, and ensure that they are returned at the top of the search results. In particular, make sure that any intranet applications are easy to find with a search. It's best to separate off the manually chosen results into a section at the top – for example, Microsoft provides a "Best Bets" section at the top of their search results.

In some cases you may find that there's no appropriate content to be returned for a search result already on the intranet – this should be a cue to write some new content or to get in touch with the relevant content owner.

Where to Look for More Information

Making a very usable site search is a substantial amount of work, but definitely pays off. Microsoft, for example, estimates that a typical employee spends 2½ hours every day using their intranet, and half of that time is spent looking for information. If that percentage can be reduced, then it benefits every employee.

It's not always necessary to buy an expensive search package from one of the big companies like Verity or Inktomi. There are several open source tools that may be more appropriate if your needs are simple – for example, Swish-E (*http://www.swish-e.org/*) is fast and free, and will index PDF and compressed files, and Lucene (*http://jakarta.apache.org/lucene/*) is a cross-platform Java-based search engine from the Apache Foundation. It's possible to get a more usable site search from a free package and some time working on HTML templates around the results, than you would from an expensive package to which you do no customization.

An excellent web site that gives more information on searching, including reviews of many site search tools, is *http://www.searchtools.com/*. It's also worth looking at the Usenet newsgroup *comp.infosystems.search*, although there can be a lot of spam to wade through.

Keep It Simple, and Keep It the Same

A common intranet problem, particularly in larger companies, is that every section of the site looks totally different. You need to re-learn how each section of the site works, and your time is wasted trying to work out where the search bar has moved to now, rather than being able to concentrate on finding the information you need.

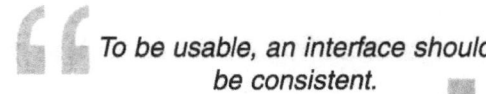

To be usable, an interface should be consistent.

To be usable, an interface should be consistent. This is as true of your intranet as it is of an Internet web site. The problems arise because in an intranet there are often a number of different content creators, each of whom works independently of the others. Each one makes their own decisions about how to structure their pages, and although these may be reasonable in isolation, it's much easier for the user if they only have to cope with one standard page design.

So, what can you do to increase usability in this situation, and how can you avoid this problem in the first place?

Creating Your Electronic Corporate Identity (ECI)

An Electronic Corporate Identity (ECI) is essentially a set of "look and feel" guidelines for the intranet. It's an intranet microsite itself, providing a set of resources to help content creators keep their own microsites consistent, and acts as a "support kit" for them. It's primarily useful for a large intranet with a number of different content creators in different areas

Usability and Information Architecture

Since the ECI is available online, it's easy for content creators to find, and easy to keep up to date. It is also an example of best practices in itself.

Things that can go into an ECI include:

- Standard page templates for whatever systems your authors use
- CSS or XSLT stylesheets
- Images, such as the company logo
- Color palettes
- Samples of code to produce page headers, navigation, breadcrumb trails, and so on.
- Best practices and guidelines including a style guide, page weight recommendations, image sizes, and so on
- Online discussion forums – it's not just a static data store, it should be more of a "Community of Practice" for content creators

and, most important of all:

- Examples!

It's really important to get the templates and examples right – content creators tend to use an ECI by copying the examples rather than reading the best practice guidelines, so if there are any problems with the examples, the problems are likely to be copied along with the good parts.

Persuading Authors to Use the ECI

If you are creating a new intranet, then you can create the ECI at the start, train content creators in using it, and ensure a consistent look and feel for the intranet from the beginning. If there are already a number of existing intranet microsites, as in most large organizations, then you'll have to win over the existing site creators to using the new standard.

If content creators dislike the idea of the ECI, and see it as a restriction of their freedom, then they'll use it reluctantly if it all. Having enthusiastic content creators is very important to a vibrant, useful intranet. Some useful approaches to convince content creators that an ECI is useful include:

- Consulting existing site authors and designers before drawing up the ECI. If site creators feel that they have had input to the ECI, and understand the compromises that went into it, then they are more likely to comply with it willingly.
- Providing "goodies" for web sites that follow the ECI. For example, professionally designed graphics, Flash movies, and templates. This is not to say that you should police the use of these goodies – but a graphic will naturally look better in the context it was designed for.
- Promoting sites that follow the ECI. For example, you might have a "microsite of the week" featured on the intranet homepage, selected from the sites that conform to the intranet ECI.

- Providing flexibility within the ECI – not everything has to be exactly specified. Remember that the goal of the ECI is to promote usability, not to enforce the "One True Way". Keep it as minimal as possible while still fulfilling your goals.

- Providing training along with the ECI. Even if a site creator is convinced that the ECI is a good thing, then she still won't use it unless she knows how to. Along with this, make sure that the ECI itself is easy to use – there's not much point trying to promote usability with a tool that is hard to use itself.

- Selling the benefits of the ECI to the content creators. One of its purposes is to save them time, reduce the amount of maintenance they have to do and let them spend more time working on the content.

Increasing usability helps everyone! Site creators want their sites to be helpful and to be widely used, and an ECI helps towards this goal. As long as it's seen as a tool to increase usability, and not as a pointless corporate edict, then the ECI will be popular and useful.

Using a Content Management System (CMS)

A CMS can be the solution to the problem of consistent look and feel – but only if everyone is using it. There may be good reasons why it's not practical to migrate every microsite into a CMS immediately, and in the meantime, it's still useful to have guidelines and examples for authors to follow who aren't using the CMS.

We'll talk about CMS systems in more depth in *Chapter 8*.

A method I've used in the past to ensure a consistent behavior between a CMS and sites that haven't yet been migrated into the CMS is:

Create individual pages in the CMS for site navigation elements, such as the header, footer, and navigation.

Then include them in the non-migrated page via an HTTP connection (in ASP, this uses the Microsoft ServerXMLHTTP *object, in JSP you read from a Socket object or use the Jakarta* HttpClient, *in PHP you can use* fread, *and similar functions exist in all other web languages).*

This is slightly risky – after all, if the server that you're pulling the navigation elements from is unavailable, then it will affect the availability of the site that's not running in the CMS. In addition, it will increase the latency of the request to the first server because it has to pull in elements from elsewhere. If either of these is a problem in practice, then you can set up a local cache on the first server to store the navigation elements, which is automatically updated.

Building a Vocabulary

If in one area of the intranet, a spade is called a "spade", but in the next it's a "shovel", and in the third a "digging implement", then a user unfamiliar with what a spade is will be confused. A user searching for "spade" via the search engine may not find all the information that's on the site, and a user searching for "shovel" will find a different, also incomplete, set of information.

A solution to this problem is to build a "site vocabulary" (sometimes called a Thesaurus or taxonomy), and make it available in the ECI. A site vocabulary provides an authoring style guide, listing the terminology that should be used for key items. It's also helpful to have synonyms and common misspellings listed as part of the vocabulary.

As well as helping the content authors, the site vocabulary is also useful when creating the site navigation, and as keywords for the search engine (more on this later).

> *A useful article detailing Microsoft's work in creating a common vocabulary and taxonomy for their intranet is at http://www.boxesandarrows.com/archives/ 002931.php.*

A standard way to provide a link to an HTML page providing the site glossary is by using the HTML "link" tag in each page header. For example:

```
<link rel="glossary" href="/glossary.html" />
```

In browsers that support it, such as Netscape 6+ and Mozilla, this will display a link to the glossary in a browser links bar so users can have quick and consistent access to it.

The other types that can be used in a link tag are listed in the HTML specification at http://www.w3.org/TR/html4/types.html#type-links. For example, you can use the link contents *type to link to a table of contents for an intranet microsite. The only widely used link type is the stylesheet type to link in a CSS stylesheet.*

Vocabularies and Search Metadata

It is common to use the HTML meta tag keywords to list the synonyms and alternative spellings for the keywords in the page. This allows search engines to find the page more easily. For example, from Usability First (*http://www.usabilityfirst.com*):

```
<meta name="keywords" content="usability, usable, useability, useable, user,
interface design, ...">
```

While this is useful on the Internet where there is no control over the search engine being used, it's less useful for an intranet search. The problem is that vocabularies change over time. For example, if a new synonym is used in a widely distributed internal publication, then users will begin to search for that synonym. If the keywords are fixed in the page, then this requires either a major search and replace task or a sophisticated CMS to add a new synonym to every occurrence.

Instead, it's preferable to store the "root word" taken from the site vocabulary in the page. Then the intranet search engine can be set to use the list of synonyms (and misspellings) taken from the vocabulary. This increases search usability, and it reduces the maintenance effort.

The Need for Speed

When you think about fast web pages, the first thought is of making them fast to download and display. While this is important, it's not the only kind of speed that matters. You need to worry about:

- Download time
- **Perceived** download time and responsiveness
- Speed of use

Why Bandwidth Still Matters

Web developers used to working on the Internet tend to assume that developing intranet pages gives a license to use large images, AVI videos, and chunky Java applets, because "bandwidth doesn't matter on an intranet". While there is some truth to this when the intranet is for a single site, what about company branch offices with slow connections? What about employees working from home via modem? What about salespeople on the road with mobile devices?

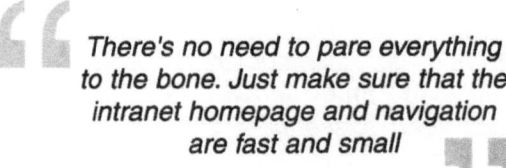

There's no need to pare everything to the bone. Just make sure that the intranet homepage and navigation are fast and small

The truth is that nowadays, bandwidth **is** important, and will remain so until we're living in the promised paradise of universal broadband and ultra-fast 3G mobile communications (don't hold your breath).

There's no need to pare everything to the bone. Just make sure that the intranet homepage and navigation are fast and small, and so is all the information that a remote user might want to use. And most importantly, make sure to test the intranet using the access methods that will actually be used, rather than just testing it over a fast internal network. For an intranet, you will have a good idea of what every user's connection speed will be, which makes testing simpler.

A good Content Management System (CMS) can help by providing a low-bandwidth version of web pages from the same content (see *Chapter 8* for more information).

Which Pages Should Be Fast?

As a rule of thumb, the amount of effort you put into speeding up an intranet application should be proportional to the amount of time that users will spend using it. This may seem obvious – but it's all too easy for a developer to get carried away tweaking a rarely used application when it might be better to add a progress indicator, or a simple warning "*This will take approximately three minutes to run*".

By making the intranet faster, you can make it more widely used. If it's faster to use an offline alternative, then people often will, even if it doesn't have all the same advantages as the intranet.

There's not enough space in this chapter, or even in this whole book, to give advice on exactly how to speed up applications. Instead, consult the appropriate manuals and web sites for your CMS or programming language.

At one company at which I worked, it took nearly ten seconds to search the company address book from the intranet. Employees tended to jot down phone numbers on Post-It notes and scraps of paper rather than use the intranet.

By optimizing the code in the page and the database query, I managed to reduce the time for the page to display to less than a second. The address book became more widely used and the Post-It notes began to disappear.

People will work around inconvenient technology – often without complaining about it. So, track what users are actually doing with server access logs and by talking to them, and you can fix the speed problems that they haven't told you about.

Increasing Perceived Speed

The time taken for all the elements of a page to download is not necessarily the same as the time taken for the page to be useful. On a well-designed page, you can start making use of the page before it has all downloaded. Some tips you can use to help design pages that appear quickly are:

> The perceived speed of your intranet may have very little to do with its actual speed. Usability expert Jared Spool has conducted research showing that people rate the download speed of a web site by how successfully they can perform tasks on it! So, when users complain about slow web sites, they may be complaining that it is slow or difficult to complete the tasks they need to, rather than that the pages are actually slow themselves.
>
> Jared Spool talks about this research, and other interesting usability topics, in an interview at http://webword.com /interviews/spool2.html

- If an HTML `<img>` tag has `width` and `height` specified, then the browser can place that image on the page and reserve space for it even before the image has downloaded.

- Internet Explorer loads images in alphabetical order of their filename. If there are images that are more important on a page, then you can provide them with names that are nearer the beginning of the alphabet to prioritize their loading.

- If all of the content in your page is within one large table for layout, then none of it can appear until the whole table has been downloaded. If you split up the table, and use `<div>` elements and CSS for layout, then you can cause the page to be displayed considerably sooner.

- Web browsers are usually capable of opening several connections to the web server simultaneously. If files such as JavaScript and stylesheets are linked to from the page, rather than included within the page, then they can be loaded concurrently with the page (and should be cached for future pages).

You can find more advice along these lines on sites such as Evolt (*http://www.evolt.org*).

Providing Feedback to the User

On an intranet, it's quite common to have "applications" that perform some lengthy task such as a query or a database update, or sending a number of e-mails. This is much more common on intranets than it is on the Internet.

If there is no feedback from the task, then the user will often be unsure whether the task is in progress, or whether it's failed. It's very common for users to hit *Back* in their browser, and resubmit the page that runs the task. This may cause the task to restart, to occur twice, or even to corrupt the data on which it acts.[7]

The first attempt at a solution should always be to speed up the application sufficiently that no feedback is needed. Unfortunately, this isn't always possible.

The easiest solution to implement, and probably the most widely used, is to add a warning (often popping up when the link to launch the task is selected):

"This task will take a long time to execute. Do not interrupt the browser until the task completes."

This example is poor for two reasons. Firstly, it doesn't give an estimate of the amount of time needed – how long is "a long time"? You should always be able to give at least an approximate estimate of the time. Secondly, it's an ingrained reflex for many computer users to click *OK* on pop-up warning dialogs without reading them. For a warning to be effective, the message needs to be visible while the user is waiting for results.

A fallback can be to put a time-based check in the application, to display a page that says something like:

"*This application was last run less than 2 minutes ago. Are you sure that you want to run it again?*"

A better solution is to provide a progress bar. This is a common idiom in desktop applications that users will be accustomed to. It's relatively easy to provide a progress bar with an ActiveX object, a Java applet, or a Flash movie.

An alternative for a multi-threaded environment is to start the task in one thread, and to have a process that monitors it in a separate thread. The web page can point at the monitoring thread, and with a meta-refresh tag update the display of task status until it is complete.

Some applications may not require a visible progress indicator, for example a task that takes five or ten minutes to execute might be better dealt with by having a "Task began successfully" message on the Web, and then an e-mail sent to the user to explain whether it succeeded or failed.

If you're using an ActiveX object, Java applet, or Flash movie, then it's not too hard to add a progress indicator – if you search on Google for "ActiveX progress bar" you'll find hundreds of examples.

If you want to produce feedback from an ASP, PHP, or Java web page, then one of the simplest ways is just to output a dot "." from the script every time it completes a step, or the name of the file that it's just processed. However, many web servers will cache script output and only send it when there's a decent sized chunk. You should be able to turn off this caching for specific pages, but if you can't, then there's a hack I've used in the past. You can send a "." and then "<!--(several KB more dots) -->". The dots sent inside HTML comment tags won't display, but they will fool the cache and make your progress indicator display immediately. This isn't a great solution, but it is better than leaving the user hanging.

Note: Adding a progress indicator often slows the operation down slightly (especially if you use the "comment" hack above). Don't worry about this too much; studies have shown that responsiveness and feedback contribute at least as much to perceived speed as the actual performance does!

Don't Waste the User's Time in Repetitive Tasks

A user experienced with a desktop application such as Word can use all sorts of shortcuts to help him use it much faster than a new user. For example, they will know keyboard shortcuts such as *Ctrl-B* to embolden text, and *Ctrl-S* to save. Although shortcuts like these are available for the web browser (such as pressing backspace rather than using the back button) it's also possible to set up similar keyboard shortcuts for the specific elements of a web site – for example, pressing "*Alt-1*" to go to the front page. However, timesaving shortcuts like these aren't common on Internet web pages, because Internet sites have few repeat visitors who would benefit from taking the time to learn them.

On an intranet site things are different. A receptionist might use an intranet phone book application several hundred times a day, and will benefit from whatever shortcuts can be provided. Likewise, a software tester might fill in bug reports via an intranet form many times in a day. There are a few simple ways of making the intranet more usable for these people, and it will increase the accessibility of your intranet as well.

Usability and Information Architecture

Keyboard Shortcuts and Tab Ordering

A little known part of standard HTML is the `accesskey` attribute. This attribute can be applied to form inputs, links, buttons, and a few other elements. It looks like this:

```
<form>
        <u>N</u>ame: <input type="text" name="name" accesskey="n" /><br />
        <u>A</u>ddress: <input type="text" name="address" accesskey="a" />
</form>
```

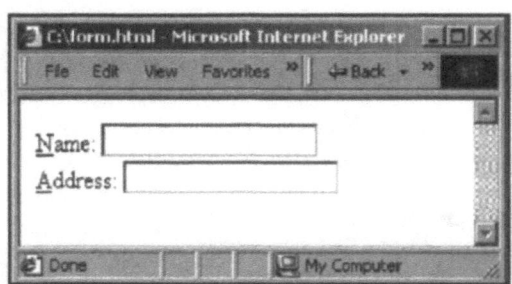

When you press *Alt-N* (or *Control-N* on the Macintosh) then the focus will be set to the *Name* text field. The convention used in Windows is to underline the access key for an item, like this: *File* (as above).

However, you have to be careful with the keys you choose for the `accesskey` — if you set an `accesskey` of "f", then *Alt-F* will no longer display the *File* menu in the browser. It's even worse if you have a multinational intranet because different countries have different menu shortcuts; for example "Tiedosto" is Finnish for "File" and so *Alt-T* normally opens the *File* menu.

`accesskey` is supported by Internet Explorer 4+ and Netscape 6+, but not Netscape 4.

In most browsers, it's also possible to use the *Tab* key to step between form elements. By default, form elements are stepped through in the order that they appear in the HTML source. It's possible to use the `tabindex` attribute to force the ordering to be different, which can be useful if you're displaying the form elements in a table. It looks like this:

```
<form>
        Name: <input type="text" name="name" tabindex="1"/>
        Address: <input type="text" name="address" tabindex="2" />
</form>
```

Internet Explorer and Netscape also support using *Enter* to submit a form – you can make this most useful by making sure that each form has only one submit button.

It's no good having keyboard shortcuts if no one knows what they are or how to use them. But if you have a separate set of instructions for a simple web application, very few people will read them, because they will assume that they already know how to use the application.

Some applications deal with this by providing a pop-up "Tip of the Day" to gently introduce features, but this is rarely appropriate for a web application unless it is very complex. Instead, you can help the user by providing a brief overview of how to use the shortcuts, perhaps in a sidebar or at the bottom of the application page. It's also important to use shortcuts consistently, so a user's knowledge of one web application will generalize to all the others on the intranet.

Google uses this technique. If you use your mouse to click on the Google Search button, Google will give you a message "Tip: In most browsers you can just hit the return key instead of clicking on the search button". To avoid annoyance, it uses a cookie to only send this message once. Note that search engines like Google are one of the few types of Internet application that have as many repeat users as an intranet application does.

Default Form Values

In most web applications, many of the fields entered each time will be the same. For example, a software tester will only rarely switch between operating systems and product build versions.

On an Internet form, usually the best that can be done is to set sensible defaults for the form elements. On an intranet, because the same users will keep coming back to the application, it's possible to help them more. Setting a cookie that automatically saves form entries and re-fills in the form when the user comes back to it can save them considerable amounts of time.

This technique is particularly useful when combined with the `accesskey` keyboard shortcut described above. The whole form can be filled out with values to begin with, and the user can jump quickly to the one or two fields that need to be altered before submitting the form.

Summary

In this chapter, we've looked at the user-centered approach to intranet design, and considered the different audiences of the intranet. We've discussed several techniques for assessing the usability of your intranet, including heuristic evaluation and user testing, and we've given a formula for estimating the money saved by increasing usability.

We've also looked at some specifics of intranet usability that will be applicable to every intranet. We've covered the design of site navigation, and the benefits of a site map and a site A-Z. We've offered ways of increasing the usability of the search. We've explained the importance of consistent navigation, and introduced the Electronic Corporate Identity (ECI) as a tool to encourage consistency – we've also talked about ways of making this palatable to existing content authors. Finally, we discussed ways to save time spent on the intranet waiting for pages to download, and the use of shortcuts to help experienced users carry out tasks quickly.

For more information on web usability, glasshaus publishes a range of books including "*Usability: The Site Speaks for Itself*", "*Usable Web Menus*" and "*Usable Forms for the Web*". There are also a number of good web sites focused on usable web site design including "A List Apart" (*http://alistapart.com/*), "Boxes and Arrows" (*http://www.boxesandarrows.com/*), and usability guru Jakob Nielsen's web site (*http://www.useit.com/*).

In the next chapter, we're going to take a look at managing intranet content. This will cover techniques for putting useful content on your intranet, encouraging authors to contribute, and how to avoid the problems of having multiple authors.

6

Usability and Information Architecture

7

- Methods of controlling content
- Typical problems

Author: Inigo Surguy

Controlling Content

The primary focus for this chapter is answering the question of who controls the intranet's content. Should there be centralized control? If so, there is the risk of the intranet becoming static and divorced from its users. Alternatively, should control of the intranet be distributed among its users? If so, the intranet can become chaotic with relevant content very hard to find.

The main area that we will tackle is how to keep a balance between these extremes of control, and how to use the strengths (and overcome the weaknesses) of each option. We will examine three common pitfalls that intranets may fall into:

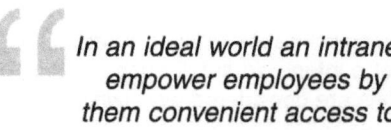

In an ideal world an intranet should empower employees by giving them convenient access to exactly the information they need.

- The "static" intranet
- The "junk drawer" intranet
- The "ghost town" intranet

The "static" intranet is one in which too much centralized control makes it hard for users to contribute to the intranet. The "junk drawer" intranet is caused by insufficient control – it contains a large amount of information, but is very disorganized. The "ghost town" intranet is an intranet that is poorly maintained and contains much out-of-date content. We will describe each of these intranet types in detail in this chapter, and present possible solutions to the problems they present.

In an ideal world an intranet should empower employees by giving them convenient access to exactly the information they need. It should connect diverse workers within the organization, allowing them to collaborate to do their jobs more effectively. Business processes should be streamlined by the intranet to be fast and cheap. The information on the intranet should always be up-to-date and accurate, and it should be easy to find relevant information without being overwhelmed with unrelated data. Any worker should be able to update the information on the intranet for the topics in which they have expert knowledge, subject to suitable checks and controls. Despite this freedom to change content, the intranet should be easy to use and consistent, and the quality of intranet content should be high.

In this chapter, we will look at some of the steps you can take to make your intranet more like the intranet described above, avoiding the common failings of the three intranet types.

The "Static" Intranet

In a "static" intranet the content is hard to change, and hard to update. The control is very centralized, the authors are separated from the users, and the intranet lacks vibrancy and community spirit.

This is often because only a few authors, often in a central "Internal Communications" or "Intranet Development" team, are able to put content onto the intranet. These authors are better trained at using the intranet tools and skilled at writing for the Web. The content that they produce is of high quality, but they are often overworked and cannot produce the quantity of content that intranet users would like. In addition, they are not the people who actually have the expert knowledge, so the content must come from the experts within the company. This takes time (especially if it is edited for the Web by the intranet authors, and must then be reviewed by the expert), and can lead to outdated intranet content.

A similar cause of a "static" intranet is if there are multiple authors around the organization, but one or more central authorities, such as an intranet manager or a legal department, must approve all changes. In this case, the workflow process can become a bottleneck, preventing the intranet from being up-to-date.

> " *In a "static" intranet the content is hard to change, and hard to update.* "

In both these cases it takes a reasonable amount of time and effort to make any change to the intranet content, so small changes and improvements are discouraged, and only significant new additions are considered worthwhile.

Do you have a static intranet?
Some symptoms of a static intranet are:

- Content requires special tools or technical knowledge to update – such as Macromedia Flash, or Adobe Acrobat for PDF, or knowledge of HTML, JavaScript, or web programming languages.

- The task of adding a sentence to the end of an intranet page is just not worth the effort.

- There is a very limited number of authors – often all in one department. These authors are often overworked as all intranet changes must come through them.

- There are lengthy workflows for changing intranet content; for example, a document must written by an author, then be approved by a departmental manager, approved by the legal department, and approved by an intranet manager before it appears on the intranet.

Central Control Can Be the Right Approach

So far, we've looked at reasons why central control can be a bad thing. However, static, highly controlled content is appropriate for several parts of an intranet. This is true of those areas where content should change infrequently, and other aspects such as accuracy, clarity, or lack of legal exposure are more important than being up-to-date.

For important documents that will be read by the majority of the company, it makes sense to use a professional writer. A good writer can make the documents easier to understand and more pleasant to read. This is particularly worthwhile for areas of the intranet such as new employee orientation – these will be read by a large number of people, and it is important that they are clear. A lot of technical authors work on a contract basis, so you can still use one even if your intranet doesn't have enough such documents to justify a full-time author on staff.

Accuracy is paramount, and has legal implications, for some areas of the intranet; for example a company's financial reports, or information on employee share schemes, policies, and records. For these documents, accuracy is more important than regular updates. These documents will often be thoroughly checked for accuracy by a number of people in a workflow. These are also the kind of documents for which legal approval may be required.

A single team that updates the whole intranet will lead to more consistency across the intranet than if there are multiple authors in different parts of the company. For example, within a small team, the vocabulary can be consistent, as can the use of acronyms and abbreviations, and the internal formatting of articles. A Content Management System (CMS) that uses standardized templates, stylesheets, and navigation can lead to a consistent interface even with multiple authors, but there will still be stylistic differences that cannot be automated away. Later in this chapter, we'll discuss Electronic Corporate Identities (ECI), which can help multiple decentralized authors produce a consistent intranet, but this is still less effective than using a team that is all in the same office, and can easily talk to each other.

A single team is also more able to focus its efforts – that is, it can take an overall view of the intranet, and concentrate on updating and maintaining those areas of the intranet that are most important to the business. Individual, decentralized authors will concentrate on the intranet areas that are important to themselves, which may not be the ones which provide the greatest ROI for the business as a whole.

> *A new intranet will often begin with centralized control, but as it grows it becomes more appropriate to use a mixture of central control and decentralized authoring.*

Note that these benefits depend on the intranet team taking an active role in producing or editing content – if their role is to rubber-stamp content produced by other authors, then there may be less justification for central control.

A new intranet will often begin with centralized control, but as it grows it becomes more appropriate to use a mixture of central control and de-centralized authoring. Exactly when this changeover should occur depends on the size of the company, the number of intranet users, how physically separated the company members are, and any number of other factors. In general, if it becomes hard for an intranet user to have content added to the intranet, or existing content amended, then it might be time to consider greater decentralization.

Avoiding the Static Intranet

The previous section described the parts of the intranet for which it may be appropriate to use a static model. Now we'll look at how to avoid the static model in those areas for which it is not appropriate. The major step in avoiding a static intranet is to ensure that more authors are actively contributing to the intranet, and to remove the barriers that prevent them from doing so.

If the content of the intranet is under the control of the people who are actually using it, then they are far more motivated to keep it up to date and to fix problems, because this helps them in their day-to-day work. In addition, the users of an area of the intranet are likely to be those people who have most knowledge of that area and so they are the people best placed to recognize good quality or inaccurate content.

How many authors should there be? That depends on the size of your intranet, and how geographically, hierarchically, and socially separated your organization is. As a general principle, every member of your organization should be able to easily get in touch with an intranet author. This may mean one author per site, per department, or per office.

So, there are two steps needed to prevent your intranet from becoming static: make it easy for authors to contribute content and make them enthusiastic about doing so.

Making It Easy to Contribute

Making it easy for authors to contribute to the intranet has several components – they must have access to the technology needed for authoring, they need to know how to contribute, and there must not be too many restrictions on what they are allowed to do.

Making the Technology Available

Whatever system you use for updating intranet content, it should be available to as many people within your organization as possible. This means that it shouldn't require special software installed on the author's machine (such as Macromedia's Dreamweaver), or require special knowledge such as HTML or JavaScript. In practice, this generally means that the intranet is updated using a web browser interface that provides a Word-like WYSIWYG editor to change the content.

In the next chapter we'll talk more about using a CMS as a technology to make the intranet easy to author for. Although many commercial CMSs are very expensive, there are also several good Open Source CMS systems that may be just as effective for your needs.

One easy way for intranet users to begin contributing to the intranet is by adding comments to existing content. This is a common practice on many web sites, such as the web developer community *http://www.evolt.org/*. Although this technique may not be appropriate for all areas of the intranet, it is certainly appropriate for articles in a knowledge base.

It is very easy for a developer to add this functionality to an intranet – and all that a user needs to do to add content is to enter it into a simple textbox. It allows users to make useful additions to the intranet with no training and no special software. Making an initial contribution to the intranet in this way can be the first step to becoming a full intranet author.

If you set up your intranet to allow comments, then consider having the page author e-mailed whenever a comment is added. It's also useful to allow the page author to remove comments – this allows the author to transfer information from the comments into the main body of the page and then remove the now-irrelevant comments.

A related alternative is to have discussion forums associated with intranet pages or intranet microsites. These allow readers to discuss ideas and thoughts based on the page. Comment threads can often become discussions, unless there is an existing forum that can be used for the discussions instead.

Training for Authors

In *Chapter 6* on Usability, we discussed the creation of an Electronic Corporate Identity (ECI) as a resource for intranet authors. The ECI is an intranet microsite that provides page templates, advice for authors, and discussion forums where authors can discuss the intranet (although these are only useful if several authors contribute – the ECI owner needs to encourage participation). Authors can be pointed towards the ECI to provide them with best practices, advice, and support for intranet authoring.

Although the ECI may be all that is needed for an author who has written for the Web before, some authors are likely to require more support. Ideally, every intranet author should receive training, both in using the authoring environment and in writing for the Web. In practice, most organizations will consider this to be too expensive, especially when the intention is to get a large number of intranet authors.

An alternative that keeps the training costs low is to provide training for a core group of "intranet champions", dispersed throughout the company. The champions can keep in touch with each other using the ECI site and share ideas. When a new author wishes to start writing for the intranet, they can get in touch with their local intranet champion and receive the help and support that they need.

It's helpful to consider the trade-off between the costs of increased intranet training, and the costs of increasing the usability of your authoring interface. Although in the previous chapter we considered usability primarily from the perspective of a user of the intranet, it is also important from the perspective of an intranet author. The intranet champions are in an excellent position to assess the usability flaws of the existing interface; if the new authors that they are helping frequently have the same difficulties, then this probably points to a problem with the interface.

Removing Restrictions

As we have discussed above, in some areas of the intranet it is appropriate to have restrictions on who can make content available and a review process in place to ensure that content is appropriate. What these restrictions should be will vary depending on how many people will see the content, what the consequences of a mistake in the content would be, how costly or time-consuming it would be to check the content, and so on. For example, before content is added to the intranet homepage, it is probably appropriate to send the edited page to at least one other person to review, because the homepage will be seen by many intranet users and will affect the trust they place in the intranet. However, for a less widely used page, it might be more appropriate just to carry out an automated spell check and link check, since the cost of reviewing the page manually might outweigh the benefit of doing so.

Consider carefully where restrictions are needed, and err on the side of making it easier for authors to contribute. Unlike your company Internet site, content posted on the intranet will only be visible internally, so mistakes are less damaging and easier to correct (although offensive content can still cause legal problems). Within a single organization there are also stronger social pressures on intranet authors to post content responsibly.

Encouraging Authors to Contribute

Although sharing information with others via the intranet will benefit the company, it won't happen unless it also gives benefits to the authors expected to do the sharing. In *Working Knowledge,* Davenport and Prusak, Harvard Business School Press, ISBN 1-578513-01-4, an excellent practical book on Knowledge Management, there are three motives identified for authors to contribute knowledge: reciprocity, repute, and altruism. In addition, authors must be given time to contribute content to the intranet.

Reciprocity – Giving in the Expectation of Receiving

Reciprocity is giving knowledge in the expectation of receiving benefits in return. These benefits may be in the form of more knowledge, or the author could receive benefits in a more indirect way. For example, if the exchange of information benefits the company as a whole, then it may increase the value of the author's stock options or increase their job security. On an intranet, if an author has benefited in the past from knowledge found on the intranet, then they are more likely to contribute their knowledge to the intranet in return. We'll talk more about increasing the usefulness of intranet content in the section on "*Junk-drawer Intranets*" later in this chapter.

One form of reciprocity that has been very important in motivating me to add knowledge to an intranet is the awareness that I will probably refer to it myself in six months time. I can guarantee that I'll forget how to do something, but as long as the information is on the intranet, I know I can find it again. This form of motivation is only useful if contributors have a reasonable expectation of both needing and being able to find the information again; this may not be true if their role or their employer has changed!

Another form of reciprocity that has motivated me is entering knowledge to receive "freedom from interruptions" in return. If you can direct people to the knowledge base to learn how to perform a task themselves, then they won't need to ask you to do it. This is the "teach a man to fish" principle. It can backfire – once you become recognized as an expert in a field, then you may face even more interruptions with questions upon that topic.

Repute – Giving for the Sake of Reputation

This motivation emphasizes once again the importance of crediting authors for their contributions to the intranet. Being known as an expert in a particular subject can increase job security, lead to promotion, or lead to projects based on a topic in which the author is interested. Some companies (such as the accountants Ernst & Young) use an employee's reputation for knowledge-sharing as a factor for evaluation in their employee review process. Other companies provide a "Hall of Fame" that lists the top contributors to the intranet, and helps establish their repute. Others award a small prize, such as a bottle of champagne, to the best intranet contribution each month.

It may be outside your remit to change your company's employee review process, but you can set up the intranet so it can be used for providing rewards. For a small intranet it is possible for one person to scan through the changes to the intranet and assess their value to find the "top contributors", but this rapidly becomes impractical as the intranet grows, and in some companies will take on a political aspect. You can assess the top contributors automatically by measuring the volume of content (for example the number of pages) created by each intranet author. The drawback to this is that it rewards quantity over quality, and is likely to lead to a lower-quality intranet as authors concentrate on producing large numbers of pages rather than making their contributions useful and concise (this is especially true if authors can expect monetary rewards for producing more content). A more effective way of assessing top contributors is by allowing intranet users to vote on the usefulness of pages as they use them.

At Xerox there is a "Eureka Hall of Fame" that lists the top contributors to their Eureka knowledge base. Users, who vote as they use the system, identify the most useful contributions. This is using peer review and peer recognition as a reward process. You can find more information at *http://choo.fis.utoronto.ca/mgt/KM.xeroxCase.html*.

Altruism – Giving Due to Generosity

Altruism is the sharing of knowledge for the pleasure of helping another. It may increase the sharer's perceived self-worth if they can help someone, or they may highly value the information that they share and wish it to be more widely known. The only way of encouraging this motivation for contribution to the intranet is by improving the culture of the company, by hiring generous people, and treating them well. This is easier said than done, and probably not something on which you can have a great influence.

The Internet is perhaps the finest example of altruism on a computer network. You can benefit from this altruism on your intranet by encouraging intranet content authors to provide links to existing Internet resources, such as FAQs, mailing lists, and USENET newsgroups.

Making Time for Authors

If authors don't have any time to contribute to their intranet then they won't, no matter how motivated they are. Authors need to be able to take time away from their immediate projects to update the intranet. As discussed above, they may receive immediate benefits from doing this, as they are interrupted less by questions since the answers are already on the intranet.

Official recognition needs to be given to the intranet; for example, by adding "updating the intranet" as a valid task in the timesheets system, by including intranet contributions as a performance criterion in employee reviews, by adding "creating intranet content" to the job descriptions of employees, and perhaps by setting aside specific time in which authors should update the intranet. This lets authors spend time contributing to the intranet without feeling that they are taking away time from their "real work".

Dealing with Documents Without Specialist Software

Even when authors are keen to contribute, you need to provide the tools for them to do so. In the case of non-HTML document types, such as PDFs, MS Word documents, or Photoshop files, this can pose problems to intranet authors unless dealt with by a centralized team. You need to decide what formats of documents are to be standard on the intranet, and how they can be produced.

Non-HTML documents have a number of drawbacks when used on an intranet:

- They require reader software that may not be installed on all computers (particularly non-Windows computers)

- They are hard for content authors to edit and update without having expensive specialist software, such as Adobe Acrobat

- Even if you've got the appropriate software, you may also require the correct version of that software. Several formats have multiple versions that are not backward-compatible (in the past, MS Word has been particularly notorious for this)

- They cause a delay while the reader software opens – this is a particular problem when you're evaluating a list of search results to see which are relevant

- Some search engines won't index non-HTML documents, or may require additional setup in order to do so

- Often, the document formats are proprietary, and may be hard or impossible to generate automatically (for example, due to undocumented file formats, complex file formats, or legal issues)

- They are prone to a whole new set of bugs that are different from the problems of HTML (for example, IE 5.0 occasionally has problems displaying PDFs in the browser)

This is not to say that non-HTML formats are wholly bad. PDFs are very good for providing pages that print well, and are good for sending documents to clients since you can guarantee what it looks like. Word documents are very easy for any author to create – far more intranet users will have experience with a word processor than with any given content management system. Other formats have their own benefits.

Of the problems listed above, the most significant issue for intranet authors is the availability of software for viewing and editing the documents.

Viewer programs for PDF, Word document, or other binary formats may not be available on all of your users' computers. This is particularly a problem if there are intranet users who are not using Windows; for example a CAD (Computer Aided Design) department that uses Unix exclusively. This is not an insurmountable difficulty as there are free viewers for most popular formats available on the major operating systems.

For Word, Excel, and PowerPoint files, OpenOffice (*http://www.openoffice.org*) is a free viewer and editor for Windows and Unix. Microsoft also supplies free viewers from the *http://office.microsoft.com/* site. Neither of these is a perfect solution; for example, Open Office does not yet deal well with comments.

For PDF files, Adobe's Acrobat Reader (although not the full Acrobat PDF creator) is available free from *http://www.adobe.com*. For both PDF and PostScript files, GhostScript (*http://www.ghostscript.com/*) is a free viewer that is available for more platforms than are supported by Adobe Acrobat.

Editor programs present more of a problem. Although most document formats have freely available viewers, the document creation tools require a license fee. When buying tools for a small central intranet team, this is unlikely to be a problem, but if every contributor to the intranet throughout the organization requires them, then it can become very expensive!

For some formats, this problem can be overcome while still allowing authors around the company to contribute. Many content management systems will generate PDFs and Word (or RTF) documents dynamically. This means that authors can edit an HTML version of the page through the normal content management system, and then the CMS can generate a PDF version suitable for printing or e-mailing to clients automatically.

Don't assume that this will solve all your authoring problems immediately. Automatically generated content invariably requires considerable tweaking before it looks just right. The main benefit of using a PDF is that (unlike HTML) it will look exactly the same on every computer, and print out exactly the same. However, this doesn't mean that it will be correct everywhere, unless you take the time to adjust the automated PDF generation tool to suit your needs.

In addition, content management systems are beginning to support WebDAV as a mechanism for updating content. This allows authors to edit intranet content within their standard tools, such as Word and Excel, and save it directly to the intranet. This support is neither widespread nor mature as yet, but has a great deal of potential. Within Windows, support for WebDAV is provided by the Web Folders mechanism in Explorer, which allows a remote directory on a server that also uses WebDAV (such as IIS, Apache using mod_dav, or some CMSs) to be edited as if it was a local directory. WebDAV also allows metadata to be added to describe files, and can support versioning. There is more information at *http://www.webdav.org*.

The "Junk Drawer" Intranet

The "junk drawer" intranet is the opposite problem to the "static" intranet that we've just discussed. Where the problems of the "static" intranet come from too much central control, the problems of the "junk drawer" intranet come from too little control. There is a huge quantity of content available, contributed by a large number of authors, but there is much duplicated work, appearing in a variety of formats and layouts, and with no way of identifying the quality of the content. There is no easy way to find the information that you need without looking through many different microsites within the intranet. Inevitably, each microsite uses a different design, uses slightly different terminology, positions the navigation in a different place and hence forces you to spend time re-learning the interface rather than concentrating on finding the information you need. The junk drawer intranet can be summed up as "Here's everything that I have" rather than "Here's everything that you need".

Do you have a "junk drawer" intranet?
Some symptoms of a "junk drawer" intranet are:

- You regularly spend a long time searching for information on the intranet, and even then you often don't find it.

- There is no consistency between different areas of the intranet.

- It's easier to write a new page for the intranet than it is to find an existing one.

When Is Decentralized Control Appropriate?

For some segregated parts of the intranet, it may be appropriate to allow complete freedom to the authors, without any of the practices to limit this. For example, in a microsite that is a technical knowledge base for a small group of engineers who know each other and their field well, there is no need to establish trust between the author and the reader. Incomplete or outdated content is not a major problem, because the readers will know the field sufficiently well that they can benefit from incomplete information without being confused by it. Consistency is easy to ensure within a small space, and consistency with the rest of the intranet is not important while the microsite remains a segregated information silo.

However, as soon as this segregated area becomes accessible to the rest of the company, then this idea breaks down. All these individual content silos may be useful in themselves, but someone who has to deal with several of them will end up very frustrated and confused.

So, while complete lack of control can be useful in a very small intranet, or in a restricted area on the intranet, as the intranet grows and becomes more widely used it begins to cause problems.

Selling Consistency to Authors

We've already discussed the importance of having a consistent intranet style in *Chapter 6* on Usability. A consistent style means that the user doesn't have to think about the layout of the intranet, and re-learn the interface in every section. This means that they can spend more time focusing on the intranet content, find what they need faster, and get more use out of the intranet.

> *A consistent style means that the user doesn't have to think about the layout of the intranet, and re-learn the interface in every section*

While it's easy to maintain a consistent appearance if there's only a small team working on the intranet, it becomes much harder when there's a large group of distributed authors. In order to have an intranet with a consistent appearance, it's necessary to convince your authors that design consistency is important and make it easy for them to comply

If authors are working within the framework of a CMS, then it is much easier to produce pages that are consistent, because they will all use standard templates. In fact it may be very hard *not* to produce pages with a consistent design. If they are not working with a CMS, and especially if they are creating microsites on separate servers from the main intranet server, then consistency is harder to achieve.

We've already mentioned the creation of an ECI (Electronic Corporate Identity) earlier in this chapter and in the previous chapter. As we said before, as long as you explain to the authors that the ECI benefits the users of the intranet, then they are more likely to use it than if the ECI is seen as an attempt to enforce consistency for the sake of the corporate image.

Duplicate Content and "Satisficing"

One of the problems of the "junk-drawer" intranet is that similar information may appear several times and in several different places. If there are various possible solutions to a given problem, it's likely that the best one won't always be found and used. This is due to a phenomenon called "satisficing". This is a word that comes from combining "satisfying" and "sufficing", and means "being sufficiently satisfied". Because intranet users don't have the time to search for what might be the best solution to their problem, they will instead use the first solution that is good enough. Hence, if there are several pages providing a solution to a problem, and the user comes across one of the less useful pages first, then they are likely to stick with it rather than bothering to search further.

So, how can you prevent this from being a problem? Before entering information into the intranet, authors should get into the habit of searching to see if similar information is already there. This requires that the intranet search is accessible from the authoring environment – if it's too hard to do, authors won't bother. If there is existing information, the author should be able to update or amend the information with as little trouble as possible – either by contacting the existing author, or by editing the content himself.

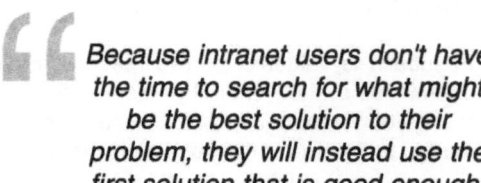

Because intranet users don't have the time to search for what might be the best solution to their problem, they will instead use the first solution that is good enough.

With an existing "junk-drawer" intranet, the problem is harder. The best approach is the "big bang" – to spend some time going through all the contents of the intranet evaluating its worth. Irrelevant material can be deleted, and similar pages can be merged. Unfortunately, this can be time consuming and expensive, and will require experts to assess the value of content.

There may be time or money constraints that prevent the "big bang fix" from being an option. In this case, the only option is "continuous renewal". When an author is updating a page, she should search the intranet to see if there are any other pages with similar content, and if so, then merge the pages. This is not a great solution, because it may take a very long time to remove or rework all duplicate documents, but it's better than doing nothing and letting matters get worse.

Establishing Trust in Intranet Content

Knowledge on the intranet is useless unless it can be trusted. In an intranet with tight central control, then intranet readers can be fairly sure that the information has been checked before it was put onto the intranet – but it may have become outdated since then. In a "junk drawer" intranet, there is no guarantee that the information has ever been checked, and the reader needs to make their own judgments about whether it is trustworthy based on what they know of the content, the author, and the intranet as a whole.

There are two aspects to trust on the intranet – first, convincing a user that the content is trustworthy, and second, ensuring that their trust is well-placed. The two can be combined by **not** attempting to convince the user of anything, but instead giving them all the necessary information for them to make an informed judgment.

Controlling Content

Establish Trust in the Content

If I know about a subject, then it's not too hard for me to work out whether an article on that subject is trustworthy. I can compare it to my own experiences, and if what the article says agrees with my existing knowledge, then I'm inclined to trust the new information that I learn from the article.

If I don't know the subject, or don't know it well, then additional cues are necessary to establish trust. The customer book reviews at Amazon are an excellent example of this. They provide a simple rating, and a space for comments. Although I don't know the individual reviewers, I can use their opinions to work out whether I'll put enough trust in the book's content to buy it, and if there are multiple opinions I can see if there is a common theme across them.

Feedback is valuable for two reasons. First, it helps the reader assess the trustworthiness and usefulness of the material presented to them. Secondly, it rewards the author for their work. Peer recognition is more important to many knowledge workers than small direct rewards (although it can lead to indirect rewards such as increased job security and promotion).

A major influence on the perceived trustworthiness of a piece of information is its presentation. Simply by making sure that information is displayed in an aesthetic, elegant manner, with correct spelling and grammar, you can make it seem more trustworthy. So, make sure that your knowledge base is using a well-designed template and stylesheet, and there is an integrated spellchecker. However, unlike the other ways of establishing trust that we're discussing, this technique does not help the reader discriminate between useful information and out-dated, irrelevant information – both will be perceived as trustworthy if they are both presented well. Therefore use it carefully.

If the information is based on other sources: people, books, web sites, or whatever, then providing a link to those sources helps the reader establish trust. First of all, it lets them evaluate the information based on the trust that they place in its original source, and secondly, it allows them to obtain further information if that provided by the author is not sufficient.

Establish Trust in the Author

The primary factor influencing whether we trust a piece of information is who tells it to us, and what we know about them. I will take medical advice from my doctor, but not from a stranger. I'm not likely to trust "Dr. Bob's Medicine FAQ" that I've found on the Internet, although I might if several friends recommended him to me. One reason for this is that I have met my doctor face-to-face, and I've seen his office, his receptionist, and other signs of his authority, whereas "Dr. Bob's" authority is not so easy to ascertain – he is an unknown entity.

We've already mentioned that the name and e-mail address of the author should be on every intranet page they've written. In a small company, this may be enough to establish trust – if I can see that the information comes from a colleague who I know and respect, then I will trust it.

However, this doesn't go far enough to establish trust in a larger company, where I don't have first-hand knowledge of all the contributors to the intranet. I need more information about the author.

It would help establish trust if I can find other pages that they've contributed to the intranet, assuming that those other pages are highly rated and have enthusiastic comments. It is possible to automate this kind of system; for example, the Slashdot community web site (*http://slashdot.org/*) gives an automatic ratings bonus to new posts by consistently well-rated authors. However, an automated system doesn't build trust, it only makes the information available so the readers can assess it for themselves.

A useful addition to the company address book is a section that can be edited by each employee, to which they can add biographical information, projects they have worked on, hobbies, or links to personal web sites. This can provide some of the context about the author that helps to build trust.

Establish Trust in the Medium

If the user has previously been disappointed by the accuracy and usefulness of what they found on the intranet, then it's going to be hard to convince them to use it again. Conversely, if they regularly obtain accurate information, then they're more likely to trust other pages from it.

For this reason, the quality of information obtained from the intranet should be obvious. This is not to say that all the information on the intranet should be thoroughly researched, checked, and evaluated by experts – even if the time needed for this approach was acceptable, then the cost certainly wouldn't be! Rather, it means that there should be a clear indication of whether the author, and whether other readers, consider the information to be accurate or not. If a reader of the intranet finds that a piece of information marked as "possibly true" is wrong, then it will shake their trust less than if they found that one marked "totally accurate" is wrong.

As described above, there needs to be a feedback mechanism in place so readers can rate pages, add comments to pages, and report inaccurate content. In addition to the benefits for increasing trust, adding a comment to a page is a good first step in becoming an intranet author.

It is generally best to simply remove content that is inaccurate, or de-activate it until the author has time to improve it. Some information may have value even if it is not perfect; for example, it may be sufficiently correct to point a skilled user in the right direction, or to suggest ideas. However, most intranets have the problem of too much information rather than too little, and anything that removes excess pages is worthwhile. If the content does remain on the intranet, it should be clearly marked as untrustworthy, and shouldn't be ranked highly by the intranet search engine (this does mean that the search engine should be able to rank pages on criteria such as this, and not all are able to).

If time or money precludes improving the quality of information on the intranet in the short-term, it may still be worthwhile to create a clearly branded "walled garden" of high-quality intranet knowledge. Information can be promoted to the "walled garden" when it is recommended by users, and the intranet search engine can be set up to return results from this area at the top of its list. Users will know that the information that has come from this area will be more trustworthy.

The "Ghost Town" Intranet

In many Westerns, there's a scene in which the hero enters a long-abandoned town. There are buildings there, but the paint is peeling, doors are falling off their hinges, the windows are broken, and the only motion is the tumbleweed rolling down Main Street. Most of all, there are no people there.

This is what the "ghost town" intranet is like. In this section, we'll look at ways of avoiding this fate for your own intranet, by keeping the intranet up-to-date and useful, and keeping page authors in touch with the page readers.

Do you have a "ghost town" intranet?
Some symptoms of a "ghost town" intranet are:

- None of the pages you look at have been updated in the last 6 months.

- There are broken links on numerous intranet pages that once linked to internal and external pages.

- It's not easy to contact the author to ask them to fix problems with a web page, or to obtain more information.

Maintaining the Intranet

Basic maintenance to the intranet can have a large effect on its perceived usefulness to readers, and on the willingness of authors to contribute to it. If there are broken links or outdated pages linked to or from important pages like the homepage, then it immediately devalues the intranet in the eyes of its users. In this section will look at how to reduce these problems.

Broken windows and broken links
Police officers have noticed that if one window in a building is broken and is left unrepaired, then it is likely that the other windows in the same building will be soon be broken. This is because a broken window sends out the message that nobody cares about the building, and there is no community that maintains high standards.

The same idea can be applied to the intranet. If there are no broken links on the homepage of the intranet, and one appears, then it will be immediately reported by numerous intranet users. On the other hand, if there is an expectation that the intranet is poorly maintained and much of the intranet is out-of-date and contains broken links, then any additional broken links are likely to be ignored. Likewise, intranet authors are less likely to check their work thoroughly, and to make sure that it is removed when outdated.

Automated tools, such as a link-checker, can help improve the intranet quality, but what's ultimately important is a community of users that values the intranet. If it is immediately possible for users to contact the page owners, for instance with a "Report a Broken Link" facility, and they can see their comments leading to a rapid improvement, then it is a sign to users that the intranet maintainers consider the intranet to be important and worth maintaining.

Keeping Links Valid

Links to other resources, both internal and external, are very useful on an intranet, but also tend to become broken over time as URLs change, web sites change name, and content is removed from the intranet. To keep the intranet useful, you need some way of detecting and fixing this problem.

Most CMS systems have some sort of automated link checker built in. If your CMS doesn't, or if you are not using a CMS, then there are a number of commercial and free link checkers that you can use. One good, free, cross-platform link checker is the aptly named Linkchecker, available at *http://linkchecker.sourceforge.net/*, which is written in Python. It shouldn't be too hard to tweak any of these link checkers to automatically contact the page owner when they detect a broken link. (One which already does is Xenu's Link Sleuth – *http://home.snafu.de/tilman/xenulink.html*).

The drawback of automated tests is that they cannot tell if the page being pointed to is useful, only that there is a page there. If a target page has been replaced by wholly different content, as happens all too often on the Internet, then an automated tool cannot detect this, only a human reader. While automated checks can reduce the problem of broken links, they cannot completely remove it.

Keeping Pages Updated

It's inevitable that pages will become outdated over time. In order to keep the intranet relevant, there needs to be some mechanism for updating or deleting irrelevant pages.

The standard approach is to set an expiry date for each page when it's created. This can be done by the author, or automatically based on the current date (for example, 6 months in the future). The purpose of this is to make sure that the pages are regularly reviewed, so they can be either deleted or updated every so often. The expiry date is stored as part of the page's metadata, and can be acted upon automatically by software.

Most of the time, it's best to have the expiry date set automatically by the content management software (and the CMS should also provide tools that warn of page expiry). Since it's not something that will normally need to be changed, then there's no point making the content author have to think about it – it just makes the page authoring process less usable, and wastes the page author's time as they think about it. However, some areas of the site might have different automatically set expiry dates (for example, a page in a "*News releases*" section automatically expires after a month, and can be moved automatically into a news archive). There are also some items, like postings of upcoming events that have a known date after which they are no longer relevant.

One possible action when the expiry date is reached is to automatically remove pages from the intranet unless they are updated. Although this is effective in ensuring that only relevant pages are found on the intranet, it has significant disadvantages. Firstly, it runs the risk of alienating the authors of the pages. Secondly, old information may still be relevant, or require only revisions to bring it up to date. If it is removed completely, then useful information will disappear from the intranet. However, in a very large, chaotic intranet, it may be worthwhile to make this trade-off because the useful pages removed will only be a small percentage of the total pages deleted (and if no-one can find the useful pages amongst all the others anyway, then they might as well not be there).

An alternative is to automatically e-mail the page owner when the page passes its expiry date, and keep on sending e-mails until the page is either deleted or edited. As long as there is a simple way for the page author to say "This page is still valid – reset the expiry date and don't bother me until it expires again" then this should help keep intranet pages up to date without imposing an undue burden on page owners.

If pages that are past their expiry date are still visible on the intranet, then there should be some visible indication of that fact – both on the page, and in any search results that list the page. Although the last time that the page was updated should be visible on the page anyway, it's easy to miss that a page is expired unless there's a large, clear indication of that fact.

It should be part of the process of removing a page from the intranet to check that there are no links elsewhere in the intranet to the page that will be broken if it is removed. A CMS will generally have this functionality built in. If the entire intranet is not in a CMS, or if the intranet is in several different CMS systems, then it may still be possible to find the linking pages.

Most web servers will store the URL of the page that was viewed before the current one. In Apache you set this up with the LogFormat configuration variable, while in IIS you can set the log format to "*W3C Extended Log File Format*" and configure it in the "*Extended Logging Properties*" dialog.

It's simple to write an automated tool that will find all the logged referrer pages for a page that's about to be removed, download and search each to see if there's a link to the page being removed, and then display each page that contains a link. It is then possible to contact each of the owners of the linking pages and ask them to remove the link (or even remove the link automatically). Of course, this requires that you store your access logs for a long period – or at least, regularly build summary files from them that list the referrers for each page.

Establishing Ownership

Authors are more likely to maintain their web pages if they feel that they "own" the pages. In order to feel a sense of ownership, authors need to be in control of the content to as large an extent as is practical. If an author is given responsibility for maintaining a section of the intranet, but they don't have easy access to the tools needed to update it, or needs to have their changes approved before they are accepted, then they will feel less of a sense of ownership than if they had immediate access to make the changes. The more intimately the author is involved with the information on the pages, the more they will tend to take operational ownership of it. The author also needs to recognize that their work is important to the company, and that the work is valued both by the organization and by the intranet users.

Connecting "Communities of Practice" Via Intranet Microsites

An alternative to having pages on the intranet owned by an individual page owner is to have a section of an intranet, such as a self-contained microsite, owned by a group.

A Community of Practice (often abbreviated CoP) is a group of people who share an interest in a topic, for example a group of HR managers who meet to discuss problems of recruitment, or a group of developers who share tips for coding. In a small company it's easy for these groups to work together and exchange information. In a larger company, particularly one spread across multiple sites or multiple countries, it is much more difficult for these groups to work together or even form, unless supported by communication technologies such as the intranet.

Using the intranet allows the CoP to have a persistent store of information in a knowledge base. It also allows the CoP to organize upcoming events, share news about their field, and other relevant information. It can store a list of CoP members and their contact details to help keep members in touch. It can also host "webinars" and other social functions to provide a social hub that helps bind the CoP together.

Small intranets have many benefits over larger in terms of ownership, trust, and community. You can bring the benefits of a small intranet to a larger intranet by using microsites on the intranet to connect communities of practice. It's much easier to motivate authors to contribute to a small intranet than to a larger one. Reciprocity is more immediate, as each intranet author is aware of who contributed what. It's also easier to build a reputation within a small group, and colleagues are more likely to become friends, and hence share information with each other from altruism.

More information on communities of practice can be found at in the following resources:

- the Yahoo "com-prac" group (*http://groups.yahoo.com/group/com-prac/*).

- A good book on the subject is "Cultivating Communities of Practice", Etienne Wenger et al, Harvard Business School Press, ISBN 1-578513-30-8 .

- There are links to more information in Google's directory at *http://directory.google.com/Top/ Reference/Knowledge_Management/Knowledge_Flow/Communities_of_Practice/*.

Paradoxically, an intranet may become more useful to its users if access to some areas of it is restricted. It can be worthwhile for teams or communities of practice to have their own private areas on the intranet that cannot be read by anyone, even their managers, outside the team. This is not an approach that will be popular with all organizations, but can be effective if your company's culture allows it.

Normally, authors are reluctant to contribute information to the intranet if they are not certain that the information is correct, because any mistake can be seen by their peers and managers, and may damage their reputation. This reluctance to be publicly wrong can restrict investigation of new ideas, and can prevent others from working with the author to refine their own incomplete ideas. If each author knows that their contributions are only visible to trusted colleagues, then they have the freedom to make mistakes and to learn from them. The content in these private areas can be more experimental and express more personal opinions than on a widely-visible intranet page.

This private information can eventually be made publicly available. Firstly, members of the team can periodically convert their private intranet documents into publicly visible intranet pages. Secondly, it should be possible to identify which private teams are working on which topics through an intranet search. Even though the content is not generally available, an interested intranet user can contact a team member to find out if there is anything relevant to their own problems in the private content.

Contacting the Page Owners

If every page on the intranet has an owner then it should be possible for the reader of the page to contact the page owner. We've mentioned this several times already in this chapter, but we haven't talked about how it can be done or what the problems are.

It is important that the reader be able to contact the page owner because not all information can be recorded on the intranet. There will always be questions that the page author hadn't considered, or weren't applicable when the page was authored, that can only be answered by talking to a human being.

The traditional method of making it possible to contact the page owner is to include their e-mail address in a mailto link at the bottom of each page for which they are responsible. On clicking the link, the reader's e-mail application will open allowing them to e-mail the page owner.

A significant improvement over a simple `mailto` link is to use a `mailto` that automatically includes the details of the page at the top of the e-mail. For example, the following rather unreadable link:

```
<a href="mailto:inigosurguy@hotmail.com?Subject=Intranet query about page titled
%22About the Mailto URL%22&Body=Intranet link
http%3A//myintranet/info/mailto.htm">Contact page author: Inigo Surguy</a>
```

will open the reader's e-mail client with a mail initialized with the subject:

Intranet query about page titled "About the Mailto URL"

and with the body content

Intranet link: http://myintranet/info/mailto.htm

There is more information on the fields that can be added to `mailto` URLs on Netscape's site at *http://developer.netscape.com/viewsource/husted_mailto/mailto.html*. Although it's described on Netscape's web site, this technique also works in Internet Explorer and with mail clients such as Outlook and Outlook Express.

As mentioned earlier another approach is to allow users to add comments to a page. As each comment is added, it can generate an e-mail to the page owner, sending the name, URL of the page, and the content of the comment. The page author can then respond by e-mail, by updating the page, or by adding a comment. This way, the usefulness of the page should increase over time, as it can provide the information to anyone reading the page at a later date. On the downside, the public visibility of questions may discourage some readers, so it should be used alongside a `mailto` URL rather than as a replacement for it.

An approach that can be used in conjunction with the two previous methods is to tie the intranet page into your Instant Messaging (IM) system. When a page reader clicks on a link at the bottom of the intranet page, then it can open an IM window that lets the reader talk directly to the page author.

This approach is more appropriate in a small company, where people know each other well and are happy with the relative informality of using IM. It also gives convenience and a rapid response to the reader at the cost of possibly inconveniencing the page author. Whereas e-mail can be filed to be dealt with later, IM is immediate and insistent. If authors find that they are regularly being interrupted by IM questions while trying to work, then this will not encourage them to write intranet pages in future. We'll talk again about the advantages and disadvantages of IM in *Chapter 9*.

Providing the author's phone number is another option. Phone calls, of course, share many of the advantages and disadvantages of IM, but are even harder to ignore.

What if the author of the page is no longer at the company, or if he has moved to a different role within the company?
Up until this point, we've been assuming that the page author is the page owner. Although this is desirable, it's not always possible. We need to draw a distinction between the "page author" who originally wrote the content of the page, and the "page owner" or "page maintainer" who is currently in charge of it.

When a page owner leaves the company, part of the leaving process should be to go through each of the pages that they own on the intranet, and either reassign it to their successor or remove it. The new owner should familiarize themselves with the contents of the pages that they are responsible for; if the intranet pages are useful, then the successor is likely to need to know the information contained on them anyway. Over time, as the intranet is maintained, the page owner is likely to replace portions of the original page content with updated material, or even remove the page entirely.

Why Should a Page Owner Agree to Be Contacted?

An author will agree to be contacted about their intranet page for the same reasons that they'll write the page in the first place. As described above, these are reciprocity (the expectation of benefits to follow from doing so), repute (the increase of the author's reputation), and altruism (providing information in order to help others). For personal contacts, these reasons apply even more strongly than when the author is in contact with readers through the intermediary of an intranet page.

What Discourages Readers from Contacting the Page Author

Even though intranet readers can contact the page author, a lot of the time they will not, even when it would benefit them to do so. There are several reasons why this is the case. We'll look at what they are, and how to overcome them.

Local Knowledge Is Preferred

In general, intranet users are more likely to ask the person at the next desk for help, rather than contact an expert that they don't know from an entirely different part of the company. This is true even when the person at the next desk has little chance of answering the question usefully.

This is related to the need to establish trust described earlier in this chapter. Face-to-face conversations are the best mechanisms for establishing trust, so you are likely to trust someone close more than someone further away. Incomplete information that comes from a source that you trust may be more valuable than more complete information from a source that you have no reason to trust. In addition, talking to someone nearby is quick, easy, and informal – while composing an e-mail is slower and more formal.

Trust in the content owner can be established using the methods described earlier in the "*Establishing Trust in Intranet Content*" section. It's also important that people consider the intranet as one of their first options for obtaining information.

I Don't Know What I Don't Know!

Users of the intranet may not know exactly what they need to know – and e-mail is more suited to asking and answering well-defined questions than it is to a broader discovery process. Until someone has at least a basic understanding of an area, then they are unlikely to be able to form useful questions relating to it.

This problem can be reduced by several mechanisms:

- By providing more information on the subject on the intranet so users can read around the subject

- The page author can provide links to background reading or Internet web pages that reference the subject

- The reader can talk to the content owner via a more immediate medium than e-mail – such as phoning the content owner, talking via IM, or meeting face-to-face

Readers Don't Want to Waste the Page Owner's Time

An intranet reader may avoid contacting the page owner to avoid wasting their time with foolish questions, particularly if the page owner is higher in the organization hierarchy. Sometimes this is justified; after all, if a subject expert is constantly interrupted by requests for answers to trivial questions, then they will be reluctant to make their knowledge available. It is often hard for a non-expert to know whether their question is trivial or difficult. Readers are not keen to embarrass themselves by asking questions that the expert might consider stupid. There needs to be a mechanism by which readers can tell whether their question is worthwhile, or embarrassingly obvious.

One solution is to use a contact mechanism that doesn't demand an immediate response from the page owner. For example, using IM is bad for this, because the author must respond immediately to an IM request if they are going to respond at all. On the other hand, adding a comment to an intranet page is less insistent, and it also allows for the possibility that another reader of the page might answer the question.

Another solution is for the page owner to establish a page of FAQs (Frequently Asked Questions) with the questions that they have previously been asked. This solution is most appropriate for a microsite owner that is responsible for a number of different pages, since most pages are unlikely to generate very many questions. Even if the reader's question isn't in the list of FAQs, then they can get an idea of the sort of question being asked from the FAQs.

On some subjects, there may already be related information elsewhere on the intranet or Internet. The page author can provide adequate and accurate links to similar articles, introductory tutorials, and existing FAQ pages. When the reader has perused these and still faces problems, then they can be sure that their problem is not too easy to bother the page owner with. In addition, the page owner can tell that the reader's problem is sufficiently important to the reader that they have spent time and effort trying to solve it, so will be more inclined to spend their time helping than they would if the problem was trivial.

These problems also apply to intranet applications like the "expert locator" or the "skills database". These typically consist of a database of people within the organization, with their skills in various fields rated. A skills database lists everyone within the organization, while an expert locator lists the top few experts within a given field. The idea is that when a member of the company has a question on that field, they can ask an expert. In addition, a project manager assembling a team for a project can search through the skills database to find people who have the talents that she needs.

Although the motivation behind these applications is good, the use of them is subject to similar problems as we've described above.

If you are assembling a team for a project, then it's often more important to know things like how well the team will work together, what sort of clients the team members have worked with before, and what similar projects the members have worked on, rather than just their skills. This is information that will not be in a skills database.

The expert locator may find an expert in the field in which you're interested, but without more background information, it gives you no reason to trust their expertise, and you will have no idea how well they will work with clients and other team members. Trust must be established using the mechanisms that we've already described in this chapter. In addition, you must overcome the reluctance to contact the expert described above, in order to make the expert locator widely used.

Summary

In this chapter we've looked at the problem of controlling the intranet and its content. We've covered the "static" intranet caused by strict central control, the drawbacks this approach brings and when such control can be appropriate. We've looked at how to move away from too much central control, by making it easier for the authors to contribute, and how to motivate authors to encourage them to do so.

We went on to consider the "junk drawer" intranet, which has lots of content but is highly chaotic. We talked about how to keep the chaotic intranet under control, and about how to convince the intranet authors of the importance of a consistent interface. We thought about the problems caused by duplicate content on the intranet and how to overcome them. We also mentioned the problem of establishing trust in the intranet when the reader doesn't know the source of all the information that they're reading, and explained ways of creating trust.

Finally, we looked at the "ghost town" intranet which has unmaintained content and no sense of ownership by the users or authors. We talked about the importance of establishing ownership and how to keep intranet content maintained effectively. We've also discussed making microsites that are owned by a community of practice rather than an individual. We then discussed the advantages of putting intranet readers into contact with the intranet authors, the best ways of doing this, and why the author should allow this. Finally, we discussed the reasons why readers may not contact the author, and how to encourage them to do so.

At the very beginning of the chapter, we described what a good intranet can be. In order to achieve this ideal, you need to find a balance between the static intranet and the junk drawer intranet, while avoiding the ghost town intranet. This requires encouraging authors, and making sure there are just enough restrictions on posting to the intranet to ensure high-quality content, without having so many that contributors find them too burdensome. The techniques discussed in this chapter should help you achieve this.

Controlling Content

8

- Why a Content Management System (CMS) is useful

- Obtaining a CMS

- Meeting intranet needs

- Other publishing technologies

Author: Gareth Downes-Powell

Content Management Systems

In this chapter we deal with various methods of organizing and storing content. Our primary focus will be on Content Management Systems (CMS), but we will also look at Portals, Document Management Systems, and web logs (blogs). We will discuss the benefits CMS can offer, and how it can make your intranet serve your staff more efficiently and save both time and money.

We look at some of the processes involved in selecting a CMS package, and some of the qualities you should be looking for. We discuss the use of CMS with both your intranet and web site, and integrating the CMS within the two to stop duplication of data.

Next we look at how the CMS needs to work with your existing intranet, and discuss some of the issues involved, and look at different approaches that can be taken. Finally we close the chapter by looking at some of the other publishing technologies and techniques available such as Document Management Systems and portals.

What Is a Content Management System?

As its name suggests, a CMS is a system for managing content. This seems to be at first fairly simple, but there is much confusion about what a CMS is, and what these systems actually do. Most people realize they are useful somehow, but unsure of how they can actually help a business, and it's usually these businesses that do not understand the potential of enhancing the sharing of information amongst their staff.

What Is Content?

Before talking about managing content, we need to first clearly define what we mean by content. Content is basically information, whether it is text, images, video, etc., anything that can be displayed on a page is classified as content.

Individual items of content can be combined to form documents. A CMS deals with the individual items of content and a Document Management System (DMS) can handle the entire document. We will take a closer look at Document Management Systems later on in the chapter. Some systems combine the two: managing content as well as documents. Web pages for the intranet would be managed by the CMS for example, whereas documents, such as Microsoft Word Documents for example, would be managed by the DMS part of the system.

Organizing Content

CMS manages information, and is responsible for storing it, categorizing it, and displaying it. This allows the staff to focus on the information itself and keeping it accurate, without having to worry about the technicalities of adding, displaying, and storing the information.

Why Do I Need a CMS?

Many businesses think that they have no need for a CMS, using the argument that their site isn't that big, and they only have a small amount of staff. However, the amount of data that the business handles is often grossly underestimated, and a content management system could actually help the business substantially.

Organizing information can be problematic; even when web sites or intranets start off fairly small, they can quickly expand and become hard to manage and maintain. This is especially true with company intranets, as they usually have a large amount of information added on a daily basis to keep employees up to date.

Companies typically have a special team that manages the intranet and uploads information to it using Web Design programs. If staff need some information added to the intranet, they supply a copy to the intranet team, then wait for it to be uploaded. This leads to wasted staff time, duplicate information, and means that the intranet will never be up-to-date due to the delay between the staff member giving it to the intranet team, and the time taken for them to add the information.

As the intranet expands the amount of information it handles will grow, increasing the time lag for information to be uploaded, especially since content can only be added by the intranet team. When large amounts of data are continually being added to the site, it will need to be categorized so that users can easily find their way around. However the intranet team won't have time to categorize the data in such depth. What happens, in effect, is that the few people who work with the intranet end up organizing the filing system for every department in the company, which is hardly an optimal situation.

We'll now look at these situations in greater detail, and explain how CMS can help in each situation.

Adding Content

To add content to the intranet you need to have an understanding of web design so that you can do things like adding new menu items for example, which typically most staff will not be able to do. Consequently, this task is usually assigned to a small team of web developers who liaise with staff to get information for the intranet. Of course, this limitation can be a problem, but this is the case with a lot of company intranets.

We mentioned earlier that this has the undesired effect of creating a delay in getting the information up onto the intranet, but there are other disadvantages that it is important to be aware of. The team responsible for adding content to the intranet is unlikely to have knowledge of what the data actually means, since it is not something they will have specialist knowledge about. This means that they will probably be unable to spot errors in the information as they enter it, they will simply copy what they have been given. Furthermore, the copying process itself may lead to mistakes that weren't present in the original information.

This can also have the effect of stifling useful knowledge that could benefit others because only a few people in each department are in charge of adding data, and there will be a limit to the amount of information the Intranet Team can add, depending on the number of staff for example.

How a CMS Can Help

CMS allows easy entry of data without requiring knowledge of web design, HTML, or specialized web design programs. This allows all staff to be able to enter data, although you then have to decide how much control they have, for instance if the staff are allowed to upload pictures through the web browser, you can limit both the physical size of the picture, and the file size that can be uploaded.

CMS separates the content from the presentational aspects of the page, allowing staff to focus on the actual information itself; the presentational aspects of the page, design, menus, links, etc., are handled by the CMS.

Allowing staff to update their own sections of the intranet through CMS makes the staff feel more involved. A message throughout this book has been that an intranet can only be effective once all the staff actively adopt it and use it; CMS allows all employees to contribute directly to the intranet, increasing their awareness of it and their enthusiasm to use it.

The advantages of this are pretty clear. CMS allows staff to enter the data themselves through a simple form in either a web page or a custom application, alleviating the need for a specialist team to enter data for the intranet. This solves the problems we mentioned earlier: there will no longer be a delay in getting content on the intranet, and the content itself will be more accurate since it will be added by staff who are knowledgeable about it.

Inefficiencies of Handmade Intranets

Intranets that are maintained by hand usually end up being very inefficient, and it can be a long process to add a small amount of information. To add new content to the intranet, a new HTML page has to be created on which the new information is entered, then all relevant site menus have to be manually updated to link to the new page.

A lot of time is wasted on these repetitive tasks. Templates can help this situation, but if the site is large, it can still be difficult to maintain. Imagine, for example, that you have a menu stored in a template. If you add a new menu item to the template, the new link will be physically added as HTML to all pages that are using that particular template. This saves a lot of time, but say you have 500 web pages using that particular template. Each time you make a change to the menu, 500 pages have to be physically changed and then re-uploaded to the server. Even when this task is automated it can still take a while and uses unnecessary bandwidth as 500 pages are uploaded to the server each time a menu item is added.

8

Content Management Systems

On intranets without CMS, information can end up being duplicated, leading to versioning problems as old and new copies of the same information exist on the Internet concurrently, and leaving users confused as to which is correct.

How CMS Can Help

CMS improves this situation by allowing contributors to manage their own content, freeing up the staff who run the system to keep the servers and networks running, design the site, and keep the technology up to date.

The staff from each department who actually use the data will be entering the data themselves, as well as managing and categorizing it, so they and other staff members in the department can find the information they need. They are allowed to add and edit content, so they can make sure that the information on the intranet for their area is always correct and up to date. Because staff are in control of their own section of the intranet, and are responsible for adding content themselves, it helps to eliminate the chances of data being duplicated, as they know what content they previously added.

Repetitive tasks such as building menus and maintaining links (within a preset framework) can be handled by the CMS, taking this job away from staff and freeing up staff time. Data for menus is usually generated dynamically in real time, so if a link is changed, it's instantly reflected on all pages. There is no need to change the HTML for the link on every page that contains the link, and then re-upload all those pages to the server, saving time and bandwidth.

With a business intranet, it's not just the data itself that's important, the links between pieces of information are also important. A page of figures may be absolutely meaningless on its own, but linked to some other content it may be much more meaningful. This is analogous to an office filing cabinet: all relevant documents are kept together in a file, rather than being stored separately, to make them easy to find.

A good CMS will allow you to link related pieces of information to each other and make them available together, so they are viewed in the correct context. Once the link has been established, the CMS takes over and even if documents are moved, it maintains the correct links, which quickly becomes extremely difficult with a hand-maintained intranet. If you are using documents from other applications, such as Microsoft Word documents, or Adobe PDF files, the CMS should be able to track versions of the documents, and maintain links as with other types of content.

It can also categorize the data faster and more accurately than a human could, and so allows for more accurate search results, ensuring information never gets "lost" in the system.

Inconsistency

Another problem that often occurs with handmade intranets is that over time, parts of the site start to alter as different people take over. Each person has their own style and way of working, and so eventually parts of the site start to look and work differently from each other and use different ways of categorizing data.

Over time the whole purpose of the intranet (that is, sharing information between staff) starts to break down, and each department becomes separate from the others, and the whole point of building the intranet is lost.

How CMS Can Help

CMS can help enforce a consistent style, and can help to ensure that the information is categorized correctly by presenting a solid framework for the information. It maintains consistency between departments, and ensures that an employee feels as at home in another department's section of the intranet, as he or she does in their own department's section.

Over time the site can still evolve, and change to meet future needs, but the CMS package ensures that all departments change in the same direction, and keeps the changes consistent.

This again is another major benefit over maintaining a site by hand. When you have a large number of pages, maintained by different people who come and go, you can quickly end up with a mix of different styles and navigation systems. Although CSS can help with visual consistency, it still allows scope for abuse unless strictly managed.

The CMS handles the presentational aspects of the page and manages the links, ensuring consistency; a user who normally uses one part of the intranet, can easily use another part if necessary, instantly finding their way around to get the information they require.

It also helps to ensure that "accidents" don't happen and incorrect or private data appears. The CMS provides a rigid structure, and data can be checked by other staff members, for example, before it actually appears live. A CMS also provides an audit trail, allowing managers to easily see who added content and when it was added. This means that staff are ultimately responsible for the content they maintain and they are accountable for any mistakes. If you compare this to a hand-maintained system, you can see it's much more secure; with a hand-maintained system it can be difficult to show who added pieces of information, and who is responsible for that data.

Need for Rapid Growth

As more and more data is now being shared between businesses such as customer bases, transactions etc., it becomes increasingly difficult to keep track of all the information and allow it to be shared between staff. Staff in charge of the intranet can become overwhelmed with data, held back by the process of having to create a new intranet page for each piece of data, categorizing it, and adding links to it.

With hand-maintained systems, as greater volumes of content need to be added to the system, the intranet team soon becomes unable to cope, and skilled IT personnel become tied up doing repetitive tasks such as creating new pages and maintaining links.

CMS Can Help

CMS allows each staff member to enter data, subject to preset restrictions, so the intranet team doesn't get overloaded and the system will always contain the latest information.

A CMS actually gets more productive when it handles greater volumes of content

The system will also be able to scale according to the number of staff, and can work just as well with 100 staff, as it can with 10 staff.

Content Management Systems

A good CMS package should scale well in terms of the amount of information it can manage, and be easy to update and expand in the future as the needs of the intranet change and evolve. If you have a hand-maintained system, the intranet will always be slightly behind the times. As the intranet content grows, the lag will be greater and greater. The hand-management system becomes a larger and larger problem the more you use it.

On the other hand, a CMS actually gets more productive when it handles greater volumes of content, and since content is entered in realtime, the lag is eliminated. The CMS becomes more helpful the more it is used.

Cutting Costs and Increasing Productivity

Although a CMS package may initially involve a large outlay to set the system up, this is easily justified by the money the system saves over time. CMS will perform many jobs that previously staff had to do, freeing them up to perform other tasks.

It also allows staff to deal with the information more efficiently, and ensures that documents don't get "lost in the system". Staff are able to apply complex searches to find the data they need quickly, they can access the information from anywhere, and related documents can be linked to each other.

A CMS also ensures that everyone has access to up-to-date information, it makes staff accountable for the information they enter, and also checks can be enforced before a document goes live. Clearly, mistakes in information could cause major problems for a company, not only can mistakes make a company look unprofessional, if prices are wrong for example, mistakes could end up costing the company money.

Obtaining a CMS Package

In this section we're going to look at obtaining a CMS package, and the various options available, how you would go about selecting a particular CMS package, and how it applies to your intranet.

Selecting a CMS Package

Selecting a CMS package can be a daunting task. There are now a large number of "off-the-shelf" systems available, for use on a variety of different computer systems, and written in a variety of different languages. There is also a huge variation in price, ranging from free (under a GPL or similar license) to systems costing hundreds of thousands of dollars.

Alternatively you can create your own custom-built CMS specific to your business. This may in fact work out cheaper than one of the off-the-shelf packages, and you have the benefit that it's specifically targeted to your business's needs.

Setting Down the Goals

Before you can start looking at the various options available, it's very important to first identify your requirements, and what you want the CMS to achieve. The best way to do this is to ask heads of all the departments who will be using the system, to compile a list of goals that need to be achieved for that particular department. Rather than just sending a memo for example, it would be much better if someone involved in the development of the system briefed the staff on what information was required to help the department managers to create their list of goals that the system needs to achieve. Many of these goals will overlap with each other and can be combined.

When you're discussing what you need the CMS to achieve, it helps to think about the future, and try to anticipate any future directions that the intranet will take so you can choose a system that will still work and cater for these future needs.

It's also important to have a clear idea of the budget you have available, so that you can select a system that stays within your budget. It's important to allow some of the budget for costs which come after the system is purchased, for example if you need to hire consultants to set up the system.

Which Package to Choose?

Which package you choose will depend upon the size of the intranet, and the goals you want the CMS to achieve.

If your needs are fairly basic, and your intranet is fairly small, you could think about building one from scratch rather than an "off-the-shelf" system. It may be that your existing IT department will be able to complete such a project, if not you could always outsource the project to professional web programmers. If your needs are fairly simple, this could be the best option, and cheaper than buying a large commercial package.

> To find out more about effective ways of designing your own CMS, see Content Management Systems (Phil Suh, et al., glasshaus 1-9041511-06-X)

Alternatively, there are many open source CMS packages available, which could be used as a base, and then customized specifically for the company's needs. Having a large part of the project already completed, using an open source solution speeds up development time if you are building your own in-house CMS. An example of an open source CMS is PostNuke at *http://www.postnuke.com/*. This system is widely used on the Internet, and there are many different modules available to add in extra functions. An open source system gives you a huge advantage if you're developing a custom system; all of the code is available to you, so it's much easier to adapt the package to your needs, and to recode the whole system, which wouldn't be possible with a commercial system.

" *Using an open source solution speeds up development time if you are building your own in-house CMS* "

Open source systems are obviously much cheaper to set up than a commercial package would be, and there are some extremely powerful open source systems around.

Content Management Systems

Even if you need a very powerful CMS, it may still be feasible to design your own system from scratch, depending on how much development time and resources are available, otherwise you can go for an "off-the-shelf" commercial system that will be quicker to implement.

If you go for a commercial system it's important to look, not just at the system itself, but also at the business behind it. When you are buying such a system, make sure the vendor provides a good after-sales service, and buy from an established company which will probably still exist in a couple of years' time when you might want to upgrade the system.

It's also important to check whether the vendor provides training, as this will be needed by the IT staff who will be administering the system and maintaining the servers.

Although an off-the-shelf system is going to be faster to set up than developing your own system, you need to have an idea of the amount of time that the system will take to customize to your specific needs before the system can actually go live. You also need to think about who will be performing this customization; if it is to be done by the vendor it will be quicker since they know the package inside out, but it can also add extra costs to the development of the system.

Who's Going to Be Using the Package?

It's also important to think of the people using the CMS when it comes to choosing one. Bear in mind that it's likely to be used by all staff rather than just the IT staff, so it needs to be usable and intuitive, even to those who may only have a very basic level of computer knowledge.

No matter how simple the system is, you will still have to provide some training to get the staff used to the system. If you're going to build the package in-house, the training can be done by the department that designed the system.

If you are using an off-the-shelf commercial system, you will have to decide whether to do the training in-house (once the training staff have learned the package), or whether the software vendor can supply training and support. Good training and support is essential, as the system will essentially be useless if no one knows how to use it.

You also need to think about the IT staff that will typically be administering and maintaining the system. The new CMS may involve more complicated hardware for instance, and the IT staff will need adequate training.

Which Content Formats Need to Be Understood by the CMS?

As well as who is going to be using the intranet, you also need to look at which content formats and hardware appliances are in use by the company. For example, if a company has staff out on the road, it would be useful for them to connect to the intranet using a browser on a PDA or some sort of WAP device to retrieve information.

If this is the case, then you would want to make sure that the CMS can output data in WAP format for example, so that all staff can connect to the intranet, no matter which device they are using.

Even if you don't currently have staff on the road, it's still worth considering. Smaller devices such as WAP-enabled phones and PDAs are getting more powerful, and it's likely that in the near future they will be used a lot more. As such it is a good idea to cover yourself by implementing a CMS that can handle PDAs and other devices, and this applies even more if the CMS will also be running your web site.

In terms of software format, the CMS should be able to use and read the formats already in use by the company. For example, if the business is using Microsoft Office, then the CMS will need to be able to read Microsoft Word documents and Excel spreadsheets so that it can index the documents and make them available within the CMS.

What Computer Hardware Will Be Available to Run the System?

An important consideration in choosing a content management system is the hardware requirements. Many of the higher-end CMS packages need powerful dedicated servers and use complicated database systems. Clearly, this can mean it takes longer to set up the system and get it up and running.

The frontend of the system should be able to run on the staff's existing PCs, otherwise a large outlay will be needed to train staff and to purchase new hardware, and would cause a major inconvenience to the business. It's important that CMS can utilize the existing computer systems for its front end as these are the systems that the staff are familiar with.

How Long Will It Take to Deploy the System?

If you need a system that is fast to deploy, then an in-house custom-designed system will probably be out of the question, although development time can be cut by basing the system on an existing open source solution.

Commercial systems are much faster to deploy, but the time taken with each system must be looked at. A system may be fast to install, but you also need to consider how long it's going to take to customize so that it fits into your business and is integrated with your intranet. This time is often mistakenly not taken into account when people choose a CMS.

If you need a system that is fast to deploy, then an in-house custom-designed system will probably be out of the question

When Should the System Be Implemented?

The answer to this is as soon as possible, the longer you wait to implement a content management system, the more data that has to be migrated into the new system, and the longer it will take to get the system up and running.

Also the sooner CMS is implemented, the sooner you will start to see the benefits for your business and allow staff to work more efficiently.

If You Already Have a CMS

If you are already using some form of CMS, it may be time to take another look at how the system is performing. CMS automatically handles all the routine tasks and administration of a web site or intranet, but because they're low maintenance, over time they can be taken for granted.

As businesses evolve, their needs change and so does the type and quantity of information that they handle. After a while the CMS can lag behind, become outdated and perform inefficiently, or it might be transferring tasks back to the staff, for example staff might be forced to convert data into a format compatible with the existing system.

Content Management Systems

It's important to periodically review your CMS, just to check it is performing optimally. As well as the IT department reviewing the system for performance, it's important to speak to the staff who actually use the system on a daily basis, as they will be most qualified to point out bottlenecks or problem areas, and it is likely that you will find problems that you were previously unaware of.

Although this sounds like a major task, the more often a review of the system is carried out, the less work is needed as minor niggles can by nipped in the bud before they develop into major problems. It's much easier to maintain the system with frequent minor updates, rather than leaving the system until it starts to fall apart.

If your existing CMS creates log files, a huge amount of useful information can be gained from them. You can use them to find out which areas of the system are most widely used, and areas which are hardly used, either because a problem exists, or they're no longer relevant. Studying usage patterns helps to see which parts of the system are most important, and which areas need to be looked at and either "revived" or removed from the system.

To find out more about web traffic analysis, Practical Web Traffic Analysis (Peter Fletcher, et al., glasshaus 1-904151-18-3) contains interesting case studies of major web sites such as the BBC and eBay, detailing how they analyze their log files.

It also helps to analyze the user patterns, and the paths people take to reach the data. Frequently used data could be made more easily available higher up the menu hierarchy for example, to make it easier to get to, without having to navigate through a network of menus and submenus. Less frequently used data can be moved down the menu hierarchy; if it is rarely used it will not matter that a longer route is needed to get to the information.

Considering One CMS for the Intranet and Web Site

It's almost certain that if you have a company intranet it's also very likely that you have a company web site. If this is the case it makes sense to use CMS for the whole system, managing both the web site and the company intranet.

Doing it this way means that you do not have to duplicate information, and publish separately for the intranet and web site. Having one centralized copy of your data is also better in terms of data integrity, and saves you having to update the same documents twice, which could lead to errors.

Even though the CMS manages both the intranet and the web site, you can still keep the intranet private for internal staff only by using a private network separated from the Internet by a firewall, whereas the web site is of course open to everyone. You need to bear this in mind when selecting CMS, and make sure that it is able to handle this scenario. Security needs to be looked at in more depth if information is being served out to the Internet.

It's important that the CMS you choose can handle the needs of both the web site and the intranet. The web site needs are likely to be quite different from the needs of the intranet, and it may have a different design to the company intranet. Alternatively, two different systems could be used, one for the intranet, and one for the Internet, but both systems sharing the same data from a central data store.

Aligning with the Corporate Platform

When choosing your CMS, it's also important to look at how well it will fit in the framework of the company: in terms of design and the way it looks, but also in the way it works, and the software it works with.

In terms of design and looks, the CMS needs to be flexible and easily customizable. Some of the lower-end CMS packages use templates for the site, and you are limited to how much you can alter the templates. A good system will be flexible in terms of page design, and should be able to be modified to incorporate the business's look, colors, branding, etc. This is especially important if the CMS will also be running the company's web site.

It's likely that most interaction with the CMS will be through a browser, so ensure the existing browser base is suitable to work with the chosen CMS package. Different browsers have different capabilities; Microsoft Internet Explorer for example, has better integration with Windows and allows you to drag and drop from other Windows programs, which can make the system more user-friendly for staff. With an intranet, you have the luxury of choosing to target a specific browser and have everyone in the company use that browser, rather than having to lose functionality by making the intranet work across all browsers.

Meeting Intranet Needs

As a CMS is usually a significant investment for a business, it's important that you choose the right system from the start, and that it can handle all the needs that will be placed upon it by the intranet, as well as allowing for future growth.

Supporting Intranet Size and Structure

It's likely that if you are using an intranet already, you'll want to keep a similar structure, since the staff will already be familiar with it, and it will be easier to integrate your existing intranet with CMS.

This should be a requirement when you're evaluating different CMS packages, as they need to be flexible enough to support your existing structure, rather than having to change your intranet structure to fit round the CMS.

> Make sure that the CMS is powerful enough to cope with the huge amounts of information that most businesses generate on a day to day basis. Bear in mind that the volume of information business's processes always rises, especially as businesses become connected to each other and to various information services. This being the case, the CMS should be designed to cope with the current volume of data, but should also have enough capacity to cope with increased amounts of data in the future.

Content Management Systems

Helping Staff Find Information

The ultimate purpose of CMS is to make data retrieval easy, and so staff members don't have to waste time searching for the information they need.

There are many different systems available, and the search facilities they offer vary a lot, usually depending on price. The search facilities are one of the most important parts of CMS, and should be extensively evaluated to make sure they can live up to your needs. The system should have the ability for custom searches to be specifically adapted for the company's needs.

We mentioned earlier that the system should also be able to understand relationships between documents so it works in a similar way to a folder in a filing cabinet: if a document is opened, other documents related to this document are linked. Take a customer's record, for example; when it is opened, the system will show links to any information that is related to that particular customer. To do this the CMS should have a good search facility and indexing system. This obviously has many benefits for staff; they always have all the information about a subject to hand, allowing them to make more informed decisions.

Simple Authoring for Busy Staff

Another important factor to consider is how usable the CMS is, and whether it can be used intuitively by people with basic computing skills: the easier the system is to use, the more staff will use it.

The CMS should offer a wide range of input options so that the CMS management staff can create HTML documents, including those containing JavaScript. However normal users of the system who work with the data and have no web design knowledge shouldn't need to know any specialist languages to enter information into the system. It's important that information already entered is easy to find and update, otherwise staff will be unlikely to update it, defeating the object of the system.

Usually with a system such as an intranet, the interface for the CMS is web-based, and allows the user to view and edit information through their web browser. Most staff will already be familiar with using a browser, so they are at home right from the start without having to cope with a new application interface.

It's important for there to be a system in place so that separate user types can be set up. The everyday staff should only be able to see the sections of the interface that they use, while the rest of the application interface for more advanced setup is hidden. There's no point in showing the staff options they cannot use, as it only serves to confuse and add extra clutter to the interface.

Mix-and-Match Authoring Tools

The aim of CMS is to draw from a wide range of authors, and it's almost certain that the staff will be using many different programs to create content: word processors, spreadsheets, graphic applications, and so on.

The CMS needs to be flexible and should be able to interpret many different forms of information and data formats, for example reading common word processor formats. The aim is for the system to convert the data from one form to another, rather than the author having to convert the data from one form to another before inputting into the system. Introducing CMS should ideally cause as little disruption as possible, and the CMS should fit round the business, rather than the other way round. This means that the CMS should allow users to continue working with the tools they were using before the CMS was introduced.

It's important that the CMS caters for all of the tools that will be used to create content, and allow users to use their tool of choice, rather than being dictated to by the system.

Centralized or Decentralized Authoring

An important decision to make before selecting a CMS package is whether to allow **decentralized authoring** (where all staff can freely add and maintain content), or **centralized authoring** (where only a dedicated CMS team enter and maintain content).

Decentralized Authoring

Most companies using CMS will opt for a decentralized authoring model, and allow all staff members to add content if required, because this is, after all, one of the goals of the CMS. Using decentralized authoring saves on having to have a specialized team that creates and edits intranet content, which saves money and allows all staff to be involved in the system so they use it to its maximum potential.

It is however important that you allow employees the time to enter new content, rather than expect them to just fit it into the schedule. If staff are busy and are not given time to enter new content, it's likely that the content will not get entered, rendering the CMS pointless; however the extra time needed to add content can be offset against the large amount of time that the system saves.

Centralized Authoring

Centralized authoring involves setting up a special team; that will solely be in charge of the CMS and entering and maintaining the content it contains.

This allows stricter control of the content, but has the disadvantage that you're limiting the amount of content that can be added, and you miss out on a lot of potential input from your staff. Centralized authoring limits the power of the Content Management System.

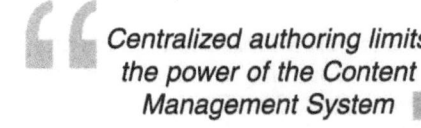
Centralized authoring limits the power of the Content Management System

Centralized authoring is typically used when there is a limit to the amount of content on the intranet, and where the information is complex, highly structured, or available to external users.

Delivering Single Sign-on

One function a CMS which runs an intranet needs is security with different user levels so that access to certain information can be controlled. Although the point of the CMS is to share information, there will be times when you want to make sure that some information, such as business accounts, for example, can only be seen by certain staff.

8

Content Management Systems

In order for a secure system to be effective, it needs to be simple for authorized users to access the information without having to spend time going through many different levels of security. If it's complicated to log in, staff will usually write instructions including their usernames and passwords, and stick them somewhere convenient such as to the side of the monitor, which renders even the best security system useless.

Most business computer system "break-ins", where a system's security is compromised and confidential information leaked, are "inside jobs" carried out by staff working for the company. Many businesses underestimate the importance of security in the workplace when it comes to accessing the company intranet, but break-ins usually occur where staff have easy access to someone else's login information.

The system is actually more secure with a single sign-on, with a username and password that are strong but also memorable. This avoids the temptation of staff to write down their passwords, and they won't need instructions to log in. It's also important for the login to apply to all areas of the system that the user has access to instead of repeatedly asking the user to input their username and password when moving between different sections of the intranet. Single sign-on also cuts down on the amount of time needed to administer users, and cuts down on the number of user accounts that need to be created.

If the CMS is going to be serving a web site as well as the company intranet, security needs are higher, since you are greatly increasing the access to the system and it will now be open to attacks from outside the company. A good firewall and virus-checking system are essential to protect the CMS. Alternatively the intranet and Internet sites could be split onto separate networks and servers (but still accessing the same central data store) to minimize the risk of the system being compromised.

Enterprise Application Integration (EAI)

We previously mentioned the importance of integrating the CMS with other applications that are currently in use in the company: the CMS should also be able to access reports generated, for example, by the accounts system, without requiring the user to convert the format of the data.

It's important that the applications used on a daily basis can communicate with the back-end servers running the CMS, and are able to use information stored in the CMS from within the application. The CMS must be able to use the company's LAN or WAN and have the correct protocols to be able to send data over the network. Businesses like to get the maximum usage out of equipment, so the vast majority of the system should run with the existing hardware available.

As we mentioned earlier, most interaction with the CMS will take place through a browser so it's important that the existing company browser base is looked at, and possibly upgraded to work better with the CMS. With browsers, most version changes typically affect the back end of the browser: the interface doesn't often change. This means that staff are familiar with the browser, even after an upgrade. Many of the earlier browsers are fairly limited in their abilities, so in this case, a browser upgrade in order to work with the CMS can be justified.

Implementing Workflow

Another factor that must be considered is the workflow, or system that is used by the CMS, and how close that is to the existing business system.

Workflow is the automation of a business process and describes the chain of events that occurs as information or tasks are transferred from one stage to the next, according to a set procedure. Each stage in the chain is referred to as an **Activity,** and an Activity could involve interaction between one person and another or a person entering data into a computer for processing.

Often when you study your existing workflow, you may finds steps which may be unnecessary, or are repetitive and are ideally suited to being automated.

The CMS should allow you to use a workflow and processes very similar to the ones the business is used to, and should allow you to create custom workflows to ensure that the system is up to date with the business's practices you use, even if they change in the future.

Before the CMS is chosen, the existing workflows should be analyzed to get a clear overall picture of the current system, and to ensure that the new CMS is compatible with the current workflows in use. It should be a case of the CMS adapting its workflows to fit with the current business workflows, rather than the other way round.

There are however, some extra workflow tasks that come with the content management system, that need to be carried out periodically by staff. Examples of these extra workflow tasks are managing users, for example adding or deleting users, maintaining log files and backups, maintaining security, and so on. Each CMS will have its own workflows, and you need to consider who will be carrying out these tasks, and how much time it will take them, and how much training they will need to learn how to carry out these tasks. Once the CMS is in place, It's important to periodically review the system to check that the CMS workflows are still aligned to the current business workflows in practice.

It's also important to decide who will implement the content management system and customize it with the company's existing workflows, and whether this will be carried out in-house or by external consultants. This will largely depend on the skills of the existing intranet staff.

CMS – Summary

Hopefully this chapter has raised your awareness of CMS, and has made you interested in finding out more about it.

To learn more about Content Management Systems, it can help to look at some of the open source CMS systems available, as they are free to download and give you a practical example of what a CMS can do. Although some may be too basic for your needs, it will help you to get accustomed to CMS before you look more a more advanced system.

Some of the most popular open source CMSs are PostNuke, which is available at *http://www.postnuke.com/* and EZ Source at *http://developer.ez.no/*. Both have a large user base, and have a large number of modules available to add extra functionality. If you are looking seriously at an open source solution an excellent resource is *http://www.cmsinfo.org* which links to a wide range of open source Content Management Systems.

There are a huge number of commercial Content Management Systems available, and many companies that have developed a custom system for themselves try to recoup some of the outlay by selling their system to others, leading to a wide range of packages, some good, some not so good. It's very important to fully evaluate a CMS before purchase to make sure it can meet all of your needs, current and future.

> *For a much more in-depth look at CMS, we recommend Content Management Systems (Phil Suh, et al., glasshaus 1-904151-06-X). You can find full details about this book from the books section of the glasshaus web site, http://www.glasshaus.com/bookInfo.asp?bookId=65, and it's an ideal guide for learning more about CMS and offers much more advice on choosing a CMS.*

Other Publishing Technologies

As well as CMS, there are also many other types of information publishing technologies, and in this section we take a look at a few of the different systems available, and how they could be useful to your intranet.

Portals

Portals are an online information gateway, and act as an anchor point to many different sources of information. Portals generally cover one type of information, and sort the links to this information into categories and bring a logical order to the information to make retrieval quicker and easier. Whereas an intranet covers a wide area in the content it contains, portals tend to be focused towards specific areas of content.

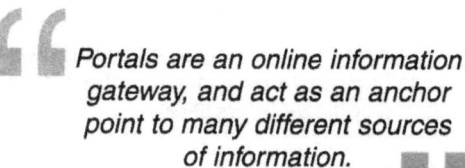

Portals are an online information gateway, and act as an anchor point to many different sources of information.

A portal is different from an intranet in that an intranet is a content site containing information that the user requires, and a portal is a site a user visits to locate a particular content site. Although most portals are focused towards a certain subject area, there are also portals springing up which are less focused, such as the ones created by Excite, MSN, and AOL. These portals provide links to other content on the Web as well as their own content.

Using an internal business example, you could create a portal for your company's sales team. This would bring together links to information specifically for that department, such as links to customer records, and customer administration sections of the intranet. It could also include links to supplier's web sites, so the sales team can check prices etc. All the information the sales team needs will be brought together into one place, organized into logical categories, to make it as easy as possible for the staff to access the information they need.

Portals have a reputation of being fairly simple, but the technology has evolved quickly and can interface with many different types of systems and applications to pull all the different data into one place. They can provide users inside and outside the business with an integrated and personalized interface to a range of business content including information, business applications, and expertise.

Many companies are now developing web portals, with information relevant to the type of business. As well as a medium for displaying the company's services etc., they also bring together relevant industry news pulled from other sources, and links to relevant information. This makes the site more attractive to the end users, because it's not just acting as a brochure, but also as a source of useful information. More users will return to spend more time on the company's site because all the information they need is in one place. It's also likely that they will tell their colleagues which increases the popularity of your site.

> *If you are interested in portals, you can start by looking at some of the existing portals available. If you simply search for the word "Portal" in one of the major search engines, you'll get a huge number of portal sites returned covering a wide range of different subjects. There are also a large number of software vendors offering portal software, for example IBM has a portal toolkit for their WebSphere software platform, please see http://www-3.ibm.com/software/info1/websphere /index.jsp?tab=products/portal for more information about portals, and how they can be used by a business.*

Document Management Systems

Document Management Systems allow a business to store all the documents they generate in a centralized repository. The Document Management System categorizes the data, and has powerful search and retrieval facilities to allow the user to quickly find the information they require. They allow users to upload and download documents, and can track user changes. They allow people in different departments to easily collaborate without overwriting each other's data, as well as maintaining version control and user permissions.

A Document in this sense is defined as a container for information. Document Management is a structured, systematic approach to controlling, describing, indexing, storing, retrieving, and sharing the information contained in your documents. With electronic storage costs so low, over time, a huge amount of documents will be archived, and without a good system it will become increasingly difficult for users to find the information they are looking for.

The Document Management System also controls security, so confidential documents can only be seen by staff with correct authentication details. Version control is also implemented, so changes to documents can be rolled back if necessary, and it ensures that staff do not accidentally overwrite each other's alterations to documents.

Document Management Systems are usually coupled with imaging systems, such as high-speed scanners, and use OCR (Optical Character Recognition) to "read" the document, classify the data it contains, and store it in the repository. This allows for the "paperless office", as all documents are stored in the computer system rather than in physical filing cabinets. This has a number of advantages:

- Backups can be taken off premises in the form or removable hard drives, tape cartridges, and so on, where it would be impossible to store copies of all paper documents outside the premises due to the volume of paper involved. Backed-up data is actually more secure if there was a fire for example and could easily be recovered, unlike if a filing cabinet is destroyed in a fire and the information it contained would be lost forever. Recent DMS systems have built-in compression routines for storing documents, and this increases the amount of data that can be stored on the storage medium, and increases document management efficiency.

- Documents are categorized and indexed so advanced search operations can be used to find any document quickly, wherever the employee is located in the company, without having to go and get a physical copy of the information from a filing cabinet.

- Documents are easily shared between departments, and are stored centrally, rather than each department having to have a separate copy of the information.

There are many different Document Management Systems available, and they need to be evaluated in a similar depth as you would with a CMS; there is a large variation in prices and abilities of the various systems on offer. Many vendors are now selling both the software and the hardware (like scanning equipment and so on) and this is usually cheaper than buying the hardware and software separately, from different vendors.

A good resource for finding out more about Document Management Systems is Comp Info, the Computer Information Center. On its document management page at *http://www.compinfo-center.com/docs/document_management.htm* there are a number of links to sources of more information about different aspects of DMS systems. There are also a large number of books available from Amazon, specifically about Document Management Systems.

Discussion Groups and Web Logs

Discussion groups are hugely popular, and there are now many different types of discussion group systems, for example newsgroups, which allows discussions through a newsreader. Alternatively, web-based forums can be used, and both of these formats are becoming more and more popular. They allow relatively quick interaction between people, either inside a business, or as a support medium for the business's clients. Information is displayed in threads, where each thread represents an individual conversation, so a message and its replies are kept together.

All discussion groups however serve the same purpose, which is human interaction. As the name suggests they are designed for discussing and sharing information, and tend to be fast-growing sources on information between a large number of people. They allow people to easily collaborate on any information, and receive fast replies. Discussions are divided up into topics and are usually threaded, and viewed in a hierarchical format so you can easily see which reply is to which message visually. Search facilities are provided so you can find all threads about a particular subject, and easily locate specific information.

One of the most common applications of discussion groups is for dealing with questions and answers. One person posts a question, and then other people who know the answer reply, usually fairly quickly, and sometimes this might spark off a discussion about the best answer to the question. It has the advantage that old messages are held in searchable archives, so people can quickly find the answer if their question has come up in the past, without having to repost the question again.

Web logs, or Blogs as they are more commonly known, are similar to journals, although in a business sense they don't contain personal information, but business information. They are fast moving and usually contain information which has a fairly short lifespan, rather than being put in "long-term storage" on a web page for example. Usually they show information for a short amount of time, a week, or a day, perhaps. Information that appears on the blog isn't necessarily lost once it has reached the expiry time, but it's no longer viewable by default.

A blog is similar to an online version of Post-it notes, where snippets of information are added by the staff regarding the latest project, for example. They tend to be more informal and are good for allowing staff to brainstorm and share thoughts and ideas.

Many companies have blogs open to the public to share information about recent company news, or answer frequently asked questions for example. It allows the business to have more freedom to share information with its clients which wouldn't normally be shared. They have the advantage that clients go there because they want to read the information contained, rather than forcing information on the client in the form of an e-mail that they are less likely to read. As blogs are usually informal, they allow a more personal relationship with the customer.

A large number of links to articles and information about Blogs can be found at
http://www.marketingterms.com/dictionary/blog/.

Web logs and Discussion forums will be discussed in greater depth in the next chapter.

Summary

Implementing CMS within your business isn't something that can be taken lightly, and may initially require a large outlay, but over time will more than pay for itself: both in the money it saves, and by making the business and staff more efficient. More and more businesses are using Content Management Systems and they're fast becoming a business essential. In this chapter we looked at the benefits of CMS and we discussed some of the different ways in which a CMS can be implemented on your intranet.

9

- Communication technologies
- Using forums to build a knowledge base
- Demonstration systems

Author: John Colby

The Intranet As Communications Platform

Many companies and organizations know that they have a problem with communications. Typically, a company will appoint people to oversee the development of communications. Their brief is commonly built round the words "effective" and "efficient" and maybe "attributable". One problem for any organization with many individuals is the organization and management of e-mail. This form of communication, although fast (efficient) and providing a record of transactions (attributable) may be taking over and the sheer volume of mail may reduce its effectiveness. The aim may be to provide a more widespread communications platform. Consider the following situation:

You are anywhere in the world. You have a question, or you've become stuck and are unsure about something you're doing in your job. You have access to a communications device with Internet facility, so you e-mail someone with the question that will solve the problem. They mail you back, and your problem is solved.

What happens when someone else has a similar question? Another e-mail, another reply. And again... and again. There is a proliferation of e-mail on the same subject which all takes time, especially for the person to whom all the queries are directed. And they have their own job to do.

Let's analyze this from an operational point of view. There is no problem with answering questions via e-mail. In fact it's a very good medium for that. However, if someone has a similar problem then you have to repeat the process. So what do you do? Copy the e-mail to everyone who is likely to need it? Hardly, as the load on the e-mail servers would be immense and the avalanche of unnecessary information would just be too much, the answer you want would soon be buried among all the other answers that you don't need. And then again, those who receive these e-mails may be a subset of those who actually need to know the information you're imparting. What this chapter does is discuss effective ways of sharing information, the software for their implementation, and managing your company's communications resource.

So what are the options for using the intranet as a communications resource? What do we want out of it? You could consider many solutions, forums, chatrooms, mailing lists, Wiki, FAQ lists, conferencing, and proprietary solutions such as NetMeeting. Some are a way of making conferencing facilities more widely and more economically available while others provide a transactional record of the messages. How you wish to implement any of these is dependent on your own needs. We'll deal with them in more detail as we proceed.

In this chapter we will cover the following areas:

- The solutions in general: – Including information on forums and discussion groups, chatrooms and messaging, and what purpose they serve.

- Concerns about the information – Security, privacy and accountability, validity and relevance, accessibility, legal requirements, moderation, and administration

- Control – How controlled is your information? Is it too tightly or too loosely managed? Who is responsible? What issues may arise from creating a knowledge base?

- Demonstration Systems – Setting up a demonstration forum or chatroom system.

Communication Technologies

Here we'll look at where each of the application mentioned fits within an intranet, and more importantly, where they don't. Be prepared to adapt anything you find here to your own situation of course. You might also find that one technology leads into another; for instance, chatrooms can sometimes lead to some other system that records information on a more permanent basis.

Forums and Discussion Groups

Forums and discussion groups are a way of managing virtual conversations with a permanent record. They require a web server and application to manage the forum. The great advantage is that they only need to hold one record of each posting and thus are more economical on disk space than mailing lists. However they do need moderation and have to be consciously looked at by the participants rather than something appearing in their mail inbox. Moderation also means that offensive postings can be dealt with as appropriate. However if the moderator is too heavy-handed then a lot of the value of a forum is lost as it will both reflect that moderator's bias and become less used. Forums usually allow linking to other web pages or downloads – a great advantage when information needs to be available – and only those needing the download need obtain it (for example mailing lists, where everyone gets it).

A forum can also be viewed as an information-gathering exercise

If used correctly, a forum can also be viewed as an information-gathering exercise and form the basis of a company knowledge base, as can other forms of communication. A forum is already part way to being a knowledge base, because the whole series of the contributions to the discussion are visible on one page rather than in separate e-mails.

Mailing Lists

It's easy to set up a discussion mailing list – everyone gets everything presented to them and they can reply to the same group of people. There are numerous Internet sites where this technology is used to great effect – and many Internet users are subscribed to several mailing lists.

There are, of course, advantages. Your users get the information delivered to their inbox without having to take any further action or having to remember to visit a web site, so there is a guaranteed delivery of information. One great and important use of mailing lists is by administrators of intranet systems to broadcast news and to promote the use of the intranet.

Mailing lists are a long-standing technology that work cross-time zones, allow for easy archiving and storing, and allow access from all areas of the world. They are easily searchable too, especially if you keep a full archive that can be imported into the mailbox of new employees. Send a question via your cellphone, check for replies with your PDA, get updates on your laptop later. It also solves the problem of accessibility as most people with disabilities already have some method to handle "reading" e-mail.

If you are trying to create a continuity of information then a mailing system falls down somewhat as there will be different retentions and deletions of previous contributors' mail, unless everyone retains all the content of all previous e-mails. Clearly this will mean an incredible waste of bandwidth and disk space. In intranet terms it means that every message is stored on every person's mail storage area, either on a mail server or locally on their own hard drive, which is probably wasteful. It also means that attachments, if you allow them, will also be duplicated. Internal network traffic will increase to be able to cope with the extra demand. Whether this is the most efficient solution for you is for you to determine. Additionally if the mailing list messages are archived onto a web site, the whole company can see the whole of the message sequence – again an overhead in storage, but one you may be prepared to accept.

Chatrooms

Chatrooms can be useful as an inexpensive conference facility, especially if the users are widely distributed geographically. For informal chats they are very good, but they do not leave a permanent record. The costs are much less as you do not have a separate telephone call charge, or, if there are more than two people, the additional cost burden of a conference call.

Wiki

According to one definition, 'wiki' is a composition system; it's a discussion medium; it's a repository; it's a mail system; it's a tool, we don't know quite what it is, but it's a fun way of communicating asynchronously across the network while dynamically sharing your ideas (from *http://c2.com/cgi/wiki*). This said – in intranet terms it's an 'anyone edit' web page. So it could be useful for your intranet as long as your users are quite confident and web-savvy and know how web pages work. If your organization falls into this category, then it is an avenue that could be explored further, but in my opinion it is only really for the minority of intranets. It is quite hard to police – as someone has to be on their toes to ensure that postings remain on topic, are correct – all the normal policing of any discussion with a permanent record however it is hosted. However, one of the necessary features of Wiki is that anyone can edit and delete anything – so you have to be sure of your audience/users.

However it is a useful development tool for the teams developing the intranet as they can share ideas and contribute. We'll leave it just with this mention.

FAQ lists

FAQ – Frequently Asked Questions – a one-way communication device. A FAQ list must be kept up to date to be of use. And how you determine what are the questions frequently asked can be a problem. All too often on the Internet as a whole FAQ lists are manufactured by the site owners and bear only a passing resemblance to real-world situations. From the use of forums you could construct FAQ lists – but this will not be interactive and probably not reflect the burning questions. However, using a FAQ for a support team may be a very good way of distributing knowledge, but essentially it is a one-way channel.

Webcasts, Conferencing, and Messaging

Voice over the intranet will save costs on phone calls for Webcasts, conferencing, and messaging. It does need sound on each client PC, something that many corporate machines do not have. If you wish to add video, then fast network connections are almost essential and you will have to add cameras to take advantage. While these hardware additions are relatively inexpensive individually, the cost of equipping the whole workforce may be prohibitive and there will be a significant bandwidth hit on your network. Several competing products (mostly not free) are available for use with your intranet. You will have to decide on how best you should proceed.

One free product that fits these purposes is Microsoft NetMeeting – more information about this product can be found at http://www.microsoft.com/windows/netmeeting/

Forums and Discussion Groups

What are forums and discussion groups in this context? A forum is an online community where visitors may read and post topics of common interest. A discussion group is a group of people who like to discuss mutually interesting topics online. For the purposes of the intranet they amount to the same thing.

In an Internet environment you would certainly commit the records of a forum to a retrievable database, but in a discussion group you may not necessarily. In the intranet, you're much more concerned with retaining that body of knowledge generated for future use by members of the company. Indeed it becomes so valuable as a resource that it should rapidly transform itself into a knowledge base. If you don't do that, what is its eventual use? Do you throw the information away? For the sake of the company it would normally be retained – because a number of questions and responses will invariably come up again.

So let's define our requirement as a virtual place where a series of discussions can occur and that are recorded so that they become a reference for others as well as the people who took part in the discussion. To do this we need a datastore. The forum software will normally define the datastore that is required, be it a database, a file, or XML. Each has its benefits and costs; relational databases are very flexible but need an administrator and management, flat files are much simpler but can grow very large and become unmanageable, and XML has the advantage of becoming a standard data interchange format but will need web-based administration to keep it in place and readable. We'll deal with software more specifically at the end of this chapter.

Whatever datastore you choose, someone in the company should have an insight into what's being stored and in what format, so that it can be extracted if necessary and form a different type of record. Let's say that you need to rewrite a procedure manual, and you decide to see what users are finding troublesome, you can search the database and find a lot of information in the form of ongoing questions, which you can refine for your procedural documentation. This, of course, is always assuming that you've set up the forums to be an information point for in-company processes, and not just message rooms where people organize Friday lunch times. There's room for that type of message on the forum, but it shouldn't be its primary purpose.

Defining the Forum

So let's define what a forum looks like. With forum software you divide your forum into subject areas and users generate threads, and replies are posted under these threads. Moderators look after the forums in their charge, maybe answering queries but making sure that the forums stay on topic and are used and not abused. They may also delete irrelevant or offensive postings. We'll deal with policing the forum in this way later in this chapter.

We will outline the setup for a typical forum. The specific details will be determined by the forum software you use or alternatively, you may want to code the forum yourself. Forums are typically designed top-down, although arriving at precisely what is included in those forums will involve an iterative design process where you may want to list all the topics that should occur. They are then grouped, and reviewed and altered as necessary. Simplicity and directness should be the key here – too complex a forum may well discourage users from knowing where to start. All design decisions, and this includes whether you will be writing your own software from scratch or not, need to take the audience into account. As with all software you should be putting yourself in the position of the user and looking at the problem from their angle. Put yourself in the place of the average user and you may be surprised at the level of simplicity they demand. We're not denigrating the user here as their prime aim in life is not to make forums but to get on with their jobs, which is what we're trying to assist them in doing. And the lower barriers we put in their paths the better for them and for the organization.

Hierarchy	Actions	Who?
Forums	Created from the forum software. Most forums demand top-down design, so a little work with pen and paper beforehand is necessary.	Administrator
Groups	Sets the framework for each forum. Groups are merely heads for sets of topics.	Administrator
Topics	Sets the framework for each group. Topics form the main operational structure of each forum, and are placed in groups for convenience.	Administrator
	Control over the postings in the forum.	Moderators
Threads	Can open new threads. Summary displays of the threads in a forum are universal in forum software so that users can quickly scan them and find out what's been posted beforehand.	Registered users
	Review the title and structure of the threads created by users. Can move threads between forums.	Moderators
Posts	Can post messages in the threads they have just created.	Registered users
	Able to review/change/move/delete.	Moderators
Replies	Can reply to messages in existing threads.	Registered users
	Able to review/change/move/delete.	Moderators
View only	Unless the user is registered they should not be able to post. The reasons are discussed further in this chapter	Anonymous/Guest

You will, of course, have to declare a purpose for your forums. It may be that it is more convenient for you to construct several forums dealing with specific aims – for instance you may wish to separate queries relating to hardware, software, procedures, training, or anything that your company requires. How this decision is reached is up to the company involved but should have leeway for change should things not work out as planned. From experience, micro-detail planning at this stage is unwise – you will have to change things as the forums develop so allow yourself the necessary freedom. As we mentioned in *Chapter 6*, asking users what they need is often the best way to start when deciding on site organization.

You may find it best to start out with a few very general topics (if you're in a computing environment you may choose software, hardware, and so on) and let more specific forums grow naturally. If 75% of the traffic is about Outlook, then you may want to make a separate forum for Outlook, but if you start out with a separate forum for Outlook and no one uses it, then you have to deal with removing it and any old references to it. It's like booking a room for a lecture; if you have a choice between a room for 100 people or a room for 150 people and you aren't sure how many people will come, take the smaller room. If you get 105 people they'll be impressed with how popular it was, if you book the larger room and get 75 people, it looks like a bigger gap. Similarly, if you set up ten forums and four are popular, it looks like a failure, but set up three and find that you have to add a fourth and it's growth. It also saves you from asking ten people to be moderators of forums when you only need four.

Having declared the purpose of the forum and set up its structure you have to tell your users what you expect of them. At the top of each forum it would be helpful if you declare its purpose and some broad limits about what would normally be expected. Along with this it would normally be necessary to put some sort of caveat about responsibility for the accuracy and acceptability of postings.

You need also to be aware of the costs of the forum – if you have chosen to moderate all postings prior to publication then this will be a cost in time to those performing the moderation service. Your ROI will have to be modified as a result. However in most public and private forums moderation of every post is seen as an expensive overhead as well as downgrading the forum as users are not then considered adult and responsible enough to make their own statements. If there are registered forum users who abuse the system then it may be necessary to moderate their posts, or you may care to moderate posts of new users. Frustration can occur and your forum may not be used if you are too heavy-handed. Be aware, however, that corporate management may not see your users as responsible and ask questions – be prepared with your answers however you see them. The way I and a colleague have had to deal with this when a user posted an question critical of company policy (born out of frustration) was to stand up for the user. We asked whether the storm in a teacup that was being brewed was really for the good of the company and whether the poster may have had a point. The objection disappeared.

One of the great things about a forum on the company intranet is that it can be international and is not time zone-dependent. Thus employees from any part of the globe can access and be party to ongoing discussions and contribute. People doing similar jobs can communicate and feed off each other's ideas. However this brings us to the realm of language – if several different languages are spoken in your organization then you will have to handle it in whatever way is practicable. Whether this means having translation engines or by declaring a 'forum language' is up to you and the way your company is structured.

Chatrooms

An intranet relay chatroom is an ideal place for informal typed-message discussion over distances. Here people can, as the description says, chat with much lower cost than a telephone conference call. Whether the chatroom is hosted by a server on your intranet or on one of the many free web services available is up to you. There's an advantage in hosting one internally as then security is less likely to be compromised. There are various chat programs around for which you have to provide a host and are usually either Java-based with applets or HTML/script-based that are generated periodically by the server. However if your chats are not going to carry sensitive information you may consider using someone like Bravenet – who provide a Java chat that's very fast but is advertising-supported. For this you will need to have Java enabled in each browser and be able to resolve any firewall issues involved.

There are advantages to chatrooms, the major one being cost. There are also several disadvantages that may, or may not, be important for you.

The first disadvantage is one of non-permanence – in the first section of this chapter we discussed the desirability of recording information for eventual possible transformation into the company knowledge base. With many chatrooms no record is kept, so if substantive discussions take place then someone should be responsible for making a note of the discussion and transcribe the conclusions onto one of your permanent forums. Whether this responsibility is imposed on one of the chatters, takes the form of a minutes secretary, or whether (and in my mind best) someone volunteers is up to you.

The second disadvantage is in the undoubted fact that this planet is an oblate spheroid spinning round a small star located in a galaxy – we have time differences between countries. To chat, people have to be online at the same time, and this may mean working odd hours in some countries. From experience in doing this there is no 'right' time to chat – someone has to get up early or stay up late. You have to schedule these things and adapt to fit. It seems to work that if you have regular chats, then the timing for them should be varied so that different people are working at 11pm their time.

If you are going to set up an international chat then you need to agree (or publish) a time for this to occur. One scheme is to try and find out the individual times that exist in each country from somewhere like *http://greenwichmeantime.com/* and express the meeting time as that time and the local times of likely participants, such as "Chat tomorrow, 16:00 BST (15:00 GMT, 10:00 EDT). Another suitable method is to use the UT (Universal Time – essentially the same as GMT) convention and let the users work it out as you may make a mistake. This is really good if your users have correctly set their time zone and daylight saving preferences so they know, but some users are known to leave their time zones set at Seattle time.

If you're going to allow people to do access out of local hours would they be more inclined to use it if they could access it from outside the office, especially at home? And if so, how are you going to arrange security and privacy? I'm talking here about home workers and people on customer sites – this is not advocating participation in forums in 'unpaid overtime' mode. If participation in your forums starts out voluntary and ends up mandatory and part of the appraisal or review processes for each employee then that seems like a backwards step. However participation in and moderation of forums should really not be a prime activity for anyone – you don't want projects getting behind schedule because staff are involved in question and answer sessions.

Messaging

The final mode of non-e-mail communication is instant messaging. Your company could run an Instant Messaging Server themselves as part of the intranet, or use an external service. It is useful for subgroups of workers who need to communicate. It is the least managed of the three groups of communications resource and is only really suitable for quick instant answers that would (or should) probably never make it into the knowledge base. There are also well-publicized security issues on externally hosted instant messaging services, so it's your choice if there is a need in your company.

As it's the least-controlled medium messaging lends itself to potentially being the most off-topic and time-wasting. A large general messaging service involving every employee would probably mean no work done for the entire company for long periods of time. Gossip about the latest soap opera episode could easily spill over into large numbers of people. I have only found it of real use in small groups such as an IT team who need to maintain awareness of what the other is doing. However for some companies larger rollouts will be useful.

Concerns About Information

We'll now concentrate on the forum, or knowledge base as it may well become. This section deals with the information held and, above all, the accuracy, usefulness, and security of that information and its use. We'll also look at how people can be encouraged to participate in a forum and share their knowledge and also the duties of the moderators and administrators. We'll look at the following:

- Security
- Privacy and accountability
- Validity and relevance
- Accessibility (from where?)
- Misleading or defamatory postings. Legal requirements
- Updating and keeping information current
- Moderation and administration
- Involvement

Security

The information being generated in an intranet forum is potentially some of the most valuable in the company. It is what concerns people **now** – not a dry set of published procedures. It's a resource of information helpful in employees' day-to-day business. Because it is useful to your employees, it will be of interest to other parties too.

Examine the information held (or potentially held) within your system. How sensitive is it? How secure is it? Does it contain anything that's useful to competitors? If you don't want the information to be seen, then pay particular attention when setting up the security on your intranet, especially when dealing with any kind of remote access.

There's also the issue of security within and between groups within the company – should the shop floor know of the workings of the payroll system? Should payroll need to know about the design of the latest widget? Do they need to know? Two groups of people will need to keep their information secure – Personnel, or Human Resources as it seems to have morphed into, and the management team. Both of these need secure information, so ask yourself whether your systems can allow this level of security. If you're setting up forums of this type, then you may consider setting up access based on username so that the presence of the forum is not advertised except to those who are entitled to access these parts of the forum. You may also consider using this form of access restriction when testing new forums or new aspects of your system.

Employees will move departments and responsibilities – and in the course of their employment will require different levels of access into the forums – so a name-based access permission would work here – you can add them to see (or not) areas relevant to their work.

There's also the converse argument – if some forums are blocked against certain groups of people then is the company going to be accused of conspiracy? This is a facet of human nature that, if not handled correctly, can give you a sticky ride.

One of the obvious answers is to make a trial setup and test all of the issues you've identified. Create some forums and see how people react – publicize what you're doing to a small group of people. Depending on how your company is structured you'll get the reaction you want and offers of help or not. But here we digress and will deal with forum setup a little later.

Privacy and Accountability

This doesn't just apply to forums, but to the whole intranet setup. Let us suppose that your systems administrator has gone forum-happy and everything on the intranet is on a forum. Yes, it's an easy option as then it gets maximum flexibility, but if someone provides personal information then that person has a right to expect privacy. Securing that information can be problematic, and for this reason alone it is one of the areas best avoided when declaring what sort of information is going to be presented in the context of a forum. So, not that you would, please don't become the forum happy system administrator – it'll get you into deep water.

Another aside, having personnel information accessible on the intranet itself is beset with security problems. A case in point came up when it was declared that all personnel information was going to be available on the company intranet. And it was all duly loaded – and everyone could see *everything*. The problem was that those who declared that the information should be so loaded had a set of tools at their disposal and made use of that set of tools. The system administrators who noticed their omission then had to put in some very long hours putting in security that should have been designed into the system in the first place. And so all's well that ends well, but unfortunately, not quite as well as could have been expected.

Obviously it goes without saying (and is easy to say with the benefit of hindsight) as with all systems, the intranet should have been designed in the correct way from the start. And even now most employees request the information by e-mail or paper record.

> *If your information is potentially personally sensitive, don't create a forum for it*

9

If your information is potentially personally sensitive, don't create a forum for it. Obviously, there will always be exceptions, for example an employment agency where the nature of the work is dealing in personal information where consultants are passing data round to each other. So you have to make judgments based on the circumstances of the company in which you work.

It also pays us to look at the **legal responsibility** for the information supplied within your intranet and within your forums in particular. Let's say a question is asked and someone gives a wrong answer which may lead to incorrect procedures being applied or worse, some safety item not working the way it was intended. Who is then responsible for the mistake? The provider of that incorrect information? You as the administrator of the forum? The moderator for not picking it up quickly enough? Or the person applying the answer? Hoping this question is never going to occur is burying heads in the sand, however trying to tie down the accuracy of the information too much by over-moderating will quickly lead to other problems. This whole question is one of the most difficult because there can be no right answer. You are reliant on the goodwill and accuracy of the information provider; not many people are going to deliberately set out to provide incorrect information, so this problem may diminish or increase in importance for your own intranet. The answer here is good and efficient (and regular) moderator involvement.

On any forum, whether Internet or intranet, you're going to get someone with a problem about using the clearest and simplest language appropriate for a site's content. If the posting has a name attached you can do something about it, if it doesn't (is anonymous) you have a detective job to do. If you only permit posting from registered people you limit the likelihood of arguments (also known as flames) occurring in the first place, but don't eliminate them entirely. What needs to be pointed out is that the intranet is a company-wide communications device and can be seen by management as well as immediate colleagues, therefore some sort of restraint is desirable.

Finally, it should also be possible to report a post to the administrator or moderator so that objectionable content can be detected and passed to the moderator or administrator. You will be much safer if you compelling your users to register so that any posting is instantly traceable and accountable. The user's name, department, e-mail address, and phone number should be required with registration, and automatically affixed to each post. Linking forum login to the users' network login is also an option. It is also more comfortable from the users' point of view as information can be seen as emanating from a names and known source.

Validity

As new users come on to your forum they may well post in the wrong place before they are familiar with the structures you placed in the forums. If not, you may have to move it. If it is moved without reference then you may end up alienating the user. A standard practice employed on many of the forums on the Internet where effective moderation does take place (and there are many where this does not occur) is that the thread is moved but a reference is left in the original place. In addition, if this is done, an e-mail is sent to the contributor so that there are no bitter feelings about being shortchanged.

Now if this is happening too frequently it is either that your user base doesn't understand where or how to post, they don't read your explicit instructions, or some other cause. It could be that your instructions are not read because users just don't understand where they are or that they're couched in terms they don't understand. It's a common problem that's easily addressed.

Another reason may be that your originally designed forum structure does not allow for the postings that they're trying to make. You may have made the structure of your forum too inflexible. As an example, let's invent the structure of a software forum.

Let's say we've got the following topics: Visual Basic, IIS, and .NET and then someone wants to ask question about: Java, Apache, and Tomcat; either they will have to ask their questions in the wrong forum, or keep silent. It would have been wiser to start off with more general forums first, then creating more specialized forums later as necessary.

So what's best? As in all things, a balance between structure and evolution, a balance between formalization of structure and flexibility to change. If you as forum administrator are too rigid then you lose much of your users' input, if you're too flexible you get questions from management. If this sounds like I'm talking from experience, then you'd be right!

Accessibility

The big issue with accessibility concerns disabled users of your intranet information. You may not know that any of your users are disabled in any way, and they may not want you to know either. So what can you do about it? And why do you need to do anything about it? The answer is quite simple – most countries have disability discriminations legislation: The UK and Australia have their own Disability Discrimination Acts, Canada has Human Rights legislation, the USA has Section 508; to avoid me going on with a long and boring list, someone in your organization is going to be affected at some time. Even if it's color blindness, which affects 1 in 20 of white males, you may have to be careful in how you design your forums. For instance, is there a set of traffic lights that indicates how a query is progressing? If so, can a person who is colorblind distinguish between the red and the green (the most common form)?

The first thing is to ensure that your forum generates code to Web Standards as recommended in *Chapter 4*. Excellent information on applicable standards can be found at *http://www.webstandards.org*. This will at least give you the basis of a good design to start. What you need to check is that the HTML pages generated by your forum programs are valid and accessible. The second thing is to test the code. You can use a non-graphical browser such as Lynx which renders your page in text-only format. This is a good emulation of speech readers and is only a small download from *http://www.lynx.org*. It's also possible to do accessibility testing with the Opera browser. Opera 6 and earlier have settings to easily disable tables, font styles, and colors with the press of a button. Opera 7 has several accessibility-minded style sheets built in.

The principles of accessible web sites are well-documented in Constructing Accessible Web Sites (Jim Thatcher et al, glasshaus, ISBN 1-904151-00-0).

> *You may not know that any of your users are disabled in any way, and they may not want you to know either*

So is all this just for the minority of people with disabilities? Well not really, because your forum may be required to be rendered on a PDA or similar device with a screen resolution of something like 160 by 160. Your people on customers' sites may have need of the information in your forums.

By having a forum that is coded to standards you will have been able to fulfill that requirement before you even know you have it, as the new toys are in the hands of senior management before any of the techies know that they're in the shops. And senior management have a habit of trying things out and then wandering along to see you if things aren't as they expect. And that sort of visit takes time.

Another related point is the accessibility of forum content to employees in various situations. Suppose that one of the employees is using the information on the intranet forum to solve a problem on a customer's site. The forum contains some technical information about the product along with troubleshooting advice about installation problems. The employee performing the installation may well have a different skill set from those who have produced the product. The employee will need to know with clarity what should happen, and what they should do when problems occur. They may be in different time zone or not understand your forum language and are using a translation engine. They may have to follow a discussion thread to find the answer if the solution has not yet reached your knowledge base.

So all this means just one thing – **clarity** and **transparency**. This should be encouraged, but it's not just going to happen without some sort of administrative control. If your forums are going to be viewable from outside the immediate confines of the company, via RAS or VPN, you will have to consider the implications of their content. You may have enabled this so that your staff can access in-house information whilst on a customer's site. It may also be that the customer can look over your employee's shoulder when they're legitimately reading posting on your intranet.

Legal Implications of Unsuitable Postings

We've already discussed the need for the information contained on your forum to be accurate. But what about the tone of the posting? That can have an effect on how the posting is perceived by other users. You may also have a flame war where parties tend to express their feelings in rude and abusive postings, despite what you declare as official forum policy. And invariably if someone posts in, shall we say, a strong way on one of your forums, it'll be noticed by senior management before you notice.

You can inadvertently make the forum look ridiculous by putting too many barriers in the way of normal discourse

In these circumstances legal requirements are important, but the "cold shoulder factor" seems even more pressing. How is Bob going to act around Ted, after Ted tore into him on the forum because Bob thought ASP was better than PHP? Who gets to have the fun conversation with Bob and Ted where they are told to shake hands and apologize? The social dynamics of active forums can be interesting to those on the outside, but may be more of a challenge to those who may have to keep the peace.

You cannot automatically detect instances of these, so it's up to the moderators to take action. As part of the conditions of use of the forum (the small print) you will have published what you do. As a suggestion in the *Control* section below we have a template for battle-tested forum conditions of use, so to speak. What this means is that after one unsatisfactory posting the user gets a warning, after two they're suspended. This is usually enough. Further sanctions would necessitate your company's disciplinary procedure to be invoked, so if you think this may be a problem check the disciplinary paths open to you. There's usually a catch-all to cover you, so it shouldn't be too much of a problem.

You may also get bad language on the forum – and your profanity filters can take care of most of that. However beware what you are doing. How about someone in your organization called Woodcock, the name of a perfectly ordinary game bird? Would your profanity filter cope with that or throw the name out. In the dictionary there are a hundred definitions for words beginning "cock", yet only one is vulgar. Also, what if your forum concerns chickens? You can inadvertently make the forum look ridiculous by putting too many barriers in the way of normal discourse, which is not what you want to do. By all means insert the usual four letters words, but be aware – are you running a business or a Sunday afternoon children's tea party?

Updating

All information gets stale. In your original design for your forums it would be prudent to budget some time for someone to regularly take the time to make sure we're up-to-date. This should be a normal moderator task, putting expired threads into an archive area so that your main front forum stays fresh. You should also remember to publicize the existence of the archive area when you set it up.

Many forum applications usually bring threads with the latest postings to the top, so your decision process can be made easier. Making decisions about what to archive is best done by the moderators of each forum – they will probably have a better understanding of their subjects than the administrator. Depending on the software, if users are allowed to rank threads themselves according to their own criteria of interest they could sort by this ranking, and you would have an idea when a thread is dead. Some of the criteria when to archive could be:

- The forum/topic is getting too big and slow

- The focus of the topic has changed

- The topic hasn't had any postings in a long time.

- There is a policy change within the company.

Moderation and Administration

Moderator

A moderator for a topic has responsibility and control for all the posts in that topic. Ideally they should be familiar with the technical nature of the items that will be discussed. Administrators will not usually have the same level of control within the topic unless they also declare themselves to be a moderator.

A moderator should:

- Promote the topic and forums

- Take responsibility for the content of the topics under their control

- If they have reason, alter the posting by deletion, moving, or editing, always contacting the original poster when they do this via e-mail and therefore make sure that only registered users can post to the discussion forum. In addition, also make sure that all member names in the posts are linked to the corresponding author (contributor) biographies – so if necessary a reader can check if the posts have come from responsible people. Secondly, also provide for a link which can report the post and the contributor's name to the administrator or moderator if the contributor has abused his rights (for instance by spamming the forum unnecessarily or by cross-posting across forums)

- Ensure that threads are answered if someone has a problem. This is important otherwise you'll get a forum where the majority of the messages are "Why doesn't someone respond to my message"

- Deal directly with people who post via e-mail or in person if necessary to sort out any problems

- Use features such as message vetting, objectionable content filters, administrative editing, and deletion capabilities

- In an ideal world there would be more than one moderator per topic where the traffic warrants. However this is a cost to the intranet as a whole and will affect the ROI if employees are busy moderating and not busy with their normal tasks

Administrator

An administrator is the person who initially sets up the forums and determines their structure. Ideally there should be more than one person of administrator status to cover for holidays and sickness and just to share the load.

Administrators should:

- Promote the forum and topics.

- Take administrative responsibility for the whole forum.

- Appoint moderators – don't try to do the entire task themselves.

- Be prepared to be the final arbitrator in matters concerning the forum.

- Appoint themselves as moderators in topics where they have an interest, but balance the workload.

- Review the work of the moderators.

- Keep the forum software up to date – modifications usually resolve security issues.

Promotion of the Forum

These points should be used in conjunction with those covered in *Chapter 11, Internal Marketing*.

Both administrators and moderators should have sufficient faith in the value of the forums to be able to actively promote them. The most important positive message that can be portrayed is enthusiasm for the subject. Here are some tips for promoting the forum:

- Put a link to the forums on the intranet homepage in a prominent position.

- Hold short training sessions (short – don't want to take up too much company time, need to prove its simplicity)

- E-mail promotion – an announcement that forums exist.

- Put a 'Forum Success Story' (when you have one) on the intranet homepage so that you can point out the value of having the forum.

There will be a number of negative points you may have to overcome. Some of these are:

- The "Not Built Here" syndrome – if one group in the company think they should have been given the construction, and not you. There is not a lot you can do about this except gracefully back away.

- The interminable case study – you may be asked to prove and prove again rather than getting on with the job. An answer is to just get on with it and prove the worth by practical means rather than case study. In other words build it and prove its worth.

- "What if our customers/competitors get hold of the details?" - you will need to prove the security of the intranet. This is a shared responsibility among many people in the organization: network folks, systems administrators, operating system, and application security people

- Someone "from above" will pounce on the first negative posting as proof that everyone in the company has a negative attitude and this sort of thing should be banned. There is very little you can do to counter negativism of this order. Having your manager firmly on your side will help in this type of case.

Fortunately the forums I've constructed have all been well received and, for the greater part, well used. They've also been the result of the personal effort of a small group of people initially to prove the concept, then a presentation to senior managers to gain approval. It really has helped that the group of people constructing and using the forums have all been enthusiasts for the mode of communication.

Involvement

A forum is no good until it is used, and used fairly extensively. It could be that the forum is the way that people are going to be encouraged to visit the intranet – it just depends on how useful, interesting, or vital to completing the normal day job the intranet is held to be. If people have reasons to post on one of your forums then they have a reason to visit the intranet.

And all of your forums needn't be just about work. There can be others about HR, employee relations, office atmosphere, in-house sports, upcoming social events, new babies, leaving parties, for sale, wanted, that sort of thing. Call it something out of the ordinary – not anything like "Employees Forum" but something like "The Bar" - after all, that's the sort of atmosphere you'd be after here. If people can discover this sort of forum then they're more likely to be interested and to use the main company intranet.

> *A live forum means that employees are involved with the intranet*

But above all, a live forum means that employees are involved with the intranet. It's part of your job to ensure that it's projected in the right way so that it does become a useful tool. Precisely how you do it will be dictated by your company setup. But experience has shown that it pays to be inventive and somewhat adventurous.

Control

The 'corporate culture' of your company can affect the kind of information you will store on the intranet. Some organizations require information to be strictly controlled, but sometimes the level of management can affect any of the usability, employee take-up, fear of posting the 'wrong' thing. It doesn't take many unpopular decisions from management to transform a culture of 'we' as a company all pulling together to a 'them' and 'us' situation in the whole or part of the company. You have to be aware of this if at all possible so that you are not drawn into the mire – other people will decide for you if you're part of the 'them' or part of the 'us' very quickly. Some of the things you have to consider:

- Responsibility for control.
- Creating a knowledge base
- Do the employees see it as another method of management control? Is there a Trade Union that has to be involved?

How Controlled Is Your Information?

If you are in an organization where there needs to be (or just is) a lot of control then you will have to make the case for freedom when using forums. Sometimes it's to do with office politics and power; maybe it's just the style of management that has been built up over the years. Both areas are maybe uncomfortable for techies who build web sites, but nevertheless even in the freest of companies you will come across it somewhere. If that sounds like experience, you'd be correct. A cynic would say that it's largely about power. I leave this part of the discussion to your own judgment.

If your management insists on seeing all postings before they are made then it's going to mean that your forum becomes very slow and stilted. The time that this is likely to be suggested is just after there's been a posting that has in some way rocked the boat. A sort of knee-jerk reaction that happens to the best of us. If control is overly heavy then this could really hurt the forums, people will feel like the Orwellian Big Brother is watching them, as in 'them' and 'us' mentioned above.

If your forums are loosely managed, what is the worst that can happen? Is it a life-threatening issue? Or is the control going to come through insisting that staff register and log in to the forum? The "Rules for Posting" should be clear and brief and visible on the launch page of the forum. A sample is shown below.

> The forum is provided for the use of (company name) employees. Anything you post here can be read by the whole company, although you have to register to be able to make postings. We ask that you keep to the topics, and please conduct discussions in the manner of normal business. Each topic is moderated. Copyright of all posting is vested in (company name).

Responsibility for Control

Who within your company is going to be responsible for the forum? Is it going to be the responsibility of IT, of other management, marketing, or of experts in the field? Let's consider the pros and cons of each.

Controller	Pro	Con
IT control	Have technical ability	May not have the knowledge how other departments work.
Management control	Can see where the questions are coming from within the company	Can be seen as overbearing and a desire for total control. Will all your staff accept this or is it going to stifle development?
Marketing Control	Can see where marketing effort needs to be directed	Marketing produces spin. Forums are one place where the presence of spin is going to be detrimental and a turn-off. There is a danger of "static" intranet – see *Chapter 7* for explanations.
Expert Control	Knows what is required (or should do)	May be too introverted and assume knowledge – but the forums are a method of dispensing knowledge. Is also prone to use jargon or acronyms without explanation. Possibly not the best choices for controllers – they're too close to the topic.

As you see, the number of cons outweigh the pros in my list above – this is intentional – it cannot be an exhaustive list – it's up to you to provide what's best for your company.

Problem Issues

Do employees see a forum as another method of management control? Is there involvement from a Trades Union?

In some companies everything has to be discussed and approved before implementation. If you work in one of those companies then you'll be well-versed in dealing with this issue, if it is an issue. As you've probably guessed I'm a great forum fan and see them as a great liberator of knowledge. By using a forum all employees can raise questions. Analyzing these questions will provide, as well as answers to do the job more effectively, the extension of the knowledge base so that others can benefit from everyone's experience.

One way of overcoming this is to provide a demonstration system. The next section illustrates one method of doing it for free.

Demonstration Systems

In this final section of the chapter we will illustrate how you can set up an effective demonstration forum system and a chatroom.

A Demonstration Forum

To build the demonstration forum, you will need a server to host it. The following is a list of the hardware and software you will need:

- A spare, no longer used PC – obviously the bigger the better but I have made this work using a P166 with 64Mb of RAM and a 4Gb hard disk

- A downloaded version of Linux – whatever flavor you require, RedHat, SuSE, or whatever. Or if your Internet pipe is going to be tied up for too long, you can buy a copy. *http://redhat.com*

- The latest Apache HTTP server for Linux from *http://www.apache.org*. Your Linux install will probably have it already, so check first

- The latest MySQL database for Linux from *http://www.mysql.com*

- PHP scripting language from *http://www.php.net*

- phpBB – a free bulletin board – software set available from *http://www.phpbb.com*. To see this in action visit the web site and log into the community section

Install the software in this order:

- Linux, following the instructions with the product you've chosen. You will need to give the PC a fixed IP address and enter the name into the DNS your company uses. Dynamic setting of the IP address will not work.

- Check the version of Apache you've been supplied with as part of Linux – you may or may not need to upgrade to the latest version.

- Load MySQL – the instructions are on the MySQL site.

- Load PHP – the instructions are on the PHP site.

- Check that PHP works – the instructions are in the downloadable manual.

- Load phpBB – as you'd expect the instructions come from the site.

Configure and set up a test forum. Populate it with test or semi-real data – enough to show that you understand the scope of the requirement. Don't forget to set up a forum like 'The Bar" mentioned earlier, where employees can have informal conversations. Let your friends use it and comment upon it. You then have the basis of something you can present.

You're not going to get it just as you want it first time, so play around with it and see how the forum postings work. The recommendation is for PHP here as it is a small download and you can control it on a small system. All this has the benefit of being without cost, assuming that you have a spare PC.

Setting Up a Chatroom System

For this there are a whole host of free software system that you can host on your own server. But in order to illustrate an external service I suggest that you use a Java applet-based chatroom, as the conversation is only seen in its complete form within the Java applet on each client PC that's in the chatroom. No permanent record is stored anywhere which makes it more secure. See *http://www.bravenet.com/samples/chat.php*.

You will need to put a link to the chatroom you create on your intranet site where it can be found, but that's really all there is to it.

Summary

What we've been discussing in this chapter are enterprise-wide communications and the ways of managing them. Each have their advantages and disadvantages and you have to decide the best way for your organization. Solutions are divided into those that leave an audit trail and those which just carry the immediate conversation. Each have their own storage and transmission requirements and demand different actions on the part of the employees and each have their own overheads in duplication of information.

Forums and discussion groups provide a web server-based viewable record that can be seen by anyone – but we suggest that only registered users can post for traceability. They do require specific actions by going to a web site to do this. Mailing lists are immediately available in the subscriber's mailboxes, and archives can be made available for general and archive viewing. Both of these are time-independent. Chatrooms need users to be online at the same time and may or may not be able to have their discussions archived. Wiki are web pages anyone can alter – and need a level of technical skill to post to and maintain. FAQ lists have to be initiated and maintained and are essentially one-way communication devices. Voice and video can be broadcast in webcasts, conferencing and messaging services – whether the frequency of use is worth it for your company or whether it would be a very good status-enhancing project for you as intranet engineer is up to you to determine.

Whatever you decide to do, any of these can be a very valuable resource on an intranet which, properly managed, enhances the company's collective knowledge, provide feedback, and encourage people to use the intranet. To test any of these concepts, it need not cost you much as the majority of software is available free – either under open source or free downloads.

Any of the software mentioned has been used, tested, or recommended by the authors and technical team of glasshaus, but these are not the only solutions available.

10

- Intranet security options

- Security policies

- User directories and personalization

Author: Jeffrey Haas

Security and Personalization

This chapter explains why securing an intranet is important and outlines a variety of approaches that can be taken. Once the decision about security has been made, you'll likely find that the personalization issue has simultaneously been decided. This is because the user identification process inherent in a security authorization scheme will naturally extend to customizing that user's experience according to their security profile or other extended settings. Then, when basic customization is occurring, it's not a very significant theoretical step towards complete personalization (by either the system or the users themselves).

It's important to remember that security can be implemented without personalization, but the opposite is not true. If your intranet's personalization engine isn't absolutely certain who your users are, customization with integrity will be impossible. That's why it's important for us to discuss intranet security first.

Intranet security isn't just about keeping people out. You should certainly consider the implications of placing sensitive business data on your intranet and what might happen if it falls into the wrong hands, but there are other aspects to consider as well. A secure intranet can empower your organization by giving employees an opportunity to freely share and exchange information for projects and corporate initiatives. If you can guarantee that limited groups of users will have access to sensitive data (year-end financial results or salary increases that are being discussed, for example), then all the benefits of interactivity and collaboration that are inherent to web-based applications can take effect.

If intranet users know that their data will only be accessible to appropriate parties, the adoption rate of functional areas will skyrocket. Strong security policies can make insecure users feel secure in their use of your intranet. Payroll, benefits, and training areas of a business, for example, could be integrated into an intranet and embraced by users if this sense of security existed, resulting in substantial cost savings for your company.

If intranet users know that their data will only be accessible to appropriate parties, the adoption rate of functional areas will skyrocket

Note: This chapter talks in absolutes such as 'guaranteed restrictions' and binary access permissions that define individual users and groups of users who can either get in or not get in to a system, but be aware that absolute guarantees do not exist in the real world. You can be careful – and you must be careful in regard to anything that cannot be made public for any reason – but you must realize that even large corporations with multi-million-dollar IT budgets, governments, and military installations get hacked periodically. Read any IT news site for news of this and realize that internal dangers are as relevant as external ones (more on this later). You should take reasonable precautions to secure your network, your data, and your company from the many dangers of a networked world, but do not put your career on the line by promising your system will never be compromised. Also, do not ever be complacent with your existing standards, best practices, and rulebooks. Constant vigilance, unfortunately, is necessary if you want to minimize risks.

Why Security Is Important

If your intranet users will have access to any data that should not be available to all of them, then having a security framework in place is essential; it should be a consideration from the start, not a last minute afterthought. Some degree of user authentication must be implemented to restrict access to only trusted users who will be responsible with it. If this isn't done – or is done inadequately – then your organization should be prepared for the possibility that one day the data will no longer be proprietary (not to mention the headaches and liability issues that can arise when your customers' personal data ends up on Google).

Another major concern to be taken into account is that the intranet can serve as a staging area for more serious attacks on the machine or network where it's hosted, or on other enterprise networks. All access to resources with a company, whether publicly available or otherwise, should be monitored and regulated. Even if your intranet isn't carrying content of much value, its lax safety measures can prove to be the weakest link in the chain fence of your entire organization's IT security policy.

If you're in charge of only a part of your corporate IT system, but that part represents a potential security risk to the entire enterprise, then your concerns are no longer limited to what happens when an intruder hacks an Internet site or has access to private and insecure data. The related costs come into the picture: help desk calls; emergency network services; data recovery experts; network analysts; a security audit; and the inevitable after-the-disaster planning for security precautions that should have been implemented in the first place.

In a worst-case scenario where the system goes down completely (cross your fingers that it's only a temporary situation and that the backup process has not failed due to laziness or ineptitude), calculate the number of people who can't use the system times the number of hours the system is down for. In medium-sized or large organizations that are entirely network-dependent, the costs can quickly become exorbitant and frightening, making any up-front security quotes paltry by comparison.

All that being said, however, it's hard to sell people on worst-case scenarios. The macroscopic consequences of an intranet breach should be mentioned to your stakeholders, but the real planning for network security issues should be the responsibility of your corporate IT team. Your role is to explain why the intranet in particular needs to have security.

The necessity for guarding information in a corporate intranet can best be explained to stakeholders through a walking tour of a real-world office. Most companies have locks on their front door and a receptionist that greets visitors and reacts appropriately. If a delivery or meeting request comes through that front door when it is unlocked during office hours, the receptionist can guide the person or package to the appropriate destination. If a door-to-door salesman or incorrectly addressed package arrives, the receptionist can send them away or call security. Outside office hours, the only people who can walk through that front door are trusted staff with their own keys. This security is all in place to regulate and authenticate traffic from the outside world into the physical space of an organization. Inside the building itself there will typically be further layers of security such as lockable filing cabinets and office rooms, where very sensitive proprietary data can be kept. These cabinets will typically be for storing and managing data for employees and departments like Human Resources, and the locks on them exist to prevent other staff, authenticated visitors, and unauthenticated visitors (who somehow bypassed the front door and reception) from accessing the data – none of which is intended for wide circulation inside or outside the company. If your company has data in a locked cabinet behind a locked door that can only be reached by someone with the right keys after getting past the front door and the receptionist, then there is no acceptable rationale for making that data available on an unsecured intranet.

Even if your intranet is on a private network that is not connected to the Internet, there will be some system users who should not have access to some data. This isn't because these users are untrustworthy, but rather because an electronic security policy should mirror an enterprise's existing information access requirements. Digital access can be defined parallel to physical access (who has the keys for a locked cabinet? The same person should have the equivalent passwords on the intranet). If someone needs to be a director to see data relating to a stock's listing on an exchange, or a manager to see staff salaries, then these information security rules – a subset of an organization' broader business rules – should be the same online as they are offline.

These rules, in the context of an intranet, are commonly referred to as a **security policy**.

> *An electronic security policy should mirror an enterprise's existing information access requirements*

Security Policy

A security policy defines the roles and responsibilities related to information access, and the procedures governing how this access is monitored and maintained over time. It will be highly dependent on your existing business rules, but will be affected by the transition into the electronic space. Typically, an organization will evolve their security policy when mission-critical business components like client contacts, timesheets, and communication systems are integrated into their intranet. Decentralized offline access and administration processes become centralized and formalized when this happens.

Developing your intranet security policy can be a complex task, more so as the systems integrated within your intranet and user numbers increase. It may also be affected by your existing security infrastructure, IT policies, and actual deployment of your intranet in context with these. Some companies have security officers who handle all aspects of security. If your company doesn't have one, your IT team will be able to tell you more about this.

> *Developing your intranet security policy can be a complex task, more so as the systems integrated within your intranet and user numbers increase.*

The other things you need to consider are legal, social, and regulatory requirements that apply to your specific business, industry, and geographic location. Allowing private customer data to be obtained can constitute a breach of contract with customers, and can cause serious hassles for any organization. In more serious cases, some courts might view your company as being party to criminal activity. Compromised security can obviously have significant consequences in these instances.

Your security policy should be a written document that has been approved by senior management and the head of your IT department. It will typically be a document of much breadth and depth. Some of its major components should be:

- A list of categorized user groups according to departments, groups, lines of business, and hierarchy (staff, management, senior management, executive, etc.). Note that this will make long-term maintenance much easier than defining access permissions for individual users.

- Defined content types and functional areas. These should be cross-referenced with the user groups that will have access to them.

- A maintenance procedure for adding, editing, and deleting user profiles when their roles change (applies to new employees, departing employees, promotions, changing responsibilities). In larger organizations, this should include a process for requisition, approval, implementation, and confirmation of changes.

- A procedure for backing-up the intranet. This should include technical details, as well as handling responsibility and storage policies. If the data is backed up to tape and that tape can be carried outside in someone's back pocket, then there is a problem with the security policy. Remember that the intranet's entire security is only as strong as its weakest point.

- A procedure for recovering the intranet from a backed-up copy when necessary. This should include information about what backup to use, how to manage the change, what the roles and responsibilities of the involved personnel will be, and the communication channel for informing the right stakeholders about what's going on.

- A monitoring procedure for real-time tracking of system usage, and for regular auditing of log files. This may involve purchasing an Intrusion Detection System. Some leading vendors in this area are:

    - http://www.iss.net
    - http://www.intellitactics.com
    - http://www.tamos.com
    - http://www.nokia-intrusion-detection.com
    - http://www.gfisoftware.com
    - http://www.enterasys.com

- Emergency response procedure for if and when the system's integrity is compromised. Detailing who should be contacted and what steps should be followed.

- An improper use procedure for when a system administrator discovers the intranet is being abused by an employee.

- Proper guidelines for using Instant Messenger applications (something that is not secure), and alternative solutions (internal deployments) for employees who do want to chat online in real time about sensitive matters.

- Regulations for use of digital signatures using PKI (Public Key Infrastructure) and/or PGP (Pretty Good Privacy) and the storage of encrypted messages and keys.

- Employee security policy education form. This should be a document that every employee signs upon implementation of the policy, or upon starting employment afterwards. It should clearly communicate what the security policy is, what acceptable use is, where ownership of intellectual property resides.

- Guidelines for choosing appropriate passwords to prevent social engineering compromises (someone successfully guessing a password that is a husband's mother's maiden name) and handling procedures (nobody should affix Post-it notes to their monitors with their password on it).

Security Framework

A security framework is your organization's identity directory and access management system. It will serve as the architectural basis of your security policy. The framework should allow for flexible, intelligent growth of your intranet over time by providing a centralized authentication system for future systems to integrate with. Instead of synchronizing directories across multiple systems, or making them redundant, a single system can be used to increase the effectiveness and efficiency of your security policy. This system, a directory service that includes profiles of each user and their access privileges (defined by individual and group permission levels), would then be accessed by various components of your intranet (perhaps on multiple systems).

The Benefits of Security You Need to Know
The theory is that the cost of implementing a security policy is less than the cost of dealing with a security breach. The truth of the matter is that you don't ever want to really be in a position to disprove that theory. If you're an advocate of insurance for your car, your house, or your health, then you're likely to be an advocate of intranet security too. Some of the benefits to securing your intranet are:

- Preventing malicious hackers from illegally accessing, destroying, or corrupting data

- Preventing hackers from illegally accessing and stealing sensitive personal and corporate data

- Prevent corporate intelligence-gathering (a nice way of phrasing corporate espionage) by hackers employed by rival companies

- Reducing the risk of denial of service (DOS) attacks

- Reducing performance problems and down-time caused by hackers and their processes

- Reducing the risk of improper use of IT systems by internal users

- Reducing the risk of privacy violations in regard to your clients and staff. This may be in accordance with fiduciary and other legal responsibilities in some jurisdictions.

- Allowing users to access the intranet from outside the organization through Virtual Private Networking (VPN)

- Preventing inappropriate use of system resources which may be inconsistent with business needs as they apply to some users

- Preventing virus attacks in many cases (though this will largely rely on enterprise security issues)

What Level of Security Do We Need?

Some level of security should always be in place, but there are situations where a lesser degree of implementation is acceptable. If your intranet is being deployed on a network that is not connected to the Internet and no sensitive data is being placed on it, then there is no need for more than a basic level of security. If all users can access all the data, then the only consideration to take into account is in regard to adding, editing, and deleting the information.

Sometimes users will unknowingly or consciously manipulate data on an intranet. To prevent this, have the system administrator set basic file/directory permissions to allow all users "read privileges" but only administrators "write privileges." This will ensure that the integrity of the data remains constant.

If the intranet will be on a network that is connected to the Internet and no specialized security precautions are taken, your intranet will only be as secure as the weakest point in your network. If a firewall is in use and improperly configured (a very common occurrence), then that would be the likeliest source of any possible trouble.

In a situation where the intranet is wide open, be very hesitant about placing sensitive information on it. In the event of a security breach, data loss would then not be as damaging. One option to consider is segregating your more valuable data on a separate machine that can only be accessed by a highly-secure connection from a pre-defined location (the IP address of an internal network machine, for example).

If the budget and schedule allow for it, define a security policy when implementing your intranet. Even if you don't build it out into a framework and start using it, this will provide a basis for future growth and development. When the time is right, there will then be a number of technology options for developing the framework.

Intranet Security Options

In a perfect world, you will have a properly configured firewall on either side of your intranet (for both internal users and external users coming in from the intranet via VPN) with a DMZ (literally, a "demilitarized zone" – a neutral computer or network between a company's private network and the outside public network) set up for good measure, a well-managed directory service, and a finely tuned server for hosting your site. The server would authenticate all incoming users and create a session that keeps track of who they are as they proceed through the intranet's content and functionality areas.

This tracking mechanism – a "session" which defines and tracks the relationship between the user's machine and the intranet server with identifying data stored in "session variables" – could also then be used to customize the intranet experience for the group(s) the user belongs to, and allow them to personalize some content and layout preferences. In situations where functional components reside on other servers, the user session could persist across servers on a network (allowing for a single sign-on, if that is part of corporate policy). Thus, a user signing on to the intranet will be able to access their e-mail, calendar, contacts, timesheets, personalized content, and customized applications in a single action.

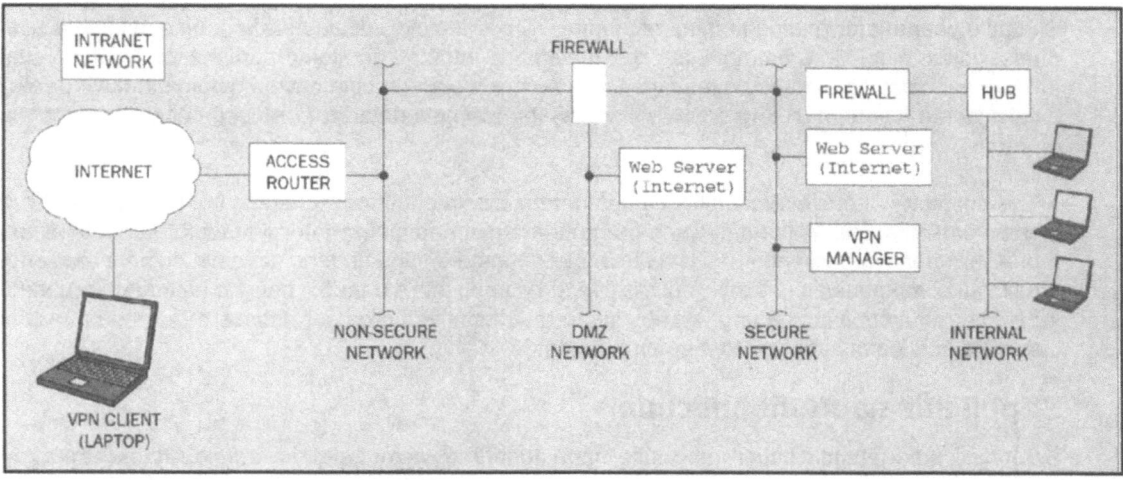

That being said, the world is not perfect and many organizations will choose other solutions. Speak with your IT department to get a clear understanding of what's in place now and what their intentions are in the future. Make them aware of your needs and bring them on board for the discussion (after all, they will be implementing whatever you decide on during this process). Keep in mind that there are numerous options to consider when selecting and developing your intranet security framework and implementing a technology solution. Some of these are:

- None
- Directory Permissions
- Simple Authentication
- Sophisticated Authentication
- Single Sign-on
- Application Service Providers
- Public Key Identity Infrastructure Providers

The first option, none, is certainly not recommended. But what do each of the others offer?

10

Directory Permissions

The first option is to use directory permissions on a central system that restricts read/write/execute access to users with the correct (universal) password. This can be used to access the entire system or its various parts. This does not take into account who the user is or what group or groups they belong to. The most significant flaws in this scheme are that staff turnover will necessitate enterprise-wide password updates and that there is no way to effectively trace security violations.

Simple Authentication

Simple user authentication and management will provide individual users with unique login IDs and passwords that allow them to access the entire intranet or major portions of it. The unique information can be stored and managed in a variety of ways to be mentioned below, but will typically exist in some type of directory provisioning system, simple database, or user identity management product.

This solution will provide restrictions on intranet access to authorized users, but is only effective for small organizations. Without defining group privileges, an administrator will need to update all user profiles whenever the system or business rules change. As the number of users, content areas, and functional components (possibly across servers) change, this data will need to be manually updated in each required instance and possibly done redundantly (if the user database resides on multiple servers and is not synchronized automatically).

Sophisticated Authentication

Sophisticated authentication and user management systems allow administrators to assign individual users to larger groups of users with **group access** privileges, **organization access** privileges, or **role-based access** privileges. This depends on their position within the company, what line of business they belong to, and what their responsibilities are. In essence, this is a fully fledged and fully featured user management system.

Some users will have administrative access to a functional component, regular access to five of six content areas, and be restricted from accessing the sixth content area and all other functional components. These privileges will be due to either their individual or group settings, and can only be changed by an administrator of the directory service.

The directory service would typically be a proprietary application or one of the pre-eminent solutions available in today's market: Novell's eDirectory (*http://www.novell.com/products/edirectory/*); Microsoft's Active Directory (*http://www.microsoft.com/windows2000/technologies/directory/*); and Sun ONE Directory Server – formerly iPlanet (*http://wwws.sun.com/software/products/directory_srvr/home_directory.html*). In any case, the directory service should include compliance with one of the two leading standards: either the Lightweight Directory Access Protocol (LDAP); or the Directory Service Markup Language (DSML). Also very worth investigating, depending on your budget and development strategy, is OpenLDAP (*http://www.openldap.org*), an open source implementation of LDAP.

This type of system allows administrators to manage user access to a large intranet in a more efficient manner now and in the future. It would not necessarily by default extend across systems (if you have distinct areas of your intranet running on multiple servers), but it could be made to do so, allowing for single sign-on privileges for application users. The issue of single sign-on is significant

Single Sign-on

Single Sign-On (SSO) is a popular system used by organizations considering allowing all enterprise users to access all their systems with a single username and password. This would allow a user to log in to disparate systems on a Local Area Network (LAN), Wide Area Network (WAN), and across the Internet with a single login. The advantages of this are obvious: a user only needs to remember a single set of credentials, and an administrator can edit all of a user's permissions in a single location. It also reduces the support time required for administrators to reset passwords and remind users of what they are when they are lost or forgotten (something that happens frequently in companies where there are two or more passwords needed for various systems that users must access). These three factors are normally enough to sell an organization on this approach – one that is currently very much in vogue.

The Gartner Group (*http://www.gartner.com*) published an analysis of help desk calls and found that users forgetting passwords not only experience costly downtime because they can't get to critical systems, but also overwhelm help desks with support calls. They reported that it costs a \$14-25 for each of the 50% of total calls due to lost or forgotten passwords. This is not only expensive, but also wastes valuable IT resources. Additionally, help desks experience high employee turnover, and when these former employees leave their jobs they take with them important access information that also jeopardizes an organization's security.

The problem with SSO is that it might not actually be all that great an idea. Should one single credential give *anyone* access to everything? Back to the analogy from earlier in the chapter, would you make a master key to every door and cabinet in your offices and give someone the theoretical opportunity to obtain it? While SSO reduces requirements for technical support, a bit of social engineering can compromise a password that might allow a malicious hacker to destroy the integrity of all the data in an enterprise. This single point of failure (compromising one system or one user's credentials) should be strongly considered before moving in this direction.

Application Service Providers

Integrating your systems with a dependable third-party Application Service Provider's (ASP) identity and access management product can be a good way to save development costs and obtain a high degree of intranet security. These products offer all the management capabilities that would be included in a sophisticated internal system and allow you to realize all the benefits of outsourcing the learning, maintenance, and 24-7 network vigilance that could otherwise be quite expensive.

The tradeoff for this, however, is that you won't be able to extensively customize (or perhaps even slightly customize) existing enterprise solutions if you attempt to integrate them with the new ASP solution. As many companies are considering outsourcing parts or their entire intranets, more ASP providers are starting to develop products to suit their needs. Some of the leading identity and access management products available today are:

- *http://www.rsasecurity.com/solutions/idmgt/*
- *http://www.caldera.com/products/volutionmanager/*
- *http://www.diasoft.net/securitymaster.asp*
- *http://www.opennetwork.com/products/directorysmart/*

Public Key Identity Infrastructure Providers

Public Key Identity (PKI) Infrastructure Providers are global directory services that allow electronic devices to authenticate the identity of people trying to use them. They function by prompting a user to enter their private key (like a password, pass phrase, or biometric input) into an interface and then comparing that input with a key that is part of their registration profile in the directory. If the keys match, then they will be authenticated as the person they profess to be. Once that happens, their access privileges on the electronic device can be retrieved from the PKI Infrastructure Provider (the less likely scenario) or defined by a separate directory service (local on the device or remote on another network). There are two primary points that need to be considered when even thinking about PKI Infrastructure Providers: technical ability and trust.

Technical ability is certainly a huge concern. With hundreds of millions of Internet users online today, what company or organization would have the resources to manage a directory service for even a small share of them? Surprisingly – to some – there are numerous answers to that question.

Note that PKI is actually more complex than this, but the particulars aren't relevant for the purposes of this section.

America Online and Microsoft, for example, authenticate tens of millions of people every day. When users attempt to access any of their systems (web mail, instant messenger, online dating, chat, etc.), the chosen system requests a password (a private key) and matches it with their respective central registries. This is something very similar to what thousands of other web sites do every day, but significantly, in many cases exponentially, on a far greater scale.

The sheer size of these market giants' registries has led them to identify becoming PKI Infrastructure Providers as a new business opportunity. They have both surpassed critical mass in respect to market share and feel their base of registered users will be attractive to any large or medium-sized web site that wants to realize all the cost savings identified in the *Single Sign-on* section above. This is a new business in an emerging market that's changing rapidly, but it does look as though it will be here to stay. This rationale is based on eBay's recent decision to start using Microsoft's Passport system for user authorization.

There are several significant initiatives underway to develop a global directory service that other companies can access to authenticate and manage their own network users on a massive global scale. Some of them are: Microsoft (Passport); Sun Microsystems (Liberty Alliance); AOL (Magic Carpet); and a number of other major software manufacturers.

The most significant issue that remains is trust. Would you rely on any of these aforementioned companies to decide whether people logging onto your system are who they say they are? Do you trust their security processes and procedures enough to "take their word for it" and let people into your enterprise systems based on them? What if the PKI Infrastructure Provider were a government that ties their passport or national ID card system into their electronic system? What if it were a Non-Governmental Organization run by the UN?

The issues of trust and technology are being debated more loudly as the business opportunity becomes more apparent. Using a Public Key Identity Infrastructure Provider may not be practical at the time of this book's publication, but it will be shortly thereafter.

This type of service would allow a company to have a user authenticated by a remote system and have their local security policy applied by a local system. The local system would then pass an "approval token" to the user's browser, which would grant the user's web browser permission to access content areas and functional components on the intranet.

The authentication system would be widely distributed (global in nature), extremely flexible and highly secure (when used in conjunction with certificates sent over SSL) to the degree that documents could be digitally signed by authenticated users.

There would probably be an initial licensing fee and recurring subscription fee for this service; unless a public domain, distributed system wins the day (which is unlikely). Watch the market space to see how it evolves in the future.

Authentication Methods

Once an intranet security option has been chosen, a decision needs to be made in regard to the authentication method. To prove who you are to a computer, you need to state who you are (your username) and provide a key (typically your password) that is an exact match to whatever data is stored in your profile. This key can be:

- A word
- A phrase
- A digital certificate
- A number from a smart card or token
- A scan of your iris
- A thumbprint
- Or a voice analysis

Whatever it is, as long as it matches the key in your profile, you will be approved.

Username & Password

A username and password is a normal, well-recognized, and quite acceptable method for determining the authenticity of a user. The problem with it is that most username and password combinations are sent by HTTP to an intranet web server for lookup in a directory. HTTP (the standard protocol for sending and receiving web documents) just transmits the text as it has been entered and, unfortunately, there are a vast number of network management tools that can sniff these passwords out from regular data traffic and intercept them. As such, regular HTTP user authentication represents a significant potential security issue.

The best way to resolve this is to create an encrypted communication channel between users' web browsers and the authentication server with a Secure Sockets Layer (SSL) connection. SSL over HTTPS is a variation of HTTP that adds the secure 's' to the prefix of a URL string. Use of "*https://*" before a URL instead of "*http://*" will indicate that SSL is in use on a web server. Using SSL of the correct level to encrypt passwords renders useless all known network-sniffing software.

10

Public Key Infrastructure (PKI)

PKI is essentially the use of a digital certificate-based solution to authenticate users and their communications. It involves planning, developing, and implementing the hardware, people, and processes necessary to provide publicly available encryption keys used for the secure, positive conveyance of confidential data to designated parties.

Using Public Key Infrastructure (PKI) to manage your intranet's security can be a very good idea. Essentially, it uses a digital certificate-based solution to verify that users and the computers they're using to access your network are who they represent themselves to be.

Every intranet user could obtain a certificate for their computer by using their web browser to access the corporate certificate authority (Verisign – *http://www.verisign.com* , RSA – *http://www.rsa.com*, a trusted certificate authority your company does business with – many banks now offer this service – or a network machine) and registering for one. The registration process would involve filling in a form and submitting it electronically to the web site via SSL. This registration submission would automatically do the following:

- generate a private/public key set
- store the private key in an encrypted format on the user's computer
- and store the public key in an encrypted format with the certification authority

Note that a delegated PKI implies some mechanism for individuals to reach out of a corporate network or "intranet" to an external host, and return information from that host to a location within the corporate network. The presence of a path from the internal network to an external entity may be deemed a generic security risk. Accomplishing the necessary communications may require the opening of specific ports on firewalls, or the admission of certain external IP addresses into the network that would otherwise not be so permitted.

Users wishing to use their certificate would just need to enter the password or pass phrase they used when registering in order to log on to the system and "digitally sign" documents. Also, because of the higher degree of security used in the PKI method, digital signatures in some jurisdictions are legally binding. This would allow users to sign e-mail messages, documents, and form submissions (that are encrypted with SSL) to conduct electronic business within an organization. The cost savings in paper alone by allowing people to file expenses and various requisitions online could be significant.

Another option for companies that want to implement PKI but have limited budgets is to configure a Certificate Authority on your own network. The CA providers mentioned above will have software that can be installed on network machines.

Smart Card

Smart Cards identify a user when they insert a credit card-shaped badge into a reader connected to their computer by a USB port. The corresponding software then prompts the user to enter their password on the screen. A user can then simply log off the network or lock their computer by removing their card.

The advantage of a smart card is that it integrates a physical item with a user password, making it twice as difficult to compromise a password.

Some of the leading developers of smart cards today are:

- *http://www.cryptocard.com*
- *http://www.datacard.com*
- *http://www.rsasecurity.com/products/securid/*
- *http://www.smartcards.net/infosec/*
- *http://www.raaktechnologies.com*

Biometrics

Biometric security refers to any type of authentication process that uses a unique genetic key to determine user authorization to access digital systems. The most-deployed biometric access devices in use today are fingerprint scanners – principally thumb scanners. These devices are manufactured by a wide variety of companies and are available for a few hundred dollars each. This low cost (considerably less than other biometric options) makes it an attractive solution for companies that worry about keys and passwords being compromised, but trust in the integrity of their users' biology.

Fingerprint scanners are now starting to be used in portable equipment like laptops (IBM is one of the first companies to provide this with their products).

The other biometric security devices available today are: speech recognition; face recognition; vein pattern recognition; iris scanning; keystroke verification; and lip movement recognition. Typically such systems are expensive.

For more information on different biometric devices and current development, visit the US government's biometric consortium web site at: http://www.biometrics.org/html /examples.html.

Some of the leading biometric authentication device manufacturers today are:

- *http://www.ringdale.com*
- *http://www.biopassword.com*
- *http://www.imagistechnologies.com*
- *http://www.biometricgroup.com*

A Brief Note About Firewalls

A firewall protects a network from unauthorized traffic that attempts to get inside for a variety of reasons. Sometimes they are put in place to simply keep search engine spiders from crawling and indexing intranet content, and keeping curious people with FTP clients from accessing any internal documentation. Other times, they are implemented to explicitly keep malicious hackers, crackers, and script kiddies (these are all terms used to describe people trying to gain unauthorized access to your networks) from getting inside to cause damage.

10

The fact is that firewalls are the cornerstones of our ability to separate our network into private and public segments. Firewalls work by limiting the types of traffic that are allowed through a pipe. A firewall program (or programs), located at our network gateway, works to protect the resources of our private network from users from other networks by examining each network packet and determining, based on a set of pre-defined rules, if to ignore or forward the network packet to a requested server. They also work by masking the identity of a computer (its IP address) when it is retrieving a web page from the Internet by acting as a proxy. This prevents people outside the network from learning anything about its internal structure and learning ways to potentially take advantage of it.

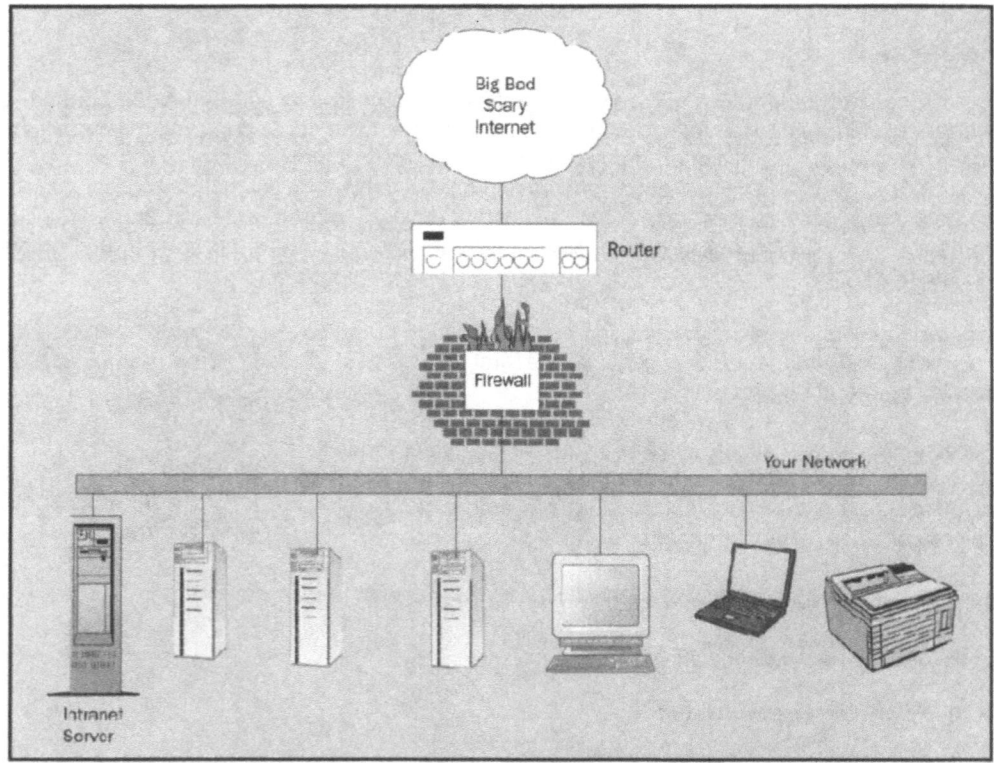

There are many obvious benefits to corporate security by having a firewall situated between an internal network and the Internet. In regard to the intranet specifically, it prevents unauthorized users from attempting to access it and stealing, destroying, or compromising information. But what if you have people inside your organization who have similar intentions? As mentioned earlier, your security is only as strong as its weakest point. Something worth considering is implementing a firewall between your internal users and your intranet, too.

If someone doesn't need – or perhaps even shouldn't have – access to parts of the internal network, then they should be explicitly restricted from accessing them. One concern that will probably occur as the scope and scale of your intranet grows is the emerging need for access to the intranet from outside the firewall. People in other offices or who are traveling will need access to vital content areas and functional components, and your firewall won't let them through (because it's meant to only let web and e-mail traffic in).

The easy solution would be to allow them to dial-up directly into the intranet server, but that would go against basic security principles – if someone obtained the dial-in information, the entire system would be compromised. Instead, implementing a Virtual Private Network (VPN) is a recommended course of action.

Some leading firewall vendors are:

- *http://www.novell.com*
- *http://www.evidian.com*
- *http://www.cisco.com*
- *http://www.cyberguard.com*
- *http://www.intrusion.com*
- *http://www.lucent.com*

Virtual Private Networks

A VPN uses software or hardware to encrypt Internet traffic between two points. If the software is properly configured on both the users' computers and the intranet, then the secure connection can take place over the intranet and through the firewall. Speak to your IT team about whether they will implement it as this may have an effect on broader corporate security issues. Also, encourage users who install VPN on their laptops and home computers to practice safe security behavior and not post their passwords on sticky notes on the sides of their computer.

Some leading VPN vendors are:

- *http://www.secgo.com*
- *http://www.cisco.com*
- *http://www.netsentron.com*
- *http://www.checkpoint.com*
- *http://www.lucent.com*
- *http://www.nortelnetworks.com*
- *http://www.sonicwall.com*

Security Audits

Many consulting companies are available to provide Security Audits or "Security Vulnerability Assessments" on your network. They would conduct a thorough examination of the existing IT infrastructure and security policies to determine what flaws, if any, exist, and make recommendations for your organization to move forward. If your intranet's functional components (as defined in *Chapter 5*) include numerous mission-critical applications, then you should consider investing in a professional audit.

A security audit will also:

- Allow you to be proactive about preventing corporate litigation (in case private customer data is compromised)
- Reduce performance problems that may arise during a hack attack
- Allow you to be proactive about preventing Denial of Service (DOS) attacks
- Test your Intrusion Detection System
- Qualify for Information Protection Insurance
- Gain confidence in your security systems

Even if you use firewalls (internal and external), an Intrusion Detection System, SSL, VPN, and a rock-solid authentication system with biometric security, a security assessment can help determine if your current configurations contain any unknown, and potentially unauthorized, network "goodies" left by previous developers or technicians. Creating backdoors are an infamous favorite of many nefarious computer villains, for situations where they depart companies on unfavorable terms and want revenge.

In addition, note that one of the most important reasons for having a Security Vulnerability Assessment performed is to enable corrective action. How can you know what to secure if you don't know what is insecure?

Take care at this stage, if you're going to put forth an initiative like this, to get written permission before you start poking around for security holes. The case of Randal Schwartz (*http://www.stonehenge.com/merlyn/*) versus Intel (*http://www.intel.com*) should serve as sufficient warning in this regard.

Information Protection Insurance

If you're really concerned about all the "what if" scenarios and the potential financial impact on your organization should one of them unfortunately come true, you may want to consider purchasing Information Protection Insurance. In the late 1990's, after the Lovebug virus and first few rounds of Denial of Service attacks crippled the e-commerce sites of many large online retailers, the insurance industry responded with options for companies that wanted to be covered in case it happened to them.

The options, while expensive, were and still are fairly comprehensive. If you choose, you can be covered for:

- Internal violations (criminal acts by employees)
- Hackers
- Viruses
- Media liability (defamation, libel, and copyright violations)
- Privacy violations
- Inadequate crisis management

- Cyber extortion

- Crisis management

- Global risks

To find out more about Information Protection Insurance, contact your corporate insurance broker.

Network Security Software

Generally speaking, your IT team will have your network security as tight as they can make it, and will be on top of all the latest news, software, and software updates. If you need to know what they're doing to proactively secure your intranet from possibly security issues, the best thing to do is talk to them about it.

Just so you're aware, however, these are some of the steps that an organization can take to optimize their chances for a long-term hacker-free existence:

- Make sure the Employee security policy education form has been read, understood, and signed by all employees. Walk around from time to time to watch what people do when they log on to the network. Are they looking somewhere for their password or do they know it? Take a walk around the office and see if you find any yellow sticky notes on the sides of monitors with passwords written on them…

- If you can see someone enter their password as you walk by their desk, other people can, too. That includes other office workers, clients, and maintenance staff with dark streaks.

- Each operating system has its own inherent vulnerabilities, many of which have to do with file sharing and administrative permissions. In addition, many individual software packages have identified security vulnerabilities. It's important that all your software subscriptions are up-to-date, and that current anti-virus updates, system software patches, and security updates are implemented on a regular basis, as they are released by the publishers.

User Directories and Personalization

Once all the security issues have been resolved and a decision has been made about the identity and access management infrastructure, you can start thinking about personalization issues.

For purposes of this discussion, think of your user directory as just a database that contains information about the people within an enterprise and the resources to which these people need access. When a user tries to access the intranet and they are authenticated, this database is queried for all its information on that user (what groups they belong to and any personal preferences they have selected). This information is then used to generate a dynamic homepage (for example) that offers the user information about content areas and access to functional components that are appropriate for his defined groups. If he has selected personal preferences that effect layout, colors, hierarchy of navigation components, or other customizable areas, then those personal choices will be apparent.

Note that personalization and customization are two separate things, and are only related in that they both result in the dynamic modification of the intranet's presentation layer.

Personalization is what the system does when it matches a user's profile with relevant content profiles. This is done according to the group specifications detailed in the directory service, and it allows for a dynamic navigation system to change as specific group needs and broader business needs evolve over time. As content relevant to their job changes, the nature of the intranet and its relationship to the user will change, and grow. Furthermore, the non-dynamic content areas that all users will have access to will remain static on the user's pages, so he can explore and learn with the traditional navigation system, too.

Customization refers to a technique that may or may not want to be employed. This refers to interface elements that can be moved and changed according to individual preferences. If a color palette has been defined inside the scope of a design, then it would be possible for several variations on a design to be created by simply moving colors around and giving users choices to select what they prefer. Also, some users find certain types of information (current stock prices, corporate news, and press releases) more important than others (new HR benefits, fundraising initiatives, and cafeteria menus). Giving users an option to customize their intranet (and really make it their own) does not require a significant technology leap beyond what will be developed during a personalization initiative, and it will have a positive impact on the level of satisfaction people get from it.

How Does Implementing Security in My Intranet Allow for Its Personalization?

When a user has been authenticated, there are three ways to track them to make sure their intranet experience is consistent across their session. A session refers to all the connections that a single user might make to a server in the course of viewing any set of pages within an intranet. Logging on to the intranet and/or making your first page request to the server will instantiate the session. Logging off the intranet or remaining inactive for a set period of time will end it. Sessions are specific to individual users. As a result, every user has a separate session and has access to a separate set of session variables.

The three ways to track session variables are:

- **Pure Session Variable (server only)** – Session variables are a convenient place to store information that all pages of your application might need during a user session. Using them allows your intranet's functional component(s) to initialize with user-specific data the first time a user accesses one of its pages. This information can remain available while that user continues to use that application. For example, you can retrieve information about a specific user's preferences from a database once, the first time a user accesses any page of an application (or after authentication is complete). This information remains available throughout that user's session, thereby avoiding the retrieval of these preferences again and again. Pure session variables are stored on the server only and they track all simultaneous users separately.

- **Cookie** – Session information can be stored in a users' browsers' cookie files when there is an expectation for numerous simultaneous user sessions that you may not want be handled by the intranet server. Setting cookies (storing a few lines of text information with the session variables inside them) will allow the server to operate with less strain, and for some variables to be persistent across sessions (like color preferences and other customizable options that aren't stored in a database).

- **Token** – When cookies can't be written to a web browser (which happens in some organizations due to a variety of corporate web browser standards), session variables can be tracked by appending a unique identifier and variable information to the end of every URL which a user accesses. This can be done automatically in most instances by enabling session management with tokens on a web server.

The decision will largely depend on the scripting language you have chosen to use during your development cycle, as some of these methods are easier to adopt in certain languages than they are in others.

The advantage of tracking a user through their session is that you can continue matching categorized content with different end users based on business rules as they proceed through the intranet. This matched content can also be presented in context with where they are in the site, what their previous actions have been, and what their customized preferences are.

> *By looking at the clickstream (the path of pages a user clicks through) of many users on an intranet, you can get a deeper understanding of how successful your GUI design was, how usable the site is and how much utility the users are getting from it.*

The other significant benefit to personalization and use of sophisticated tracking mechanisms is that user sessions can easily be logged and analyzed. This analysis would typically not look at individual sessions unless they indicate system abuse, but rather aggregate them for advanced analysis by designers and usability personnel. By looking at the clickstream (the path of pages a user clicks through) of many users on an intranet, you can get a deeper understanding of how successful your GUI design was, how usable the site is, and how much utility the users are getting from it. Also, when and if the site is re-launched, this data can be cross-referenced with solicited feedback to more clearly define future direction.

Integrating Personalization

Once you know who your user is and how you're going to keep track of their information, you need to integrate their unique information with the relevant graphical interfaces and information structures. Based on the user's group memberships and unique access permissions, you would probably have a dynamic left-side navigation system that gives them access to all the generic company-wide content areas and functional components, but also includes specialized areas to which they have special access. The differences that you know exist between them will not matter to the average intranet user because they won't likely know about the content and components they don't have access to.

Beyond simply allowing a user to have access to certain areas of the intranet, it is recommended to provide them with options to select size and placement of information areas (the number of content headlines, for example, and their placement on the page relevant to press releases, financial information, and weather updates). Additionally, flexible color options are almost always appreciated because people do have personal preferences. If you have a set of defined colors within a corporate palette, ask your design team to recommend alternative schemes for color selection within their design. If it's just a matter of creating three Cascading Style Sheets and letting users select among them; the technology isn't difficult, and the reward will be substantial.

Giving a user control over even slight aspects of their interface from an information layout perspective (while keeping all possible options within the greater framework of your designed templates) empowers users to customize their experiences and make it personal. When this happens, their satisfaction and utility from the site will likely increase as well.

Summary

After reading this chapter, you should understand the importance of intranet security and be nervous about what might happen to your job if you take the issue lightly. Hopefully, you will take adequate measures to reasonably protect yourself, your organization, your network, and your data. If you're careful and meticulous, even the damage caused by a catastrophic failure triggered by a malicious hacker can be minimized through a solid process that includes well-communicated procedures for dealing with such incidents.

And never underestimate the value of good, accurate, regular back-ups.

The unfortunate reality is that most companies don't invest in security until after a breach has already occurred. Try to minimize your risk of that happening through constant vigilance, thorough preparedness, and good contingency plans. If you do that, then all your users will be happy with their personalized intranet and surf happily ever after.

11

- The challenges of intranet marketing
- Promoting intranet use
- Keeping users interested

Author: Frank Pappas

Intranet Marketing

After countless delays, months of exasperating fights between HR and marketing and the folks in your technology group – not to mention a significant investment in both financial and human capital – your brand-new corporate intranet will be ready for launch in few short days. Congratulations!

What now?

How do you get the word out to every corner of the corporate universe that there's a new intranet on the horizon? How will you convince hordes of employees to cozy up to once-familiar policies, procedures, and practices that have now been re-engineered as part of the intranet development effort? More importantly, what's the skinny on how you'll leverage the intranet in the future as part of your comprehensive employee-communications strategy?

I'm guessing that the deer-in-the-headlights look that you're wearing right now means that you might not have considered many of these issues, and that perhaps the entire scope of your post-launch plan for "selling" the intranet to your employees was (up until about five seconds ago) pinned to the "If you build it, they will come" strategy. Not exactly what we'd call an awe-inspiring plan, but not to worry. There's still plenty of time to tinker with your plan and spruce things up just a bit.

"What now?" is an important question that lots of really smart people forget to ask when it comes to launching a new intranet. If you're still with me, I'm probably correct in assuming that you're the go-to person for pitching your company's new intranet to your coworkers, or that you've got a minion reporting to you somewhere on the organization chart who'll be doing the pitching instead, and you'd like to be able to wrangle said minion somewhat more efficiently. Either way, great! My goal throughout the next few pages will be to bring you up to speed on a handful of useful concepts that can help you to achieve three high-level goals:

- Get the word out
- Encourage use and adoption of the intranet
- Integrate the intranet into ongoing employee-communications efforts

Of course, along the way I'll also point out some of the really BAD ideas that often pop up when discussing intranets and intranet marketing, just to ensure that you don't wind up enthusiastically recommending one of these ideas in your next marketing meeting.

Intranet Challenges

There's one important lesson that to learn that applies brilliantly to our discussion of intranet marketing, and it's one that we should review before we get too far into things: *you can't turn lead into gold.*

Put simply, if your intranet is a disaster – for whatever reason – there's only so much that even a masterful marketing plan will be able to achieve. There are a wide array of factors that can undermine your intranet even before it is first presented to your employees, and you'll not necessarily be able to compensate for any of these shortcomings prior to launch, if at all, simply through snazzy tag lines or custom mousepads. You may simply have to put on a brave face, work diligently to market the most appealing intranet elements to your audience, and hope for the best.

Of course, marketing is based as much on hard facts and consumer research as it is on the touchy-feely intuition and gut-feelings that guide some marketing groups. This can come in handy, especially in instances where your intranet's initial reveal was less than well received. Via the traditional tools of marketing – customer surveys, collection of feedback, focus groups, etc. – you can collect solid quantitative and qualitative data that will, over time, allow the marketing and intranet development teams to turn their insights into the wants and needs of the company's employees in order to foment improvements to the intranet. Even if your intranet's early days are plagued by some of these problems, all is not lost. Simply apply some of the techniques and tips provided throughout this chapter and you'll stand a good chance of getting your intranet back on the right track.

The Intranet Is a Corporate Afterthought

Intranets, just as with extranets or public web sites, are not inexpensive endeavors. Depending on their scope and complexity, it's possible for intranets to consume significant amounts of time, staff, infrastructure, and financial resources.

If your intranet has been launched on someone's seven-year-old desktop computer that can barely boot up without catching fire, there's a storm on the horizon. The same is true if your lead intranet developer is a 15 year-old kid from the local high school – not necessarily a good sign that your managers really give a hoot one way or another that your intranet launches successfully, thrives, or even survives!

Unfortunately, we're not necessarily dealing with a simple lack of sufficient hardware or hands-on support. An even more difficult hurdle can be when senior management doesn't view the intranet as worthy of *attention*, let alone support. Once that tone is set by the managers, such an attitude can trickle down through the ranks and convince other employees to disregard the intranet as a serious business resource, undermining attempts to elicit content updates or feedback from coworkers, bog down efforts to integrate new functionality that is dependent on a particular team's input, and so on.

Alas, there's no quick-fix or otherwise universal solution for such a problem. The best strategy for addressing such a scenario is to identify the top 2 or 3 features of the intranet that are the most exciting or useful to your audience and market the heck out of them, almost to the point of over-exposure. Over time – with a good bit of hard work and a little luck – you can hopefully build a grass-roots movement of sorts that will integrate those core features that you initially presented into their daily lives. From this point, you can step up your efforts to solicit input from your audience (focus groups, message boards, suggestion boxes, etc.) and start the employees actively considering how the intranet can best enhance their productivity, integrating the employees more closely into the development process, and lending the added weight of their collective opinions to your own when negotiating with management for future intranet enhancements.

The Intranet Was Not Designed to Satisfy Employee Needs

It's often the case that an intranet will be designed based on artificial technology constraints or will focus on fulfilling management's pet projects, rather than on providing the core content and functionality needed to facilitate cost savings and increase efficiency among the largest number of employees.

For example, companies will often dictate that a strategic business partner's software be used as the platform for the intranet, while the intranet team's protestations of foreseeable usability problems, technology incompatibilities, or their evaluation of the software as simple garbage, fall on deaf ears. Additionally, managers will often manipulate intranet development efforts in order to streamline the operation of their particular fiefdom (marketing, logistics, etc.) at the expense of others, with little regard for the enterprise as a whole. Of course, if you've already read the earlier chapters, you know that working through the proper development stages can assist with creating a plan that *does* address employee needs, and can help you in justifying them up-front. (If you haven't read the earlier chapter stick a bookmark here and go read them!)

It's important to note that it's not *always* the case that a software solution recommended by management will be garbage. If you're lucky, your company has a strategic business relationship with an organization that produces an excellent web server, or authentication system, or e-collaboration tools. And if your bosses can obtain preferential pricing, or training, or other freebies, so much the better!

However, we'll frequently find that managers force employees to use platforms for internal computing needs based on arrogance, questionable *guesstimates* of potential efficiencies, etc. AOL-Time Warner, for example, mandated that the employees of ALL companies with the AOL-TW family would – post-merger – be forced to use AOL's proprietary client software as the backbone of their internal electronic communications. Nice idea, save for the fact that AOL's e-mail system was designed for leisure use and did not meet the needs of big business in terms of scalability, functionality, or reliability. After months of frustrating struggles with this new system, many AOL-TW business units staged an internal "coup" and reverted to Exchange servers and traditional clients to reliably solve their mail needs.

Not only did the migration to a management-mandated platform not *enhance* productivity or otherwise benefit the enterprise in any significant way, it actually *cost them money* both for the initial switch *from* their original solution, then *again* when they were forced to switch back to their original system from this supposed "upgrade".

"Usability" Is a Concept Foreign to Your Intranet Developers.

Even if your intranet has benefited from an enthusiastic and well-meaning sponsor from within the ranks of management **and** was built *specifically* to address employee needs through content and functionality, there's still the possibility that the folks designing your intranet's user interface or its information architecture are simply sub-par, hindering users' efforts to utilize the intranet. Not to mention that your developers may have completely disregarded generally-accepted web development standards, leading to other unforeseen problems down the road. (If you think this is the case, perhaps you should leave this copy of *Intranet Development* on the desk of your lead developer, casually opened to our *Usability* chapter.)

Some of the usability problems that can plague your intranet can include:

- An intranet that works on only certain computers within your company, perhaps on all the PCs, but only on certain Macs, and not at all on the Linux boxes
- Web pages that cease to function in newer versions of web browsers
- A visual interface that fails to anticipate the need for a flexible interface that can be easily modified without changing the underlying (back-end) technology of the intranet, requiring massive effort to implement even the most modest of changes

Hands-on Intranet Marketing, Down & Dirty

Of course, just because your intranet (fortunately) hasn't fallen victim to one or more of the "big three" challenges that we've just covered, it's not quite time to rest easy: you're not in the clear just yet. In order to successfully position your intranet for its initial launch and (eventual) acceptance by your colleagues, you'll have to anticipate and deal with a variety of other hurdles.

The specific tactics that you'll use to address each of these hurdles will vary from company to company, and will depend in large part on the amount of management support you receive, your available budget, the size of your organization, etc. And it's important to remember that not every red-flag issue *has* a direct solution – a particular problem might not have a quick fix, but might instead simply require time, patience, and continued upselling across a variety of communications channels to dispel any myths, preconceived notions, and other institutional or procedural prejudices concerning your intranet that are present in your workplace.

What Intranet?

The first (and most obvious) issue to tackle is "Intranet? What intranet?" This is a problem that *every* company faces when they first deploy an intranet within their organization: employees often don't even know what an intranet is, let alone understand how an intranet might impact their daily work lives. As such, it's important to address employees' questions as quickly, thoroughly, and as proactively as possible.

Educating your employees about intranets right before launch can often be a painful and frustrating experience. A better strategy – if practicable – is to ensure that at least some of your employees are intimately involved with the development and launch of your intranet from the earliest stages possible. That way you'll not only gain additional insight and suggestions that may improve the intranet, but you'll also have a well-trained team of intranet ambassadors who are ready to hit the ground running and can enhance your efforts to integrate the intranet into the workforce. This, of course, is a strategy that works in tandem with the other ideas we'll talk about shortly, such as using more traditional marketing channels (newsletters, e-mail, etc.) to keep the general employee audience in the loop concerning the intranet's development, and purpose.

Culturally, intranets (or any new technology that impacts the workplace, for that matter) tend to be less of a problem for younger employees, who often have attained at least a minimal comfort level with using the Internet, are conversant in the lingo, and so forth. However, for some of the more senior employees within an organization, the transition to a more technology-dependent business process can sometimes be quite challenging, even to the point of being unsettling and disruptive to their performance. For both the junior and senior employees alike, it's exceedingly helpful to follow a few simple steps to prepare the staff for the intranet:

- As early as is practicable, start educating your employees about your intranet, and give them "teasers" or other sneak-peeks into both the design process and scope of the nascent intranet in order to whet their appetites for what's to come. (If your marketing team is involved early enough, you can always turn to focus groups, individual or group interviews, questionnaires, etc., to both educate your target audience and capture feedback that can be used to channel the direction of the intranet's development.)

- Using your current communications channels – employee newsletters, the CEO's speech at the company picnic, periodic e-mail updates, canned demos at department meetings – seize as many opportunities as possible in order to define intranets in general, as well as to lay out your top-line vision for how your company's intranet will eventually provide tremendous advantages, efficiency, and cost savings.

- As your planning continues to evolve, so too will the breadth and depth of the information that you'll be able to share. For example, let your employees know that they'll eventually be submitting their weekly timesheets, expense reports, and leave requests online, perhaps even offering focused storyboards or other procedural walk-throughs to both set expectations, and to begin to retrain your employees to think of the intranet as their first-line resource for solving problems and accomplishing tasks.

I can't stress enough that it's important for you to *communicate early and often*. It's not sufficient to send out an e-mail a few days before launch and expect employees to eagerly stampede the gates in order to make use of the intranet, or to mention the coming intranet offhandedly in a speech 13 months before the intranet is due to arrive. For maximum impact, there must be a concerted effort over a number of weeks (or, better yet, months) designed to gradually educate employees and prepare them with the knowledge and skills required to effectively use the intranet in their daily efforts on behalf of the enterprise.

Co-Opt Your Employees

Beyond simply telegraphing to your employees that an intranet is on the way, you'll also need to focus on securing their buy-in, or acceptance, of the intranet. One of the best ways to co-opt your employees and to transform them into champions of your intranet initiative is to make them feel as though they've had a hand in the creative process leading up to the launch of the intranet.

It's critical to understand that as smart and as experienced as your management and intranet teams may be, there's another source of significant knowledge, expertise, and ideas within your company that MUST be tapped in order to provide a solid foundation for the success of your intranet: employees. (Remember those stakeholder interviews we talked about back in *Chapter 3*? No? Then take a break and go back for a quick refresher.)

As part of your communications strategy, provide ways (an e-mail address, or even simply an anonymous drop-box somewhere in the office) for employees to voice concerns, ask questions, and make suggestions. Not only will this be a significant boost for morale, it may also prove useful in identifying opportunities for intranet features or functionality (also known as, potential increases in cost savings, efficiency, and profitability) that your team hadn't initially considered. Remember that it never hurts to *solicit* input and feedback from your employees, even if you don't get a chance to make use of more than a little of it. However, it's important that you emphasize your appreciation for their input, acknowledge their effort, and encourage their continued contributions. And as you implement iterative revisions to the features and functionality of the site, you're then able to circulate the newly updated components to your captive audience to gain your endusers' thoughts on your "improvements".

> *Never underestimate the innovations and insight that can be captured from the collective experience of your employees*

What's more, as your intranet teams work to develop solutions for *specific* intranet components (time reporting, expense and leave requests, scheduling conference rooms, and so on) you can also make use of your traditional communications processes to ask your employees for their help in creating powerful and creative solutions *tailored specifically* to the needs of your workforce. A sometimes more successful technique in some circumstances can be to bring in employees for hands-on testing of certain components, either as part of a final beta-test stage (extra eyeballs never hurt) or in earlier alpha-test stages, when features and functionality are still somewhat mallable. Involving your employees in the development cycle in this manner can make them feel like "insiders" of sorts and can often prompt them to feel a sense of responsibility to contribute forcefully to the eventual success of the project.

The bottom line is that you should never underestimate the innovations and insight that can be captured from the collective experience of your employees, as this knowledge can translate into significant cost savings, efficiencies, and competitive advantage for your company – especially when you consider that your users will decide whether your intranet is, in the final analysis, a success or a failure.

The Intranet As Fluff

Another problem that you might have to deal with is that your employees may view the intranet as a superfluous make-work project that is irrelevant to their role in the workplace, and as such, not worthy of their time or attention. This is especially the case when intranets are designed to showcase technology for technology's sake (the gee-whiz factor – things like showing the local weather or the webcam view from the office roof), when they include functionality that disproportionately focuses the intranet on social topics (chat rooms for employees to discuss hobbies), or when a core goal of the intranet is ever determined to be "to make the intranet *fun* for our users".

The honest truth is that *business*, by and large, has never been intended to be a primary source of *fun* – and neither should the intranet. The intranet, just like business as a whole, should be focused on enabling productivity, increasing cost savings, and enhancing profitability. As a manager, it shouldn't be your goal to get your employees *excited* about the intranet as they would about a new movie, or to convince them that using the intranet is as thrilling as a roller coaster ride.

It *should* be your goal, however, to design a focused, well-envisioned intranet that accomplishes these three business goals as quickly and with as little distraction as possible, and to tell a compelling story via your internal marketing efforts that helps to underscore for your employees:

- WHAT the intranet is

- WHY the intranet's content and functionality support the company's mission

- HOW – in terms of real-world examples – the intranet will benefit the workers on a daily basis

This will greatly reinforce to your employees that your intranet initiative is not only of significant value to the overall organization, but has particular relevance and potentially many benefits to themselves, as well.

Fortunately, you'll find that throughout the balance of this book there are presented a host of ideas, strategies, and real-world examples of how intranet developers, managers, and other corporate stakeholders have managed to successfully work in concert to negate these (and other) pitfalls that can frustrate the adoption and acceptance of a corporate intranet

Getting the Word Out

So, let's pretend that you've followed our advice so far and have been communicating with your employees on a regular basis concerning your budding intranet project. Once the intranet is nearing completion, however, you'll suddenly find yourself facing a whole new set of questions. How do we handle the launch – is it a big affair, or something more reserved? Does the intranet need a name? If so, how do we come up with one? Should there be a launch party? The list of questions is potentially limitless!

Now, it's completely true that throughout much of the 1990s, the launch of intranets (heck, even the launch of a new time-reporting system) often triggered a mad rush to plan triumphant parties, with free food, booze, commemorative plaques, and so on. Fortunately (or unfortunately) the bravado and unchecked spending that accompanied projects in the earlier days of intranet development have gone the way of the dodo, replaced instead by much more reserved management practices. This doesn't mean, however, that you enjoy *no* wiggle room whatsoever in shaping a slate of activities surrounding the launch of your intranet. What it *does* mean, however, is that, unlike in recent years, you *do* have to be responsible and not go to any particular extreme in structuring your launch – spend money where it's needed, but try to remember that this is a *business*, after all.

Loud or Quiet Launch?

Whether you choose to introduce your intranet through a loud or quiet launch is mostly up to the personal preferences of you and your management, based on your corporate tastes, budget, etc. However, *louder* generally translates into *more expensive*, and given the realities of the current business economy, might not be the best direction in which to focus your activities. That's not even mentioning that there is really little evidence to support that parties or custom hats and mousepads contribute in any significant fashion to a successful intranet launch.

It *is* possible, though, to have a boisterous set of events surrounding the launch of your intranet without having it break the bank, so to speak. Well-timed messages from your CEO, still distributed via traditional marketing channels, can christen the intranet, and can be coupled with updates from individual departments (introducing new intranet resources or describing how a traditionally-offline process will be handled via the intranet). What's more, enthusiastic quotes can be selected from your beta-test group of employees and can be used as part of the promotional messaging. And if your budget and timeline allows, you can even create online demos that can assist in not only *spreading the word* but also in training your users, simply by presenting how typical tasks or scenarios are handled, all while illustrating how each "improved" process saves the company money, and saves the employee time and frustration.

Keep in mind that you don't have to wait until after your launch to recruit intranet ambassadors. As we mentioned earlier, if you recruit small groups of users and bring them into the fold early in the project's life for user testing, focus groups, sneak previews, etc., you can proactively create intranet ambassadors that can be your "street team" for convincing other employees en masse of the value and excitement surrounding your intranet project.

Of course, it's still perfectly reasonable to opt for a quiet launch instead. This gives the intranet development team a little extra time to work on the overall implementation and quality-assurance testing of the intranet, with more eyes and keyboards poking and prodding the system. If things break in the first few weeks, so much the better that the launch was quiet – there's plenty of time to fix problems as they arise without taking a huge PR hit. Plus, as individual users begin to discover the advantages of using the intranet (remember, you'll still be sending out updates to entice users via traditional channels like e-mail or through an offline newsletter, at least for a short time), you'll begin to see a grassroots recruiting effort emerge as your first users become *intranet ambassadors* of sorts, bringing their colleagues into the fold.

Naming the Intranet

You'll have to excuse me here for a minute, because the naming of intranets is one of my pet peeves. Seriously. I've dealt with *so many clients* over the years who have gone to great pains – including such insanity as hiring high-priced branding and naming consultants – to craft catchy or serious-sounding names for their intranets: WheeNet, GWIS (an acronym that ends up being pronounced 'gee-whiz'), and so on. Names that make little sense, have no meaning, and serve no significant purpose – and certainly not providing any tangible *business* benefits to the company. Just be sure that your employees can fire up their web browsers and access the intranet by typing *intranet* in the address bar, and you'll have taken care of all the intranet naming tasks you need to worry about.

To be fair, it's probably not *the* silliest, most wasteful thing I've ever seen. But it's certainly in the top three.

I won't even begin to dignify this topic with a discussion of the point of developing a brand. But let's consider this: when was the last time your boss told you to check with, say, *HR*, to see whether the new tax forms were available? Were you confused by the lack of snazzy branding or logos associated with your human resources group? Did you become confused and call the company two-doors down, or maybe even your key competitor, and ask *their* HR department where those new tax forms were? *Of course not.*

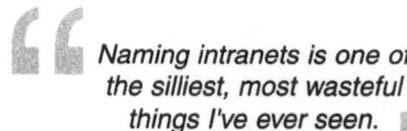

Naming intranets is one of the silliest, most wasteful things I've ever seen.

It's exactly the same with your intranet – there's pretty much ZERO opportunity for your employees to confuse your intranet with, well...anything else. The bottom line? Save the money and effort of developing a cute name for your intranet and channel those resources either into the *development* of the intranet, or perhaps into bonuses for your employees.

Look, I'm not completely against the idea of having a cool, classy name for your intranet. It's just that, almost without fail, companies manage to brand their intranets with names more appropriate for a six year-old's toy ray gun, which can put a serious ding in the credibility of your intranet. I like branding – I've been doing it for nearly a decade. But this is one area where branding is not only somewhat tricky, but also (generally) pointless. So, if you do manage to come up with a great brand name for your intranet, then by all means, please use it with my blessing. (And do let me know about it!) But don't kill yourselves and waste valuable resources if you don't have a good one at the ready, since the corporate intranet is as sufficient a brand as you'll likely ever need.

Offline Marketing, E-mail Messaging, and SWAG

As we've discussed, while your intranet is still under construction you'll still need to rely on some of your more traditional offline marketing channels for communicating with your employees concerning the development of your intranet. This holds true right up to – and even for a little while following – the public launch of the intranet, because even once launched, you're going to still need to target the employees lagging behind the early adopters.

The offline and e-mail marketing opportunities are limited only by your creativity, budget, and good business sense – that is, no more shaving your company logo into the side of a goat that gets paraded around your office. Strategically-placed posters, flyers, and brochures – all generated from in-house printers for cost-effectiveness – can all be useful in hammering home that there's an intranet on the way, and that it will bring a bevy of benefits along with it. What's more, updates from the intranet team, management sponsors, or department heads during staff meetings or retreats can also help to enforce your intranet messaging.

You can even (I can't believe I'm encouraging this) look into generating custom-designed trinkets, like T-shirts, mousepads, yo-yos, and the like. But here's the only way I'll let you get away with it: find a sponsor *outside* your company who is willing to underwrite the cost of whatever doodads you want to create.

It's not as hard as you might think – there are tons of companies, everyone from Dell to some of your business partners, to random mousepad companies in Taiwan – who'd be willing to provide free, customized SWAG in exchange for a little bit of co-branding space on whatever particular item you have in mind. So if you're *really* into giving away freebies, just break out the Internet yellow pages and start sending e-mail messages and making phone calls. Who knows? Maybe you'll get lucky!

Holding a Launch Party and User Training

So, given what we've talked about relative to launching and naming your intranet, can you guess what I'm going to have to say about launch parties? I've been to lots of launch parties ever since I got into this business. And while the extravagance has been quite impressive, I'd be lying if I said that my closet wasn't currently filled with a few thousand dollars worth of trinkets and baubles celebrating projects and companies that have since been acquired, shuttered, or otherwise withered away.

These days the reality is that such extravagance is somewhat repugnant. And given how tight some corporate budgets are as of late, high-end launch parties can mean the difference between keeping a lower-paid staff member employed at the end of the budget cycle or having to give them a pink slip.

But – and I'm going to repeat this because I feel a little bad for raining on your parade – I'm **not** a killjoy. Launch parties **were** great, and I'm sorry that they're almost a thing of the past. So, perhaps we can find a way to combine a launch party of sorts with some other important tasks relating to the intranet in order to kill two birds with one stone, and maybe find an excuse to slip in some free food for good measure?

A launch party for the sake of a launch party is something I'd try to avoid. But, since you can never have enough user training (and you'll inevitably need a good bit of it even if your pre-launch marketing efforts have been superb), why not double-up your launch party with a user-training session? Then (can you see where I'm headed?) schedule the launch/training around lunch time, and bring in some food and soda for your staff members. In one fell swoop, you'll have:

- Managed to provide an exciting launch for the intranet along with an overview of all the key areas of content and functionality

- Empowered your employees to use the intranet via hands-on training, either through web tutorials, mini-conference style events run by a professional instructor, or through periodic user group meetings

- Boosted morale thanks to the free lunch!
- Made the employees first encounter with the intranet a memorable one.

Not all that bad for an honest day's work! (Not to mention that it's worlds easier to convince your boss to fund a training session than it is to get a *party* authorized!)

Promoting Intranet Use

So far you've managed to learn a good bit about the first two phases involved in the successful marketing of your intranet to your employees or co-workers. We've talked about a number of ideas that should help you to lay the foundation for an effective intranet launch even while your new intranet hasn't moved much beyond the confines of the drawing board, and we've also knocked around a few concepts about how to handle the launch itself.

But what happens after your intranet is up and running? What's left for the marketing folks to do after your intranet becomes part and parcel of your daily business experience, once all those logo-embossed intranet stress-balls and custom T-shirts are simply a fond, yet distant, memory?

Promoting intranet use over the longer term depends less on any particularly revolutionary marketing strategy than it does on a comprehensive and omnipresent adherence to what I like to call "housekeeping" marketing initiatives. The idea behind housekeeping marketing tasks is pretty simple: they're essentially like regular housecleaning chores in the real world, tasks that you may need to be shown how to accomplish once by someone in-the-know, but then are able to be performed by rote time and again, usually by subordinates.

As applied to our intranet, housekeeping marketing efforts are really ongoing mini-initiatives that require just a wee bit of creative thinking either in the very early planning phases, or perhaps infrequently from time to time just to ensure that our messaging and bigger-picture marketing efforts remain synchronized. And, of course, our HM efforts can be successfully handed off to lower-level employees for daily operational management. We'll now take a look at some good ideas for ongoing marketing attention.

Ensuring Project Sponsorship

One important task that the marketing team can focus on following the launch of the intranet is ensuring that project sponsors – senior managers and other influential stakeholders – remain enthusiastic, supportive, and committed to the continued success of the intranet.

The FactSheet

One of the most successful ways to accomplish this is to establish a monthly, single-page FactSheet that can present carefully chosen qualitative and quantitative data to selected managers and other VIPs. Content to feature should include a combination of:

- Basic metrics – total page views, unique user sessions, popular sections of the site, etc.
- Qualitative data – some of the more touchy-feely data, including your thoughts on why certain tools or content may be popular, updates on progress in deploying new content and functionality, positive or constructive quotes pulled from user feedback, and so on.

It is crucial that you limit this executive briefing to no more than one sheet of paper, perhaps going so far as to use both sides of the page. While I have encountered successful implementations of such briefings that have been as long as four single-sided pages overall, in my estimation successes in such circumstances are few and far between. The longer and meatier your briefing, the less, well, "brief" it becomes, and you run the risk of losing your target audience's interest. Remember, as you target an audience that is higher up the management food chain, the less time they'll likely have to read and digest the important pieces of data that you've made available. Make the most of the limited attention they're able to devote to your briefing, and concentrate on data elements that will most effectively capture their attention and promote their continued support.

FutureScape Briefings

Beyond the FactSheet, which helps to convince managers of the power and utility of the intranet based on *where we've been*, FutureScape Briefings provide a regularly scheduled, face-to-face opportunity in which to introduce executives to the future potential of the intranet, as made possible by new technologies, business plans, feedback from users, or other developments.

A typical FutureScape Briefing might include:

- a demonstration of how a Bluetooth-enabled PDA can surf the intranet wirelessly when paired with a Bluetooth cellphone (or other Bluetooth access point).

- A primer on XML, and how such a standard can benefit specific segments of your company in terms of overall productivity, cost-savings, etc.

- Highlights of users' intranet wish-lists, along with a brief vision of how such wish-list items might be successfully developed to the benefit of both the corporation and the employee.

Not only will you have an opportunity to press for *your* agenda with the full attention of your corporate executives, you'll also be able to solicit their input, field their questions, and make them feel more at ease not only with the technology itself but also with the ongoing role of the intranet within the overall business environment.

Include the Intranet in Staff Orientation

Another housekeeping task will be to ensure that your intranet is featured prominently and effectively throughout all staff orientation and continuing education materials. It's perfectly wonderful that you brought your existing employees into the intranet fold when you first launched it 11 months ago, but it's incumbent on the marketing staff to work in conjunction with human resources and other appropriate groups to "get the word" out even for new recruits, keeping in mind that the intranet is a living, changing creature – you'll need to revisit the orientation and related materials occasionally to ensure that they're complete and up to date.

Letterhead, Business Cards, and More

It's long been a well-accepted business practice to give special executive perks to certain managers, including custom-printed letterhead, notepads, etc. With the rise of the Internet as a core business and branding channel, many of these items have been further customized to include company logos, URLs, unique department taglines, and so on.

Once again, we'll fall back on our position that your intranet doesn't strictly need its own branding, so we'd recommend avoiding the added expense and complexity that go hand in hand with such custom printing. If your intranet has a particularly long or convoluted URL, perhaps it's reasonable to include the intranet address on some HR material, or the intranet team's business cards. However, a much better idea is mandating that your intranet simply be accessible from any web browser (password-protected at least, though you can also use more advanced SecureKEY technologies to reinforce your intranet's security – see *Chapter 10* for more information on intranet security) at *http://intranet.yourcompany.com* – which will make life much, much easier for everyone involved.

Setting the Default Browser Homepage

Another tactic you can use to promote knowledge and ongoing use of your corporate intranet is to set the default homepage in your employees' browsers to the intranet's URL. You can reach out to your information technology or desktop support group – the folks who are in charge of installing and supporting your desktop computers. They can easily change a few settings to ensure that your intranet is the first thing a user encounters when they start their browser application for the first time. A great companion idea is to add shortcuts to your users' desktop or quick-launch toolbar that will take them directly to the intranet. These are just as useful and are more likely to survive in the long term than their browser's default page settings.

*While it's OK to set the default browser page to your corporate intranet, **you shouldn't force users to keep the intranet as their default page**. (Companies will often do this by making special changes to Internet Explorer/Netscape or Windows settings to disable a user's ability to edit their start page.) This can really anger your user base. So unless your intranet is the coolest, most exciting, most wonderful web property ever, I'd recommend setting the browser to your intranet initially, but giving your employees wide latitude to change their settings at their convenience.*

Maximizing the Value of the Homepage

An area that deserves your attention – but that can prove somewhat tricky – is maximizing both the perceived and actual value of your intranet's homepage. This virtual real estate holds great rewards – and potential perils – for the ongoing utilization of your intranet, and it requires a careful balancing act to bring all the various pieces together in an effective manner.

Part of the difficulty lies in the simple fact that making your homepage valuable bridges a number of disciplines, including usability, editorial, and marketing, to name but a few. So the chances are that, as the marketing rep (or as the tech guy who's been hijacked into being the *de facto* marketing expert for the intranet), you won't have the freedom or the authority to act unilaterally in selecting the content to promote on the front page.

However, what you *can* do is two-fold. First, you should strive to work closely with the editorial, usability, and other representatives who "own" various parts of the front screen – allies are usually a good thing, and their additional support can often help achieve your nefarious – and not so nefarious – intranet goals.

Second, you should advocate the establishment of a special, marketing-controlled area of the main intranet page, as well as a marketing-controlled content silo (also sometimes called a "vertical") through which you can communicate directly with employees, encountering as few procedural roadblocks as possible *in your own corner of the intranet universe*. In this way you can ensure that at least part of the content on both the intranet's main page as well as in a deeper section is up to date, compelling to your users, and provides ample motivation for users to frequently make use of the intranet.

Keeping People Interested

We're closing in on some of the final issues that we need to discuss about internal intranet marketing and how it can help to support the acceptance and ongoing success of your intranet. But there are still a handful of additional items that are worth covering, so bear with me for just a few more minutes.

We take for granted that many of the business practices and marketing theories that we've discussed have come straight from Western cultures – mostly from the UK and the US, arguably the central pillars of Internet, intranet, and extranet development across the globe.

One of the best non-Western business philosophies that is especially relevant to our discussion of intranet marketing and how it can be utilized to continually improve your intranet (and your business as a whole) comes from the Japanese: *kaizen*. As it was first described in Masaaki Imai's book "KAIZEN, the Key to Japan's Competitive Success" (I'll keep the school lesson short, I promise!), *kaizen* was described as follows:

> *KAIZEN means improvement. Moreover, KAIZEN means continuing improvement in personal life, home life, social life, and working life. When applied to the workplace KAIZEN means continuing improvement involving everyone – managers and workers alike.*

Over the years, the concept of kaizen has evolved into something beyond a simple theory and has become, arguably, a holistic way of life that guides the Japanese in their approach to business systems, procedures, and challenges. Kaizen helps to focus the efforts of Japanese corporations and to unite both management and general workers alike in their quest to achieve a higher goal: eliminating all wasteful or superfluous excess within the business environment and in striving to attain the highest possible levels of quality, efficiency, and profitability.

Now, I certainly don't expect that you'll be running out to start a kaizen support group in your office, or that you'll even go out of your way to read up on kaizen after you turn the page. HOWEVER, what you *should* take away from my little cultural exposé is that there are a variety of different approaches that you can take to keep your intranet – or any business system, for that matter – fresh, relevant, and useful to your business. You simply need to keep an open mind and be receptive to new ideas as they cross your path.

Building Brand Identity

If you poke around on the Internet, you'll likely find lots of "experts" who talk about building a strong brand *for* your intranet. As we've discussed, that's patently dumb.

What you probably *won't* find lots of talk about is using your intranet to continually convey to your employees – or to refine your employees' understanding of – the brand identity, values, and macro-level goals espoused *by your corporation*. The better informed your employees are about every aspect of your operation, the better empowered they'll be in working to achieve your corporation's goals.

From time to time, take the opportunity to make available brand identity documents, host discussions of your company's mission, goals, and beliefs, and highlight other aspects of your organization's business practices as appropriate, including new lines of business, products in development, potential clients that you're targeting, etc. This can help to expand your employees' understanding and appreciation of the fundamental attributes of your corporation, and will unquestionably result in their being able to be more effective while working on your behalf.

An added bonus is that – by leveraging the intranet's ability to act as a two-way conduit for near real-time communication and collaboration, you'll not only be able to talk to your employees about your brand identity, you'll also be able to hear from them, giving employees a sense of buy-in while simultaneously tapping their knowledge and expertise to help keep your corporate identity fresh, relevant, and powerful.

Keeping the Intranet Fresh

Another critical item to keep at the tip of your brain is that you *must ensure that the content on your intranet is both current and comprehensive.* If your information is out-of-date, it's essentially useless to your employees. They'll figure it out pretty fast, too, and will find other avenues to obtain the information they need. It's important to establish an *editorial calendar* – a set schedule upon which certain areas of content will be developed, edited, and posted to the intranet – and to stick to it. It's less important whether this schedule involves daily, weekly, or even bi-weekly updates, so long as it meets the needs of both your corporation and your employees. As long as you embrace the concept of *anticipatory marketing* – namely the practice of providing marketing and other creative content at regularly defined intervals known by your audience – you'll be able to maintain a less-than-daily refresh schedule without an excessive risk of alienating your users.

Similarly, if you only post half of your HR policies and procedures, or don't quite include all the forms needed to accomplish a certain goal, say booking a trip to an industry conference, there will be a natural reticence that develops among your users that will hinder the adoption of your intranet. It's less important to provide *some* information on every topic within your company, and more important that what you *do* provide is comprehensive, useful, and functional for your employees. Even if your resources are limited, focus on small, bite-sized tasks – and do them well – and your intranet will enjoy far greater success.

Relaunching the Intranet

Every now and then your intranet will undergo some major growing pains, with your typical small, incremental updates morphing into a quarterly (or annual, etc.) re-envisioning of the user interface, information architecture, or significant portions of your intranet's content and functionality. How do you prepare your users for the shock – and potential usage nightmares – associated with deploying major changes to a well-established, familiar intranet? A relaunch.

Intranet Marketing

11

Realistically, a relaunch doesn't require any more tactics than we've discussed, but it's an often-overlooked opportunity that gets intranet teams in hot water. In fact, preparing users for the relaunch of an intranet is oft-times even easier than preparing them for an initial intranet deployment, as your intranet is a new and powerful communications channel that can be used to spread the word. What's more, you can feature online tutorials, or old versus new comparisons to illustrate how old processes and procedures (how to search the intranet, complete a form, reserve a conference room) are completed.

Not to mention that a relaunch gives the intranet team a proverbial *second bite at the apple*. Features and functionality that didn't fare well in the initial version of the intranet can be enhanced and tailored to more closely address the wants and needs of the user group, and can be upsold aggressively as part of the relaunch, as the more popular intranet components don't necessarily compete for attention.

Regular Usability Testing

Depending on how duties are segmented in your company, you – in your capacity as marketing lead – may or may not be responsible for providing initial or ongoing usability testing for your intranet. This is a valuable resource not only in terms of how functional the current site is, but also as a means for soliciting real-time, task-oriented feedback from users concerning both current and future content and functionality requests.

To ensure that your usability testing yields the most useful results, make sure to fill your testing pool with victims…I mean, *users*, from across the corporate spectrum, in terms of seniority, job discipline, and technical savvy.

Intranet As the First Point of Contact

As your efforts to provide timely and comprehensive intranet content and functionality are successful, employees will soon view the intranet as their primary point-of-contact, or source, for solving the problems they encounter each workday. Whether it's finding a particular form for an upcoming employee evaluation, looking up the phone number for the in-house courier service, or in booking a hotel room through the corporate travel agent, users will consciously begin to view opening a web browser and surfing the intranet as a more efficient and preferable course of action than the more expensive and less efficient manner of using the telephone.

Integrating into Daily Usage

Another significant avenue to explore in your efforts to foster the integration of the intranet into your employees' daily routine is to constantly highlight a small set of basic functionality that users would traditionally have accomplished multiple times each day via offline resources. This might include such tasks as locating phone numbers in the corporate directory, submitting timesheet data, reserving an overhead projector, or other common "workflow" tasks such as document trafficking, approval of expense reports, etc. By focusing your marketing efforts on some of the more pedestrian, but high-volume, activities that can be accomplished more efficiently via the intranet, you'll find that your users very quickly integrate the intranet into their daily usage patterns.

Budget for Incremental Development

Just because you've built and successfully launched your intranet doesn't mean the work is finished. Far from it! And the work of the marketing expert (also known as, you) is just beginning. One of the many additional ways that you can provide value to your employers is by intermittently sponsoring (or simply performing) a cost-savings or a time-value-of-money analysis, which can help to illustrate to management how the intranet saves the corporation money, not necessarily in direct cost savings (for example, less staples purchased – although those metrics are there, too) but also through the sheer savings in time cycles: invoices are processed 30% faster, we save 22 hours a month (multiplied by someone's salary and benefits) in tabulating payroll, etc.

As you work to calculate the return that your corporation's intranet investment will generate, be sure to attempt to capture at least a portion of the overall cost savings that can be channeled toward ongoing, or *incremental*, development. Whether it's 10% or a flat dollar amount, one of the best ways to secure added funding is to strike a deal with your managers: for every dollar we save the company via the intranet, you'll allocate x percent of such savings toward the next year's research and development projects.

Feedback Mechanisms

As the final thought for the chapter, it's paramount that you *constantly* provide avenues of communication – whether via e-mail, sticky notes, vmail, or through a Q&A period at the weekly staff meeting – that can capture a user's questions, comments, and concerns on an ongoing basis. Not only will this help to keep your users happy by providing them with a means through which to sound off, but it will also serve as a leading indicator of what sections of content or particular areas of functionality are becoming tired and dated, requiring either removal or a creative update, resulting in an intranet that constantly evolves to stay fresh, relevant, and valuable to the organization it serves.

Summary

Unlike the earliest days of intranet development, when intranets were left to succeed or fail basically on their own, today's corporate intranets often demand much more aggressive marketing efforts to promote widespread acceptance, let alone basic use. As we've discussed, this can be both a blessing *and* a curse. But as long as we're stuck building the intranets, it will often fall upon our shoulders to also make sure that the intranets *are successful* in the long run – not to mention that it's good to occasionally remind our bosses that we're busily adding value in these days of frequent and unexpected layoffs!

As you prepare to structure your assault on a marketing plan to promote your intranet to your coworkers, there are three key points to remember:

- **Identify challenges, big and small:** Early on, it's critical to identify the myriad challenges that will face your intranet marketing efforts – everything from a funky user-interface to a disinterested management team. Understanding the challenges that face your intranet will not only help you craft better short- and long-term marketing plans, but will also help you to focus your (always) limited resources on those challenges that are not so terribly daunting or entrenched as to be outside the reach of even the savviest marketing efforts.

11

- **Map out your core marketing strategy**: With your challenges in mind, begin to craft a marketing strategy that brings to bear all the "best practices" and other marketing techniques likely to negate such challenges and lay a foundation for a successful intranet property. Anything is fair game here, and includes the whole gambit of marketing tips and tactics – launch parties (big or small), user training, offline marketing through newsletters and corporate events, even co-opting employees early in the process to serve as intranet ambassadors who'll reach out to other employees as part of a grassroots marketing effort – nothing is off-limits that will help to ensure the successful launch and widespread acceptance of the intranet among your coworkers.

- **Work to keep users and management interested over the long term**: But it's not enough to launch the intranet and then hit the beach. A successful intranet is a living, breathing entity, and requires ongoing support not only to maintain the intranet as it exists in its initial form, but also to identify opportunities for growth and to secure the support and sponsorship from the appropriate stakeholders (or better yet, from the bean-counters with check-signing authority) in both management and from among the general worker pool.

  Whether you opt to host FutureScape Briefings or distribute printed factsheets to keep executives apprised of the intranet's progress and potential, it's paramount that the executives be targeted in addition to courting the rank-and-file employees through ongoing focus groups, questionnaires, usability testing, etc.

By applying the best marketing practices that we've detailed throughout this chapter, you'll enjoy far greater success in your initial efforts to deploy a new intranet property within your corporation, be more effective in soliciting ongoing feedback from employees throughout all levels of your organization for the ongoing operation of your intranet, and will become exceedingly adept at securing the support from both management and workers required to continually evolve your intranet as your corporate needs change over time.

12

- How big is too big?

- How did this situation arise?

- Solutions

Author: John Colby

When the Intranet Gets Too Big

What is "too big"? Big can mean "absolutely huge" or it can mean "too big to be able to know where everything is" or anything in between. The person who defines the "bigness of big" will probably impose their own views on the situation. They may have their own agenda, be involved in a power struggle, be a senior manager, or any combination of factors. The skill you will have already developed is to recognize this and deal with it, but let's say that for the purposes of this argument that "it's too big" means "it's got to change and become more manageable.".

What we'll do in this chapter is to assemble a collection of strategies that can work together to bring your intranet under your control and include sites that are part of an internal web resource that had not been widely publicized. In this type of case you may not have been aware of their existence. Of necessity you will have to tailor any strategy to suit your local conditions and management. This is not an exact science – there's no magic cure to intranet consolidation that will satisfy everyone in the company, so compromises have to be made somewhere. There's no guarantee that the final solution you adopt will even be the best one as you see it, but that's the art of compromise.

We'll be using case studies in this chapter to illustrate some of the concepts I'm trying to put over – and your own situation may have certain similarities them.

- How did we get into this situation?
- Where are you now and where do you want to be?
- Think before acting
- Setting the foundations
- Communication and marketing are key
- Design matters
- Transition strategies
- Future-proofing

How Did We Get into This Situation?

Without proper planning the intranets can easily become dispersed and uncontrolled. How you initially identify what "dispersed" and "uncontrolled" actually mean is up to the organization in question. The example we will describe shortly is a story of how one organization tried to consolidate a set of web sites that had been built to cater for specific information demands when the main intranet proved too slow or too conservative to respond. Bear in mind that, during the period of this example, corporate, personnel, and management changes altered the way in which the intranet was managed.

The definition of "dispersed" in this case was interlinked with the definition of "uncontrolled". The intranet was considered "dispersed" because there was more than one place to look for information, and "uncontrolled" because management, who defined what was meant by "uncontrolled", was possibly influenced by a corporate strategy that was not communicated to the people on the ground who had already built the sites.

Case Study: How We Got Here

You may have an internal intranet site or two. Then more appear. Or maybe you have an 'official' intranet and web servers start appearing, individual or departmental. These may be the result of someone's 'good idea' and they're used both in the department and outside, or they may be a way of documenting what an individual, team, or department does. Whatever it is, you get satellite web servers appearing for either general or very specific audiences. These are in the main good ideas and effort expended by people working independently to what they see as enhancing what they do and providing information about what they do – maybe the company has said "we're not very good at communication", and these people have done something to address that.

So let's plot a time chart – units are arbitrary. Links can be one- or two-way, adding to the confusion.

Time: T

The intranet begins life as a simple intranet, centrally managed and reasonably well-used. Others perceive the limitation, but don't say, or don't have the mechanism to say. The Server in this case is a designated server (or server cluster) that is the host of the main intranet. We're using a simplified 'black box' diagram approach here.

Figure 1: simple intranet

Time: T + 1

A manager has been asked to produce documentation for a project. This involves loads of paper, revisions and collation of several people's efforts, and time, which they haven't got. Then someone says, "Why don't we build a web site?". So a new server is built that the department can control. In this case server may mean something like a Linux or Windows Server with Apache, a Windows server with IIS or Windows workstation with PWS, or any other conceivable method of web serving – it really doesn't matter for the purposes of this explanation.

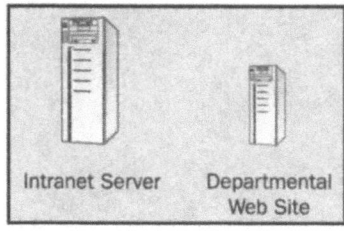

Figure 2: intranet and departmental server

Time: T + 2

So the web site is built – and it gets talked about at peer level. It becomes something of a feather in the cap of the department, and because it's good the idea gets copied. Departments talk to each other and interlink their own web site homepages. However this interlinking can be quite random

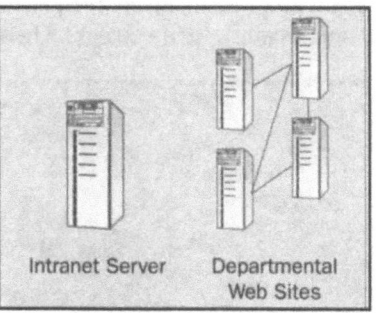

Figure 3: interlinked departmental web sites

Time: T + 3

Individuals get in on the act – they want to learn the technology of web sites, build them on their own PCs and build web servers and become very skilled at doing so. The authors have the same sort of personal links as the departments, and random links develop, and the existing sites find more to link to. The intranet administrators have heard of some of these sites and try to link into some of them. But they can't find them all.

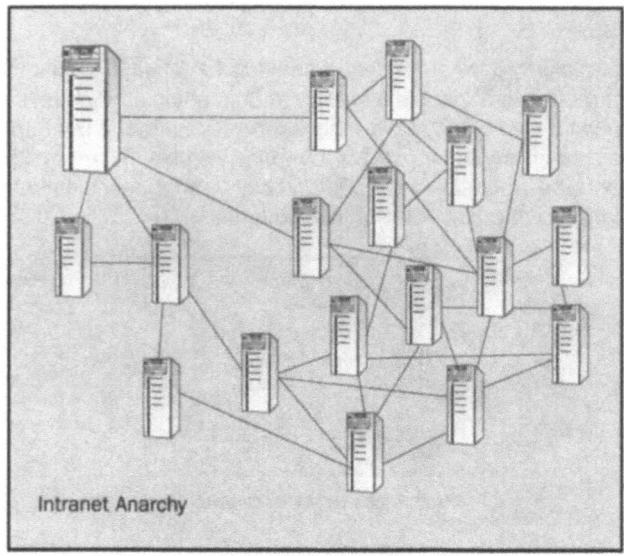

Figure 4: chaotic intranet

Time: Today

The result is a widely dissipated set of information held on a variety of servers with links that get confusing. The intranet managers recognize the value of having all this information and try to provide a link to everything. They fail. Even trying to maintain such links is getting to be a fulltime task, as they have both to discover the sites and talk to the owners. Then keep track of changes.

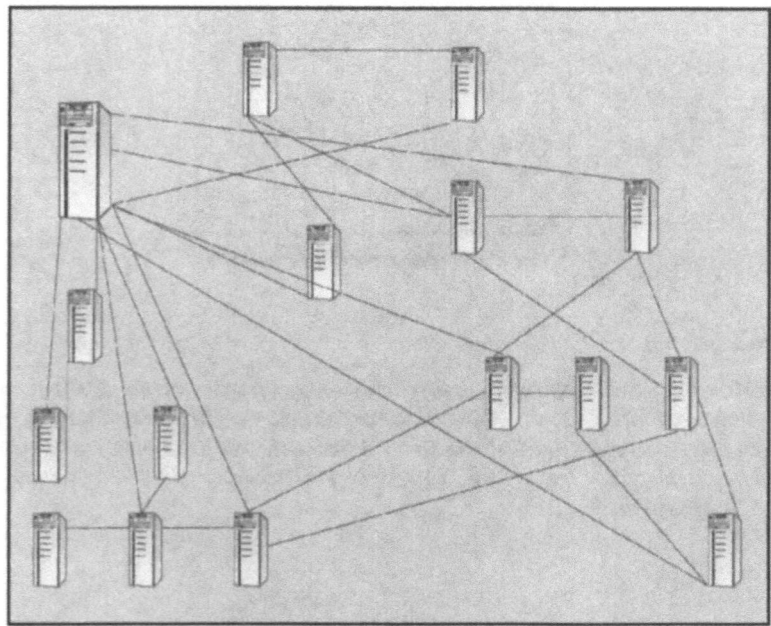

Figure 5: uncontrolled and anarchic intranet

Relax, You Are Not Alone

The vast majority of companies have an intranet that is fragmented to a greater or lesser degree; there is no perfect intranet. Whatever exists in your company is the result of various pressures and compromises. And of course, the intranet is not static; new content needs to be added the whole time, not only to keep the intranet live, but because business is dynamic. The best that can be achieved practically is to design your perfect solution and attempt to move towards it, always aware that the goalposts are going to change as new functions are found for the intranet. So in this chapter we won't present a foolproof solution, instead we will present an open-ended approach allowing yourself to promote a coherent structure and giving yourself the framework in which it can operate and allow for change.

Reasons Why You May Be in This Situation

We've given a broad example of the scenario you may find yourself managing – but let's just examine for a while how this has developed. Identifying the elements of the scenario that you are facing will assist you in dealing with the people who have put it in place. There may have been very good reasons why this situation developed. It may be because the controllers of the intranet were not receptive to new ideas or took too long to implement them, or didn't want to let go of the power. It may be any combination of these factors. Whatever led you to this juncture, it is now your job to bring some sort of order into the chaotic anarchy that is now in place. You've probably identified it as chaotic anarchy because it's not working well – and you have navigation, content, or duplication problems. We'll deal with each of these later in this chapter.

Organic Growth

Your intranet may have grown organically, without a development plan in place. This is a natural consequence of unplanned and uncontrolled development, but often has the advantage of adding valuable content quickly. I'll be talking later about the way that this effort is utilized – if you go about it the wrong way it is very easy to alienate the people who have put in the work to get their sites up and running. Assuming that their content is useful, alienation is not going to help in your efforts to make a coherent intranet. However in this organic growth there is the danger of content duplication – or worse, different solutions for the same sort of problem that will lead to confusion amongst users.

Organic growth will have brought a rich diversity of information content into the wider realm of your users. It is worth thinking that even though the information contained on those sites may have been repeated by others, that the audience for those sites may not appreciate that there is another source of that information.

Sub-Brand Ownership

The ownership of an intranet site may have become a status symbol where departments have created their own 'sub-brand' within the company. A sub-brand may be a statement of identity or an element in the power struggle within the company. You may not be aware that there is a power struggle, so objectivity and tact must be the order of the day. You could find yourself unwittingly drawn into inter-departmental politics that you never knew existed! Sub-branding may be important to the department or people in question, as they may see their collective or individual identity within the company as not as high-profile as they would like. This must be considered in how you handle any change process for the intranet.

Introduction of a CMS

Has the diversity of web sites and web site content come to light as a result of the implementation or consideration of a new Content Management System? In the analysis prior to its implementation any duplication or diversity would have come to light. If, as does happen, a CMS is imposed on a division by the corporate management, it may well have come to light as those charged with implementing the CMS are part-way through the job. This will cause angst to those who thought that their plans were well-developed. A well-thought-out CMS will be able to cope with this problem, however on most occasions this is not the case – and either the CMS or the content (or both) will have to be shoehorned to fit.

Publishing Controls Didn't Exist

It is almost inevitable that in a diverse organically grown intranet that there will be little compliance with a corporate design or adherence to standard uses of the code necessary. It is inevitable that designers of the disparate sites will have used whatever tools they feel comfortable with – Frontpage, Dreamweaver, Arachnophilia, Homesite, TopStyle, Word, hand-coding, what you will. What is virtually certain is that very few of these sites are going to have a DTD (Document Type Definition) so that the browsers will have to enter 'quirks' mode to deal with a language they'll have to interpret before being told what it is. Also, while the intranet is subject to accessibility requirements, it is likely that only a few of these content producers will have adhered to them.

There will be reasons for people using a variety of tools – probably because they know no other way and have acquired the tools to do the job. They probably do not know about or appreciate the importance of standards – they'll use the ones that the first book they bought about HTML coding tells them. They'll use convoluted table-based layouts and spacer graphics to achieve what they want, often because that is what the tool is doing for them. So their content will be bloated and not as trim as it may be.

There is a considerable school of thought that sees the coding style as unimportant – unfortunately this pervades a large number of commercial web sites. In any redesign, if you are not able to use the latest coding standards then you're only causing trouble for yourself in the future when markup standards like XHTML 2.0 make an impact.

So where does this leave publishing controls? Much as it will be resisted, you will have to implement them and win the authors round. We'll deal with how a little later.

It Doesn't matter, It's Only the Intranet

The intranet is often perceived as a poor second cousin to the Internet. The Company's Internet presence is, after all, the public face of the company. Only employees use the intranet, so it may be considered that they must manage as best they can. There are more important things to do, like producing products for sales, than look after the internal systems. However you look at it, development of an effective intranet solution will reflect on the eventual cost-effectiveness of the way that people work within the company.

> *Refer to Chapter 2 concerning Return on Investment for a detailed discussion on this.*

Does this sort of argument really hold water? Is not the goal of organizations to make things run as smoothly as possible for all concerned? And where has this view come from? Presumably it was not current when the original intranet was first conceived. Has anything changed? Consider the following:

- Have there been management changes so that the focus of the business is different?

- Have there been changes in the fortunes of the company?

- Are the original site designers and architects still with the company, or still in the same sort of positions?

- Have there been any redundancies? Those left within the company will probably need re-motivating.

- Has everyone just got fed up with criticism?

- Has the person who was the driving force lost the support of their manager?

This is all very well as an argument – except that you have to ask yourself how much extra effort is being expended in producing those extra sales because the information systems on the intranet are not readily accessible. Let's assume for the purposes of this argument that the intranet is important to the company and allows your employees to do a better job. If there is the perception of the intranet being a second-class citizen then you have to promote it. You'll have to justify it to the business. Be realistic on how it can be used and why it should be used. Presumably you are an intranet fan, and don't want to see its use terminated. One of the ways is to make sure that it is viewed as a strategic resource.

The Intranet Is Not a Strategic Resource

If the intranet is not perceived as a strategic resource within the company, before embarking on any redesign you have to question whether the perception will change – otherwise what's the point of doing the redesign?

So before going any further, try making a list of what makes a strategic resource and discover some reasons why your particular intranet doesn't fit into the correct category. Here are some of the questions:

- Is the intranet used?

- For what purpose is the intranet used?

- Can you identify an improved ROI?

- Is it an information repository, or an information black hole?

- Are any questions being asked on any intranet forums being answered? If not, why not? Is it down to the moderators or administrators having better things to do?

- What was the last time that a question was asked on any of the forums? If more than a few days ago ask why.

- Have alternatives been developed to using the intranet because information can't be found? Have the information systems been hijacked?

- Is everyone who wants use the resources able to do so?

- Are remote users excluded because they're, well, remote? Are home workers given full access into the intranet? Is this a problem you have to take up with your infrastructure people?

- If you allow sales people and engineers access to the intranet, are they using it or are they embarrassed to use it because it takes up too much time or looks awful – are they phoning up the office to get information because of this, therefore tying up two people's time?

This list is not closed – in fact it is very open-ended – you can go on for ages developing a hobby of intranet-bashing. So identify the key points and work on them. Above all you have to get the resource recognized as strategic and important to the future working of the company. Otherwise you may find yourself in a position of closing the whole thing down because you don't have a justification for its maintenance.

So let's assume that you can make a case for the intranet being strategic, we can now proceed.

Perspective – The Intranet Wasn't Too Big, It Just Got Very Fragmented

Following on from the previous case study where we declared the results of intranet construction anarchy was the cause of our problems, we didn't take into account what was happening inside the first box we drew that was labeled Intranet Server. It's easy and comfortable to blame everyone else outside the 'official' intranet, but if there was a policy and welcome in place for new information to be put into the 'official' intranet then the number of diverse web sites may not have developed in the first place. Or maybe the intranet server itself has become a little difficult to manage with the resources that were granted.

Let's look at another slant on how the intranet can have grown. As a reminder let's take a second look at conceptual diagram of the organically grown, fragmented intranet:

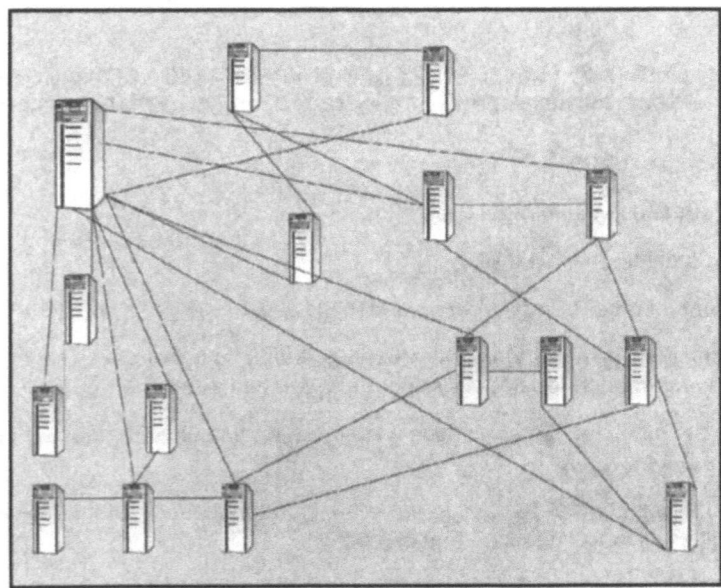

A reminder of the initial situation you could be starting with

But what if the intranet server itself has become unwieldy? Not because of the size of the server, although that may be a contributory factor, but because of random additions and changes to the menu navigation system. Two of the multitude of possibilities here are trying to put everything on one page or trying to organize things by author or department rather than popularity or task.

Maybe also the maintenance of the existing intranet server has become fragmented, and the directory structure no longer represents the content. People may have had good ideas and have placed bits of the site in directories that are meaningless to anyone else but the original author. There could also be dead files out on any of the sites. Here are some instances gleaned over the years of directories and filenames that make little sense. I've also included what they were renamed to.

Directory	What it meant	Rename
sue_lambert.htm	Staff list (you would have guessed?).	staff_list.html
g_input	Directory of graphics files – you had to know that g_ prefixes meant that the directory contained .gif images.	graphic
p_input	Directory of photograph files – you had to know that p_ prefixes meant that the directory contained .jpeg images.	images
d980714	Directory of content for a customer conference (you'd have had to know the date of the conference to relate this).	cust_conf_98
mike-htm	Directory of .html files worked on by (you've guessed) Mike. This had to be divided up and remapped so that the subjects of the files were reflected in their names. Not only was the name meaningless but it was also confusing – it was a directory but may have looked like it should have been an HTML file.	

These may have meant something to the original development team, but it was unmaintainable once the team changed.

There was also the case of the people who put the lengthiest description possible on files and directories, such as Jean Smithson Conference Presentation July 99 - New Products and Future Developments.ppt – a filename length of 87 characters. If you need to distribute these files especially by CD, then you may have trouble cutting them as some software for CD burners have been known to choke on filenames longer than 64 characters (or with directory trees more than eight levels deep).

Symptoms of an Overgrown Intranet

It may be that the only thing that users perceive wrong with the intranet is the length of time that it takes to find anything. This can often be solved by a simple case of signposting and navigation. Here are some of the typical signs of a "too big" intranet:

- You get phone calls and e-mails as users complain of being unable to find anything. How often have you received an e-mail asking if you know where a particular piece of content is on the intranet? The question to be asked first here is "does it exist?" – is the user trying to find something that just isn't there – is there a content hole?

- If users are disillusioned then usage of the intranet will decline, even if essential information is only available on that medium. Users will not bother to look on the intranet because of the disillusionment, and bad-mouthing may well occur. This may not only be a symptom of an overgrown intranet but of some other condition.

12

- If there is duplication of information then users may well be confused where to go. This is a frequent occurrence of organically grown intranets where different authors have detailed a complete process, some elements of which are common to a number of processes. For instance, a software house with products written by a number of departments may each have told the users how to configure a Windows server. If the ostensibly duplicate information gives different instructions then this can be at best confusing and at worst dangerous.

- Information may be inconsistent and patchy. You have to determine the level of detail that is appropriate to the page, not always an easy task with a diverse user base. If, for instance, a common procedure known to everyone in the company is omitted, what happens to the new employee? How do they find out what to do? This content gap should be plugged. Inconsistency of design will force users to educate themselves on how the individual bits of the site work each time a new portion is launched. This is not only confined to the technicalities of menu systems but the general arrangement of the page. However, too similar looking pages with indistinct titles and navigation may also result in the user being confused.

- Has the discovery that the intranet is overgrown been prompted by other factors, for example the result of an internal audit or survey? Do you have to give an immediate answer or excuse? If it's an excuse should you not have known? How could you not have known? Have you known and reported on it but your report has been ignored?

- If a significant amount of content is out of date or inaccurate then it's time that someone did something. That someone may be you! The intranet can be a boring place if there's nothing new. The content must be live and dynamic reflecting the perception of the company by the workforce.

- Fragmentation – we've already illustrated this in the case study – if it's difficult for users to discover what's there let alone navigate round it then the intranet tends to be less used than it may be for maximum efficiency. In a fragmented intranet the current perception, integrity, and trust of the facility is probably low.

So when you have identified signs and symptoms, what can you do? Assuming that "nothing" is not an option, you will probably have to prepare cost/benefit analyses of why you should be spending more of your time on the resource that senior management may not see with the same clarity of vision that you have. You'll have to do some convincing and selling to ensure that you get the resources to make it work this time. The remainder of this chapter is concerned with looking at how the existing intranet can be brought up to scratch and become worthy of the company so that it'll be used much more.

You will also have to become something of a visionary and evangelist.

The Benefits of Re-Developing Your Intranet

The intranet you have created or inherited is, whatever its state, a valuable company resource. It contains at the very least some important braindumps from your skilled employees – but one of your problems is finding out just what is useful and what isn't. We'll leave that for the moment and take a look at the overall picture. You have to define certain criteria that the new intranet will be designed to meet.

- The new intranet must support agreed business objectives.

- Make the intranet more user-centric.

- Can you offer a better internal service?

- By providing better business-oriented information you can provide your business with better adaptability to the marketplace.

- With information in one place, there is a faster induction process for new employees, especially if that information is background.

- Faster communication will be enabled through your new intranet

- You will have better informed, and consequently empowered, employees since your new intranet will be an organizational asset containing business information and knowledge.

- The new intranet reinforces organizational training and development initiatives.

- For organizations that have geographic diversity the intranet can be used as an online community.

We'll now discuss each of these in more detail.

Supporting Agreed Objectives

We said that the new intranet must support business objectives. What are the business objectives? Can you define them? The short and self-evident answer is that you must be able to define the business objectives, otherwise you'll have a hard time justifying (to anyone) any change that you propose. How they apply specifically to your company can only be up to you; see *Chapter 2* regarding Return on Investment to refine your arguments here.

Making the Intranet User-Centric

If users have been complaining, listen to their concerns and what they're complaining about. It may be that the information they need is well hidden, too complex, not in the right form, or simply isn't there. You'll have to tailor the intranet to be more user-centric. If the current intranet is just a knowledge base, consider whether the new intranet should be able to serve up information about current customer requirements and project progress; in other words, make the resource much more dynamic and responsive to users' needs.

Improving the Internal Service

Can you offer a better internal service? Can you define a service level that you expect the intranet to achieve, such as 80% of all queries being answered by reference to the online resource? Can you measure a service level, or is the exercise in quantifying this part of the criteria not cost-effective as the effort that would be expended in the definition exercise is out of all proportion to a foreseeable return? Is the conformance to your proposed service level achievable? Because if not, aim for a lower target. If you don't know what your base figures are for the current intranet, you'll have to carry out analysis to determine those figures before offering an improvement. However this is one of the measures of lesser importance unless your company require such detailed quantification.

12

Business-Oriented Information

You could aim to provide better business-oriented information (your CMS designers should have something to input here) in order to provide your business with better adaptability to the marketplace. By knowing what is happening in, say, development, marketing, and sales you will have a better idea about targets. Conversely Development can read about the promises that Marketing have been making. If you are putting in a CMS this will require that you have certain standards in place such as page and document templates so that information is presented in a consistent manner.

Employee Induction Processes

With information in one place, there is a faster induction process for new employees, especially if that information is background. The employee will have to go through Health and Safety, and Fire Drill procedures, but things like how to submit an expense claim, notice to give in respect of holidays, the names of people to contact in Payroll and similar less frequently used items of information can be left as a searchable record rather than taking up valuable trainer time. If the whole information were to be printed out and given to the employee at the start of their employment it will become out of date as soon as the first piece of information changes.

Faster Communication

Faster communication will be enabled through your new intranet – if it is designed correctly, and especially if a good workflow system is integrated with the intranet. This is not just the sending e-mail but the discovery of who to send the e-mail to in the first place. If you have your internal telephone directory on the intranet, that will save hundreds of bits of paper being stuck on monitors or walls. But if you do have an internal phone book, make sure that the users can construct a favorites list – those people with whom they frequently confer. It saves both the bits of paper and the endless searching for the correct information.

Benefits to Employees

You will have better informed, and consequently empowered, employees – as long as your company subscribes to the idea of employee empowerment. Most forward-thinking companies do, but it will not hurt to spell this advantage out. This is because your new intranet will be an organizational asset containing business information and knowledge. It will also contain the knowledge base of the company, so you'd better start thinking about security and backups.

Reinforcing Organizational Development Initiatives

The new intranet reinforces organizational training and development initiatives. When such initiatives are being discussed, the new intranet should be the first place that they are made public. This will increase the usage of the intranet – presumably what you want. If you're doing your job properly and people are reading the intranet then these new items will jump out at them – if they don't they're not being sold correctly.

Online Community

For organizations that have geographic diversity the intranet can be used as an online community. We discussed the use of the intranet for discussion forums and the formation of the Knowledge Base in *Chapter 9*. It's also the place where far-flung people can keep in touch. With home-working becoming more popular, it can also be isolationist. The use of an effective intranet is a way round this isolation.

In summary, what are the overall Business Objectives? Can we yet define them? The answer is yes, using selections from this list where relevant. How they apply to your company can only be up to you.

Where Do You Want to Be?

If you have never undertaken research of this nature before, put yourself in the position of a market researcher who stops you in the street. When they approach you their manner will determine how well, or if at all, you answer their questions. People like being asked their opinions as long as there is no compulsion to 'get the answer right'. What you have to do is ask the right questions to the right groups of people. All these lists are open-ended – you have to tailor the questioning to your own situation.

Research, Research, Research

Researching what you need may be a little alien to you if you are a hands-on coder and think you can see clearly the path you want to take. However in order to refine your system specification you need to involve the people or groups of people who are your audience. This serves two purposes – first it enables you to refine your ideas and second it makes the users feel involved. Remember that an intranet is used by a closed and relatively well-defined set of users compared with the Internet. Iteration is the key – once you have your initial research results go back and involve your users once again. There's a double benefit to this. First you are getting closer to your audience and enthusing them more, and second you're refining your model so that you stand a chance of producing a better product.

- You have to determine who are the key major stakeholder groups in wishing to get the intranet right. There may also be some major groups who want you to get it wrong, maybe those who think they should be controlling it in the first place.

- Get some really honest research conducted. Ask the questions that may hurt. Don't be scared of poor results, it only serves to support the project you're about to undertake. In a sense, the worse comments are the better!

- Make sure that you are able to understand the issues from a user's perspective. If the users have difficulties, make sure you understand where they are. When you go back with your redesign, address the solution to those difficulties directly with the people who brought them up. That will get them on board for your solution and make them your ambassador.

- You could think about running an anonymous survey where the answers are not attributable. Although this may have been a more acceptable practice in the office environment of the 1950s, the more you can get people to identify the problems with the intranet personally the better you can commit to giving them service. If there is no other choice then get the survey anonymously, but in my opinion it is very much a last-ditch option. Also if you adopt the anonymous survey approach you will not be able to either ask for clarification or give follow-up except generally.

- Sometimes in this process it is absolutely critical to get senior management onboard. Without them you'll get nowhere. However you have to choose your moment and your subject carefully. If one member of senior management could be thought of as having an interest in what you're aiming for, target them. If you get one person on board, there's your ambassador for the rest.

- Ask what is your intranet costing you now? If you can drop the duplication factor by x percent, you'll be reducing the cost of managing the content by the same percentage. If, by implementing standards, you can reduce development costs or by implementing Linux servers over Windows servers you reduce the licensing costs your accountant's going to listen at least.

- But also take time to find out what's good about the intranet as currently arranged. In performing all your miracles (you'll feel like they are once you've finished) you definitely don't need to throw the baby out with the bathwater. Take the example of the person we identified above who has given you some useful feedback about what's wrong – also ask what's right. Taking back a solution to their problem alone you may find that you've just gone and inadvertently removed what they really liked – and in so doing you've just lost an ambassador. It may have been something simple like the color scheme – and they may be color-blind – you weren't to know and your new sleek scheme has reduced the contrast for them so the pages are more difficult to read. If you know about this, you can compensate for them in their browser by supplying an alternative stylesheet, assuming you're taking the Standards route for writing web pages.

- In your research, find out just who has web sites hidden away. What do they do, how are they maintained, and who uses them? We'll be using this information to make some instant improvements.

So listen to your users – they're the only ones you've got, and they alone will determine whether your regeneration project is going to be a success. This may seem obvious, but maybe ignoring the users got the intranet to where it is, fragmented and difficult to use. We'll be addressing user buy-in and selling and marketing your solution later on. Just be aware for the moment that it's the way you're going to have to go. Enthusiastic user support does not come without effort. And without that you'll have a slow take-up for your new designs.

The Joined-Up Intranet – Leaving Things As They Are But Improving the Mapping

Let's return back to the example company mentioned earlier. They first carried out a survey, and then started by making the navigation of the existing intranet easier by redesigning the main page of the existing intranet as a portal to the existing server and all the other machines scattered around. That is the start of being both able to organize the intranet, and show users an immediate improvement.

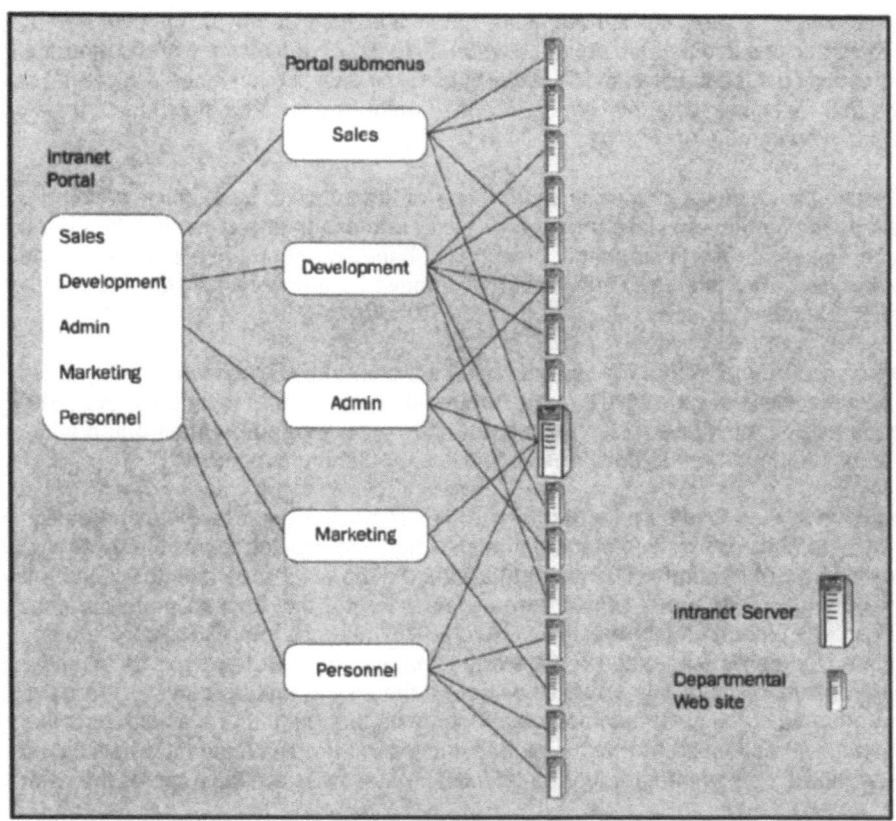

Figure 6: organizing the intranet

Having gathered information about the web sites that exist and what they do, construct a portal page that will improve the navigation. The links between departmental and individual machines are not shown – they are the same as before. The portal is sensibly organized with respect to menus – it's one of the developments that was necessary to start making inroads into the redesign.

Applying It to Your Company

By constructing a very simple web page the issue of navigation can largely be solved – at least temporarily. What you have is a very simple quick and dirty fix – publicize the address of the portal and encourage its use. Publicize it personally to the ambassadors you've selected from the research stage – this need not be time-consuming, maybe a personal pre-announcement e-mail. If you do this you start keeping them attuned to the intranet.

At this stage you've done nothing to remove any of the functionality or links that already exist even on the existing intranet server – you can still have people work the same way. So you also pre-announce the changes to the owners of the departmental and individual web sites you found during your research – it shows you value their contribution and want to make more of it.

So now onto the next phase as you've finished the research.

Hold on, have you actually finished? Or is this just one stage of an iterative process that you're going through? Maybe you add items to the portal gradually as you find out what they are whilst performing the research and then you get feedback so that modifications to the design become easier. Whatever you do you have to apply all this to your own company – so there's no absolute right and wrong way as long as it works for you in the end.

Do you "launch" after this change? In my opinion, no – you announce it as a minor change to improve navigation. Singing about success too early is going to make the real launch harder. And please retain all the research – this phase has been crucial and you need to be able to justify the effort that will be involved. At this stage each server will have its own look and feel, you've only changed a couple of pointers.

So now you can start on the real work of redesign. Now's the time to start plotting what you want done. You can now more easily review what's out there, and you'll find that people will start telling you about their sites as you may have missed some and they don't want to be left out. It takes a pretty isolationist mindset not to want to belong, so this is a pretty natural process.

In any design you have to start with some sort of vision. Is making all sites use the same design structure important? Are accessibility and standards an issue? Do you want to give the owners of the existing sites a degree of freedom? Think of the pros and cons. If all sites look the same the intranet may look boring and it's more difficult to navigate as you have to read more carefully where you are. So paint a picture of where you want to go – what does it look like? Are you using any existing company standards – indeed are there any that you can use or are you defining the standards in what you are doing? Only you can decide, there's no magic formula. You have a fragmented intranet, but do you have the immediate resources to bring it under a single machine, for instance. How would you cope, both with the loading and the extra administration work? Would it be better to plan stage by stage integration and let existing site owners take some of the work off your hands.

Is it necessary to throw everything away and start again? Sometimes it may be the course of action that's required, but that's rather drastic. How many people would you lose while on this path and would it all really be better when you've finished? Unless you are in a real position of dictatorial power with a load of resources at your disposal then this is probably not an option. So how do you decide what to do?

One way is to run workshops or brainstorming sessions. These are some of the most powerful ways to get honest feedback and attendees feed off each other's ideas. Members of your workshops should include the departmental and individual web site owners. They're the ones who had the inspiration in the first place. You also need to include some of the users, the ambassadors, so that you can both show them that you mean business and that the provision of a portal doesn't mean that the job's done, and get their input in the same room as the designers. And listen – you can learn much from what people don't say as well as what they do. And have your own questions – throw in some really outrageous ideas and see if anyone takes them up – it's surprising how wacky you can be – get some humor going – if nothing else it gets people to relax. All this requires some skill in leadership, but it's not daunting. Once you have got the discussion going you can relax a bit. So for any session set some sort of private agenda – not hidden agenda – so that you are able to cover all the topics you believe are necessary. And when you've covered them, ask if there's anyone who has something else. You could conceivably have missed something.

While doing a brainstorm start off with a blank page – a blank, clean (large) whiteboard, nothing else. Your attendees will then feel compelled to fill it – don't start off by doing any work for them, let someone from the floor start the ball rolling – a single word will do – then the ideas will start flowing. You'll find that the board will quickly become filled. And don't try to lead the discussion all the time – try handing over the marker pens to someone else so that you have time to be part of the audience and absorb what is being said. In the end you'll have a whole load of information that you'll have to reduce to something manageable, but do it with the co-operation of the attendees at the time – if you take it away to analyze then you'll lose them and their support. Make a result from your brainstorm – that way it will have the agreement of everyone and they'll feel that something has been achieved. They'll achieve a sense of belonging to and ownership of the solution.

I know that this has been about something more general than the new intranet design process, but brainstorm sessions are a great way of channeling energy. You have to be something of an energy source to start off with, but there rarely fails to be a synergy and even if those partaking have never met before, the sense of belonging to the team is heightened more than they or you expected. Strange but true. Once you've been part of a brainstorming team you can go back months or years later, even after you've forgotten their names, and start talking to them. They'll remember you as well.

That's only one way and probably by far the most effective. There are formal methods of obtaining feedback:

- Realize that not everything is bad about the existing intranet. There's the old wisdom that developers see only the problems in the product and that salespeople see only what's good. Embrace what's great about your current intranet, build on these strengths.

- Do you have an internal Market Research resource you can deploy internally?

- If you are considering using a range of existing design templates, research users' views. Conduct some usability and heuristics tests to determine what you are proposing is going to work.

- Analyze your technical architecture and infrastructure. Is it up to the job if you're going to move all web serving onto one system? Or would you be better off distributing it?

- Interpret usage statistics to assess most and least frequently used areas and identify trends in user behavior, for example peak times. By running a portal this may be a way of collecting those statistics. You also need analysis of the departmental and individual sites themselves – a way of checking what proportion of visitors are using the portal and how many are going direct.

- Are there other project teams already trying to resolve this issue? This type of activity is often found in Knowledge Management or Internal Audit teams.

- Put in some time to listen and watch what's going on. Spend time away from your desk (do you really need an excuse?) with users and find out about the operation of other parts of the company. Very few people are going to begrudge a ten-minute chat about how you can help them improve their working life.

- Are there elements of your existing intranet that are the worlds best kept secret? Finding out is a different matter – and you can only do this by being aware of what your users are telling you, so keep listening.

- Can you get feedback from each of these activities you're undertaking. If really necessary can you give incentive for feedback? One thing here – if you do this you may get people telling you what they think you want to hear. It's not an option to be used lightly. This type of incentive can be anything from entering a prize draw (pretty crude) to having their name in the acknowledgements on the intranet (name in lights syndrome) which reinforces their sense of belonging to the final product. (Yes, and I'm pretty pleased to have my name on the cover of this book – it works at all levels)

- Identify any business critical facets of the intranet – these must be guarded during the development process.

- You might be re-developing the intranet but it still needs to function. You may try the approach of using your portal and changing links when they're up and running, a process of gradual change. In any phase of your switch over, be sure that you leave the original intact so that if you do make a mistake and it falls all over the floor that you have the reassurance of the original to fall back on. If you don't it could be problematic for you. Leaving alone what works is your insurance policy.

Think Before Acting

This could be viewed as yet another self-evident heading, but it's easier to say than live up to. Under pressure from all sorts of people you may be pressured to implement a solution. You will not be able to satisfy everyone but the more time, within reason, that you are able to consider an answer the better your solutions may become. Conversely too much time spent in thought may alienate your audience.

Create a 'Strategy' Rather Than a 'Fix'

A fix is for a one off, a strategy allows you a path of action and growth. The initial fix will of course be consistent with your strategy, won't it? If it is a fix for an unusual set of circumstances that will change then your strategy has got to say so. Any strategy you develop will be dictated by any number of circumstances, not least the performance of the company in its chosen marketplace and the general economic climate. You should be in a position to review your strategic intranet objectives with relation to the overall company objectives, performance and strategy.

- You won't solve the problem if you just tidy up what you've got. All the portal menu has done thus far is to bring any shortcomings more into the open. You'll still have the lack of standards, the different designs, the different navigation. You have to look at the content as well to determine that duplication and holes do not occur. It needs a rethink. Look at the next case study to find out how one rethink failed.

- In this process you'll have to create solid foundations for the future – and you have one chance to do it. To take something that isn't working well to convert it with a load of time and effort into something else that doesn't work well is not really an option. If this seems like stating the obvious, then it is, but it really is amazing how many organizations limp from one redesign to the next without coming up with a solution. More of the Dilbert factor, I fear, or maybe not being allowed to complete the task, or having an inadequate model to start with.

- One way to ensure that you do activate a redesign is to instigate standards for the future. If you adopt something that's going to improve the browser, Internet device, and user accessibility, you're going to have to force a redesign and not be tempted to "leave it as it is, it's OK". My own preference is to take a radical approach and remove all frames and layout tables and really separate content and presentation using XHTML 1.1 and CSS2 (or whatever are the latest standards to apply when you're reading this book) – and this will force you to redesign. If you do this then you make it easier to ensure that your designs will be current for the next generation of browsers, which are at the time of writing making the transition from version labels 6 to 7. Another advantage is that using the standards approach minimized file sizes, useful for traffic reduction on the network. You'll only want to re-engineer once. The old adage 'An ounce of prevention is worth a pound of cure' applies here as it does in all aspects of life.

- Failure to re-engineer correctly will involve you in continuing work similar to painting the Forth Bridge. Once you've finished at one end you'll start again.

- However in all this remember that you're creating a strategy. Be aware that standards change and that technological advances may occasionally outpace you. If you create a fix then you'll have run yourself into another dead end that's worse than the one you've just come from – they'll have someone to blame for this one!

- So use all the research you've gathered and collate into tangible recommendations. Make sure that you can account for all the reasons why you chose one course and not another. You'll not have to justify this all to your managers but you may well have to justify it to the ambassadors you've been preparing. If they feel alienated then you not only stand the danger of losing them but having them work against you. In this area you can't afford to be dismissive of anyone's efforts. Take a deep breath and remain calm and only swear about it while you're on your own.

- What you're doing is creating a change model at this stage of the game. You can set standards, but if you go into specific page redesign at this time you're in danger of making your model too inflexible. Retain all the options you can at this stage – as you change things because of external pressures then you want to leave yourself enough degrees of freedom.

So how do you actually make sure that you're not just creating a fix? The one question I would ask is "can changes in the company be handled without changing the model you've created with your strategy?". Play round with your model of change by looking at potential changes and how it copes. If the answer has an unreserved "yes", that is a pretty good indication that your model is going to stand up.

You're going to have to be a bit ruthless with yourself. As we've already said you can't afford to run into another dead end, so before presenting it make sure it works. Recruit some of your developers and ambassadors to assist you in this task – let them pick holes. If you've recruited them correctly then they're on your side and want to see the project succeed. In this arena people with lateral thinking skills are the most valuable, so if you can discover who these people are, and use them.

How to Alienate Your Key Workers.

This is a short tale of politics and the stifling of initiative. It comes from a company with a number of departmental and individual web sites all running successfully and all being used. One day they were noticed and came the decree from the senior management: "We are going to have to reduce the number of web sites". So everyone waited with bated breath. A meeting was convened between the person making the declaration and a number of others, none of whom had actually designed or owned the sites. Out of that meeting came the resolution that yes, there were too many web sites and one person was designated to oversee their consolidation. This person had no involvement with any of the web sites prior to this.

A year later, there were still the same number of web sites. The only difference was that before the original declaration they had been live and kept updated. After that declaration no work whatsoever was done on any site. There was an instant loss of pride and ownership because of really bad handling and a lack of understanding of what people were striving to achieve.

Eighteen months after the meeting the rationalization program had still to see the light of day. One web site had closed because the machine hosting it had failed. It was not replaced, neither was the information it contained.

And if this wasn't bad enough the developers were being asked to prove their competence by taking tests - on web site development.

Manage Expectations

It's fairly natural to want to show quick results. It's also easy to give promises under pressure that you later regret. When you've designed your strategy you can start applying specifics to see if you can build a workable initial solution.

- Manage the expectations of your colleagues, the organization's, and especially your own. Be realistic in the development plan. Make realistic demands of your own and other people's efforts – there are only a certain number of hours in the day.

- Plan to take on a pilot project to see what it looks like. Remember that the intranet is still being used. See how your pilot looks before putting anything more concrete into time-scales.

- Build the pilot if you can before saying too much publicly – test your own theories in private and make sure they will work.

- Is the pilot going to provide you with the templates or are you going to design the templates and build the pilot on them? Either way will work, but you have to be clear which way you're doing things. If you find it necessary to change a template, make sure you do it and not leave it till later – the change will get forgotten.

- Time the development – create a prototype first. Make sure that what you eventually promise has a realistic chance of working.

- Most importantly have a realistic plan – don't neglect the maintenance time for the stuff you've already built.

- Set clear goals for the intranet long-term. When these are done set the goals for this project.

- What's the business cost of not doing these changes? You should have already identified the amount of duplication and holes.

- Impress upon everyone that this is not a quick fix – it's intended to set your organization up with a strong basis for going forward for intranet development for the next X years.

- Go for the low-hanging fruit first. After the pilot, plan to tackle the obvious ones, the ones where there have been the most complaints and the most problems, but at the same time where you can be sure of success.

- Talk to others about the pilot, especially the other developers of the departmental and individual web sites, showing them what the first delivery looks like. Involving them will work wonders for acceptability and they're going to have to be your workforce if not for building, for maintenance.

- Modify the pilot as you think fit – it's only the pilot and think of it all as a phased or iterative process, with simultaneous activity streams that you manage but not necessarily execute.

- Give example time-scales – we'll achieve such and such in one year, two years. Don't be pressured and say that you'll have it done in time for Christmas.

Don't Underestimate the Human Factor

Set out to deliver a renewed intranet that will delight the people in your organization. You have a significant opportunity to touch the lives of each person inside your organization, so respect it and use it wisely. They may not realize it in those terms, but they certainly feel it even if unable to express it. You're not going to win friends for the jazzy interface, the superbly executed Flash movie – these will pall in a very short time, as will the extensive logos at the top of the page. Your users want a straightforward entry into information that takes the least time to find. That way they'll be able to add value to what they're doing as their everyday job and add value to the organization.

However be prepared for some resistance to change. In changing the intranet you may affect someone's carefully organized list of bookmarks on their browser. You can counter this by replacing every page you remove with a page directing to the new location and remind the users that they need to update the bookmarks or provide the necessary code to automatically bookmark the new page. You will also have resistance from those for whom any change is anathema.

If you've used a color scheme that's not really clear then those working under less than ideal conditions may not thank you for it. Remember also that 5% of the white male population is color-blind. Deal with it, don't ignore it. Either provide an acceptable color scheme on startup or make a stylesheet available that will change the colors for them alone on demand.

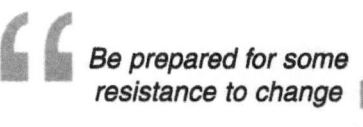

Be prepared for some resistance to change

Setting the Foundation

This should really go without saying. As with any project, if you have a clear set of objectives and a clear method of achieving those objectives, then you have the foundation of being able to cost the project. This is sometimes the most difficult part for people charged with web design and implementation – they have to pit themselves against the language of accountants. These are some of the factors that you should consider. Again these are open-ended lists.

- Decide on some metrics and make sure that they are achievable within your change process. We've been suggesting pilots and bringing people on board to ease both the workload and the acceptability of the whole project to the user and developer community. From these activities you should be able to realistically estimate the effort involved and hence the labor cost of changes.

- Calculate what proportion of content duplication you could remove – the page count should drop by XXXX and hence you can quantify the effort saved in maintaining them. Your pilot should give you an indication of how much smaller your intranet may become, although you should be careful in stating that the figure was arrived at during the pilot study of such and such a site. If the site you're piloting from has used coding that does not separate content and presentation, you will probably find that intelligent use of external stylesheets will significantly reduce the size of files, hence download time, hence network pressure even if you're unable to reduce page numbers significantly.

- Do you want to win an award with your re-developed intranet? Why – is it anything unusual? If you follow the guidelines of The Plain English Campaign then it may be. Find them at http://www.plainenglish.co.uk/ and especially their web site design guidelines at http://www.plainenglish.co.uk/webdesign.html. As the objective we've already stated is to make communication as easy as possible within your organization, clarity of language will only serve to aid this requirement. The argument may be expressed that all this attention to grammar and syntax is a waste of time and that this is a modern world, so all that sort of thing is outmoded. However, if your intranet has the possibility of being international then automatic translators may be used. If the syntax and grammar is of a recognized standard then translations may be better understood.

- When you are clear about objectives go back to your stakeholders and get their buy-in, the managers, the developers, and the ambassadors. You could do this in another meeting following on from your brainstorms – with luck they'll each be able to recognize their own input into the whole process and feel more motivated to continue to assist. This meeting should really be confined to the developers and ambassadors so that from among them you can recruit supporters. Then you and these supporters can present to senior management to get their OK. This is the stage where you should get an approval to continue with the entire project.

But how you organize all this depends on your own circumstances. Above all, make your objectives clear to those who matter, then you'll get their support.

Determining the Associated Costs

When you do finally present your objectives there will always be questions about costs. If you can demonstrate cost savings then this will work in your favor, but be sure to be able to back your arguments up with calculations. If one of those people you already have 'on your side' has some experience of doing this (or is the company accountant) then run the cost saving by them before presenting. See if they can pick holes.

Here are some of the aspects you should consider:

- Even if you're not implementing a CMS there will be costs of development, of maintenance, and of infrastructure.

- There will be internal costs and a corresponding return on investment (ROI). Can you determine what this is likely to be? You'll have to take into account both the costs savings from changing and the costs of leaving thing as they are.

- There's also the time cost from internal development – when developers are doing things for the intranet they're not doing other things.

- If you can quantify any of these it will probably be easier to get budgetary approval. But you have to estimate confidence limits in your calculations and say what these are.

- One of the questions you're bound to get is "I don't see the problem, why change?"; how you deal with this is up to you. Either the person does not see the need for change because they don't use the intranet or you haven't explained the reason for change very well. Or they're just testing you.

The Costs of Not Changing

The company we mentioned earlier in the case study was faced with the need to rationalize its server base. Not only were the licensing costs about to rocket because of new licensing policies being brought in by one of the suppliers and but also because a whole raft of the security of the whole network was being called into question.

An exercise had been completed to reduce the number of servers operating under the licenses mentioned above as infrastructure servers. Parallel with this there was an exercise to see if the number of web sites could be reduced and also reduce the number of license-carrying servers that they sat on. It proved easier to reduce the number of license fee-attracting servers than the number of web sites purely because of the time and administration involved. By the time the costs had fallen the number of web sites ceased to become an issue. The only issue then was one of maintenance costs rather than tangible costs like licensing.

There were, of course, vital personnel with the necessary skills already in place in the company for this to occur and their respective managers gave them the permission to change, and the freedom to make the changes. The only criterion was – keep the thing running.

The cost savings at the time the changes were made were $600.00 per server, and five were changed from a Windows NT server to Linux server in this exercise. The company would have had to bear the additional licensing costs when they came up for renewal.

Another advantage of the change was the lack of time chasing and applying critical updates – the estimate was an hour for each of the five servers per week. Then in eighteen months there was only one security update for Apache.

The purpose of this study is to illustrate cost savings at a certain point in time. We could have gone on to reduce the number of servers to reduce the maintenance costs even further, but circumstances did not permit that. I've also put this in to illustrate how items outside straight web costs can have a significant influence on projects. Investigate other operating systems that will fit on the same hardware and how you could deploy them, as you may be pleasantly surprised by the results.

Getting the Right Infrastructure

If you are going to try to host all of the diverse variety of web sites on a single server, how is the network and machine infrastructure going to cope? You'll already have done some traffic analysis from the portal and the satellite servers, so now's the time to do the sums. Do you need to employ a load-balancing cluster, or do you just need to integrate a number of satellite web sites into one or two other servers? There are advantages to each approach and of course disadvantages. It is assumed that normal system administration functions such as backup would be implemented on all servers.

The advantages of using one large intranet server are:

- One point of administration
- Expensive hardware can be concentrated in a secure area
- Only one place to hack

And the disadvantages are:

- Single point of failure
- More server power required to host traffic
- Bandwidth can be a problem for high-usage sites
- I/O operations similarly can get choked

On the other hand the advantages of using several distributed servers are:

- Possible to arrange failover in case of faults
- Bandwidth restrictions less of a problem especially if you can locate servers on different network segments
- Can mix servers close to authoring areas – distributed administration can reduce the workload on a single person or department

And the disadvantages of this arrangement are:

- Greater administrative requirement
- Security must be applied in a number of places

Getting the Right People on Board

You won't have time to do all the changes yourself. So it's a matter of getting the people to do the changes. You could recruit more staff to your department, but that would require extra expenditure. So involve the existing designers, they've got the experience in providing the content; in fact, they probably wrote most of it. You get them on your side but you must let it be known by this that you appreciate their efforts. This is most important – you're changing their working pattern, so a little word of thanks will enthuse them to help what you're doing.

Another reason for involving the existing people who understand the content is that you don't have to learn what they've already done which is less of a learning curve for you, and because they won't need so much training the cost is going to be reduced.

You may, however, run up against the "my boss won't let me" factor. It may have been all very well putting up the web site in the first place on the departmental server, but to now lose that control is not what they'd intended. This is a symptom of what you're going to face in trying to achieve the change. However you may like to play to this by requesting that some of that web server's power be brought into the intranet – and leave the person administering more. It's all in the politics of the situation, unfortunately. It does depend on how you handle it, but doing so is not an easy job.

Here are a few points to bear in mind:

- Gaining senior management support – can you? Have you been able to prepare the ground well enough? Have you been able to get enough converts? The more the merrier in most cases.

- Bearing in mind what we've been saying about recruiting existing web site authors if you have the budget for doing so, do you have or can you get the right people in place and have the resources necessary to support them?

- If you are getting stuck, do you need an external agency to guide you through the initial stages? This may not necessarily be a commercial consultancy – try negotiating with a local university. A consultant may only try to sell you something. A university doesn't usually have any product to sell except its knowledge. Also consider whether having a university report adds or detracts from the perception of your reports internally. One caveat is the university might not necessarily have the personnel and enough experience of business to advise you correctly. Some university personnel have entered the academic environment after a period of employment within industry, so you should look at the CVs of the individuals before deciding. Employing outside people may be valuable as a way of 'seeing the wood from the trees' and getting a fresh perspective on your situation.

- Another benefit of consultants is that an intranet is often a direct representation of a company's internal politics. It's often easier for external consultants to say things that are politically sensitive, as well as bringing in fresh ideas, enthusiasm, and the befit of experience.

- Have you thought of trying to create an Intranet Renewal Steering Group to more closely focus on the issue? To make this a success you must ensure that they are supported by senior management and have both responsibility and authority to carry out the tasks assigned to them. Of course this could get out of hand and just delay things for you, but you must assess this requirement with a mind to your organizations' own policies and practices.

- You'll need to get the necessary technology on-board sooner rather than later. Build once rather than build and copy – which takes time. The engineering adage "measure twice, cut once" applies.

- What's the impact on existing web developers if you can't use them directly? They might feel threatened by the re-development, so you will need plans to deal with this type of situation, such as forming these people into small teams to get various aspects of the intranet working.

- With the new intranet you're going to create new roles of Content Publisher and Content Author. Ensure that you have some definitions so that you can define who does what.

The web is a live, modern medium. After implementation of a CMS and intranet you give publishing power to various members of staff. However the intranet you so carefully designed can become a laughing stock if you allow what happened in this case study to occur.

Restricting the Input

The question about who to trust for putting content onto the intranet CMS exercises the mind of many executives. In this case, the intranet developers were asked to provide a simple method (they did) and the management decided that it was too dangerous to allow the common software developers to post items directly onto the intranet – they may post some inflammatory or defamatory material. So the only people in a position to post material were those used to handling sensitive issue –the secretaries of the senior managers, who unfortunately were not web-oriented people. A procedure was set up such that these secretaries would be mailed the stuff you wanted put onto the CMS. So they were put on as attachments. They also put on the CMS an explanation of what was on the attachment.

But it was soon found that people were not reading the intranet. It hadn't been sold well enough. So the secretaries started sending round the document as supplied as an attachment in an e-mail to everyone.

This rather defeated the object of having a single document on the intranet. So to solve this problem, e-mails started going round saying please read the posting just made, with a link. Then it was a case of open the link, read the message, and take the necessary action. The result was double the number of links in the CMS and also a circular e-mail and a load of time wasted, all for the want of a bit of training.

This example represents, in my opinion as an intranet advocate, gross mismanagement and under-utilization of the intranet – caused by lack of trust.

Communication and Marketing Is Key

Clarity in communication is a very big hurdle in a lot of companies. Many people recognize bad communication because it doesn't work, but fewer recognize good communication because it is inconspicuous. It's often only later that you realize that you've experienced good communication. So make communication work for you in your marketing of the new intranet.

From your research work you will have identified both the failings and the good points of the existing intranet setup. You will by this stage have a very good idea what the new intranet you are making will look like and how it's going to work. It's now your job to sell the solution.

You have to be very clear:

- About what your objectives are and communicate them effectively. Not only must you say "It's going to be better" but say why you have confidence that it's going to be. Define what will make it better, what will change to make it better, how it will ease the lives of the users. However be wary of using too much spin – employees are marvelously attuned to spin and usually each have advanced qualifications in cynicism. Tell the truth.

- What the key messages to the organization are. You have to be able to push the right buttons to illuminate those messages.

The actions you need to take before making your communication:

- Identify any "killer apps" – anything that's going to revolutionize the working lives of the staff. If you don't have anything it doesn't matter – don't be tempted to invent something for the sake of it. People are well-practiced in the reading and dismissal of spin.

- Create an intranet site that outlines what the project is about. Construct it with the design you'll be implementing for the new intranet.

Whether you want to or are able to involve your company's marketing department is up to you. It does depend on how the department is perceived internally. If you're going to create your own marketing effort then concentrate on the objectives outlined above. And use plain language – employees generally don't like hype as they may have been subjected to too much. Besides, hype can also lead to downfall where the project is concerned – unnecessary expectations and then not being able to meet them is the bane of all marketing strategies and sales pitches.

See Chapter 11 for detailed advice on how to market your intranet internally.

Staff Involvement

You need to involve your people for the project to succeed. But it's amazing how many web designers are reluctant to do that. Involving people reduces the inevitable resistance to change you may encounter. Not everyone will have your vision and commitment to the New Improved intranet. You have to be prepared to put up with that resistance. The more people you have on your side the easier it will be, and you have been preparing people since the start of the process when you conducted the surveys and research. Just remember that this part of the exercise is not about technology, it is about communicating.

In order to communicate effectively you have to identify your audiences. There's not just one audience, so you have to tailor your message so that it hits home. For each audience you have to consider:

- What's in it for them?

- Identify any perceived threats to them.

- Identify the benefits of the project to them.

- Identify what you want them to do differently.

Each of the "them"s being the different parts of the target audience. For the majority of the staff you're marketing to, the message will almost be the same. There are several identifiable sets of people where the message may have to be different. The ones I can think of are:

- The "difficult"-Owners – those who are seeing "their" web site as a status symbol.

- People who have created a sub-brand – the logos, the different look.

- The senior managers – they need to see things from a different perspective.

- The ambassadors and developers you've already brought on board.

How you treat these people will be dictated by your own circumstances, but you could try the following:

For the "difficults", stressing how the intranet has depended on the content they've been able to provide but say that for reasons of network efficiency it is necessary to incorporate their ideas into the intranet. They may have used their intranet presence as a status symbol for example "...and my intranet site's bigger than yours.". Frequently a lot of their content is duplicated. It's not necessarily bloat, but it's already been said somewhere else. Get them to understand that they can actually be perceived as heroes if they supply half of the information that will become more useful to the majority.

For the "sub-branders" they've spent some thought on creating their site. If it does say something about the content of the site and is not just a logo for design's sake, why not allow the logo on their parts of the page but in a specific position alongside the main company logo. It'll give continuity, a way of users distinguishing what part of the intranet they're addressing (remember we said that users will get confused if everything looks too much the same?) and will give some pride in the system as it is developed.

Both of these will be involved in maintaining the content for their section anyway – so remember this because you need them more than they think they need you.

The Senior Managers probably use the intranet the least of any employee group. For them you may have to stress that the information source you are creating will benefit the company with greater efficiency. You don't need to say anything about profitability, let them make their own decisions.

The ambassadors and developers need to be involved in all stages of this process we've mentioned – they will ease your load and will be on hand to field some of the questions at coffee time during the meetings. Because they are from other parts of the company they will be identifiable to others in your introductory meetings and make it look less like a "them" and "us" situation.

Create Converts Early On

You've already started creating converts, disciples, and ambassadors. Build on them.

One way of doing this is to invite people to meetings. Make them non-compulsory but ensure that you have also asked some of your ambassadors and developers to attend. Present the new concepts and ask them for support. Give the opportunity for questions and ask them for support. Let them play with example intranet sites and ask for their support. OK, so this all seems a bit obvious written down in this way, but unless you ask you won't get the support you need. You're dealing in some ways with a hearts and minds issue here. I'm emphasizing these techniques because it may be unfamiliar territory to those who are charged with doing the job of getting the intranet running effectively.

While we're here, consider the words you're using. I'm not asking you to put spin across – just choosing words for maximum impact. Consider how you speak during presentations and use words to convey the correct tone. For instance you could use the word "effective" rather than "efficient". Efficient has an aura of treating people like machines. Think about the meaning of words. Politicians have a way of using words effectively – that's how they get elected!

Selling the CMS

If you are renewing your intranet because you are implementing a CMS ensure that you communicate the bigger picture to the organization. The CMS will feed content to web page templates but don't forget that most people using the intranet won't actually recognize that there is a CMS driving the content. Ensure that the message they receive is wrapped around issues that are relevant to them. These could be a way to ensure they get less e-mail or create a quantifiable asset to the organization, for example intellectual property.

But what you have to do is make sure that those responsible understand that the CMS will be no good unless correctly maintained. And make sure that the tools serving the information present well. This is beyond the scope of this chapter, refer back to *Chapter 8* for more details on CMS, or *Content Management Systems* (Phil Suh, et al., glasshaus, 1-904151-06-x).

Design Matters

By consolidating a diverse intranet, you're probably going to be making some radical changes to the way that people are able to work. For the users you're going to offer greater effectiveness, for the content provider a different way of working that they may find more restrictive. What matters here is the way you design the interface to cope. Remember that you started on the exercise because the intranet was overgrown, remember this in your design.

Change Perceptions

While building your content, don't be afraid to challenge things – you may find multiple systems actually doing the same thing. Several people may well have attempted to write jargon busters and duplicated certain elements. Combine them into one list by all means, but you should credit the original authors.

You may also find that, especially on some of the larger departmental sites, there is a lot of irrelevant content. Note it and discuss it, but you are not compelled to take it. Set up some monitoring to find out who is visiting that part of the site. If it is, as you suspect, no one, then you have the evidence you need to archive it. If it has activity, as long as it is not just activity for the sake of it, you were wrong.

Standards

You will have probably considered standards for your re-engineering in your design process – and this book has already covered the basics of standards-based implementation. If you decide to adopt web standards in the shape of separating content and presentation ((X)HTML and CSS stylesheets) you will find that the size reduces considerably; 40% is not uncommon in pages that I've converted. This holds true unless all your other page authors have adopted web standards – a pretty unlikely eventuality.

Your Ambassadors

We've already talked about involving your key audience, the existing publishers. In order to implement this new strategy you'll have to ensure that they are trained in the technology, whether in the CMS or to your standards of writing web pages. Likewise you'll have to select content publishers and content authors and train them to your standards. These are your prime ambassadors.

If you create an online area for current developers and encourage them to populate it with whatever they like, it becomes both their test bed and their online presence. Make it public both as a reward and as a self-policing mechanism. If they know it can be seen by everyone in the company, excesses may well not occur. Keep it a little bit exclusive – not everyone gets to play with the public intranet. If you have people who want to learn web technologies you can create an area that's not public and set them projects – when they've proved themselves then they can be rewarded by being allowed to publish in public, as it were.

The others you've recruited may not have an initial responsibility for creating web pages, but initially they can become centers of questions for their local areas or departments. Encourage others to direct questions at them and if they're unsure they contact you. That way you ease the initial support load when you start making things public.

The ambassadors and developers will have to know about and be able to communicate:

- The business rationale and why it's key to have a consistent intranet. They'll also have to have knowledge about standards and why it is important to keep to them.

- Moving from just 'publishing' to 'managing content' – and why – this applies to both CMS and non-CMS installations.

- And why it's important that they realize that they're creating an asset for the organization, and that they themselves are facilitators.

In return, you can ensure that you both understand their motivations so that you can assist where necessary and have what they're doing written into their job specifications. This will ensure that they get recognition for their efforts.

Transition Strategies

Whatever you hope, any transition from distributed web servers to a more centralized system is going to be aiming at a moving target. During the period of time that you've allocated for the transferal task, web site content, people, and company policy may well change. It would be difficult to envisage a company where this didn't happen. So any strategy you choose must obviously be flexible enough to cope. It would be sensible to write into your strategy a means of reviewing the strategy as time goes by – a regular self-examination. In this way the nasty surprise element is, while not being eliminated, at least somewhat controlled. It also provides for avenues for feedback from the users to enable that feedback to be incorporated into the revised strategy.

Revising any strategy for change is another iterative process, but with the added benefit of fitting your revisions to a moving target (or should that be challenge). The balance is very hard to achieve and will undoubtedly give you headaches. How you go about this obviously depends on your own organization's situation, but in general your initial plan should have taken this into account, as we've already mentioned. Your own flexibility will both be needed and be called into question: it will be needed for the adaptation to take place and will be called into question. Those questioning your changes will often be senior managers who were 'sold' on the initial plan and think that since it's been agreed by them, the plan is immutable. Employ your caveats when you initially present carefully and with sufficient inbuilt leeway to cope – easier said than done.

We all know how sudden global changes can greatly influence economic activity and confidence. Although you cannot hope to build this type of change into your plan a regular review schedule will assist you to cope. And once you have a review schedule, stick to it and don't let it slip – even if you conduct the review and see that there's nothing to change. That way you have a positive plan instead of something less so.

So one of the words you should be considering when designing your plan is flexibility. However there is a world of difference between flexibility and woolliness, or fudge. Unless the published plan is couched in terms of some positive action with a schedule, then any holes and uncertainty will be quickly seen by your audience and you'll not be off to a very good start. As we mentioned a couple of paragraphs ago, the nature of the moving target that is your grand plan will also influence the type of action that you can take. But action is required and hopefully your grand plan will not be too much off course.

You'll also no doubt have heard of Buzzword Bingo, the game played by people who have had just about enough of corporate marketing speak at company meetings, marking the words used on a score card. Some readers of this book will have played this game (guilty) in order to stay awake during some of these events. If you have heard of this, then the people of your target audience for your plan have undoubtedly heard of it as well. So keep the plan positive but be prepared to change through regular reviews. And say that there will be a review process when you publish the plan.

So what actually makes an effective transition strategy? My answer is controlled flexibility. The ability of the system you design to adapt to and adopt changes that are inevitably going to be forced on you. And if you get questions like "when's it going to stop changing?" or "when's it going to be finished?" the truthful and possibly reasonably effective answer you can give is "when the company stops changing". And if the company stops changing and does not react to current conditions that's the time the company stagnates and contracts, maybe to a point where the point of the intranet is not necessary because there are too few people to use it.

The bleak prognosis at the end of the previous paragraph is all too common, but if you see your intranet as a way of maintaining the vitality of the company then you may well be an agent for positive change – proactive rather then reactive. The difficult thing is to keep the balance and that unfortunately is beyond the scope of this book – you are the one who has to have the vision – all this book can do is guide.

Navigation Development

The navigation from your main start page will either make or break the intranet. If users can find what they want quickly and easily using obvious links, then you have the makings of a success on your hands, otherwise success will be more difficult to obtain. If you are using the initial model we discussed in earlier, navigation will be a problem in that it will not be consistent. If you are completely restructuring the intranet architecture then you are more in control of the navigation style. The navigation style would have been presented and agreed upon when you obtained buy-in from your stakeholders, so you have the framework. Developing this into a practical navigation system needs thought and you may have to make minor design changes, but major changes to the navigation structure, however easy that is to achieve in your programs, will put users off as they will have a stylistic sea-change to assimilate. So carefully think through if there is any real benefit to such a change, and be aware that even though your navigation system is less than perfect, it's consistent and the users are familiar with it.

If, of course, you have managed to follow web standards and separated content and presentation with external stylesheets, whether CSS or XSLT, then changing your structure is more simple and you can provide users with a choice by giving them access to different stylesheets. For an example of this see the homepage of the expert in this field, Eric Meyer, Standards evangelist for Netscape, at *http://meyerweb.com*. His stylesheets are selectable from his page, and as long as you're using a browser that recognizes standards you'll be able to vary the look and feel of the page, including the positioning of the page elements.

You can also put considerable barriers in the way of easy access to information by asking your users to log on before each use. Security of your intranet *is* important, but consider whether putting a logon screen in front of everyone who tries to use your intranet to find a phone number is really efficient. Sure you have to protect sensitive and private information (like personnel details), but the point at which you ask for the authentication can be vital. It can speed up or slow down your user's experience and create annoyance at delays in getting into the system. You could also consider the use of cookies – but this may be counter-productive if you have screens in public areas – if your last logon was from an administrator then there's a danger that the cookie will grant the next person the same access rights. Think carefully how you want information to be used or secured.

If you have a firewall-protected network with only employees able to access machines inside the network, and maybe VPN contact from your sales force and home workers, then when they log onto the network will this give sufficient information protection? Consider the areas you want to protect from every user access: individual personnel files, intranet administration, or departmental staff planning. Then let everyone have access to all other groups. Let's just construct a sample intranet with these groups and a few more:

Intranet Function or Resource	Access
Phone book	Everyone
General Company Information	Everyone
Marketing	Everyone
Company Admin	Everyone
Personnel	Everyone
Individual personnel file details	The person, their manager, their manager's manager, Personnel officer(s) either as individuals or as a group
Intranet Administration	The Intranet Admin group. This may also be hierarchical with some people allowed to do more than others, which will depend on your organization
Departmental Information	Everyone
Departmental Planning Information	Members of that department and their manager, and their manager's manager.
Product information	Everyone

If we consider the frequency that several of these areas of your intranet will be accessed, then it's fairly obvious that the restricted areas will be accessed less frequently than others. So putting an access restriction at the front end of the intranet will just waste time, even though you are able to arrange a single sign-on. Just put the restriction where it's going to be needed. It's also going to be easier to resist the idea of cookies being used to hold passwords if you can do this. If you force everyone to sign on every time, you will be pressurized to use cookies to remember passwords. This is exactly what you should avoid, especially for parts of the intranet containing sensitive data where users should have to log in every time.

Back now to navigation. After entering the system you are usually presented with a global menu. How this is presented is important as well. You have to start designing this with your users' needs in mind rather than any organizational convenience. The language must be simple and straightforward and use terms that are understood generally. It's a good idea to avoid acronyms, as then you'd have to provide a dictionary for users unfamiliar with the company structure. To illustrate, a couple of samples. First a silo menu, organized on departmental lines, and then a user-oriented menu organized on logical lines for ease of use.

When the Intranet Gets Too Big

12

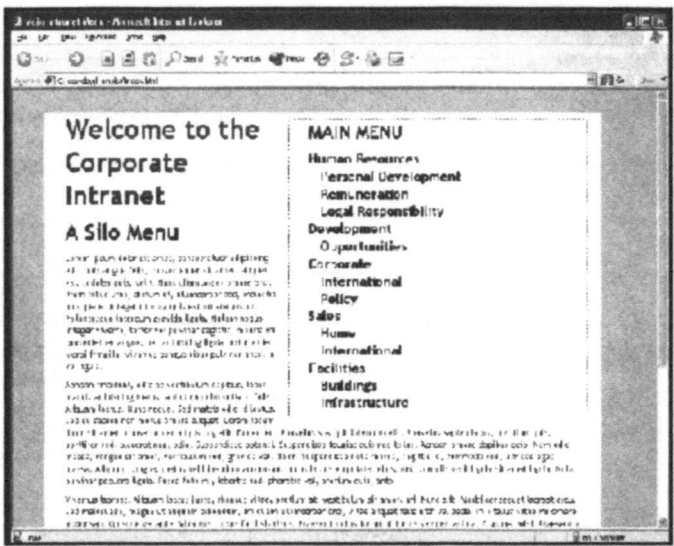

The menu is organized according to departmental constraints – some of the functions are obscure and the language used is corporate-speak rather than English. Compare this with a very similar menu organized along functional lines and using plain English. The same information is conveyed, but with language that normal people use. The structure is not that different, except that Development Opportunities becomes Job Vacancies, and that International and Sales have reorganized themselves along more logical lines. Titles have been reworded to sound less corporate and more understandable.

New User Requirements

So let's look at this in a little more detail. As the intranet develops it's going to be more and better used. As it becomes better used, new and modified user requirements will be raised. The fact that more people can see more of the content means that there will be better awareness of the potential of the intranet, so user expectations and requirements change accordingly. You have a duty to be aware of those expectations (you will be, if you've put the correct feedback solutions in place) and modify your own plans and designs accordingly. Again we mention that radical change of design halfway through will tend to alienate your user base so it is best avoided, unless there is a compelling reason to do so. However design adjustments can be dealt with. And if you do make design adjustments it would be a good time to publicize the intranet to your staff members by the same type of e-mail circulation that you used to launch the new intranet in the first place. This way it keeps the user community aware that you're still alive and functioning.

A bit of research is called for here before you make wholesale changes – use your ambassadors as a test bed, it'll keep them involved with the intranet. You can't rely on previous traffic figures because some important piece of information may have been hidden, and you will almost certainly have provided new facilities within your redesign. So you have to look afresh at traffic figures.

Thus far we've talked about changes to the intranet as redeveloped. In this whole process you need to consider the users of the existing microsites and how they have been finding information on their own site. Incorporating them into the general structure can be problematic – especially if you break up the navigation too much. If you can keep the same groupings then all will be well, but this will not be possible if you have significant duplication of information that you can usefully prune. You won't be able to please everyone, so it'll be up to you to explain your actions in one of your launch e-mails. Asking for feedback and review will assist in the adoption of your standards. From experience many objections are raised for the sake of raising objections even though there are benefits to be had from the modifications. The majority of users will see your reasons and accept them, as long as they're well-considered and well-argued.

One of the common menu structures on any intranet is the silo route. This places all access menus in the same structure as the organizational structure of the company, so from a user's perspective this demands that they know the organizational structure before they are even able to access information!

Silo Menus

So there was a big company meeting – posh hotel, free lunch, free drinks – a new MD had been appointed six months beforehand and he'd been the new broom, the product line had been re-launched and new revitalized budgets and presentations were seeing the light of day for the first time. Some people who used to be there six months ago were no longer there. There was an air of expectancy.

Near the end of the proceedings the person in charge of Human Resources steps up. He presented his bit of the change process, the new Personal Development scheme. Using this we could develop our careers within the company, the sky being our limit. One of the questions from the floor was about training policy and courses. And we got told that this information was available from the company intranet.

Next day, still enthused, back at the office a few of us tried to find mention of training on the company intranet. It took some time. It was hidden in a silo. We all thought that training was pretty important to the company, and should really smack you in the eyes. However the people who designed the intranet menu system didn't see things from our perspective. To find information about training you had both to identify the jargon used and jump through five hoops:

- *Human Resources*
- *Personal Development*
- *Education*
- *Training*
- *Training courses*

A few months later, when a couple of us were running internal weekly training courses, the menu item was still the same and we had to use other methods of publicizing. It wasn't anything to do with the developers being unapproachable, they didn't ask the questions and there weren't facilities in place for user-feedback.

So you have a difficult task. What you do first time out will be wrong. When you change it that'll be wrong as well because some users will have become used to the menu hierarchy you defined previously. And if you then change it back that'll be wrong because you're changing it too often. So any menu hierarchy must be user needs-driven, remembering that 100% happiness is unachievable – there will always be compromises, even in your own designs and ideas.

Here are some things to bear in mind when re-designing the navigation:

You may find it more convenient to have your menu structure follow the directory structure of the web site. It might be worth considering designing the directory structure alongside or a little after the menu structure. At least the directory structure should be designed for change and not fixed.

- To overcome the silo your structure should be needs-based
- Your menu structure should do what it says
- Try to make your access hierarchy needs-based
- Get your ambassadors and developers involved by asking them how the menu hierarchy should work and get them to ask their local users
- Call an ambassadors meeting and come up at that meeting with a first menu structure
- Have a real, not fictional, pilot site
- Put a feedback mechanism in place so that you can get comments

Your structure should be needs-based organized by subject, task, and activity. This should get over the silo effect. You should by this time have defined in your own mind what's in the sites you're bringing into the intranet so classifying them should not be too difficult. However in making the classification you have to perform some lateral thinking. You may have a product site designed by a product division and they're going to hand it all over. So it'll go in under the product category of your new system. But the content of the site is actually about the technical details of product installation. People wanting to know about the product are going to be bamboozled, and installers are not going to be able to get their information where they expect it to be.

"Does exactly what it says on the tin" is an advertising slogan used in the UK for the 'Ronseal' wood preservative range. If you can make your hierarchy do just that, having sensible headings in plain language avoiding jargon then you're well on the way to succeeding. Clever menu headings do no one any good. If you mean "training" say "training " and not "personal development". If you mean "self study" say so and not "personal self-development".

Try to make your access hierarchy needs-based. The silo case study above was a case in point of how not to do it. But how do you find out what your users need? This is one way that starts with a top-down design. Get your ambassadors and developers involved by asking them how the menu hierarchy should work and get them to ask their local users. But don't give them very long to do it – you need to retain momentum. You'll now have defined in your own mind that the developer and ambassadors groups have now become one, so we'll deal with them as one group from here on in. If they want, provide them with a simple outline menu to get them started and put what you think are going to be the most frequently used items at the top, and ask them to do the same when they make their suggestions. Then call an ambassadors meeting and come up at that meeting with a first menu structure. Implement it. That'll give you an important advantage in future dealings with the ambassadors group. You could also create an "Intranet Ambassadors" e-mail group.

You will have pilot sites. If they are completely fictional then effort will have been expended into something that's not going to continue. Try to pilot on a real site that you want to have as part of the final intranet. If you use a site that's already on the intranet then you'll give yourself an easier job. But if you use a site from one of the satellites then you'll be testing yourselves in a real-world situation. This has the psychological advantage of involving the people you want and testing the effectiveness of your transition strategy.

Put a feedback mechanism in place so that you can get comments. If you use e-mail feedback, respond to all those comments with at least an acknowledgment at first – but don't make it automated. You could operate a feedback forum and have the comments on display. You'll have to make sure all comments are attributable otherwise you won't be able to get back to the people who have given the feedback. But having attracted the feedback, don't change things round too often, you'll only confuse your users. You could consider publishing a schedule against which you'll make changes so that there is a warning. That also looks like good planning.

When the Intranet Gets Too Big

12

Handling New Microsites

This is almost a section that could be entitled "How to prevent this happening again". Naturally as your intranet develops you will find it expanding and you will have new sites and possibly microsites to plan. Would you consider an embargo on new sites? If so, you'll have your development smoothed but at the risk of

> *The worst thing you can do is stifle initiative, you'll force people out of the company and those are the ones you want to keep*

annoying some staff. You'll have to set priorities for development. You could do this by writing into the review process a provision for changing the priorities for handling new sites. How you do all this will be dictated by your own organization's circumstances, and the urgency with which the request for a new site is needed, and probably by whom. The only thing you can do is plan to recognize for when you spot this happening. Really the worst thing you can do is stifle initiative, you'll force people out of the company and those are the ones you want to keep. So if you can design an iterative process and keep reviewing the situation then you'll stand more chance of maintaining control of the situation.

Whether new sites are hosted on your main servers or on a satellite is up to you. Whatever method is adopted you should ensure that they conform to the standards you've declared. Elsewhere in this book there has been talk of templates, whether for use with CMS or for 'normal' web pages. This is the perfect time to introduce them for your site. Some of the common tools, DreamWeaver, for example, allow the creation of templates for use, but wholesale introduction of this technology across the company could be expensive. If people still hand-code web pages, as many do, then an outline code would be just as well understood and probably more effective. If you have chosen to adopt separate external CSS stylesheets then the imposition of templates and styles become easier. A little training for your people will allow them to construct pages to our declared style with little hassle.

One way of doing this is to set up a "Center of Excellence" where the principles of creating sites are laid down with examples to follow.

Summary

This chapter has not been so much about technology as psychology and interaction with people. It is also about managing change within a technological environment, but above all, common sense in dealing with people in your organization.

We started off by defining an overgrown intranet and how we have come to inherit one. Then we looked at a variety of methods for consolidating the information, making it more widely available, reducing duplication and bringing the structure into a more coherent whole, all the while maintaining good relationships with the users and people who developed the information in the first place. The decision-making and refinement process was examined in some detail as well as looking at the involvement of some of the stakeholder groups, managers, and decision-makers, and justifying the changes you are proposing. The continuing case study and perspectives highlighted some of these processes in a real-life situation, and in some of these cases where the process went noticeably wrong.

The processes discussed can only be described as iterative – there is no one fix, there is not one way of getting it right first time. You have to define a strategy that encompasses change and allows for changes in company direction, not the easiest thing to plan for as people who design intranets are usually not party to the level of discussion that affects company policy. Companies also react to national and world economic changes so changes of direction or emphasis are likely. Planning for this type of change is difficult if not impossible. Budgetary constraints may limit your freedom of action, but by showing what benefits reorganization of the intranet can bring to the company, you will gain friends within the hierarchy.

The most common theme of this chapter is the adoption of a strategy with inbuilt review processes at defined periods and not being afraid to hone the goals and direction that the intranet takes. Rigidity of approach has been proven not to work. Life's not like that. Along with the involvement of the users and site developers you can win – but it's neither easy nor straightforward with plenty of potential pitfalls on the way.

If you have this problem and want to solve it please accept my heartfelt wishes of good luck.

13

- Remote access
- Supporting handheld devices

Author: Inigo Surguy

Where to Go from Here – Remote Users

In this book, we have described how the intranet can be of vital importance to a company and the day-to-day work of its employees. However, today's workers need to be able to work anywhere – from home, on the train, and on the plane. How can you ensure that they have access to the intranet wherever they need it?

In this chapter, we will answer this question by looking at various ways of accessing the intranet remotely, and accessing it offline. The solutions presented in this chapter are practical and useful now, but will become even more important as home working increases and the capabilities of mobile devices grow.

We will begin by looking at several methods of providing external access to the intranet for your organization's employees. We will go on to discuss the provision of offline intranet access, for those situations when a network connection of any sort is not available. Finally, we will consider handheld devices such as the Palm and Pocket PC, and access to the intranet via mobile phone.

External Intranet Access

Working from home is increasing in popularity for many companies. In the US, 25 million people spent at least some time working at home in 2001 (increased from 22 million in 1997), and of these, 80% used a computer for their work (see *http://www.bls.gov/rofod/1460.pdf*). For the employees, home working can allow them to spend less time traveling, and to work in more comfortable surroundings. For the employer, it can save money on office space, and may increase productivity. Intranet access from home can enable the home worker to solve problems more rapidly than if they did not have access. It can also help alleviate the feelings of isolation that can be caused by home working.

Another situation in which external intranet access might be required is when there is a consultant working at a client site for a period of time. The consultant is likely to benefit from access to their employer's intranet, although there may be problems of privacy and security to overcome if using a computer provided by the client, such as making sure the consultant is only given access when and where (and for as long as) needed.

If you are supporting any form of external intranet access, then you need to be aware of the bandwidth available to your external users. If the majority of them are using modems, then make sure that you're testing your intranet designs via a modem as well. We discussed methods for making the intranet faster, and appear faster, in *Chapter 6* on *Usability*.

Using a Virtual Private Network (VPN)

A VPN is a secure network that uses the Internet for communication, but uses encryption to authenticate and secure each end. VPNs have grown in popularity because it is much cheaper to set up a VPN than a private network. We have already briefly mentioned VPNs in *Chapter 10, Security and Personalization*. An employee outside the office can use a VPN to access the company intranet securely, as well the rest of the internal business systems. In addition, different offices can be connected via VPN to share the same servers.

VPNs are a large topic, and in this chapter we will provide a brief overview and consider a few of the intranet-specific aspects of a VPN. Because of the potential that a VPN has for exposing your company to data loss and hacker attacks, it's vital to consider any move to a VPN very carefully and to consult a security expert on your exact setup.

VPNs are broadly divided into three types:

- The remote access VPN
- The intranet VPN
- The extranet VPN

The intranet VPN links together remote offices and partners, using secure tunnels across the Internet between specifically designated VPN gateways. The extranet VPN performs the same task for customers, suppliers, and other external communities. The remote access VPN allows access to a corporate network for employees that are away from the office – for example at home or on the road. The technologies used by all three are quite similar.

There are three major forms of VPN technology. These are IPSec (Internet Protocol Security), PPTP (the Point-to-Point Tunneling Protocol), and its successor L2TP (the Layer Two Tunneling Protocol). PPTP and its successor L2TP are primarily associated with Windows, whereas IPSec is more common on Unix systems (although it is now available on Windows 2000). Of the three, PPTP is the easiest to use, since the PPTP client is included with Windows since Windows 98SE, and PPTP is easy to set up on a Windows NT, 2000, or XP server. Encryption with PPTP is optional – and it must be turned on in order to provide a secure VPN. However, PPTP uses less secure encryption than the other two options, and has had several security-related bugs in the past. There's a good article on setting up a Windows VPN on the Microsoft web site at *http://www.microsoft.com/ technet/columns/profwin/pw0201.asp*.

If employees are accessing the VPN from home, they may need to check the details of their ISP's (Internet Service Provider) contract. Some ISPs do not allow the use of the network connection for business purposes, such as VPN, without signing up for a special "Business" or "Professional" contract.

> *A good, but rather dated, reference for VPNs is Virtual Private Networks (Erwin, Scott and Wolfe, O'Reilly; ISBN: 1-56592-529-7).*

Using SSL for Secure Remote Intranet Access

You may already be familiar with SSL (Secure Sockets Layer) – it's the technology used by web sites using the "HTTPS" protocol to make sure that communication with them is secure. In the way that it is used by most secure web sites, it verifies the identity of the server based on its server-side certificate (so your banking details are not sent to an untrusted server impersonating the bank's server), and it encrypts the communication between your web browser and the server.

It is possible to set up remote access to an intranet in the same way that you'd normally set up a secure web site – using a server-side certificate to provide encryption, and a username and password combination for each user. Alternatively, SSL can be used with a client-side certificate in addition to the server-side certificate. The client-side certificate is used to verify to the server that the client is trusted. It is more convenient and secure than a username and password, but it also makes it harder for a user to access the intranet from a different machine (although most of the time, this is an advantage). This also means that if anyone else gets access to the user's machine, they will be able to access the intranet. For particularly sensitive intranet data, and for computers such as laptops that are particularly vulnerable to theft, it may be worthwhile to require both a client-side certificate and a username and password.

Unlike a VPN, using SSL doesn't provide access to other computers on your intranet, but only to the intranet web pages itself.

SSL intranet access can be problematic if the intranet is running on a number of different servers – each must be set up for secure access. Using SSL to access the intranet also requires that SSL traffic to your intranet servers is allowed through the firewall – which may allow vulnerabilities in your web server to be exploited by attackers. If you are using SSL to allow remote intranet access, then consider positioning the intranet servers in a DMZ (de-militarized zone) that cannot access the rest of your internal systems.

There is no need to pay a certificate authority (CA) such as Verisign to provide an SSL certificate for each intranet server and remote client. Most web servers that work with SSL will provide a certificate generation tool so you can make your own. The advantage of using a CA normally is that the CA's certificate will already be installed in users' browsers, so certificates signed by the CA will automatically be trusted. When you issue your own certificates, they will not automatically be trusted and instead each user must install your certificate in their browser themselves. However, since this is your company intranet, the users know they can trust you, so this is not an issue.

Dial-Up Access

An alternative to a VPN is having modems connected to a computer behind the organization firewall. Employees can connect to the internal computer from home using their own modems, over the phone line.

Dial-in setups are becoming less popular than VPNs. They are more expensive, both in terms of the initial setup and the ongoing maintenance costs. In addition, with the increasing penetration of broadband Internet access, a dial-up modem connection may be considerably slower than the employee's normal Internet access speeds. Users may not be able to effectively access high-bandwidth intranet content such as video, audio, or graphics even if there is intranet access, because of the bandwidth constraints.

13

The dial-in connection from a remote user to a company's intranet server usually takes place over low-speed and sometimes unreliable communication services. Users must frequently recover from line drops and other communications issues. The combination of connect-time charges and the opportunity cost of non-productive user time can be substantial for a large field organization.

For a small intranet, it is possible to use standard PC server hardware, with one or more modems installed, connected to dedicated phone lines. Users dial in to the server via their own modems, and the server provides connectivity to the intranet. Software is also required for this, of course. Windows comes with Remote Access Service built in, and Linux uses PPPD for the same task.

> *There's more information on the support within Windows for RAS at http://www.microsoft.com/technet/itsolutions/network/Default.asp. For Linux, see the PPP documentation at http://www.samba.org/ppp/documentation.html.*

If there are many remote users, it becomes difficult to cope with the number of phone lines required. At this point, it's necessary to switch to using ISDN-PRI (Primary Rate Integrated Services Digital Network) lines. These allow the phone company to bundle 23 or 30 (23 in the US, 30 in the UK) connections down one line. This requires a RAS adapter in the server that has interfaces for ISDN-PRI connections.

It is also possible to buy dedicated RAS servers, running on proprietary hardware. This is generally a better option when there's a need to support more users – although the initial costs are higher, the servers are more integrated, use less power, and are more reliable than standard servers adapted to remote access, so support costs should be lower.

Providing Security for Remote Intranet Access

Providing security for remote intranet access is a question of assessing and minimizing risks. Allowing any sort of remote access, either over the Internet or via RAS, means that the intranet is not impenetrable by a determined and skilled attacker. However, you can reduce the vulnerabilities and ensure that security problems can be recovered from.

At the very least, a username and password should be required for intranet access. However, this only provides a minimum of security. Users will often choose poor passwords that are easily broken by automated password-guessing programs. If effective passwords are enforced (for example, with an automatic check to invalidate passwords that are too short, or dictionary words, or do not contain enough non-alphabetic characters) then users will write down the password or store it on their computer. Although this reduces the risk that a random attacker somewhere on the Internet can penetrate your systems, it increases the chance that an attacker with access to an employee's home computer can do so. If intranet security is of great importance to your business, then you should consider using a system that requires a password and a token, such as the RSA SecurID (*http://www.rsasecurity.com/products/securid/*), or even a biometric scanner that checks fingerprints or retinas. However, for most companies, simply using secure passwords is good enough, combined with limiting the damage that an authorized user can do.

If it is only possible to read the intranet remotely, without making any changes to it, then the potential for damage via remote access is low. The worst that can happen is that a competitor can gain access to confidential material. Although this is a risk, it's probably less likely that a competitor would illegally hack into a company intranet than it is that they would simply try to hire some of your company's current employees to obtain the same knowledge legally. However, if it is only possible to read and not to update the intranet remotely, then it becomes less useful when being used for legitimate purposes.

If it is possible to upload files to the intranet remotely then there is the danger of virus infection. By uploading a virus-infected file or a Trojan horse to the intranet that is downloaded and run by computers within the company, an attacker can potentially take control of computers within the organization, destroy files, and severely damage the company systems.

Viruses may also be uploaded to the intranet by accident. Although computers within the organization are likely to have a virus-checker, this is not necessarily true of employees' home computers. Therefore, if you allow executable files or MS Office documents to be uploaded to the intranet from employees' home computers, make sure that you have some form of virus-checker in place to check uploaded files. Many content management systems will interface with a virus-checker. At the very least, it's easy to write a piece of server-side script that will automatically call a virus-checker when a file is uploaded. If the VPN allows access to network drives as well as allowing intranet uploads, then virus-checking will be needed on all networked machines – most virus-checkers can be set up to automatically scan everything written to the machine they are protecting, or some firewalls can be set to scan all data that passes through them for viruses. It's also a good company policy to provide employees with a virus-checker at home for free; it benefits the company and it benefits the employees.

If remote editing of intranet content is possible, then an attacker can deface the intranet. A more subtle attacker can edit critical data based upon which intranet users will make decisions, and possibly cause more damage. You can reduce these risks with backups and with logging. If the intranet is regularly backed up, then defacements can be quickly removed. If all changes to intranet content are logged by the username and IP address that carried them out, then it's possible to check what changes are being made, and find all of the changes that have been made by the attacker. However, this requires that the logs are checked, which can take a considerable amount of work for a large intranet. It's more likely that the logs will be stored, and then when unusual data is spotted on the intranet, any other changes made by the same attacker can be undone.

Of course, if there are security holes in the intranet web servers or other services running on the same machine, then it may still be possible for an attacker to crash the intranet or gain control of the intranet servers. Microsoft's Internet Information Server has historically been subject to more attacks than other web servers, but all web servers and operating systems need to be kept up-to-date with security patches.

> **By placing the intranet server in your network DMZ, and not allowing the intranet server access to the rest of your network, you can reduce the risks of remote access**

By placing the intranet server in your network DMZ (De-militarized Zone), and not allowing the intranet server access to the rest of your network, you can reduce the risks of remote access. If the intranet server is compromised, then the attackers will still have no access to your internal systems, such as mission-critical database servers. The only damage that can be done is that the intranet web pages can be deleted or defaced. Although this is annoying, as long as there are regular backups of the server it need not be a serious problem.

Offline Access

Although remote access to the intranet may be useful for many of your users, there are still plenty of places where network access is difficult – for example, on trains, on planes, and sometimes on client sites. To enable users to work in these situations, they need to be able to access the intranet offline, when there is no network connection present.

In this section, we will look at several ways of providing the intranet offline – using Internet Explorer's offline synchronization, with Active Channels, and using Lotus Notes. We will also take into account some questions to consider when evaluating a CMS for its offline capabilities.

The drawback of all these forms of offline access is the obvious one – they cannot be dynamic. Intranet applications that depend on server-side scripting will not work. It also may not be possible to edit pages offline, unless using a technology such as Lotus Notes replication or SQL Server synchronization that has the ability to synchronize pages edited offline when an online connection becomes available.

Keeping It Simple – Internet Explorer Offline Synchronization

Most intranet content can be made available offline and at no additional cost by using Internet Explorer's "Offline Favorites" facility (as yet, there is no implementation of this feature in Netscape).

To use this, browse to the page that you want to be available offline, select *Add to Favorites* from the *Favorites* menu in Internet Explorer, and select the *Make Available Offline* checkbox. You can customize the way in which the page is made available offline, for example by changing the depth of links that are followed from the page, and by setting up the schedule that determines when the pages are automatically updated. You can also access these settings using the "*Synchronize*" option in the "*Tools*" menu.

What Internet Explorer is actually doing here is downloading and saving the initial web page, scanning it for links to other pages, and then loading those in turn, up to the depth specified by the *Download pages N links deep from this page* property. It is acting as a web spider.

This simple approach has a number of disadvantages. First, as with all offline access to pages, the dynamic content of the intranet such as intranet applications will not work. Second, this approach can put considerable strain on your intranet server if widely used. Third, there is no easy way to set this up for users. However, it is very simple, and may be appropriate for smaller intranets.

An alternative, still using Internet Explorer, is to use **Active Channels**. This uses a Channel Definition File (CDF) to define a batch of content that should be available offline, and how it should be synchronized. This file is an XML text file on your server that denotes what you have made available on your intranet site. This makes it very easy for a user to set up offline content – they only need to click on a *Subscribe to channel* link that has been set up on the intranet to link to a CDF file.

> *There's more information on Active Channels available from the Microsoft web siteat http://msdn.microsoft.com/workshop/delivery/channel/channel_node_entry.asp.*

When Internet Explorer is downloading pages with "Offline Favorites", it includes the string "MSIECrawler" in its HTTP user-agent identification header. With server-side scripting, you can check for this string, and serve slightly different pages to be used for offline browsing – for example, removing links to intranet applications, or sending smaller, lower-quality graphics.

You can also use a robots.txt file on the server to determine which areas of dynamic content should not be downloaded by IE. For more information on robots.txt, see http://www.robotstxt.org/wc/robots.html. Not all web crawlers respect robots.txt, but most do, including Internet Explorer.

Offline Access Via Lotus Notes Replication

Lotus Notes (*http://www.lotus.com/*) is a well-established groupware and Content Management System that has an extremely good process for offline access to content, and offline content generation. It has probably the most mature and fully-featured offline facilities of any current CMS.

With Lotus Notes, a user can make a local "Replica" of any Notes database simply by right-clicking on it and selecting *Replicate.* This replica has all the same code that is part of the original database, although obviously while the computer it is running on is not connected to the network, the replica will not be able to access network resources. Documents can be added to the replica while offline and edited, provided the user has the necessary access rights. When the replica is again connected to the network, it will synchronize the updates made locally with those made to the original database. In this way, multiple offline readers and authors can all add and edit content simultaneously. If changes are made to the same document by several different authors, then on the next synchronization the document is flagged as a "Replication conflict" and must be manually edited to resolve the conflict. Notes replication is very rapid, even for very large sites, because it only transfers the differences between the databases, so there is no reason not to replicate very frequently.

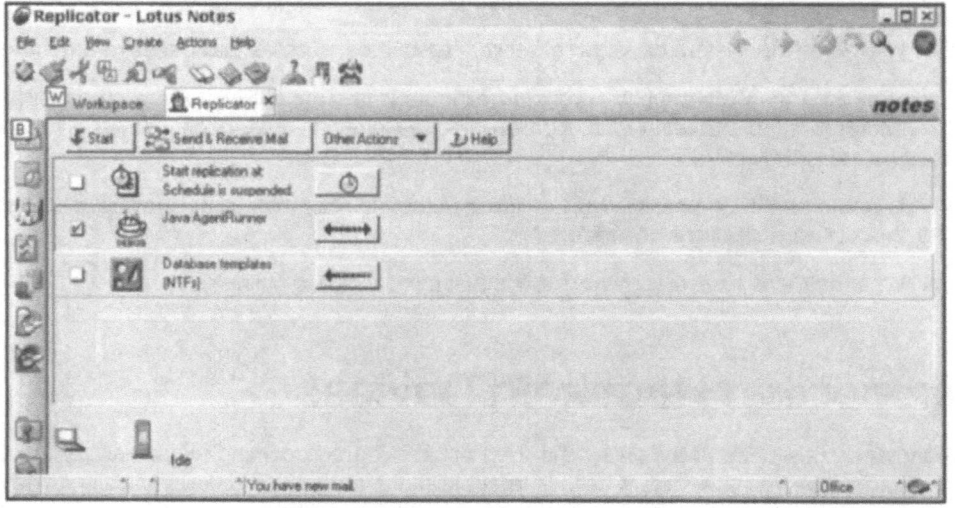

The Lotus Notes client displaying the Replicator control panel

If offline access to your intranet, and particularly offline content creation by multiple authors, is very important to you, then consider using Lotus Notes. This requires that you base your intranet around Lotus Notes – there is no way to take advantage of the Notes replication features without having your intranet server running Notes. However, Lotus Notes is a large product with a steep learning curve, and switching to it is a major step that requires careful consideration. Also, although the Lotus Notes server is cheap compared to other CMS systems, a Notes client license is needed for each computer that needs the offline replication features.

Groove (*http://www.groove.net/*) is a newer competitor to Lotus Notes that offers many of the same advantages, but is not yet as widespread or as widely known as Notes. It is designed by Ray Ozzie, the original author of Lotus Notes, and aims to be "Notes done right". It has better integration with Microsoft products, including .NET, than Lotus Notes does, but poorer support for Java, and it doesn't have an integrated web server – instead it requires that users have the Groove client software installed. As such, it is rather different from the other intranet technologies that we have discussed in this book, but it aims to solve the same problems.

Evaluating CMS Offline Access Capabilities

Several other CMS systems offer some form of offline access and offline authoring tools. Going through all of the contending systems here would be impossible – especially because each vendor is constantly changing the features that they offer, and new vendors are constantly entering the marketplace. Instead, here are some questions to consider:

- How secure is the content when stored offline? Can it be made to require a password access, and can the data be encrypted so it is not possible to circumvent the security measures by looking at the data files directly?

- How efficient is the synchronization process? Is every document transferred across, or only the changes (differential synchronization)?

- Is it easy to set up the synchronization process to run automatically?

- How does the system cope when network resources, such as databases, are not available?

- How does the CMS cope with very large intranets that are too big to be stored offline in their entirety? Is there an easy way of partitioning the intranet so users only have offline access to the areas they require?

- Is offline authoring possible? Does offline authoring require special software, and if so, does this software require a license fee?

- What happens if several authors edit the same document offline?

Supporting Handheld Devices

Handheld devices such as the Palm and the Pocket PC are becoming increasingly popular. They allow their owners to have instant access to applications and stored data practically anywhere. By making your intranet available on handheld devices, you can make it possible for employees to work more productively, wherever they are.

Who Uses Handhelds?

Does your company have sales professionals who are frequently out of the office? Can they access product information, account details, service requests, and sales data while at a client site? Does your company have technicians or consultants who work on client sites? Can they access your organization's knowledge bases, bug databases, parts inventory, and technical information while with a client? Yes, it's possible to do this with a laptop rather than with a handheld, but there's a big difference between taking half a second to pull a handheld out of your pocket, and taking several minutes to take a laptop out of its case and boot it up. If the information isn't immediately available, then in many cases it might as well not be there. Having immediate access to information from your intranet could be very useful to these sales professionals. If these are useful to your employees then you have a strong case for including handheld support on the intranet.

In addition, many handheld owners use them to read newspapers or other news feeds using a system such as AvantGo (*http://www.avantgo.com*). As well as reading a newspaper, they could also be reading your organization's news, or keeping up to date with intranet discussion forums.

The examples so far have been about viewing intranet content on a handheld. It's equally useful to be able to synchronize your handheld's address book with your intranet address book so you always have access to phone numbers of your colleagues and your clients.

The good news is that it's neither particularly hard, nor expensive, to enable sections of your intranet to be read on a handheld device. However, it does take some setting up, both in terms of software on the handheld, and in terms of changes to the intranet in order to make it more usable on small-screen devices.

> *According to a survey of handheld owners conducted by AvantGo, 68% of users believe that having access to their corporate portal or intranet via a PDA would improve their productivity, 47% think it would help them make better decisions, and 68% think that it's important or very important that they can access their intranet with their PDA. The intranet areas that they were most interested in accessing were personnel directories, training materials, and company news. There's more information at http://www.avantgo.com/news/press/press_archive/2002/release 06_11_02.html.*

If there are only a few people in your organization who require access to intranet information outside the office, then it might be more cost-effective to buy each of them a laptop, rather than to spend the development time making your intranet handheld-friendly. However, if many people need access to the intranet, then the lower price of handhelds in comparison to laptops might make them a more desirable solution. In any calculation of the ROI from laptops or handhelds, consider the time it takes to consult one, as well as the additional uses that could be made for either device.

A note on terminology

When I refer to "handhelds", I mean the generic class of handheld Personal Digital Assistants, such as the Palm, the Sony Viao, the MS Pocket PC, and the Compaq iPAQ. I'm not including mobile phones in this category, although devices like the Blackberry and the latest mobile phones have some overlap. I'm not referring specifically to the "Handheld PC" (HPC) that Microsoft produces, although it is included in the group when I'm referring to handhelds.

When I refer to the "Palm", I'm referring to the Palm from Palm Inc., and the various handhelds that use Palm OS such as the Sony Viao and the Handspring Visor.

When I refer to the "Pocket PC", I mean the Microsoft Pocket PC and the Pocket PC 2002, and the various handhelds that use Windows CE such as the Compaq iPAQ and the HP Jornada. I'm not referring to the Tablet PC – in size, power, and cost, these more closely resemble a laptop than a handheld.

The Downsides of Handhelds

There are many downsides to accessing an intranet via a handheld. Some are starting to be overcome, while some are inherent in the size and portability of the device.

The problems of mobile devices include:

- Screen size and resolution – resolution will improve over time, but screen size is unlikely to change (about 6cm by 6cm is standard)

- Color support – only the more expensive models have any colors at all

- Poor quality input devices – the stylus or keyboard on handhelds is not as good as a desktop keyboard, although they are still much better than a mobile phone keypad

- Limited software support for popular document formats. This is becoming less of a problem, as both Palm and Pocket PC handhelds support PDF, and the MS Word and Excel formats

- Dependence on batteries (especially a problem for the powerful but power-hungry Pocket PC handhelds)

- Limited support for synchronizing with desktop computers that are not running Windows – both MacOS and Linux have some support for synchronization with handhelds, but it is not as complete nor as reliable as under Windows

And for interactive, online intranet access, the handheld is handicapped by:

- Slow network transfer rate.

- Poor network latency – there is a several-seconds delay establishing a WAP connection. With GPRS (General Packet Radio Service – a newer transport mechanism that is 'always on' and has higher data transfer rates), this is not so much of a problem. However, although GPRS has been around for a few years now, it hasn't yet achieved very great market penetration and whether it is available is dependent on the network service provider.

Because of these limitations, a handheld cannot be a replacement for a web browser on a desktop PC or a laptop. However, it has its own strong points:

- Very portable.

- Very fast to turn on

We will look at how to make reading the intranet useful on a handheld by leveraging these strengths and working around the weaknesses.

How to Access the Intranet

There are two different ways of accessing the intranet via a mobile device.

The first is to access the intranet interactively, by using the equivalent of a web browser on a mobile device. If using a mobile phone, this is the only generally available way of accessing an intranet at the moment. It is limited by the bandwidth available to the device, as well as the limited screen size and limited input possibilities.

The second is to access the intranet offline. This requires a device that has a reasonable storage capacity, and a reasonably powerful processor to render the stored content. At the moment, this means that it is limited to palmtop devices such as the Palm and the Pocket PC, and phone/palmtop crossover devices such as Blackberry.

In this section, we will look at accessing the intranet using palmtop computers, both online and offline. We will delay discussion of WAP on mobile phones until the next section.

Offline Viewing on a Palm

The major advantage of viewing the intranet offline is that you are not limited by the networking speed and connectivity. Except for very time-critical content, a synchronization every day or two is probably just as good at keeping the content up-to-date as an interactive connection. Choosing to view the intranet offline rather than online is a trade-off between the memory size required and speed – viewing the intranet offline is faster than doing it interactively, but requires more memory on the Palm.

There are a number of options for viewing an intranet offline on the Palm. These include:

- AvantGo (*http://www.avantgo.com/*) – one of the standard pieces of software that comes with the Palm, and usable for Internet web sites via AvantGo Custom Channels. For intranets, you must purchase the AvantGo Server.

- Plucker (*http://www.plkr.org/*) – free software described below.

- iSilo (*http://www.isilo.com/*) – commercial software, worth the price for an individual user, but less useful for an intranet.

- SiteScooper (*http://www.sitescooper.org/*) – free software, but more limited than Plucker (in particular, it doesn't have the sophisticated Palm client program that Plucker uses).

If your users are running a mix of Palm OS and Windows CE, then it may be worthwhile to buy a cross-platform commercial product such as AvantGo server. This may reduce your maintenance costs since you can use the same software on all of your users' handhelds. If you only have to support one handheld operating system, or if your budget is limited, then one of the free alternatives might be more suitable.

We'll look in depth at one specific piece of free software that allows you to access your intranet offline. This is Plucker. It consists of "Plucker Viewer" the Palm-based reader application, and "Plucker Distiller" that downloads, parses, and compresses the web pages into a database suitable for use by the viewer. There are versions of Plucker Distiller for Windows, Macintosh, and Linux computers.

Why Plucker?

Plucker is the most useful Palm application for reading an intranet offline for two reasons. First, it's free and open source (unlike most of its competitors), and second, you can use an application to do the bulk of the work on the server.

The way that most of the offline viewing applications work is to have the user's desktop computer downloading all the web pages that are to go onto the Palm, converting them to an appropriate Palm format, and then transferring them across to the Palm when it is next synchronized. There are two problems with this approach. Firstly, it can be slow, especially if there are a large number of documents to be downloaded, parsed, and converted. Secondly, if there are a large number of people doing this, then it can be a heavy load on the server.

The alternative approach that is made possible by Plucker is to have Plucker Distiller running on the server. This way around, there is only one process doing the downloading, parsing, and converting task, and the client machines simply use the resulting Palm database file.

Setting Up Plucker on the Server

Plucker Distiller is the server-side half of Plucker. There are versions in the Python, Perl, and Java languages. Of these, the Python version is the best to use – the Perl version is older and lacks certain features, and the Java (actually Jython) version is new and hasn't yet been widely used. The Distiller is effectively a special-purpose web spider that downloads pages from a web site, following links to the depth that you specify, and stores the data in its own compressed form suitable for reading on the Palm.

There are full instructions on setup in the Plucker documentation (*http://docs.plkr.org*). To "pluck" an intranet, you need to create a file that defines which areas of your intranet should be plucked. By default this file is called home.html in your Plucker directory. It should look something like this:

```
<html>
   <head><title>Intranet home page</title></head>
   <body>
     <a href="http://intranet/news.html" maxdepth=3 stayonhost>Intranet news</a>
     <a href="http://intranet/phone/" maxdepth=1 stayonhost noimages>Phone
list</a>
   </body>
</html>
```

This specifies that Plucker should download the intranet news and the intranet phone list from the specified URLs, and convert them to its own format. Links in the "*News*" area should be downloaded to a depth of three links deep from the original news.html page, but not followed off the intranet server. There are a number of other options for the Distiller that are fully described in the Plucker documentation. The special attributes maxdepth stayonhost and noimages that appear above are not valid HTML, but only need to appear in the home.html file.

To invoke the Distiller, you need to call it with Python (the Python runtime is included with Plucker):

```
python spider.py -f IntranetForPalm
```

which will create a Palm database IntranetForPalm.pdb. On Windows you can set Plucker up to run regularly via the Task Scheduler, or on Unix you can use Cron.

Setting Up Plucker on the Client

Plucker Viewer is a standard Palm OS application. The easiest way to make it available to your users is to put the Palm .PRC files on an intranet web page – users that have the Palm Desktop installed should be able to click on them to have them installed to their Palm on their next HotSync.

There are several options for transferring the Plucker database of your intranet to the Palm.

First, Plucker comes with a desktop application called "Plucker Desktop" that downloads and parses web pages on a schedule. The disadvantage of this is that it requires that the user sets up the channels to download themselves, and the downloading and parsing is done on the user's computer rather than on a central server. It may be appropriate if you have quite a small number of users, or if the users want to download other web sites apart from the intranet to be read on their Palm.

Secondly, you can generate the Plucker database on the server using the technique described. The simplest way of getting it from the server to the user's Palm is having the user click on the generated database on a web page (using a browser on their desktop computer) every time they want to update the content. This is inconvenient for the user, but if the intranet pages that need offline access are only rarely updated it may be an acceptable approach.

Alternatively, you can generate the database on the server, and then have a script running on the user's desktop computer that downloads the database locally (using software such as wget (*http://www.gnu.org/software/wget/wget.html*)) and then installs it using the Palm instapp executable. A DOS batch file to do this that could be put into the user's *Startup* folder would look something like this:

```
@echo off
wget http://intranet/palm/theintranet.pdb
instapp theintranet.pdb
```

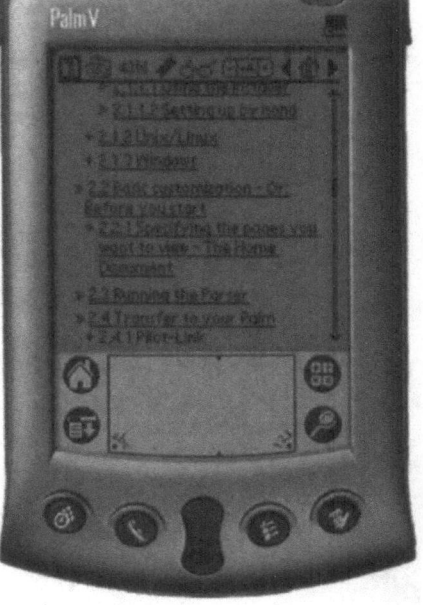

It wouldn't be too hard to write a Palm conduit that would automatically download a pre-compiled Plucker database from a specified URL on the intranet every time the Palm was hot-synched. Unfortunately, such a thing doesn't yet exist, but it is being worked on, so keep an eye on the Plucker web page (*http://www.plkr.org*).

Plucker running on a Palm V. It is displaying part of the Plucker user manual.

13

The Palm graphic displayed above is a screenshot of POSE, the PalmOS Emulator. It's available as a free download from Palm at http://www.palmos.com/dev/tools/emulator/. It is a complete emulator of Palm hardware, including memory constraints, and you can get a complete set of Palm ROMs so you can run any version of PalmOS on it.

When setting up your intranet to be used from a handheld, then it's very useful to be able to test it on a emulator – it allows developers without handhelds to do the testing, and it gives access to many more models of handheld than you're likely to have easy access to.

An additional use for the emulator is in producing documentation. Because the emulator runs under Windows, you can use the normal Alt-PrintScreen keyboard shortcut to make a screengrab of what it's showing. This is very useful when you need to provide instructions on setting up and using the software on the handheld.

Customized versions of POSE are also available from licensees of Palm OS, such as Sony and Handspring.

Viewing Other Intranet Information Offline on the Palm

Plucker is well-suited for viewing content-managed intranet pages, and for acting as an offline web browser; however, an offline web browser cannot take advantage of the server-side scripting that creates intranet applications. Some intranet applications would require custom programming to duplicate on a handheld, but it's possible to use off-the-shelf Palm applications to replace a lot of intranet functionality.

There isn't the space in this book to look at every Palm application that can be used for this purpose. One particularly useful one, though, is Pilot-DB (*http://pilot-db.sourceforge.net/*), a free and open source database program. This is very useful for storing data such as address books, contact lists, or product databases. Using Pilot-DB and its associated tools (*http://sourceforge.net/projects/palm-db-tools/*), you can convert CSV, Excel, or XML files from the intranet into Pilot-DB format, and make them accessible

Another alternative way of keeping contact lists is the standard Palm address book. The standard Palm software allows you to synchronize this with Outlook. Although this is useful for small address lists, it doesn't cope well with the thousands of addresses that would typically be held in the contact list of a medium-sized organization.

Viewing the Intranet Offline on a Pocket PC

The easiest way of viewing the intranet offline on a Pocket PC is to use "Mobile Favorites". This is an application that is installed on your desktop PC when you install ActiveSync. When you do so, a "Pocket PC" icon is added to the Internet Explorer toolbar on your desktop PC.

To use Mobile Favorites:

- Connect your Pocket PC to the desktop PC with ActiveSync.
- Browse to a web page in Internet Explorer on the desktop PC.

- Select the "Pocket PC" icon on the IE toolbar.

- Choose the name of the Mobile Favorite and how frequently it is updated.

- Select Favorites > Organize Favorites from the IE menu and adjust the depth to download links to, the schedule, the passwords to use, and other details for that favorite.

- On your Pocket PC, open Pocket Internet Explorer, and select the Favorites button on the taskbar at the bottom of the page.

This then allows you to view the pages that you have marked as Mobile Favorites on your Pocket PC. You can set a schedule on the desktop PC to update the pages regularly, and you can set the link depth to download pages that are linked to from the pages you select.

Unfortunately, there is no way that I know of to perform the parsing and downloading of web pages on the server, as you can with Plucker for the Palm. As a result, if you have many Pocket PC users, then each will have to set up their Mobile Favorites to download the intranet individually, which may lead to increased user-support problems, and an increased load on the intranet web server.

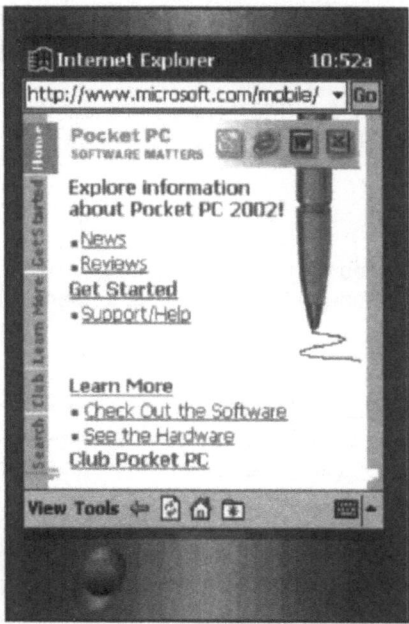

Pocket IE (PIE) running on a Pocket PC 2002

Just as with the Palm screenshot earlier in this chapter, the Pocket PC screenshot on the left was taken from an emulator. The Pocket PC emulator is a free download from Microsoft at http://www.microsoft.com/mobile/devel oper/downloads/ppcsdk2002.asp.

It requires that you also install Microsoft Embedded Visual Tools, which is another free download from http://msdn.microsoft.com/downloads/s ample.asp?url=/msdn-files/027/001/ 963/msdncompositedoc.xml. Don't download this over a slow connection – it's over 300MB! You can order it from Microsoft on CD if this is too large a download for you.

This download includes Pocket PC, Palm-size PC, and Handheld PC Software Development Kits, as well as the emulators for each of these devices.

Viewing the Intranet Online with Palm and Pocket PC

Although browsing the intranet offline, as opposed to browsing the intranet online, has advantages in terms of speed, it may not always be suitable. Only the smallest intranets can be stored on a handheld in their entirety, and there are always likely to be situations when the right piece of content is not stored offline, in which case the intranet will have to be viewed online.

Some web browsers for the Palm are:

- EudoraWeb (*http://www.eudora.com/internetsuite/eudoraweb.html*)

- Palm Web Browser (*http://www.palm.com/*)

- AvantGo Web Client (*http://www.avantgo.com/*)

- Xiino (*http://www.ilinx.co.jp/en/products/xiino/index.html*)

Each of these has different levels of support for JavaScript, frames, images, and so on. If you are supporting Palm users, then it is best to evaluate a number of Palm web browsers to find the one that suits your needs best, and then standardize on that browser. This isn't to say that the intranet web pages you use should only work on one browser, but it makes web page maintenance significantly harder if you have to test every page in five or six different handheld browsers.

For the Pocket PC, the major option is Pocket Internet Explorer (PIE). There are a few other browsers available, but these are not nearly as widely used as PIE.

Designing for Handheld Viewing

Although handheld web browsers can display most web pages with no changes needed on the server, by making a few changes you can make the intranet a lot more usable for handheld users.

Creating Handheld Homepages

Pages written to be read on a handheld need to emphasize different things from normal intranet web pages. They should be much more concise, and have a minimum of "decoration" – like headers, footers, and navigation. The latter is easy to achieve by using a different template, but the former depends on the pages being rewritten manually.

It is impractical to produce two different sets of intranet content, one for handheld users and one for the Web. However, you can create "gateway pages" that act as homepages for handheld users, that are specifically written to be useful to handheld users.

Not all of the intranet is necessarily useful to view on a handheld, particularly offline. For example, intranet applications will depend either on server-side scripting, which is impossible offline, or on client-side JavaScript, which may not be supported on a handheld browser. Particularly large pages will be hard to read on a handheld, and may cause bandwidth problems. The handheld gateway page can provide links to only those parts of the intranet which are seen as useful for handheld access.

Personalization is more important for handheld browsers than it is for normal intranet users. As there is so little space on a handheld (both in terms of screen space and in memory), it is valuable to be able to remove unwanted content. If users are collecting the offline version of the intranet client-side (as with Mobile Favorites), rather than server-side (as with Plucker) then it's useful to allow your users to customize what appears on the handheld homepage. This allows them to change what they are downloading using a simple web-based interface, rather than having to learn a new software program interface. It also allows every client-side computer to be set up with the same offline browser settings, thus reducing maintenance costs, while still allowing users to store different information on their handheld. However, if the intranet is being spidered server-side, for example using Plucker, then the best you can do is provide several different spidered versions, and allow the user to choose which one they install.

Using a CMS to Serve Different Content to Handhelds

Just as a web site can serve different content to Netscape browsers and to Internet Explorer, it can serve different content to handheld browsers. One way to do this is by checking the User-Agent HTTP header in server-side script. Pocket Internet Explorer will always contain the string "*Windows CE*" in its user agent header. Other handheld browsers have a variety of different user agent strings.

Alternatively, you may be able to set your CMS up to use some sort of "virtual directory". For example, on the main intranet site you might access HR information by going to the URL *http://intranet/hr/index.html*. You may be able to set your CMS up such that clicking on the URL *http://intranet/handheld/hr/index.html* will open the same page, but served with a different template.

A template for handheld users should be as minimalist as possible. Items which do not provide an immediate benefit to the handheld user should be removed. This may include standard headers, footers and sidebars, the company logo, and most images. Form controls (such as a search textbox) take up space that could be used for content – and if the intranet is being read offline, then such forms are likely to be useless in any case. The intranet navigation is likely to need the most alteration; one option is to have a link to a separate site map on each page, rather than display the navigation on every page.

> *There is a useful but incomplete web page listing some user-agent strings for mobile devices at http://www.zytrax.com/tech/web/browser_ids.htm, but you may need to work out what your user agent is by writing some server-side code (or by using the link on the URL just referenced).*

Making Sections of the Intranet Easier to Read Offline

There are several techniques that can be used to make parts of the intranet easier to read offline.

Offline browsers are generally set to download links to a certain link depth – for example, only following links that are two deep from the originating page. This has implications for the way that you structure your articles. If an article spans multiple pages, then you need to provide an initial table of contents that links to each page, rather than having *Previous* and *Next* links on each page. If you don't do this, then the offline browser is required to fetch pages to a link depth equal to the number of pages in the article. Any CMS should be able to create such a table of contents automatically.

You can use the page URL to help the offline browser distinguish different sections. For example, if every part of the intranet sales information is beneath the URL *http://intranet/sales/*, then the offline browser can be told to follow only those links that begin with *http://intranet/sales/*. Likewise, if all the sales information is on the server "sales.intranet", then the browser can ignore those links which lead to other servers.

If you are using browser detection to serve different content to handheld user agents, as described above, then make sure that you're also checking for the user agent used by your offline browser.

Intranet Technologies That Are Safe for Handhelds

Whichever handheld device you use, it is going to be less functional than the latest desktop browsers. Although different handhelds have different levels of support for web page technologies, there are a number of technologies that you need to be careful with. As always, you need to test the intranet on all the browsers that it is intended to be viewed with.

Frames

Frames are supported on Pocket Internet Explorer (PIE), but not on many Palm browsers (although Palm browsers will often provide a list of available frames so you can at least view them one at a time). In any case, the limited screen size makes them mostly useless unless you are very careful. They are best avoided.

Images

Handhelds will usually automatically scale images down and reduce their color depth, so the images can be seen, but you need to consider whether they'll be useful to handheld users. Only the most functional images should be used on a handheld – they not only take up valuable screen space, but they also take up the limited memory space of the handheld. alt text for images is not just useful for the partially sighted – it is very useful for handhelds as well.

HTML/WML

Most handheld web browsers are broadly HTML 3.2-compliant. Some will also support WML (the Wireless Markup Language) – but WML is more limited than HTML, and there's little reason to use it for handhelds that will support HTML. There's more detail on WML below, in the section on Supporting Mobile Phones.

JavaScript and DHTML

Several handheld browsers support a subset of JavaScript – but not necessarily the same subset. DHTML is supported only on the Pocket PC 2002, and not on early Pocket PCs or on the Palm. In any case, DHTML coders often make assumptions about screen size that may not be true of the Palm. Avoid JavaScript if you can – but if it cannot be avoided then test it thoroughly. If the intranet navigation is DHTML-based, then you will probably need to provide an alternative navigation for handheld browsers.

Flash

Flash is currently supported on the Pocket PC 2002 and on the Sony CLIÉ (running Palm OS). It's not yet widespread on handheld devices.

CSS

Very few handheld browsers have any support for CSS; Pocket Internet Explorer doesn't, and nor do the most widely used Palm web browsers. However, this is in no way a recommendation not to use CSS on your intranet – the handheld browsers that don't use CSS can just ignore the links to the CSS stylesheet.

Java

Java applets are unsupported on any handheld web browsers. However, Java 2 Micro Edition (J2ME) is a version of Java targeted at mobile devices (both handhelds and mobile phones), and might be usable as a replacement for any intranet applications that require Java. As long as Java isn't used as an essential part of the intranet, for example as intranet navigation, then this is unlikely to be a problem.

ActiveX

ActiveX is not supported on any Palm OS devices. It is partially supported on the PocketPC – ActiveX controls will not auto-install, but web pages can use ActiveX controls that are already present. In addition, some ActiveX controls may make assumptions about the environment in which they are running (for example, assuming that they have network access) that will not be true when they are running on a handheld. As with Java, this shouldn't be a problem unless ActiveX is being used as an essential part of the intranet.

Support for ActiveX is a clear advantage for the Pocket PC over other handhelds if your intranet has ActiveX-based applications, but you do need to check each one carefully to see if it will work on a handheld, and some ActiveX applications may need some amount of rewriting to make them work.

.NET

There are two options for .NET development for handhelds.

The first is to use the Microsoft Mobile Internet Toolkit (MIT) for ASP.NET development on the server-side. This simply uses ASP.NET controls to generate HTML or WML suitable for handheld devices, rather than for desktop PCs, without requiring any code changes for the developer. This is primarily targeted, as you would expect, at the MS Pocket PC handhelds, but there's no reason why it shouldn't work on many Palm web browsers too. There is more information on the MS MIT at *http://msdn.microsoft.com/vstudio/device/mobilecontrols/*.

The second is to use the .NET Compact Framework and the .NET Smart Device Extensions to produce code that can run on a handheld. This offers similar possibilities to running ActiveX controls on a handheld, but only works on Windows CE-based handhelds such as the Pocket PC. There is more information on this approach at *http://msdn.microsoft.com/vstudio/device/compactfx.asp*. The .NET Compact Framework is new, but could become an interesting option for handheld development over the next few years.

> *An overview of the two approaches, and their relative merits, is available at http://msdn.microsoft.com/library/en-us/dnppcgen/html/mobdevtools.asp.*

Where to Go from Here – Remote Users

13

Supporting Mobile Phones

Why would you want to access the intranet via a mobile phone? The answer, most of the time, is that you wouldn't. Mobile phones are slow, have a very small screen size, and the numeric keypad is a very poor input device for anything other than phone numbers. In addition, the WML browsers on mobile phones are much less sophisticated than HTML web browsers on handhelds.

However, mobile phones do have some advantages that may make them suitable for accessing small amounts of intranet data:

- Mobile phones are ubiquitous – many employees will not have laptops or handhelds, but almost all are likely to have mobile phones (although they may not all be WAP-capable).

- Mobile phones are appropriate for accessing small amounts of time-critical information on the intranet.

- Mobile phones can send and receive SMS messages – therefore they are appropriate for "push" applications based around the intranet.

Mobile phones are best suited to using custom-written intranet applications rather than browsing the intranet as a whole.

One possible use for a mobile phone intranet application is for a user who is frequently out of the office to find information on their schedule – this might be appropriate for an engineer who travels to a number of client sites. Support staff at the engineer's office can enter the appropriate information into a database via the normal intranet web interface, and then the engineer can access their schedule and the details of the client via their phone. In addition, the intranet application could send an SMS (Short Message Service) message to the engineer if the schedule changes.

An open source server for sending SMS messages is Smash, available from http://sf.net/projects/smash/.

WML

WML is the equivalent of HTML for mobile phones. Just like HTML, it is used for displaying content and for specifying user-interface elements such as forms. It uses XML syntax, so every WML page must be a valid and well-formed XML document. It must also include the XML declaration and the DOCTYPE declaration. A sample WML file looks like this:

```
<?xml version="1.0"?>
<!DOCTYPE wml PUBLIC
    "-//WAPFORUM//DTD WML 1.1//EN" "http://www.wapforum.org/DTD/wml_1.1.xml">

<wml>
    <card title="Intranet">
        <p align="center"><b>Welcome to the mobile intranet</b></p>
        <p><a href="news.wml">News</a></p>
        <p><a href="addressbook.wml">Address book</a></p>
    </card>
</wml>
```

By analogy to HTML, it should be fairly clear what's happening here. This creates a WML page that contains the text "*Welcome to the mobile intranet*", and two links, one to the news and one to an address book. Although in this page there is only one <card> element, it is possible to have several small cards defined in one page, that can be quickly swapped between, a bit like a deck of cards, or relative links in an HTML page. This improves application responsiveness at the cost of initial download time.

Although it shouldn't be too hard to create a template that will automatically generate WML rather than HTML from your CMS, it's also not very useful. Because the screen size and allowed file size is very limited, automatically converted intranet pages are barely usable. Instead, WML should be hand-written for those pages which must be accessed from mobile phones. This means that accessing the majority of the intranet content is impractical – most authors will not be able to spend the time writing a highly condensed mobile version of their page. Instead, the only real use for mobile phones accessing the intranet is to access a few custom-written intranet applications.

Entering data (for example, to fill in forms in a web application) on a mobile phone is particularly painful. The only form of data that is easy to enter is purely numeric information. You may be able to exploit this. For example, a customer search that bases its searches on the phone number of the customer would be easy to use for a sales executive, because phone numbers are both easy to enter on a phone keypad, and likely to be stored in the phone.

> *For more information on WAP, see* Professional WAP *(Arehart C., et al., Wrox Press, ISBN: 1-86100-404-4).*

The Nokia 7210 phone emulator

This screenshot is of a Nokia 7210. It was made using the Nokia 7210 Mobile Handset Simulator, available for free from http://www.forum.nokia.com/.

All the major phone manufacturers provide similar emulators that are available from their developer web sites.

It is well worth using a phone simulator (in addition to actual phones!) to test your WAP code, rather than just a desktop web browser that understands WAP. Some phones have limitations that will not show up in a desktop browser – for example, some early models of Nokia phones wouldn't accept WML files that were over 1.4 kb in size.

13

Voice Recognition and Synthesis

An alternative to accessing intranet information using WAP is to use VoiceXML. A VoiceXML gateway uses voice recognition and speech synthesis to provide a voice interface to a computer over the phone. It uses VoiceXML files that describe the words that can be understood by the system at each point, and what the response should be. It's similar to the "Press 1 to access your account balance, press 2 to pay a bill, etc."-style menu that is used by telephone banking systems, but uses voice recognition rather than the numbers on the keypad.

VoiceXML is backed by a number of major companies including IBM and Sun. An alternative, backed by Microsoft and Intel, is SALT (Speech Application Language Tags). SALT is more recent than VoiceXML, and so far VoiceXML seems better supported, but it's certainly far too early to discount SALT.

In this section, we'll concentrate on describing VoiceXML, but bear in mind that much of it is also relevant to other forms of voice recognition and speech synthesis.

The advantage of VoiceXML over WAP is that talking into the telephone is a more natural interface than using the WAP browser. It's accessible from any employee's phone, rather than just those that support WAP, and it can be used hands-free if necessary. However, as with WAP, it's only suitable for conveying quite small amounts of information at a time.

The VoiceXML file that determines which words are recognized and spoken can be generated on-the-fly by server-side script. For example, a VoiceXML gateway could be used as an interface to a company's client database. A company sales professional could phone up, and say the name of a client. This would trigger the same search that entering the client name into the "*Client database*" search box on the intranet would give. If the results from that search are returned in XML format, then they can be automatically converted to HTML for display on the intranet, or automatically converted to VoiceXML to be read to a user on the phone.

Another possibility is that a technician could use the VoiceXML gateway to perform searches on the intranet's technical support database. The results of the search can be read back to the technician, and he could use it as a step-by-step prompt to perform some support task.

Both of the previous examples could have been solved with a handheld, or a laptop – but providing all employees who are out of the office with handheld computers or laptops may be more expensive than the cost of a VoiceXML gateway and mobile phones. In addition, the hands-free access to information may be valuable to the technician.

A very simple VoiceXML file looks like this:

```
<?xml version="1.0"?>
<!DOCTYPE vxml PUBLIC "-//W3C//DTD VOICEXML 2.0//EN"
"http://www.w3.org/TR/voicexml20/vxml.dtd">
<vxml version="2.0" xmlns="http://www.w3.org/2001/vxml">
   <form>
     <field name="news" type="boolean">
       <prompt>Hear intranet news?</prompt>
       <filled>OK.
         <if cond="news">Loading news now
           <goto next="news.vxml" />
```

```
        <else />
           Going to next page.
           <goto next="other.vxml" />
        </if>
     </filled>
   </field>
  </form>
</vxml>
```

This will say the words "Hear intranet news?" and if the user replies "Yes", then it will redirect to the news page. Otherwise it will redirect to another page. This example is using the built-in "Boolean" type that will accept only "Yes" or "No" as answers. A more sophisticated page would include a specific grammar, or reference an external grammar file, that listed a number of options that would be accepted.

There are obvious security concerns in allowing voice access to sections of your intranet. VoiceXML gateways will typically allow you to limit the valid users of the system based on the phone number from which they are calling, or by using a user ID and password system.

> *VoiceXML is of limited use for intranet access, but it is an option that may be appropriate in some circumstances. You can find more information on VoiceXML in the book Early Adopter VoiceXML (Breitenbach, S. et al, Wrox, ISBN 1-86100-562-8), or online at http://voicexml.org/.*

Summary

In this chapter, we have considered the question "How can you access the intranet when not in the office?". We have found three ways to provide access.

First, we looked at external access to the intranet, from home or from a client site. We discussed VPNs, SSL, and dial-up access.

Then, we looked at providing offline access to the intranet, using Internet Explorer's offline synchronization, Active Channels, and Lotus Notes replication. We didn't evaluate the offline access solutions provided by other CMS systems, but we did discuss what to look for in a CMS that provides offline access.

Last, we looked at accessing the intranet from a handheld device, such as a Palm or Pocket PC. We discussed downloading the intranet to a Palm, and how to use Plucker to do this. We also considered using Mobile Favorites on the Pocket PC to do the same thing, and discussed web browsers for the Palm and Pocket PC allowing online access to the intranet. We went on to talk about making the intranet readable on a handheld device, and the technologies that should be avoided. Finally, we discussed accessing the intranet via a mobile phone, using WAP and VoiceXML.

13

14

- Designing modern extranets
- Planning the extranet

Author: Frank Pappas

Extranets

In the earliest stages of the commercial development of the Internet, companies rushed online, moving large segments of their marketing operations to the digital stage. This was a good way of reaching customers, as they could access a much larger audience with smaller capital investments, and enjoyed more flexibility than in broadcast or print channels. Soon e-commerce began to flourish, showering companies with even greater returns. Since public web sites were having such a positive impact on the corporate balance sheet, businesses decided to search for other ways to benefit from the lessons and technologies from their early Internet initiatives.

As Internet-based technologies matured, the second phase of Internet commercialization found managers focusing on *internal* corporate operations. Functions from just about every discipline within a company were moved within the domain of the *intranet*. Document repositories were created, basic transactions (timesheets, leave requests, etc.) were moved online, and collaboration tools were created. In many cases, corporations became more efficient and realized significant cost savings. Not surprisingly, executives couldn't leave well enough alone: after all, they had just fostered *amazing successes* with public Internet and private intranet sites.

Enter the extranet – well, extranets as they were envisioned back in the mid- to late-1990s. Extranets were to be "the next big thing", vast business-to-business electronic marketplaces in which multiple companies could bid to buy or sell raw materials, provide services, and so on. The vision was grand, the investments even greater. Suppliers, manufacturers, and random intermediaries all created super-sized, complicated (and hugely expensive!) electronic bazaars in the hopes of realizing windfall profits from these new business channels.

Unfortunately no one came. This was in part because the extranet model (at the time) was disjointed and focused on limited transactions that did little to streamline or facilitate the broader needs of enterprise supply chains. The disappointing performance of the first generation of extranets was also due to another important factor: most executives and analysts failed to notice what was to be the *actual* "next big thing", the collapse of the Internet economy.

Thankfully, the global economy has started to improve somewhat in the last year. Companies have once again become more aggressive in investing in e-business services. And extranets – though not quite receiving the same fanfare they did their first time around – are quietly working their way into the e-business strategies of companies around the globe, with a renewed focus and much greater success.

Modern Extranets

Before we can tackle some of the more advanced issues related to developing and harnessing the power of extranets, one of the first orders of business is to answer what *ought to be* a very simple question: what is an extranet? Unfortunately, there is quite a bit of confusion in the business world as to what specifically constitutes an extranet; ask 10 executives to define the term and you're liable to be confronted with 17 strikingly dissimilar answers!

> *Unfortunately, there is quite a bit of confusion in the business world as to what specifically constitutes an extranet; ask 10 executives to define the term and you're liable to be confronted with 17 strikingly dissimilar answers!*

Now, we'll get to a working description of a modern extranet in just a moment. Let's take a brief look at three factors that help us to understand *why* extranets have proven to be such a troublesome concept for the business world. This may be just a bit helpful in framing your thoughts should you ever need to convince your management of the necessity of an extranet – but if the next few paragraphs seem patently obvious to you, feel free to jump ahead to the next section.

First and foremost, extranets are still a relatively recent addition to the "holy trinity" of e-business services. Extranets are so new, in fact, that most managers (even those with plenty of Internet and intranet experience) have had little to no exposure to even the *concept* of an extranet, let alone gained any first-hand experience with or benefited from one. Only as more time passes and extranet successes and failures become better known, will executives be able to intelligently address the theory and practice of deploying extranets in enterprise environments.

Second, the basic building blocks used to create extranets – specifically, the programming languages, hardware, software, database systems, and so on – are essentially identical to those used in Internet and intranet development.

Third is the simple fact that *there are only so many ways* to reduce costs, enhance productivity, and increase revenue through the use of Internet-based products and services. As it stands, by 2003 (nearly eight years since the rise of the "commercial" Internet) we've identified and adopted the vast majority of the ways in which Internet technologies can benefit the business world. From real-time customer service solutions that reduce corporate reliance and expenditures on call centers, to online collaboration tools that eliminate the need for costly travel or video-conferencing, to portals and e-commerce that provide for targeted marketing and 24-hour sales opportunities, there aren't many revolutionary ideas waiting to be discovered – at least until new generations of wireless platforms and other infant technologies mature significantly.

So how then, how can we define the core characteristics of an extranet and end up with a reasonable framework for deciding what is – and isn't – an extranet?

An extranet:

- Is targeted specifically to business-to-business (B2B) markets

- Involves multiple companies within a single, focused supply chain

- Provides controlled, secure access to one or more of the following: strategic data, transactions, and collaborative tools that enhance the overall effectiveness of the enterprise organization

> *An extranet facilitates communication and transactions between groups both internal and external to your company*

Essentially, an extranet facilitates communication and transactions between groups both internal and external to your company that support your core business – vendors, corporate customers, consultants, and so on. The extranet connects your employees with people who work on behalf of your organization but are not, themselves, employees of your company – yet still require access to your proprietary information and other systems in order to keep your supply chain (or segments thereof) running smoothly. Or to put it another way: an extranet services the various corporations across an enterprise in much the same way that an intranet supports the various divisions within a single business.

Extranets in Action

Let's talk a little bit more about the *why* of extranets – what's the point in spending even more money on yet another computer system for your enterprise, especially when so many companies are hurting financially these days? We'll also talk about a few of the ways in which businesses are applying extranet systems in order to address ongoing business needs.

It is an unfortunate fact of life that the unpredictable economy and raucous business climate in recent years has forced many companies to tighten their belts. With these kinds of desperate cost-cutting measures in place at thousands of companies world-wide, it's a wonder that more managers haven't aggressively pursued the adoption of extranet systems to improve the financial health of their operations. The potential benefits of an enterprise extranet include, but certainly aren't limited to:

- **Universal Access** – As rapidly emerging technologies greatly expand both the manner and locations from which users are able to access the Internet, the opportunities to seize real-time competitive advantage becomes paramount. By embracing well-accepted Internet standards, extranets allow your enterprise to offer access to timely and accurate information to your partners whether via tablet PC, PDA, cell phone, or other nascent technologies.

- **Open Architecture** – As your extranet moves to replace many of your legacy systems – including your publications library, human resources systems, help desk, and other EDI systems – the open architecture inherent in the standards found in Internet technologies will provide virtually limitless flexibility and adaptability as you seek to expand the utility of your extranet beyond its initial design.

Extranets

14

- **The Almost Paperless Enterprise** – While the myth of the "paperless office" has yet to be realized in any serious fashion, a tremendous intermediate step can be realized by moving forms, catalogs, and other traditional paper documents online, whether as web-based interactive forms or as PDF files. Printing of the vast majority of these documents instantaneously shifts to an on-demand basis, while simultaneously increasing the efficiency of workers (by reducing time spent searching for documents) and decreasing printing and distribution costs for paper assets.

- **Unified Interface** – As your organization works to provide enterprise-wide access to formerly segmented applications and services from individual business units, a single web-based interface will serve to increase overall user-efficiency across a wider range of extranet tasks. This will also reduce training costs by eliminating the need to cross-train users on a number of disparate systems – allowing, for example, all enterprise inventory management duties (or supply requisitions, order processing, etc.) to be handled by one master system rather than a collection of systems with disjointed interface and data requirements, etc.

- **Self-Service** – Empowering your business partners to solve their own problems allows your organization to spend more time worrying about more strategic matters. By implementing smart editorial controls on your extranet, you can ensure that up-to-date, critical business information – everything from logistics information to FAQs and help-desk services – is available via no more than a click or two to those in your supply chain, freeing up your human resources to focus elsewhere.

- **Enhanced Communication & Collaboration** – The extranet also provides a single-source solution for distributing information (new product specs, proposals, etc.), facilitating discussion, and then rapidly and accurately channeling feedback from partners and other stakeholders back to the relevant users involved (project managers, marketers, sales teams, etc.)

You will probably notice that these benefits are very similar to those of the intranet, and again the reason for this is that the two are essentially very similar. The main difference is that the extranet is bringing these benefits to your clients or strategic partners in their work with your organization.

Designing the Extranet

As we've discussed, building an extranet isn't significantly different from developing an intranet or public Internet site. If you have had the opportunity to develop either a public web site or an intranet for your company in recent years, you're probably familiar at least to some degree with the technologies, processes, and resources that you'll need to effectively bring an extranet together. But just in case you haven't been exposed to 'net development projects in the past, never fear! We'll touch on some of the high points here, and you can always flip back to the earlier chapters for more in-depth discussions of specific topics.

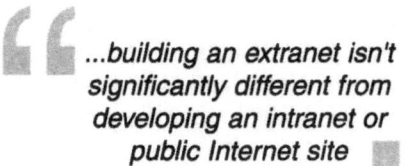

...building an extranet isn't significantly different from developing an intranet or public Internet site

Now, way back in *Chapter 1*, we spent some time discussing the type of teams you'll want to assemble when building an intranet. Not surprisingly, you'll use very similar resources when designing your extranet.

It isn't realistic to expect to find one or two employees who can handle the entire range of development tasks for an enterprise-class extranet – after all, it's no longer 1995, when a single "webmaster" was all that was required to develop and manage basic web sites. However, it *is* reasonable to expect to control headcount and costs by hiring staff whose expertise bridges multiple, related disciplines.

For example, your graphic designer will probably have a good amount of experience with usability (AKA "human factors") design, while your project manager may be adept in developing internal marketing plans for promoting your extranet. And of course, there's always significant overlap among the technical disciplines. The key is to ensure that your core needs are met (or better yet, exceeded) with the smallest team possible.

- **Project Manager** – The project manager serves as the point-person for the development of the extranet and will oversee all tasks performed by the technology, creative, and other staffers assigned to implement the extranet. The project manager ensures that the project adheres to budget, timeline, and other constraints, and acts as the liaison between management and all partner companies to make certain that the business requirements and unique needs of each business unit are addressed in the development of the extranet.

- **Usability Expert / Information Architect** – The usability expert, a specialist whose skills often also encompass the role of *information architect*, is responsible for ensuring that the visual presentation **(user interface - UI)** and the segmentation of data throughout the site **(information architecture - IA)** are optimized for your target audience(s) based on a number of factors. The usability expert will take into consideration a number of variables, including the types of data that will be presented, the tasks which your users will complete via the extranet, and the methods through which your users will access the extranet – all of which can impact tremendously both UI and IA concerns.

- **Graphic Designer** – The graphic designer or art director will work in concert with the project manager and other stakeholders to determine the visual identity of the extranet (colors, logos, typefaces, style, and so on), drawing upon branding and related identity work from the various companies within the enterprise. With an identity in mind, the designer will then work with the usability expert to apply a finished visual treatment, or "look & feel" to the user interface.

- **Database Administrator** – The database administrator will be responsible for recommending the appropriate database solution for your extranet, as well as for architecting the initial design, or schema, of the database itself. This staff member will also work closely with partner companies to establish standards and practices for ongoing data exchange between companies, and will monitor this exchange on a continuing basis.

- **Network Architect** – The network architect will be responsible for planning the physical technology infrastructure that enables your extranet. Working in close contact with the project manager and security and systems specialists, the network architect will develop a plan for the layout of your network (routers & switches, firewalls, servers, etc.) to ensure the highest levels of reliability (uptime), security, and efficiency.

- **Security Guru** – The security specialist is charged with one of the most important roles relative to your extranet project, overseeing the one key technology area in which extranets rise to a new level of complexity, far beyond intranet and public Internet sites. Unlike when dealing with an intranet or a public Internet site, which (respectively and generally) allow either NO external traffic or ALL external traffic into a site, an extranet requires a much more rigorous and delicately tuned security apparatus. With an extranet, the trick is to find a perfect balance between access and security, providing just enough access to allow only trusted partners into the site, but also putting into place stringent security systems that prevent both malicious as well as accidental damage to the system from either unauthorized users or even trusted partners.

- **Systems Administrator** – The system administrator is responsible for the operational health of the software and hardware (servers, application software, etc.) that power your extranet. This person (or a team if your extranet and business requirements so require) will be on call 24/7 to support users, troubleshoot problems, and perform ongoing maintenance.

- **System Developers** – These developers are responsible for the creation of all custom software that will comprise your extranet, including developing programs to integrate legacy systems into the extranet, or in developing the front-end interface (HTML coding) that will be visible to users.

- **Marketing Manager** – The marketing manager is responsible for effectively promoting the extranet to all target audiences throughout the enterprise through both offline (newsletters, presentations, etc.) and online (targeted email, intranet articles, etc.) channels. Additionally, the marketing manager keeps an "ear to the ground" in order to collect feedback from users concerning the extranet, requests for changes/enhancements, etc.

The same holds true for the many technology concerns that we've addressed in *Chapters 3* to *8*. You guessed it – the fundamental building blocks are essentially *interchangeable*. As you begin to discuss the implementation of the underlying technology plan for your extranet, it's important that you consult with the groups charged with managing your public Internet and intranet properties. You'll often find numerous efficiencies in aligning as many of your technology decisions as are practicable with the systems that are already deployed for your corporate intranet and Internet sites. Be certain to discuss:

Be sure to take full advantage of any technologies for which your company has site licenses. As long as the technology meets your needs, this is an excellent way to control costs!

- Web hosting solutions (Is there space available on current servers, and if so, do the extranet's security, functional, or technical demands prohibit us from sharing space on servers providing intranet or Internet sites? Is there a Hosting Solutions Provider that is approved by the corporation?)

- Internal development resources (infrastructure issues, development platforms)

- Web servers, database systems, etc

- Technology, creative, and other staff that can be shared across projects.

- Contracts with outside vendors, contractors, etc., that may be of use during extranet development.

What *does* change, however, when developing an extranet, is how you *apply* these technologies to the needs of your enterprise, your industry, and the specific business challenges faced by your organization on a daily basis. Which is why we can't give you *specific* recommendations for how to design an extranet that's custom-tailored to your situation. You need to first understand the real-world needs of your enterprise, then look for ways to apply Internet technology to reap some specific advantage, be it added efficiency, incremental revenue, cost savings, or something else entirely. In just a few minutes we'll share some of the ways extranets can be developed in order to address some common, but rather generic, business situations.

In the meantime, here are a handful of questions you can consider that will assist you in identifying areas in which extranet services may benefit your organization, as well as how to position your extranet for success.

- What are the high-level corporate goals or objectives for your extranet? Are you trying to control costs, increase revenue, enhance efficiency, or counter a direct threat from a competitor? Perhaps a little of each?

- What are the three top business goals for this initiative? Such goals could include reducing in-person meetings that consume valuable time and capital, containing costs from video- and tele-conferencing, enhancing the timeliness of cross-enterprise communication, retiring expensive and inflexible client/server infrastructure or EDI systems.

- What are the top three functional goals for the site? (Move paper documentation online, establish e-communication queues for partner support, or enable e-commerce for transactions within the enterprise).

- Who are your primary and secondary audiences? How comfortable is each audience/segment with varying levels of technology? How will they access the site – wireless, desktop, PDA? And keep in mind that before you start adding or killing off various pieces of content or functionality, it just takes your boss (or your boss's boss's boss) reading one article in the Financial Times to start demanding that certain extranet features be cut because of some columnist's advice or that you have to start providing **right now** wireless access via PDAs. *Think forward.*

- What is the budget and timeline for this project? (Is the budget reasonable given the scope, or vision, of the project? Are there any specific timelines or functional requirements that will drive the implementation schedule?)

- What cultural or institutional issues will need to be addressed in order to ensure user acceptance of the extranet? (Push-back from people who are used to traditional processes, changes to roles and responsibilities, eztc.)

- Which enterprise partners will be affected by the development of an extranet? Enterprise partners should be intimately involved in the development process to ensure emotional acceptance as well as successful technology and process integration.

- Who owns each area of content or functionality that will be included as part of the extranet? (How will updates be handled, where does responsibility lie for timely and accurate updates of data?)

Extranets

14

One sure way to prevent *feature creep* – your boss or coworkers demanding random new features in order to curry favor or embrace the latest techno-trend – is to develop a well-reasoned project specification before you begin work. This spec will lay out in black and white a variety of important information: target audiences, hardware and software platform requirements, core content and functionality, etc. Draft your document, then make sure it's circulated *and approved in writing* by all the crucial stakeholders, and you've got all the cover you need when deciding whether (or not) to embrace the Marketing VP's wacky wish list of extranet development projects.

However, even though much of the fundamental work in establishing an extranet may be familiar to you, there are a handful of issues that can trip up even the most experienced Internet strategist, and it's important to keep these issues in mind while crafting your extranet plans.

An Extranet Is a Consumer Product!

This cannot be stressed enough! It's incredibly easy to forget that your extranet is, in fact, a *consumer product*, and should be designed as such. Though intranets are sometimes sloppily engineered by a few technology staff members(though hopefully the other chapters in this book will have changed that!), intranets generate value primarily in the cost *savings* they facilitate. Extranets, however, not only contribute to savings through operational efficiency, but also directly impact the operation of core business functions *as well as* commerce and other transactions within the enterprise, influencing the productivity and profitability of the business. As such, the extranet **must** be designed to satisfy the needs of *all* the anticipated user groups. This should be accomplished by frequent meetings (see below) with representatives from throughout your enterprise, and should be overseen by senior members of the business group(s) contributing to the extranet.

Collaborative Design

Developing *any* web property in a vacuum is generally a bad idea, but it's an even worse idea when developing an extranet that will facilitate business communication and transactions to outside an enterprise – especially in cases where the extranet will impact the ability to conduct business. Cutting partners out of the design loop during an extranet project can have a number of unpleasant side-effects, including:

- Incompatibility between your extranet and the web browsers (or other technologies) at one or more of your partners' facilities, preventing them from utilizing some or all of your extranet. This can't be resolved simply by choosing to support one or more of the most popular browsers, as it's often the case that browser developers will implement non-standard tags or other functionality that will diverge slightly from published specs – and may in fact change from one release to another. It's more important to focus on strict adherence to published, current web/HTML standards, then test rigorously on your target platforms.

- Increased risk of error or downtime due to lack of coordination among partners.

- Causing strife among your long-time partners who may feel slighted or placed at a disadvantage against other vendors, etc. within the new operating paradigm.

- Missed Opportunities: Your partners understand their segment of your supply chain at least as well as you do, if not more so. It's very possible that they can identify and recommend significant improvements to the extranet systems you've envisioned, thus saving more money and increasing the competitive advantage enjoyed by the enterprise as a whole. And don't forget that it's always easier and cheaper and less stressful to incorporate feedback and insight at the beginning of a project – waiting until your site is in "beta" unnecessarily complicates things and adds additional costs and delays to the project overall.

Standards

We've mentioned the issue of developing based on accepted Internet standards in a variety of places throughout this book, and for a good reason: it's the smart thing to do, and it's often ignored even by the savviest of developers. Why is sticking to a solid standard a good idea when developing your extranet? We reiterate:

It saves *money*, reduces training costs, increases future development flexibility, allows you to potentially take advantage of other web infrastructure and resources within your organization, and (with the proper planning) ensures that all users within the enterprise have the ability to access the extranet both now and in the future.

Return on Investment

On the business side of things, one of the other many wonderful aspects of an extranet is that there are a good number of ways in which you can justify your request for development and operational resources. In fact, in calculating the ROI, the metrics for determining "success" are limited (within reason) to just about any measurable figures you can point to having been positively impacted by the extranet. Even if you don't choose to work "outside the box" and prefer to be much more traditional in your approach to calculating ROI, you can still assess direct cost savings (printing and distribution costs saved, travel costs eliminated), increases in productivity (jump in widgets produced), or increases in total sales or overall revenue.

Keep in mind that you're not required to solve ALL of your enterprise's extranet issues in one go. You're often constrained by tight budgets, limited management appetite for aggressive growth, a lack of resources, etc. Even if you can't move rapidly on ALL the items on your extranet wishlist, you can selectively implement those items within your grasp that will bring the most benefit to your organization, resulting in real, tangible value that will likely translate into additional resources, funding, and support in the future.

Another important consideration is that because an extranet does not strictly demand that a business completely re-engineer the architecture of their applications OR their business processes in order to enjoy marked benefits, the potential for ROI is much greater than other methods. As many corporations will often dedicate 20% (or more) of their allocated resources toward the integration of existing systems with "band-aid" solutions, an extranet – often a cheaper, more robust intermediary between existing systems – can help companies to save significant financial and human resources.

It's important, though, to understand *how* you intend to prove the extranet's value as you start out on the project so that you can appropriately set the expectations of all involved – as well as to know what factors to monitor as you move forward. It never hurts when, six months into the project, you identify an unexpected way in which the extranet has benefited the company. However, you'll look foolish if you just jump in feet-first, hoping that *something* will arise to justify the lavish office and cute assistant you requisitioned for the project!

Extranets

14

Extending the Extranet to Future Platforms

Wireless devices, new forms of computing tools (tablet PCs) and other technologies (such as WSDL, a standardized XML grammar for describing network services that you can learn about at *http://www.w3.org/TR/wsdl*) are emerging at a frantic pace, each promising new and useful avenues to access the Internet/extranet. As you follow the guidelines we've established for you – including adopting Internet technology standards (DOM and W3C come immediately to mind) you'll have significant flexibility when it comes to presenting your extranet data across a wide range of devices.

Equally important to making your extranet's content and functionality available to next-generation computing devices is knowing *which* pieces of content and functionality are best suited to which platforms. Rich multimedia presentations that look stunning on a 21" flat-screen display are poor candidates for display on a PDA. Long, multi-field order forms are ill-suited for use via a cellphone.

The content and services offered via wireless and other emerging devices must not only be useful in and of themselves, but must also take into account how and why your users will be accessing the data. Rely heavily upon your usability specialist to help guide the evolution of your extranet offerings onto these new devices.

Positioning your extranet's content and functionality requires that much though be put both into the back-end systems (how data is stored, segmented, processed for presentation) as well as on the user-interface issues that determine how data is displayed through a variety of devices to distinct, often disparate audiences.

Application Integration

Many corporations have significant amounts of capital and human resources invested in the development and maintenance of internal applications, applications whose content and functionality could easily be of use to others within the greater enterprise. This is especially important when you recognize that one of today's most pressing business issues concerns the integration of existing enterprise resources and legacy applications into one common, extensible, robust, and cost-effective platform. Technology and business executives must immediately begin considering two issues.

First is security. Traditionally, internal applications have been just that, internal, and have required little in the way of application-level security. Should such datastores be made available via the extranet, application-level security becomes essential to simultaneously providing access to the data while ensuring its integrity.

Second, technology managers must consider the portability/accessibility of data. This, of course, ties into many of the usability and standards issues we've raised throughout this chapter. Emerging technology standards such as XML and XHTML, WAP, SMS, and the like are rapidly replacing older forms of data presentation and transmission, and must be factored into any planning relative to system upgrades or new development.

The Project Plan

As the final step before forging ahead with the development of your extranet, you'll want to be certain to assemble a project plan, a living document that establishes the many details that will eventually define your extranet, including scope, timeline, and budget (among others). This project plan should be crafted once input has been gathered from all stakeholders within the enterprise, and the final draft of the document should be circulated for review and approval by all appropriate managers and employees.

Within this project plan, you should aim to achieve consensus on the following topics:

- **Overview** – Sets expectations within the enterprise concerning extranet goals and for which general content and functionality will be included in the initial launch.

- **Content and Functionality Plan** – Identifies the specific content and functionality that will be included in the extranet at launch, along with sources and owners for each type of content or functionality. As we're long past 1997 and the often-prevalent "know-it-all" attitudes that prevailed at the time, I'm not going to give you a bullet-point list of the features, content, and functionality that you should include in your extranet. After all, you intimately understand the needs of your business (or enterprise) certainly better than I do, so here are three universal rules that you can use to determine what will (or won't) be included in your extranet:

  - Increases efficiency
  - Saves the company money
  - Generates incremental revenue

  By identifying processes and practices throughout your enterprise that can enjoy one (or more) of the above benefits as a result of moving online, then you've found exactly what needs to be included in your extranet.

- **Technology Blueprint** – Defines all technology-related aspects of the extranet, from physical infrastructure to security, to software (servers, applications, etc.), and development tools.

- **Staff Structure** – Identifies, generically, the types and number of specialists needed for the project.

- **Timeline** – The timeline for development of each stage of the extranet, from initial concept, through development and testing, to launch.

- **Budget** – All costs anticipated for the development of the extranet.

- **Caveats** – A well-defined caveats component will ensure that all parties are aware of the importance of providing timely feedback, prompt and complete delivery of assets, etc., and the impact upon the development of the extranet should they fail to comply with the schedule or other responsibilities defined within the project plan.

By taking into consideration some of the many issues we've raised throughout this chapter, combining them with your solid business sense, a good dose of determination, and by relying on the support and expertise of your colleagues, your enterprise extranet will no doubt position your company within short order to enjoy significant cost savings, increased efficiency, and tremendously increased revenues.

Summary

In this chapter we have given you a brief overview of the subject of extranets. We defined an extranet as: facilitating communication and transactions between groups both *internal* as well as *external* to your company. We learned that the most important factor is that, from a technological point of view, extranets almost identical to an intranet, but that it requires a slightly different way of thinking. We then covered various issues that are important to take into account when developing an extranet, including: standards, application integration, and project planning.

A Guide to the Index

Some subentries also occur as main entries, whenever it's considered useful. Asterisks (*) denote multiple endings of similarly starting names when occurring together. Tildes (~) replace unnecessary name part repetitions, except in clear-cut enumeration cases (e.g. FirstChild and LastChild methods mentioned together become "First/LastChild" and not "FirstChild/Last~"). Commonly used acronyms are preferred to expanded forms and cross-referencing only happens when both are in common use. Identical page numbers accompanying both a main entry and its subentry indicate the presence of relevant information about the former, followed by a particular aspect of it in the latter (such as an example). Your feedback about this index is very welcome at **indexers@glasshaus.com**.

J2ME (Java 2 Micro Edition)

J2ME (Java 2 Micro Edition)
handheld devices using, 303
JavaScript, developing intranet using, 96
handheld devices using, 302
IE browser support from IE5, 68
job listings, 79
developing intranet containing, 79
JPG files
GUI design, converting into HTML, 95
'junk drawer' intranet, avoiding, 147
'satisficing' causing duplicate content, 149
preventing, 149
symptoms, listing, 147
trust in content, establishing, 149
kaizen, marketing using, 238

keyboard shortcuts, see shortcuts, keyboard.
keywords HTML meta tag, vocabulary, 132
intranet usability shortcomings, 132
storing root word within page as alternative, 132
killer apps, creating/choosing, 50
advantages, 50
CRM example, 51

L2TP (Layer Two Tunnelling Protocol)
VPN using, 286
language/jargon, site
heuristic evaluation, usability, 111
large groups, developing intranet testing, 99
launching site, 231
developing intranet, 100
launch party & user training, combining, 234
advantages, 234
loud/quiet options, choosing, 232
naming intranet, 233
offline/e-mail marketing & SWAG, using, 233
relaunching, 239
legal responsibility, forums, 192
tracing forum users, 192
unsuitable postings, handling, 194

licensing scheme, choosing, 45
Linkchecker automatic link checker
broken links, detecting/fixing, 153
links, <link> tag, 132, 166
broken/expired links, detecting/fixing, 153
CMS creating, 166
Linux/BSD OS
choosing, pros & cons, 43
Lotus Domino, IBM
intranet integrating, 14
Lotus Notes
replication, remote offline access, 291

mailing lists, 185
pros & cons, 185
mailto link
contacting page owners, 156
maintaining intranet, 152
broken links, detecting/fixing, 153
CoP, connecting via microsites, 155
establishing ownership, 154
'ghost town' intranet, avoiding, 152
updating/deleting pages, 153
management
intranet role, 10
sponsorship for intranet, ensuring, 235
overgrown intranet re-development,
supporting/NOT~, 263, 270, 272
maps, site, see site maps.
marketing intranet, 225
challenges faced, 226, 228
interest in intranet, maintaining, 238
brand identity, building, 238
budget for future development, obtaining, 241
feedback mechanisms, maintaining, 241
integrating into daily routine, 240
intranet as primary point of contact, 240
relaunching intranet, 239
ROI, calculating for management, 241
updated/comprehensive content, maintaining, 239
usability, testing regularly, 240
launching site, 231
naming intranet, 233
overview, 225, 241
kaizen, using, 238
key issues, listing, 241

inaccurate content, removing, 151
'junk drawer' intranet, avoiding, 149
medium trust, establishing, 151

Also from glasshaus:

glasshaus
web professional to web professional

Constructing Accessible Web Sites

Paul Bohman, Michael Burks,
Shawn Lawton Henry, Jim Thatcher,
Mark Urban, Sarah Swierenga

1-904151-00-0

April 2002

US: $49.99
C: $74.95
UK: £36.99

Accessibility is about making a web site accessible to those with aural, visual or physical disabilities - or rather, constructing web sites that don't exclude these people from accessing the content or services being provided.

The purpose of this book is to enable web professionals to create and retrofit accessible web sites quickly and easily. It includes discussion of the technologies and techniques that are used to access web sites, and the legal stipulations and precedents that exist in the US and around the world. The main body of the book is devoted to the business of making web sites and their content accessible: testing techniques, web development tools, and advanced techniques. The book concludes with a quick reference checklist for creating accessible web sites.

This is a practical book with lots of step-by-step examples, supported with a Section 508 checklist enabling developers to refer to the book as they work as well as a complete list of accessibility testing and approval sites.

Also from glasshaus:

Practical XML for the Web

Dave Addey, Chris Auld, Oli Gauti Gudmundsson, Jon James, Allan Kent, Jeff Rafter, Alex Shiell, Paul Spencer, Inigo Surguy

1-904151-08-6

US: $39.99

C: $61.99

UK: £28.99

You've heard the hype and the excitement - now here's a book that brings practicality to the party. In context, but avoiding lengthy history lessons, we show you why XML is great to get into, and how to get up and running with it quickly. Using XML appropriately can make your markup future-proof and standards-compliant, enhance accessibility and usability, and allow data to be shared between almost any language/platform combinations and rendered in any future browsers.

What you'll learn:

- Using XML client-side and server-side
- USing XHTML to future-proof markup
- Transforming and styling XML with CSS and XSLT
- Manipulating XML with client-side JavaScript
- Generating and manipulating XML with server-side scripting

Also from glasshaus:

glasshaus

labor-saving devices for web professionals

1-904151-02-7
Usable Web Menus

1-904151-09-4
**Usable Forms
for the Web**

1-904151-14-0
Usable Shopping Carts

1-904151-15-9
**Web Graphics for
Non-Designers**

1-904151-03-5
**Usability:
The Site Speaks for Itse**

1-904151-05-1
**Practical JavaScript
for the Usable Web**

1-904151-04-3
Cascading Style Sheets

1-904151-22-1
**The Web Professional's
Handbook**

1-904151-17-5
**Fundamantal Web Design
and Development Skills**

1-904151-10-8
**Dynamic
Dreamweaver MX**

1-904151-11-6
**Dreamweaver MX:
PHP Web Development**

1-904151-19-1
**Dreamweaver MX:
Advanced PHP Web
Development**

1-904151-13-2
**Dreamweaver MX:
ASP.NET Web Development**

1-904151-21-3
**Dreamweaver MX:
Advanced ASP Web
Development**

glasshaus books: labor-saving devices for web professionals